THE WITCH-HUNT IN EARLY MODERN EUROPE

THE WITCH-HUNT IN EARLY MODERN EUROPE

BRIAN P. LEVACK

Second Edition

Longman
London and New York

Addison Wesley Longman Limited
Edinburgh Gate,
Harlow, Essex CM20 2JE, England
and Associated Companies throughout the world.

*Published in the United States of America
by Addison Wesley Longman, New York*

© Longman Group UK Limited 1987
This edition © Longman Group Limited 1995

First published 1987
Eighth impression 1992
Second Edition 1995
Fifth impression 1996

ISBN 0 582 08069X

British Library Caraloguing-in-Publication Data

A catalogue record for this book is
available from the British Library

Library of Congress Cataloging-in-Publication Data

Levack, Brian P.
    The witch-hunt in early modern Europe / Brian P. Levack,—2nd ed.
        p.   cm.
    Includes bibliographical references and index.
    ISBN 0–582–08069–X
    1. Witchcraft—Europe—History.   I. Title.
    BF1571.L48 1995
    ,133.4'094—dc20   94-14607
                                                                         CIP

Set by 5BB in 10/12pt Sabon
Produced by Longman Singapore Publishers (Pte) Ltd
Printed in Singapore

CONTENTS

LIST OF TABLES

LIST OF MAPS

LIST OF PLATES (between pages 148–149)

PREFACE

The idea for this book originated in the lecture courses and seminars I have given on the history of witchcraft during the past ten years. In teaching these courses I became aware of the need for a one-volume study of the entire European witch-hunt – the accusation, prosecution, and execution of thousands of persons for the crime of witchcraft between 1450 and 1750. On this depressing but important subject much has been written, especially in recent years. The sheer volume of this work, however, has created problems of digestion, and the proliferation of theories regarding witch-hunting has created more confusion than enlightenment. My aim has been both to present a coherent introduction to the subject and to contribute to an ongoing debate.

This essay attempts to explain why the great European witch-hunt took place. It also attempts to explain why it reached its peak in the late sixteenth and early seventeenth centuries, why it was much more severe in some countries than in others, and why it came to an end. There are no simple answers to these questions. One reason for this is that the European witch-hunt was not a single historical event or episode but a composite of thousands of individual prosecutions that took place from Scotland to Transylvania and from Spain to Finland over a 300–year period. Although these prosecutions shared many common characteristics, they also arose in different historical circumstances and they often reflected witch-beliefs that were peculiar to a certain locality. Another reason is that witch-hunting was an extremely complex enterprise. Since it involved both the educated classes and the common people, it reflected both élite and popular ideas about witchcraft. It had both religious and social dimensions, and it was conditioned by a number of political and legal factors. It is not surprising, therefore, that mono-causal explanations of the witch-hunt have proved to be singularly unconvincing, if not demonstrably false.

In discussing the witch-hunt I have taken pains to emphasize both its complexity and diversity. Four chapters are devoted to the different causes of witch-hunting throughout Europe. Chapters 2 and 3 discuss the two main preconditions of the great hunt:

the formation of the cumulative concept of witchcraft and the development of legal procedures that were capable of convicting witches in large numbers. Chapters 4 and 5 deal with the general religious and social developments which served as inducements to witch-hunting, especially in the late sixteenth and early seventeenth centuries, when the hunt entered its most intense phase. In Chapter 6 the focus of the book shifts from the general causes of the European hunt to the specific hunts that it comprised. My purpose there is both to explain why individual hunts began and to show the different ways they developed and eventually came to an end. Chapter 7 places even more emphasis on the diversity of witch-hunting, suggesting reasons for the uneven chronological and geographical distribution of prosecutions. In Chapter 8 the focus of the book shifts back to the entire European hunt in an effort to explain its decline. There too I have emphasized the complexity of the process, showing that the reduction in the number of prosecutions was the result of legal, intellectual, religious and social developments.

Although this book covers a very large geographical area and many centuries of European history, it does not pretend to be a comprehensive history of European witchcraft. With the exception of some background material on the Middle Ages and a few observations on witchcraft in modern times, it is concerned exclusively with the early modern period. It also deals more with witch-hunting than with witchcraft, if by the latter term we mean the beliefs and activities of the witches themselves. There is certainly a need for a synthesis of popular witch-beliefs and practices in the various parts of Europe, but this book does not attempt to provide one.

I should like to express my gratitude to the University Research Institute of the University of Texas at Austin for the financial assistance that enabled me to write a large portion of this book. I also wish to thank Myron Gutmann, Richard Kieckhefer and Guy Lytle for reading drafts of various chapters of the manuscript and for giving me much valuable criticism. I am likewise indebted to Travis Hanes for reading the entire manuscript and making a number of helpful suggestions. In developing my ideas regarding the legal aspects of witch-hunting I have benefited from the thoughtful comments of Edward Cohen, John Langbein, Bruce Mann and Edward Powell. My greatest personal debt is to my wife, Nancy, who gave me both criticism and support when I most needed them.

B.P.L.
Austin, Texas
July, 1985

PREFACE TO THE SECOND EDITION

In preparing a second edition of this book I have made an effort to take into account the large volume of scholarly literature on witchcraft that has appeared since I completed the first edition eight years ago. The process of revision has led to the inclusion of a significant amount of new information, a rewriting of some sections, and the expansion of both the Notes and the Bibliography.

The appearance of numerous regional studies, many of them dealing with witchcraft on the periphery of Europe, has only served to underline my argument regarding the complexity and diversity of the great witch-hunt and the difficulty of establishing a single explanation of its origins and development. The same can be said of those thematic studies which have emphasized different aspects of the subject, especially gender and popular beliefs. I have tried to take these works into account in presenting my own multi-causal approach to the problem. At the same time I have not seen fit to reduce my own emphasis, greatly neglected in other treatments of the subject, on the judicial aspects of the great witch-hunt, especially in explaining the geographical distribution of prosecutions. I am also more convinced now than I was eight years ago that the original impetus for prosecution came mainly from the localities rather than from the centre and that the central authorities of the state had more to do with the restriction of witch-hunting than with its spread.

B.P.L.
Austin, Texas
November 1993

For their specific permission to reproduce plates in the text, acknowledgement is made to the following: (Plate 5) the British Museum (copyright holders); and (Plate 11) the Mary Evans Picture Library.

Whilst every effort has been made to trace the owners of copyright material, we take this opportunity to offer our apologies to any copyright holders whose rights we may have unwittingly infringed.

For Nancy

I   INTRODUCTION

During the early modern period of European history, stretching from roughly 1450 to 1750, thousands of persons, most of them women, were tried for the crime of witchcraft. About half of these individuals were executed, usually by burning. Some witchcraft trials took place in the various ecclesiastical courts of Europe, institutions which played an important role in regulating the moral and religious life of Europeans during the Middle Ages and the early modern period. More commonly, especially after 1550, the trials were held in the secular courts – the courts of kingdoms, states, principalities, duchies, counties and towns. The geographical distribution of cases throughout Europe was extremely uneven. In some jurisdictions there were very few prosecutions, if any at all, whereas in others hundreds and sometimes thousands of persons were tried over the course of three centuries. There was also an uneven chronological distribution of witchcraft trials. A gradual increase in the number of prosecutions during the fifteenth century was followed by a slight reduction in the early sixteenth century, a dramatic increase in the late sixteenth and early seventeenth centuries, and finally a gradual decline in the late seventeenth and early eighteenth centuries. Within each jurisdiction there were even more pronounced fluctuations in the number of trials. Instead of a steady stream of prosecutions we often find some periods when large numbers of witches were prosecuted and others when the crime does not appear to have been a problem.

Although the number of witches who were tried varied from place to place and from time to time, all of these witchcraft prosecutions can be considered parts of one very large judicial operation that took place only in Europe and only during the early modern period. This general but nevertheless clearly defined historical development is usually referred to as either the European witch-craze or the European witch-hunt. The former term, which is the one most commonly employed, should be used with great caution. It is appropriate only to the extent that European authorities and communities harboured such deep fears of witches during this period that they often manifested

1

frenzied, irrational or manic forms of behaviour in pursuing them. In some instances the number of suspected witches was so large, and the fear of them so profound that entire communities became caught up in a panic. The problem with the word 'craze', however, is its implication that the set of beliefs which underlay the prosecution of witches was the product of some sort of mental disorder, which was certainly not the case.

The latter term, witch-hunt, is preferable to witch-craze because all witchcraft prosecutions, even those that gave no indication of collective psychoses, involved some sort of search for malefactors. Witch-hunts did not usually involve the physical pursuit of a named individual, as in the case of a man-hunt when a prisoner escapes from gaol or evades the law. Occasionally witches who escaped or went into hiding were hunted in that way, but the essential process in combating witchcraft was discovering who the witches were rather than where they were located. Witch-hunting involved the identification of individuals who were widely believed to be engaged in a secret activity. Witches were hunted, therefore, in the same way that members of an underground movement or secret organization would be hunted today. This was a task undertaken by various individuals, usually judicial authorities but sometimes professional witch-finders. Acting on the basis of accusations, denunciations or sometimes mere rumour, these men arrested persons whose names came to their attention, interrogated them, and did everything in their power to extract confessions from them. Sometimes judicial authorities continued this investigation by forcing confessing witches to name their accomplices, the type of legal prosecution most commonly associated with the word 'witch-hunt' today.[1] The final stage of the witch-hunt was, in most cases, the formal conviction of the accused, followed by their execution, banishment or imprisonment.

The main purpose of this book is to explain why the great European witch-hunt took place. On this historical question there is no consensus of opinion. Indeed, it is difficult to think of any other historical problem over which there is more disagreement and confusion. During this century alone the witch-hunt has been attributed, in whole or in large part, to the Reformation, the Counter-Reformation, the Inquisition, the use of judicial torture, the wars

---

1 Contemporary witch-hunts also involve the pursuit of individuals more for their beliefs than for their actions. See C. Larner, *Witchcraft and Religion* (Oxford, 1984), pp. 88–91.

of religion, the religious zeal of the clergy, the rise of the modern state, the development of capitalism, the widespread use of narcotics, changes in medical thought, social and cultural conflict, an attempt to wipe out paganism, the need of the ruling class to distract the masses, opposition to birth control, the spread of syphilis, and the hatred of women. This book does not endorse any one of these all-encompassing explanations of the hunt. Rather it adopts a multi-causal approach which sees the emergence of new ideas about witches and a series of fundamental changes in the criminal law as the necessary preconditions of the witch-hunt, and both religious change and social tension as its more immediate causes. Only by studying all of these factors, which will be the subject of the next four chapters, and by seeing how they reinforced each other, can we begin to understand why the hunt occurred. Even then, however, it is necessary to go beyond these general causes of the hunt and explore the specific circumstances and events that triggered individual witch-hunts, for the European witch-hunt was really nothing more than a series of separate hunts, each of which had its own precipitants. Each of these hunts also had its own dynamic, and therefore we must also try to explain why witch-hunts, once they had begun, followed many different patterns of development.

The complexity of the great European witch-hunt is evident not only in an analysis of its causes but in a study of its chronological and geographical development. Since witch-hunting was more intense in some areas than in others and at certain times than at others, it is imperative that we explain why these variations occurred. Only in this way can we appreciate the relative importance of some of the more general causes of the entire European witch-hunt. Throughout the book, therefore, an effort will be made to explain this diversity, and in Chapter 7 a more systematic approach to the entire question will be adopted.

The final chapter of this book deals with the decline of the great witch-hunt. Although magic and sorcery are in a certain sense universal phenomena that occur in all societies at all periods of time, the European witch-hunt was a time-bound phenomenon, which did not begin until the fifteenth century and ended by the middle of the eighteenth. A study of its termination can, therefore, deepen our understanding of the conditions that both made it possible and sustained it. Such a study can also help us to appreciate the differences between European witchcraft during the early modern period and various contemporary phenomena with which it is often compared.

THE MEANING OF WITCHCRAFT

In dealing with such a complex issue as witchcraft, it is important to establish what the word means. Since contemporaries themselves assigned different meanings to the word, and since they also used many other terms as the equivalents of witch and witchcraft, this is no simple task. When early modern Europeans used the word witchcraft, however, they were almost always referring to either or both of two types of activity. The first was the practice of harmful, black, or maleficent magic, the performance of harmful deeds by means of some sort of extraordinary, mysterious, occult, preternatural or supernatural power. This type of magic would include the killing of a person by piercing a doll made in his image, inflicting sickness on a child by reciting a spell, bringing down hail on crops by burning enchanted substances, starting a fire by leaving a hexed sword in a room, and causing impotence in a bridegroom by tying knots in a piece of leather and leaving it in his proximity. These acts were usually referred to in Latin as *maleficia* and in English were sometimes called witchcrafts.[2] The agents of these deeds were usually referred to as *malefici* or *maleficae*, the Latin words that were commonly used to identify witches during the late medieval and early modern periods.

It was in the performance of *maleficia* that European witchcraft most closely resembled the practice of witchcraft in primitive and non-European societies today. In all witch-believing societies witches are regarded as individuals who possess some sort of extraordinary or mysterious power to perform evil deeds. The essential characteristics of these deeds are that they are magical rather than religious and harmful rather than beneficial. These distinctions, however, are not always clear and call for some sort of explanation.

In its purest sense magic is a power that is activated and controlled by man himself. The power is very much the magician's power, which he uses to produce readily observable, empirical results in the world. He almost always uses this power in critical situations and he usually acts secretly and individually. The assumption of the magician is that if he practises his art correctly, it will automatically bring about the desired result. If he fails, he concludes that he has not performed his art properly. In practising religion, however, man, whether he be priest or layman, does not exercise the same type of control over the power he is using. He merely supplicates spirits or gods, who

---

2 On the distinction between 'ordinary witchcrafts' and bewitchments in England and New England see R. Wiseman, *Witchcraft, Magic and Religion in 17th-Century Massachusetts* (Amherst, 1984), pp. 47–9.

he hopes or trusts will achieve the desired result. If he fails, it is because the gods did not deign to satisfy his request. The ends that he pursues, moreover, are generally non-empirical, 'supernatural' goals, such as the achievement of life after death. Religion is also a more communal, organized form of activity than magic, and its practice is not confined to critical situations. Unlike magic, religion uses the arts of persuasion in attempting to realize its goals, and since it deals with superior beings, it is more capable of filling man with a sense of awe.[3]

Although it is possible to draw clear distinctions between magic and religion in their purest or most ideal senses, in practice these distinctions are often blurred.[4] This should not surprise us, for many religions have slowly developed out of magic, while others have often deteriorated into magic.[5] One example of the way in which religion can resemble magic is the fact that the priest sometimes recites prayers or performs rituals with the magician's certainty that if he acts according to form the result will automatically ensue. The results of religious activity, moreover, are very often empirical, worldly benefits, just like those of magic, and they may have been sought in order to solve an immediate crisis. Magic, on the other hand, can easily become conflated with religion whenever it uses the powers of gods or other spirits to achieve its intended effects. In ancient Greece and Rome, for example, the very same gods who were the object of supplication and who inspired awe in their worship played an important part in the practice of magic. And as we shall see, the early Christian Church insisted that all magical activity involved the power of the pagan gods, who were considered to be demons.

Because of the frequent blurring of the distinctions between religion and magic, it is worthwhile to imagine a continuum of activities which involve the use of some sort of preternatural, supernatural or non-empirical power. At one end of the continuum would be magic in the purest or ideal sense, in which the gods would not be involved and in which the objectives would be immediate,

---

3 See H. Sebald, *Witchcraft: The Heritage of a Heresy* (New York, 1978), pp. 147–57; E. Nottingham, *Religion: A Sociological View* (New York, 1971), pp. 88–91.

4 The distinction was first made only at the time of the Reformation. See K. Thomas, *Religion and the Decline of Magic* (London, 1971), p. 77.

5 See D.L. O'Keefe, *Stolen Lightning: The Social Theory of Magic* (New York, 1982) for the argument that magic derives from religion and not vice versa; A.A. Barb, 'The Survival of Magic Arts', in *The Conflict between Paganism and Christianity*, ed. A. Momigliano (Oxford, 1963), pp. 100–25.

worldly and empirical. At the other end would be religion in its most organized, public, supplicatory and theological sense, its objectives being essentially non-empirical and other-worldly. Between the two would be various forms of magic that are public and involve the intervention of gods or other spirits and various forms of religion that exhibit 'magical' characteristics.[6] Within this continuum, however, it would still be possible to distinguish between magic and religion on the basis of the criterion of compulsion.[7] Those forms of activity in which man commands or manipulates mysterious forces, supernatural or otherwise, would be essentially magical; those in which he supplicates and leaves the power to the spirit or god would be essentially religious.

The second essential characteristic of *maleficia* is that they are by definition harmful, not beneficial. They are intended to bring about bodily injury, disease, death, poverty or some other misfortune. They are to be contrasted, therefore, with acts of white magic, the purpose of which is to bring about some benefit to oneself or another. White magic can be productive, in the sense of helping crops to grow or women to bear children; it can be curative, in the sense of healing a person who is ill; or it can be protective, in the sense of preventing some misfortune from occurring or warding off some evil spirit or witch. The distinction between black and white magic can easily become blurred, especially when the magician harms someone in order to protect himself, or when he cures someone by transferring the disease to another person. Acts of love magic very often fall into this grey area, since one person's gain in love might easily be another's loss. Amatory magic could also be considered harmful, at least by communal standards, when it resulted in an adulterous liaison but beneficent when it reunited an estranged husband to his spouse.

Our concept of *maleficium* comes very close to, but nevertheless cannot be equated with, that of sorcery. There is no universally accepted definition of sorcery, but in virtually all contexts the word denotes the practice of magic by some sort of mechanical, manipulative process. Sorcery is an acquired skill. It might involve the destruction of an image of a person in order to bring him harm, the pronunciation of a spell, or the use of a potion. Sorcery can be distinguished from *maleficium* on two possible grounds. The first is that in the view of

6 Nottingham, *Religion*, p. 91; Sebald, *Witchcraft*, pp. 150–2; W. Goode, *Religion Among the Primitives* (Glencoe, Ill., 1951), pp. 52–5.
7 E. Peters, *The Magician, the Witch and the Law* (Philadelphia, 1978), p. xv; Barb, 'Survival', p. 101.

some scholars, sorcery can be beneficial as well as harmful.[8] In that sense it is a broader category. The second is that some maleficent acts do not involve the use of any particular technique, substance or paraphernalia. In that sense it is a more limited category. *Maleficium* can be the result of a witch's general power to inflict harm rather than her practice of any particular art. One example of this type of *maleficium* in Europe was the harm allegedly caused to individuals by the witch's evil eye. Another was the harm done to a person by some completely internal act of the witch, such as wishing that a person were dead. These actions were certainly *maleficia* in every sense of the word, but they were not acts of sorcery.[9]

One further distinction should be made regarding the magic performed by witches. All magic, whether beneficial or harmful, can be classified as either high or low. Once again the distinction is not always clear, but high magic is a sophisticated and speculative art which requires a certain amount of education. The most common forms of high magic are alchemy, which is the changing of base metals into precious ones, and divination (also known as conjuring) which is the use of various means to acquire secret or otherwise unknown knowledge. Astrology, the use of the position of the stars to obtain such knowledge, and necromancy, the use of the spirits of the dead for similar purposes, are the most commonly known methods of divination, but more than a hundred different methods, including scapulomancy (divination by inspecting animals' shoulders), dactyliomancy (by means of a finger-ring) and oneiroscopy (by the interpretation of dreams) have been employed by various societies. Low magic requires little if no formal education and can be learned by oral transmission, apprenticeship or even individual experimentation. It usually takes the form of simple charms and spells. Most of the *maleficia* ascribed to witches in the early modern period fall into this category of low magic, both because the overwhelming majority of witches came from the lower levels of society and also because most high magic is white. It is important to note, however, that practitioners of high magic did occasionally incur accusations

8 See, for example, C. Larner, *Enemies of God: The Witch-hunt in Scotland* (Baltimore, 1981), p. 9; R.A. Horsley, 'Who Were the Witches?: the social roles of the accused in the European witch trials', *Journal of Interdisciplinary History*, 9 (1979): 696. For an opposite view see F.E. Lorint and J. Bernabe, *La Sorcellerie paysanne* (Brussels, 1977), p. 25; Macfarlane, *Witchcraft in Tudor and Stuart England* (New York/London, 1970), p. 4.

9 Horsley, 'Who Were the Witches?', p. 701 emphasizes this distinction. See also Macfarlane, *Witchcraft in Tudor and Stuart England*, p. 4.

of witchcraft and that the practice of divination was specifically prohibited by many witchcraft laws. Moreover, a particular type of learned or semi-learned magic, the ceremonial art of summoning up demons, played an important role in the development of witch-beliefs in medieval Europe, as we shall see in Chapter 2.

The performance of *maleficium* is only one of the two types of activity contained in the early modern European definition of witchcraft. The second concerned the relationship that existed between the witch and the Devil, the supernatural foe of the Christian God and the personification of evil. A witch was a person who not only performed harmful magic but who also made a pact with the Devil and paid some sort of homage to him. Witchcraft was therefore diabolism, the worship of the Devil. The two types of activity that witches were accused of – magic and diabolism – were closely related, for at this time it was widely believed that a witch acquired her powers to harm people magically by making a pact with the Devil. The alleged connection between magic and diabolism derived from the writings of theologians, who ever since the fourth century had argued that magic could only be performed by demonic power. During the Middle Ages this idea that magicians had some sort of commerce with demons underwent a significant development. As an increasing number of people began to practise ceremonial magic, scholastic philosophers argued that magicians made face-to-face pacts with the Devil and were therefore heretics and apostates. They also began to argue that magicians, just like other heretics, worshipped the Devil as their God in large nocturnal assemblies, to which they often flew. At these sabbaths, as they were usually called, witches not only paid homage to the Devil but also engaged in a variety of gluttonous, lewd, infanticidal and cannibalistic practices, all of which represented an inversion of the moral standards of society.

The emergence of the belief that witches were not merely magicians but also Devil-worshippers changed the nature of the crime of witchcraft. It made witches not simply felons, similar to murderers and thieves, but heretics and apostates, intrinsically evil individuals who had rejected their Christian faith and had decided instead to serve God's enemy, the Devil. Now it is true that throughout the history of Christianity magic had been viewed as the work of the Devil, a form of heresy and a lapse in one's faith. But by the late fifteenth century the heresy and apostasy of the witch had become much more deliberate, organized and threatening to society, and were recognized as a new and especially virulent form of heresy. As that change took place, the diabolical practices of the witch – the pact with the Devil and the collective worship of him – assumed much greater significance than her practice of harmful magic. Indeed, many lawyers came to regard the pact as the essence of witchcraft, while many theologians, especially those in the Protestant camp, claimed that witchcraft was a purely spiritual crime. Consequently many individuals tried for witchcraft were not accused of performing any *maleficia* at all; their crime was simply worshipping the Devil.[10] Whenever large witch-hunts took place, those persons who were implicated by confessing witches were almost always accused simply of attending the sabbath, not of practising specific acts of magic.

It is the diabolical component of early modern European witch-craft that distinguishes it most clearly from the witchcraft of many primitive societies in the world today. The belief in magic, even harmful magic, exists in virtually all primitive societies, but the belief in the Christian Devil, defined as he was by generations of medieval theologians, is unique to western civilization and its derivative cultures. Many primitive societies do, of course, believe in evil spirits and gods, and some believe that these spirits can assist magicians in their work. Some of these societies also believe that witches engage in activities that reverse or invert the established norms of society. But none of them has developed a set of beliefs that duplicates or even approximates those of late medieval demonologists, and none of them has nurtured the belief that a large sect of flying magicians worships demons secretly in orgies characterized by cannibalistic infanticide. In this regard late medieval and early modern European culture is unique.

There were therefore two quite different but related types of activity denoted by the word witchcraft as it was used in early modern Europe, one being the practice of *maleficium*, the other being diabolism. Both notions were contained in the prevailing stereotype of the witch, so much so that the presence of one usually implied that of the other.[11] Nevertheless, it is important to note that the word witchcraft sometimes connoted only one of these two ideas. On the one hand, some persons were accused of witchcraft simply on the basis of having attended the sabbath, without any evidence that they had performed *maleficia* or 'practised witchcraft'.[12] On the other hand,

10 H.C.E. Midelfort, *Witch-hunting in Southwestern Germany, 1562–1684: The Social and Intellectual Foundations* (Stanford, 1972), pp. 52–3.

11 See, for example, N. Rémy, *Demonolatry*, trans. E.A. Ashwin, ed. M. Summers (London, 1930), p. vii.

12 Henri Boguet, *An Examen of Witches*, trans. E.A. Ashwin, ed. M. Summers (London, 1929), pp. 203–4.

some individuals were accused of performing *maleficium* but avoided the additional charge of diabolism. This latter situation usually occurred in countries where witchcraft accusations came from below, which means that they came from the witches' neighbours rather than from judicial officials, and when they were not embellished by judges and prosecutors who were preoccupied with diabolical fantasies. Neighbours of witches were generally much more concerned about the misfortunes that they thought they had suffered as a result of a witch's magical power than they were about the witch's alleged dealings with the Devil. They were not completely ignorant of such things as the witch's pact with the Devil and her alleged worship of him, and during large witchcraft panics they often received instruction from clerics regarding these matters.[13] But ideas of diabolism were shared mainly by scholars, lawyers, judges and magistrates – the literate and ruling classes of society – and witches were generally accused of such activities when these members of the upper classes either brought charges against witches of their own initiative or used judicial torture to force people accused of *maleficium* to confess to diabolical activity. In England, where judges had none of these legal powers and where virtually all witchcraft prosecutions came from below, the crime of witchcraft remained essentially one of performing harmful magic, not one of worshipping the Devil. In other regions, such as Russia and Norway, the crime was viewed in the same way, either for legal reasons or because the ideas of diabolism that were current in France, Germany and Italy never fully penetrated these peripheral regions.

The word witchcraft, therefore, will be used in this book to denote the practice of either *maleficium* or diabolism, and when it is used in the fullest sense of the word it will designate both. The word can, moreover, be extended to cover two other types of activity that are very closely related to witchcraft. The first is invocation, in which a person calls upon the Devil or more commonly one of the lesser demons to obtain instruction or assistance. This invocation was usually performed as part of a ritual or ceremony, the purpose of which was to practise some sort of magic, usually divination. Ritual magicians were not generally classified as witches in the sixteenth and seventeenth centuries, but in certain instances they were prosecuted as such. These trials usually occurred when the magic that was

---

13 D. Hall (ed.), *Witch-hunting in Seventeenth-Century New England. A Documentary Collection, 1638–1692* (Boston, 1991), p. 9; G. Henningsen, 'The Papers of Alonso de Salazar Frías', *Temenos*, 5 (1969): 105.

being performed was maleficent and when the relationship between magician and demon appeared to be that of servant and master. In fact that was rarely the case. Ritual magicians almost always sought to establish a contractual relationship with the demons they conjured up. Nevertheless, as part of this contract, they often made offerings to these demons that appeared to be signs of reverence, and this made them vulnerable to prosecution.

The second activity that can be included within a broad definition of witchcraft is that of 'white witchcraft', which in early modern Europe denoted either the practice of magical healing or the use of rather crude forms of divination in order to foretell the future, locate lost objects or identify enemies. By definition white witchcraft did not involve the practice of *maleficium*, but because all magic was believed to involve the agency of the Devil, white witches could easily be regarded as having made pacts with him. In those witchcraft treatises which viewed the pact as the essence of witchcraft, very little distinction was made between white and black witches.[14] In actual practice, however, white witches were usually treated more leniently than black witches. In England they were usually prosecuted in the ecclesiastical rather than the secular courts and given only spiritual penalties. In some areas they were not even prosecuted. Nevertheless, many white witches, being known to cure the sick, were also suspected of harming them and thus became assimilated to black witches.[15]

THE REALITY OF WITCHCRAFT

Witchcraft is often referred to, at least by sceptics, as an imagined crime, an elaborate fantasy that has no foundation in reality. Those who were tried as witches, therefore, are viewed as innocent victims of a deluded judiciary and an oppressive legal system. Are these

14 W. Perkins, *A Discourse of the Damned Art of Witchcraft*, in *Works*, (Cambridge, 1613), III, p. 638, considers the white witches the most dangerous of all. The definition of witchcraft given by Joseph Glanvil in *Saducismus Triumphatus* (London, 1681), II, p. 4, would accommodate either white or black magic.

15 On white witches see G. Henningsen, *The Witches' Advocate: Basque Witchcraft and the Spanish Inquisition, 1609–1614* (Reno, 1980), p. 303; Thomas, *Religion and the Decline of Magic*, pp. 212–53; Wiseman, *Witchcraft, Magic and Religion*, p. 61; C. Ginzburg, *The Night Battles: Witchcraft and Agrarian Cults in the Sixteenth and Seventeenth Centuries*, trans. John and Anne Tedeschi (Baltimore, 1983), p. 78; Monter, *Witchcraft in France and Switzerland: The Borderlands during the Reformation* (Ithaca, 1976), pp. 167–90.

assumptions valid? Did the European witch-hunt produce thousands of criminals who had not committed any crimes, or did witches actually perform some of the deeds for which they were prosecuted? In addressing these questions we need not determine whether magic works or whether the Devil actually exists, for such problems lie outside the realm of historical investigation. But historians can and must ask whether those persons accused of witchcraft did in fact engage in any of the *activities* for which they were prosecuted. The answer to this historical question inevitably affects the answer to the related question of the witches' legal guilt, since guilt is determined at least to some extent by the historical reality of the alleged crime. If witches did not in fact perform the various deeds of which they were accused, and if they did not actually attempt to perform them, then they could not have been guilty as charged.

In discussing the reality of witchcraft it is necessary first to distinguish between the two main components of the crime: *maleficium* and diabolism. The first has a solid basis in reality, in that certain individuals in virtually all societies do in fact practise harmful or evil magic. Concerning the reality of such deeds in the past there is an abundance of physical, legal and literary evidence. In ancient Rome, for example, individuals were known to inscribe curses on lead tablets, dedicate the tablets to demons, and then drive nails through the tablets. We know that this form of sorcery, which is called *defixio*, was actually practised, since the tablets themselves have survived.[16] In similar fashion the dolls and other paraphernalia used in image magic have survived from many societies in the past. When necromancers were prosecuted in the Middle Ages, the tools of their trade were usually produced as evidence of their guilt. And the literature of magic – the hundreds of manuals and guides to the practice of both white and black magic that have survived from many different historical periods – all provide ample proof that people have in fact practised sorcery and continue to do so today.

Whether any of the European witches of the early modern period actually practised sorcery is a little more difficult to determine. The tools of their alleged art were rarely produced in court, and since they were for the most part illiterate, they could not be expected to

---

16 For examples of these curses see, H.A. Harris, *Sport in Greece and Rome* (Ithaca, 1972), pp. 235–6.

have books of black magic in their possession.[17] The legal evidence for their sorcery consisted of their confessions and the depositions of neighbours who accused them of harm. Both types of evidence are suspect: the confessions because they were very often adduced under torture, the depositions because they were made by hostile parties. Nevertheless, the depositions do often contain records of spoken curses, spells and even the use of the tools of image magic, all of which suggest that at least some of the people accused of witchcraft did in fact try to harm their enemies by magical means. Indeed, sorcery was one of few means by which women, especially older, unmarried women, could protect themselves in early modern European communities. In a study of the well-known witch-hunt that took place at Salem, Massachusetts, in 1692, Chadwick Hansen has argued that at least three of the women prosecuted for witchcraft were in fact practitioners of sorcery.[18]

Even if some of the witches of the early modern period did actually engage in the practice of maleficent magic, we must not assume that all of them, or even a majority of them, did likewise. We shall never know what percentage of the thousands of executed witches were in fact practising *maleficium*, but it certainly was very low. A somewhat larger number, but still a distinct minority, were probably guilty of practising some form of white magic, which their neighbours and superiors misinterpreted or perhaps deliberately misrepresented as being maleficent. The majority of accused witches did not practise any sort of magic at all but were either accused of causing harm by magical means when unexplained misfortune struck one of their neighbours or when they were named as the accomplices of other witches in the course of a large witch-hunt.

When we turn to the subject of diabolism, the problem of establishing the reality of the witches' actions becomes more difficult, for the only evidence we have regarding such deeds are the confessions of the witches themselves and the accusations made by their alleged accomplices. These pieces of evidence are suspect for a number of reasons. First, they frequently contain references to the performance of manifestly impossible deeds, such as flying through the air. Such

---

17 For a few rare cases in which accused witches used books see Sebald, *Witchcraft*, p. 44; C. Garrett, 'Witches and Cunning Folk in the Old Regime', in *The Wolf and the Lamb: Popular Culture in France from the Old Regime to the Twentieth Century*, ed. J. Beauroy et al. (Stanford, 1976), p. 59. For the case of Jean Michel of Moulins, see Humanities Research Center, University of Texas at Austin, Pre-1700 MS 142.

18 C. Hansen, *Witchcraft at Salem* (New York, 1969), pp. 94–104, 284–6.

statements do not by themselves invalidate the entire testimony, but they do call its veracity into question and require supporting evidence.[19] This evidence has never been produced in any recorded case of diabolism. Never once, for example, did the neighbours who accused witches of *maleficia* testify that they had witnessed the collective worship of the Devil or even the conclusion of a formal pact between a witch and the Devil. Even more important, no impartial or detached observer ever testified or claimed in writing that he had witnessed such an act. Even the rather credulous Italian inquisitor Paulus Grillandus, writing in the early sixteenth century, admitted that he had never seen or heard of any witch caught *in flagrante crimine*.[20] Never once did authorities conduct a raid on a witches' coven, even though the same authorities showed that they were quite capable of breaking into the meetings of other subversive groups. In fact, whenever independent, impartial investigations were conducted into the alleged practice of diabolism, they produced negative results. When, for example, the Spanish inquisitor Alonso de Salazar interrogated hundreds of witches from the Basque country who had confessed to attending sabbaths in 1610, he concluded on the basis of numerous retractions and contradictions that the entire affair was 'nothing but a chimera'.[21]

A second reason for calling the confessions of witches to acts of diabolism into question is that they were often extracted under torture or the threat of torture. Confessions obtained in this way contained evidence that was contaminated, since it was more likely that the confession would indicate what the torturer wished to hear rather than what the accused had actually done. Most clerical judges and secular magistrates in Europe during the sixteenth and seventeenth centuries had a fairly clear, preconceived idea of the diabolical activities that witches engaged in. When accused sorcerers were brought before them, they assumed that these people, in addition to practising magic, were also members of a secret, heretical, Devil-worshipping sect. Using highly effective methods of torture, they often forced them to confess to having made face-to-face pacts with the Devil and to having worshipped him collectively. In an effort to wipe out the entire sect of witches, moreover, they then used torture once again to elicit the names of their alleged accomplices.

19 See N. Cohn, *Europe's Inner Demons* (London, 1975), p. 115.

20 R.H. Robbins, *The Encyclopedia of Witchcraft and Demonology* (New York, 1959), p. 236.

21 Henningsen, *The Witches' Advocate*, p. 247.

The best evidence we have regarding the close connection between torture and confessions to diabolical activity is that accusations of Devil-worship usually did not arise in witchcraft trials until that stage of the proceedings when torture was applied.[22] Sometimes this was in the early, preliminary stages, shortly after the arrest of the witch, but at other times it did not take place until after witnesses had made their depositions. These depositions were almost always concerned exclusively with *maleficium*, not diabolism. Once torture was employed, then charges of diabolism arose. For this reason it is valid to claim that torture in a certain sense 'created' witchcraft, or at least created diabolical witchcraft.

The crucial role that torture played in securing confessions to diabolism is most clearly illustrated in a trial of three witches in the Channel Island of Guernsey in 1617. In this trial torture was not administered until very late in the proceedings, after the defendants had been convicted and sentenced. Up to that point the trial had dealt only with charges of *maleficia*. Numerous witnesses had testified that the three women had cast spells on inanimate objects, inflicted strange diseases upon many persons and beasts, cruelly hurt a great number of men, women and children, and caused the death of many animals. On the basis of this testimony, which made no reference to the worship of the Devil, the three were convicted and sentenced to death.[23] As soon as the sentence was pronounced one of the witches, a widow by the name of Collette Du Mont, confessed that she was a witch, but since she refused to specify which crimes she had committed, she was taken to the torture chamber.

It was at this point that diabolism entered the trial. Once Collette was put to the question, she admitted that the Devil had appeared to her in the form of a cat on numerous occasions and that he had incited her to take revenge on her neighbours. In this way a connection was established between her relationship with the Devil and the *maleficia* with which she had been charged. Her confession, however, did not stop there but went on to describe diabolical practices that were very often associated with witchcraft:

---

22 See R. Kieckhefer, *European Witch Trials: Their Foundations in Popular and Learned Culture, 1300–1500* (London, 1976), Chapters 3 and 5; M. Madar, 'Estonia I: Werewolves and Poisoners', in *Early Modern European Witchcraft: Centres and Peripheries*, ed. B. Ankarloo and G. Henningsen (Oxford, 1990), p. 272.

23 J.L. Pitts, *Witchcraft and Devil Lore in the Channel Islands* (Guernsey, 1886), pp. 9–10.

That the Devil having come to fetch her that she might go to the Sabbath called for her without anyone perceiving it: and gave her a certain black ointment with which (after having stripped herself), she rubbed her back, belly and stomach: and then having again put on her clothes, she went out of her door, when she was immediately carried through the air at a great speed: and she found herself in an instant at the place of the Sabbath, which was sometimes near the parochial burial ground: at other times near the seashore in the neighbourhood of Rocquaine Castle: where, upon arrival, she met often fifteen or sixteen Wizards and Witches with the Devils who were there in the form of dogs, cats and hares; which Wizards and Witches she was unable to recognise, because they were all blackened and disfigured: it was true, however, that she had heard the Devil summon them by their names, and she remembered among others those of *Fallaise* and *Hardie*. ... Admitted that her daughter Marie, wife of Massy, now condemned for a similar crime, was a Witch: and that she took her twice to the Sabbath: at the Sabbath, after having worshipped the Devil, who used to stand up on his hind legs, they had connection with him under the form of a dog; then they danced back to back. And having danced, they drank wine (she did not know what colour it was), which the Devil poured out of a jug into the silver or pewter goblet; which wine did not seem to her so good as that which was usually drunk; they also ate white bread which he presented to them – she had never seen any salt at the Sabbath.

The confession concludes with a report of the way in which the Devil, on leaving the sabbath, gave Collette certain black powders which she could throw on persons and cattle to cause harm.[24]

Collete Du Mont's account of the sabbath can readily be dismissed as the product of judicial coercion. What are we to do, however, with those confessions to diabolism that are reported to have been free or unforced? Some of these voluntary confessions were not free at all, having been made shortly after the conclusion of one stage of torture and before the next. Nor can we consider as free the confessions of those who decided on rational grounds that it was preferable to confess and be executed than to endure the excruciating tortures that awaited them if they remained silent. These people might very well have recognized that the situation was hopeless anyway and elected therefore to avoid some of their agony by confessing. Even when the accused thought she might survive the torture and be acquitted, the intolerable prospect of social isolation and communal hatred occasionally induced 'voluntary' confession.[25]

24 Ibid., pp. 12–14.

25 Sir George Mackenzie, *The Laws and Customs of Scotland in Matters Criminal* (Edinburgh, 1678), p. 87.

In all of these cases, confession led to what we might call judicial suicide, an alternative to the completely self-inflicted suicide that many witches resorted to while in jail. Whenever a witch committed this type of suicide, the evidence contained in her confession lacked credibility, for in making her statement she was at least to some extent willing to tell her interrogators what they wanted to hear. The same problem arises in dealing with those confessions that witches made in the hope of obtaining judicial leniency. In some cases that hope was based on false promises of the authorities or the unwarranted expectations of the accused; in others it rested on the established judicial policy of giving reprieves to those who confessed. Whatever the rationale, however, these confessions could easily be fabricated in order to win acceptance and therefore cannot be relied upon for their factual accuracy.

Not all 'free' witchcraft confessions represented conscious efforts to avoid some form of pain or suffering. Some, for example, were almost certainly the result of senescence. We need not accept the argument of Johann Weyer, the sixteenth-century critic of witch-hunting, that witches were afflicted with melancholy to appreciate the fact that many of the old women who were prosecuted for witchcraft were senile and of unsound mind. Such women were capable of developing a variety of fantasies and providing their interrogators with material that could easily be shaped into accounts of diabolical activity. We also know too much today about people who confess to crimes they did not commit – and even to crimes that no one *could* commit – to dismiss the possibility that some of the individuals who made free confessions to diabolism were mythomaniacs.

Even if witches who made free confessions were not psycho-logically disturbed, they might very well have confessed to having performed activities that they merely dreamed they had done. Some-times these dreams were conditioned by cultural traditions, such as when children dreamed or imagined that they had been taken to places where they had been told witches usually gathered. At other times the dreams may have been conditioned by drugs. In the sixteenth and seventeenth centuries it was widely believed that witches facilitated their flight to the sabbath by applying magical ointments to their bodies. The recipes for some of these flying unguents have survived and have been shown to contain such substances as atropines which, when administered in appropriate doses through the skin, have a mind-altering or hallucinogenic effect.[26] It would be rash to base

26 See M. Harner, 'The Role of Hallucinogenic Plants in European Witchcraft', in *Hallucinogens and Shamanism*, ed. M. Harner (London, 1973), pp. 125–50.

a comprehensive interpretation of the great witch-hunt on the use of such narcotics, but it is quite possible that some of the witches who confessed to attending the sabbath either had experienced something like flight under the influence of drugs or had entered a deep, drug-induced sleep in which they had experienced fantastic or depressing dreams.[27] The content of such dreams could easily have been transformed, under questioning, into a stereotypical account of what went on at the witches' sabbath.

Although confessions to diabolism are highly suspect as accounts of historical reality, they were not completely the product of people's imagination. Some of the individuals who were accused of witchcraft probably did, for example, make pacts with the Devil. We need not believe that the Devil actually exists or that he actually appeared to witches and conversed with them to admit this possibility. All we must do is recognize that in the early modern period many poor, old women, realizing that their plight was desperate and believing that the Devil often offered people material pleasures in exchange for adoration, pledged their service and sold their souls to him.[28] Other witches may have invoked his aid in critical situations. If such people did in fact believe that they had made pacts with the Devil, inquisitors would have had a relatively easy time convincing them that they had engaged in other, less credible forms of Devil-worship. The same people, it should be added, would probably have appeared in the trial records as feeling a deep sense of guilt and remorse for their actions, which is exactly how many witches have been described.[29]

Although individual witches may have actually made pacts with the Devil, there is no foundation to the widespread belief that they worshipped the Devil collectively. Unless independent, non-contaminated evidence can be produced to support the existence of a witch-cult, we must take the sceptical position that all such activities existed in the minds of the accused or their prosecutors or both.[30] Nor can we argue with any degree of certainty that people accused of witchcraft organized themselves for some other, non-diabolical purposes which were interpreted by judicial authorities as the collective worship of the Devil. There is no shortage of historical theories that look at witchcraft in this way. The most famous is that of Dame Margaret Murray, an anthropologist who in three different

---

27 See Monter, *Witchcraft in France and Switzerland*, pp. 199–200.
28 See Thomas, *Religion and the Decline of Magic*, pp. 516–26.
29 Monter, *Witchcraft in France and Switzerland*, p. 137.
30 See Henningsen, *Witches' Advocate*, pp. 93–4.

studies argued that the witches of the early modern period were really members of an ancient, pre-Christian fertility cult whose beneficent rituals were misrepresented by alarmed clerics and judges as harmful and diabolical.[31] Other scholars, sharing a romantic interpretation of witchcraft, have interpreted the witches' assemblies as organized protests against either the established economic and social order or against patriarchy. One historian has seen the witches' sabbath as the work of goliards parodying the current ecclesiastical order.[32] The problem with all these interpretations is that there is no proof that witches ever gathered in large numbers for any purpose, diabolical or otherwise. The fear of collective Devil-worship may have been based on the reality of the secret assemblies of other groups. We know, for example, that heretics did gather in fairly large numbers for purposes of religious worship. But witches, if they ever practised any of their craft at all, did so individually or in small groups.

Murray's theory appears to have received some reinforcement from the work of Carlo Ginzburg, who discovered that a number of witches from the Italian province of Friuli in the late sixteenth and early seventeenth centuries were in fact members of a fertility cult. The *benandanti*, as these persons called themselves, wore their cauls around their necks as amulets and claimed that they went out at night to battle the witches, the enemies of fertility. Under the pressure of the Inquisition these men came to believe that they themselves were witches and confessed. Ginzburg claims that his discovery confirmed a 'kernel of truth' in Murray's thesis, for the *benandanti* prove that 'witchcraft had its roots in an ancient fertility cult'.[33] That may very well be true, if 'witchcraft' is taken to mean the witch-beliefs or myths held by the common people. But Ginzburg's book does not support the position that witches were pagans or that they actually practised their religion. Not only did the *benandanti* frequently profess their loyalty to the Catholic Church, but even more important, they never actually travelled at night to fight the witches. Instead they went out in spirit, while their bodies entered a cataleptic state. Ginzburg entertains the possibility that the *benandanti* may have actually gathered under some circumstances, but there is no evidence that they ever did so.

---

31 M. Murray, *The Witch-Cult in Western Europe* (Oxford, 1921); *The God of the Witches* (London, 1933); *The Divine King of England* (London, 1954).

32 E. Rose, *A Razor for a Goat* (Toronto, 1962).

33 See Ginzburg, *Night Battles*.

The possibility that witches dreamed or imagined that they were engaging in certain activities is the only legitimate basis for a romantic interpretation of witchcraft. The peasants who were accused of witchcraft had their own fantasies, just as their inquisitors did, and these fantasies could easily reinforce those of their prosecutors. We know, for example, that many women believed that they flew at night and copulated with demons, beliefs which reinforced the conviction of inquisitors that the same women engaged in these activities at the sabbath. We also know, from the work of Emmanuel Le Roy Ladurie, that many of the peasants of Languedoc imagined an inverted social order as a form of symbolic protest and that the revelation of their fantasies could easily have been interpreted as accounts of the sabbath, where everything was believed to be upside down.[34] But we must keep in mind that the reality of this inversion was mental, not physical. We still do not have any evidence that either a witch-cult or a group of persons performing some ritual that was interpreted as witchcraft actually existed.

The fact that the great European witch-hunt involved so much fantasy – the fantasies of the witches themselves as well as those of their accusers – has led many historians, mainly those of the liberal or rationalist school, to regard witchcraft as a massive delusion or illusion, which was dispelled by the growth of scientific knowledge and by the general enlightenment that occurred in Europe in the late seventeenth and eighteenth centuries. This characterization of witchcraft as a delusion is inappropriate both because it impedes an open-minded investigation into the functions that witch-beliefs served in early modern European society and because it suggests that witchcraft, as it was viewed at this time, had no foundation in reality. As argued above, that was not the case. There were clearly individuals who practised magic, even harmful magic, and others who made pacts with the Devil. One might contend that the magician and the diabolist were deluding themselves; such a contention would depend upon one's beliefs regarding the effectiveness of magic and the existence of a Devil who could converse with humans. But when writers and judicial authorities tried to wipe out witchcraft, they were not dealing with an entirely fabricated threat.

34 E. Le Roy Ladurie, *Les Paysans de Languedoc* (Paris, 1966), pp. 407–13.

THE SIZE OF THE HUNT

Because so many judicial records have been destroyed or otherwise lost, and because the trials of many witches were never even officially recorded, the total number of witchcraft prosecutions and executions cannot be determined with any degree of accuracy. Some estimates, ranging as high as nine million executions, have been grossly exaggerated.[35] The totals have been inflated both by the claims of witch-hunters themselves, who often boasted about how many witches they had burned, and by subsequent writers, who for different reasons wished to emphasize the gravity of the process they were discussing.[36] Detailed scholarly studies have generally led to a downward estimate of the total numbers of victims. It has long been believed, for example, that an early seventeenth-century witch-hunt in the Basque-speaking Pays de Labourd in France resulted in 600 executions, but it now appears that the actual figure was closer to eighty.[37] In Bamberg, where another 600 witches were allegedly burned between 1624 and 1631, the totals are probably closer to 300.[38] And in Scotland, where Henry C. Lea claimed that 7,500 persons were executed for witchcraft, the actual tally is probably less than 1,500.[39]

In estimating the size of the hunt it is also imperative that we distinguish between the number of trials and the number of executions. There were some witch-hunts in Germany in which virtually all suspects were tried and executed, but these were exceptions to the rule.[40] Table 1 establishes the execution-rate of

35 See, for example, A. Dworkin, *Woman Hating* (New York, 1974), p. 130. W. von Baeyer-Katte, 'Die Historischen Hexenprozesse: Der Verbürokratisierte Massenwahn' in *Massenwahn in Geschichte und Gegenwart* (Stuttgart, 1965), ed. W. Bitter, p. 222, estimates close to one million cases on the basis of lost records and unrecorded processes. For a late eighteenth-century estimate see H.C. Lea, *Materials toward a History of Witchcraft*, arr. and ed. Arthur C. Howland, 3 vols (New York, 1957), III, 1075.

36 Luis de Páramo boasted that inquisitors alone had executed 30,000 persons for witchcraft before by the middle of the sixteenth century. H.C. Lea, *A History of the Inquisition in the Middle Ages* (New York, 1955), III, p. 549.

37 Henningsen, *The Witches' Advocate*, pp. 23–5, 480–1. R. Briggs, *Communities of Belief* (Oxford, 1989), suggests that the figure may be as low as thirty.

38 Larner, 'Crimen exceptum?: the crime of witchcraft in Europe?', in *Crime and the Law*, ed. V. Gattrell et al. (London, 1980), p. 52.

39 H.C. Lea, *History of the Inquisition in Spain* (New York, 1906–07), IV, pp. 246–7; C. Larner, *Enemies of God* (London, 1981), p. 63.

40 Midelfort, *Witch-Hunting*, p. 147.

witches in a number of European regions.[41] The numbers of trials upon which these rates are calculated are very small, since they include only those cases whose outcomes are known. In most regions the execution-rate was less than 70 per cent and in some areas, such as Essex county, Ostrobothnia, and Geneva it was less than 25 per cent. Only in the Pays de Vaud did the execution-rate reach the severe level of 90 per cent.

Even if we make allowances for trial records that have been lost or destroyed, the total number of persons who were actually tried for witchcraft throughout Europe probably did not greatly exceed 100,000. About half of these persons lived in German lands within the Holy Roman Empire. A project organized by Heinrich Himmler in the 1930s to obtain information regarding persons tried for magic and witchcraft in the past yielded a file containing data from some 30,000 prosecutions, the great majority of which took place in Germany. Since some of the entries in this file contain the names of more than one person, and since the records of many prosecutions are for one reason or another not included in the file, the total number of German prosecutions could easily be 50,000.[42]

The other heavy concentrations of European prosecutions were in the lands surrounding Germany. To the east, Poland, where very little systematic work has been done on the trial records, was the site of perhaps 15,000 trials.[43] To the south, Switzerland, long recognized

41 Sources for Table 1: Monter, *Witchcraft in France and Switzerland*, p. 49; M. Dupont-Bouchat, 'La Répression de la sorcellerie dans le duché Luxembourg aux XVIᵉ et XVIIᵉ siècles' in M. Dupont-Bouchat et al., *Prophètes et sorciers dans les Pays-Bas XVIᵉ–XVIIIᵉ siècles* (Paris, 1978), p. 127; Pitts, *Witchcraft and Devil Lore*, pp. 28–32; C. Larner, C.H. Lee and H.V. McLachlan, *Source-Book of Scottish Witchcraft* (Glasgow, 1977) p. 237, Table 2; A. Heikkinen and T. Kervinen, 'Finland: The Male Domination', in *Early Modern European Witchcraft*, p. 321; H.E. Naess, 'Norway: The Criminological Context', in *Early Modern European Witchcraft*, p. 371. Macfarlane, *Witchcraft in Tudor and Stuart England*, p. 57; G. Klaniczay, 'Hungary: The Accusations and the Universe of Popular Magic', in *Early Modern European Witchcraft*, p. 222.

42 G. Schormann, *Hexenprozesse in Deutschland* (Göttingen, 1981), pp. 8–15, 71. Schormann is confident that the number was less than 100,000. Wolfgang Behringer has calculated that there were certainly more than 15,000 and perhaps more than 20,000 *executions* in Germany. W. Behringer, '"Erhob sich das ganze Land zu ihrer Ausrottung . . .": Hexenprozesse und Hexenverfolgungen in Europa', in *Hexenwelten: Magie und Imagination vom 16.-20. Jahrhundert*, ed. Richard van Dülmen (Frankfurt, 1987), p. 165.

43 B. Baranowski, *Procesy Czarownic w Polsce w XVII i XVIII Wieku* (Lodz, 1952), p. 178. Baranowski's estimates of 10,000 legal executions and 5,000 illegal ones may be too high, but I have used these figures for the total number of prosecutions.

Table 1   Regional Execution-Rates in Witchcraft Trials

Region	Years	Persons tried (fates known)	Executions	% Executed
Fribourg	1607–83	162	53	33
Geneva	1537–1662	318	68	21
Neuchâtel	1568–1677	341	214	63
Pays de Vaud	1537–1630	102	90	90
Luxembourg	1509–1687	547	358	69
County of Namur	1509–1646	270	144	54
Isle of Guernsey	1563–1634	78	33	46
Dept. of the Nord, France	1542–1679	187	90	48
Finland	1520–1699	710	115	16
Norway	1551–1760	730	280	38
County of Essex, England	1560–1672	291	74	24
Scotland	1563–1727	402	216	54
Hungary	1520–1777	932	449	48

as a centre of the witch-hunt, tried at least 10,000 witches,[44] while to the west a string of autonomous states within the Empire (including Lorraine and Franche-Comté), together with the kingdom of France, held another 10,000 trials. France was in many ways the cradle of the great witch-hunt, and although Germany eventually surpassed it in this regard, French courts continued to prosecute witches in large

44 G. Bader, *Die Hexenprozesse in der Schweiz* (Affoltern, 1945), pp. 211–20, gives a total of 8,888 persons tried and 5,417 executed, but subsequent research has shown that these totals are too low. Behringer, 'Erhob sich das ganze Land', pp. 161–2, estimates that the number of executions may be as high as 10,000.

numbers. Between 1565 and 1640 the *Parlement* of Paris, which had jurisdiction over about one half of the country, heard 1,123 cases on appeal, and since appeals were not automatic until 1624, one can assume that the total number of original trials was much higher.[45] The areas of most intense prosecution in France, moreover, lay to the southwest and the southeast, outside the jurisdiction of the *Parlement* of Paris.

In addition to these areas of relatively intense witch-hunting, there were about 5,000 trials in the British Isles (more than half of them in Scotland) and another 5,000 in the Scandinavian kingdoms. There were even fewer trials – probably not more than 4,000 – in Bohemia, Hungary, Transylvania, and Russia. Finally, in the Mediterranean countries of Europe – the Spanish kingdoms and the Italian states – there were about 10,000 prosecutions.[46] Many of these trials, however, were for relatively minor forms of magic and superstition which in other jurisdictions might not even have been considered witchcraft. Very few of these prosecutions, moreover, resulted in executions.[47]

These very rough figures give us a European total of just under 110,000 trials. On the basis of the statistics in Table 1, the average execution-rate for Europe was 47 per cent, but that table does not include data for any German or Polish regions, which together accounted for a majority of European prosecutions and which appear to have had relatively high execution-rates. In the city of Kiel, for example, at least 67 per cent of the witches tried between 1530 and 1676 were executed, and the figure may have been as high as 81 per cent.[48] The number of unauthorized trials, which usually resulted in summary executions and which are not reflected in Table 1, would push the execution-rate for all of Europe even higher. It would not

45 A. Soman, 'The Parlement of Paris and the Great Witch-Hunt (1565–1640)', *Sixteenth Century Journal*, 9 (1978): 35.

46 G. Parker, 'Some Recent Work on the Inquisition in Spain and Italy', *Journal of Modern History*, 54 (1982): 529, gives a figure of 3,687 persons tried in Spain between 1560 and 1700. That figure does not include prosecutions by the secular courts. The Italian prosecutions appear to have been more intense than the Spanish.

47 Most of the executions in Spain and Italy occurred in the early sixteenth century, although there were a few in the seventeenth century. There were also a number of executions in the secular courts throughout the period. See W. Monter, *Frontiers of Heresy* (Cambridge, 1990), pp. 255–75.

48 These figures are based on the data in D. Unverhau, 'Kieler Hexen und zauberer zur zeit der großen Verfolgung (1530–1676)', *Mitteilungen der Gesellschaft für Kieler Stadtgeschichte*, 68 (1981): 45–6.

be unreasonable to conclude, therefore, that European communities executed about 60,000 witches during the early modern period.[49]

A total of approximately 110,000 witchcraft prosecutions and 60,000 executions may be significantly lower than many previous estimates, but these figures still represent a grim reality, especially if we keep in mind that most witches were either tried for crimes they did not commit or for crimes that were greatly exaggerated. The total figures, moreover, do not convey the full dimensions or the intensity of the great witch-hunt. The number of persons brought to trial does not, for example, reveal how many people lived under suspicion of witchcraft or became the object of informal accusations. We know from church court records, where individuals who were called witches brought charges of slander against their accusers, that there were many more witchcraft accusations than actual witchcraft prosecutions.[50] We can also be fairly certain that many individuals who were called witches did not bring counter-suits against their accusers. Witchcraft accusations, therefore, were a much more common feature of early modern European village life than the number of formal accusations and trials would suggest.

There were also many individuals who were formally accused of witchcraft but never brought to trial. Many of these persons were named as witches by their alleged confederates, usually under torture, but for one reason or another they were not themselves prosecuted. In some cases the failure to prosecute can be explained by the decision of judicial authorities to bring the hunt to an end before all suspects had been tried. In other cases the time and cost of imprisoning and prosecuting hundreds of suspects may have tested the resolve of even the most zealous witch-hunter or taxed the financial resources of the local community. In any event, a comprehensive study of witch-hunting cannot ignore these accused but untried persons, who shared much of the terror of those who were actually prosecuted, and who often endured social ostracism and continued suspicion after the hunt ended.

The figures regarding total prosecutions and executions also fail to provide any indication of the effect that witch-hunts had

---

49 These figures are roughly equivalent to those in Monter, 'The Pedestal and the Stake: Courtly Love and Witchcraft', in *Becoming Visible: Women in European History*, ed. R. Bridenthal and C. Koonz (Boston, 1977), p. 130. Behringer, 'Erhob sich das ganze Land' also calculates fewer than 100,000 executions. J. Klaits, *Servants of Satan: The Age of the Witch-Hunts* (Bloomington, 1985), estimates a total of 200,000 trials.

50 Macfarlane, *Witchcraft in Tudor and Stuart England*, pp. 60, 66–75.

on individual towns and villages. Only when we break down the composite figures year by year and village by village can we appreciate the full intensity of the witch-hunt. When we learn, for example, that 274 persons were executed for witchcraft in the Prince Bishopric of Eichstätt in just one year, and that 133 witches were executed in the lands of the Convent of Quedlinburg in just one day in 1589, we gain a much better sense of the toll that witch-hunting could take than when we calculate figures for an entire country during a 300–year period.[51]

For men living in the sixteenth and seventeenth centuries the main statistical question as far as witchcraft was concerned was not how many witches had been executed but how many were still loose. Some of these estimates were astonishingly high. At the height of a particularly intense witch-hunt in 1587, the judge of the French village of Brieulles claimed that he had evidence of 7,760 witches in the single duchy of Rethelois.[52] In 1571 a French witch by the name of Trois-Eschelles told King Charles IX that there were 300,000 witches in his realm, and in 1602 the demonologist Henri Boguet used this figure to project a total of 1,800,000 for all of Europe. According to Boguet, there were 'witches by the thousands everywhere, multiplying upon the earth even as worms in a garden'.[53] The number of participants at the witches' assemblies was estimated to be at least 500 by one demonologist and as high as 100,000 by another.[54] These estimates help to explain why the educated classes in Europe were so frightened of witchcraft. They also help to explain why they prosecuted witches with such ferocity. A threat of this size could not be ignored; it had to be met head-on with all the judicial power that European states could muster.

51 H.C. Erik Midelfort, 'Heartland of the Witchcraze: Central and Northern Europe', *History Today*, 31 (1981): 28.

52 A. Soman, 'Witch Lynching at Juniville', *Natural History*, 95 (1986): 10.

53 Bodin, *De la Démonomanie des sorciers* (Anvers, 1586), p. 365; Boguet, *An Examen of Witches*, pp. xxxii, xxiv.

54 Rémy, *Demonolatry*, p. 56; Lea, *Materials*, III, p. 1297.

2 THE INTELLECTUAL FOUNDATIONS

By the end of the sixteenth century most educated Europeans believed that witches, in addition to practising harmful magic, engaged in a variety of diabolical activities. First and foremost, they believed that witches made an explicit, face-to-face pact with the Devil. This pact not only gave the witch the power to perform *maleficia* but also initiated her into the Devil's service. The conclusion of the pact was a formal ceremony which took place after the Devil had appeared to the witch, usually as a handsome, well-dressed man, and enticed her with the promise of material reward or sexual pleasure. The witch agreed to reject her Christian faith, often symbolized by her trampling on the cross, and to be rebaptized by the Devil. She then paid homage to the Devil, either by bowing down (often backwards) before him or by kissing his buttocks. As a sign of her allegiance the Devil imprinted a distinctive mark on the witch's body, usually in a concealed spot. He then gave her careful instructions for the performance of her maleficent work, equipping her if necessary with the potions, unguents and images she would need to ply her trade.

A second witch-belief that most educated Europeans subscribed to in the late sixteenth century was that the witches, having made a pact with the Devil, gathered periodically with other witches – sometimes numbering in the hundreds or even thousands – to perform a series of blasphemous, obscene and heinous rites. At these meetings the Devil would appear in various forms, together with subordinate demons. The witches would very often sacrifice children to the Devil, feast on the bodies of these infants and on other unsavoury dishes, dance naked, and engage in sexual intercourse with the Devil and the other witches. At some time during these assemblies a parody of the Christian eucharistic celebration might very well take place, and throughout the entire affair witches would make preparations for continuing their maleficent work. Closely associated with all these activities was a belief that witches could use the power of the Devil to fly through the air and thus gain quick access to assemblies that often took place a considerable distance from their homes.

Now it is important to note at the outset that these witch-beliefs, all of which concern the relationship between witches and the Devil, were mainly the property of the literate and ruling classes and not the common people. Although popular beliefs in demonic spirits, *incubi* and *succubi*, orgies and cannibalism had provided some of the raw material out of which such ideas had been fashioned, the actual formulation of those ideas had been the work of theologians, philosophers and lawyers, and the men who subscribed to them were judges, clerics, magistrates and landlords. Peasants could gain a limited amount of information about the diabolical activities of witches from the public reading of the charges against them at the time of their execution and from the deliberate efforts of authorities to instruct the populace regarding witchcraft during a witch-scare or hunt. Once these ideas were presented to them, they had little difficulty accepting them; the idea of a miserable peasant making a pact with the Devil in order to improve his lot and of attending a shocking orgy in order to gain culinary and sexual pleasure was hardly alien to a peasant mentality.[1] But illiterate peasants could not fully understand the sophisticated theories of the demonologists, nor were they likely to become as frightened of diabolical activity as did monks and theologians. Their concern with, and fear of, witchcraft centered on the witch's ability to cause harm by occult means, not her relationship with the Devil. Identification of the Devil as the source of the witch's magic probably aggravated lower-class fears, especially after the Reformation heightened their consciousness of the Devil's powers, but their primary concern remained the magic rather than the diabolism of the witches.[2]

The great European witch-hunt could not have taken place until the members of the ruling élites of European countries, especially those men who controlled the operation of the judicial machinery, subscribed to the various beliefs regarding the diabolical activities of witches that we have briefly described above. The mere belief in

1 See Ginzburg, *Night Battles*, p. 135. C. Holmes, 'Popular Culture?: Witches, Magistrates and Divines in Early Modern England', in *Understanding Popular Culture*, ed. S. Kaplan (Berlin, 1984), pp. 100–01, argues that in England the propaganda of the clergy eventually resulted in the limited acceptance of the satanic pact in popular culture.

2 On the gap between popular and learned beliefs see Kieckhefer, *European Witch Trials*, pp. 27–46; R. Muchembled, 'The Witches of the Cambrésis: The Acculturation of the Rural World in the Sixteenth and Seventeenth Centuries', in *Religion and the People, 800–1700*, ed. J. Obelkevich (Chapel Hill, N.C., 1979), pp. 232, 240; Wiseman, *Witchcraft, Magic and Religion*, pp. 53–72.

the reality of the magic that witches practised was not capable of sustaining the systematic prosecution and execution of large numbers of witches. The crime of *maleficium*, as allegedly practised by early modern European witches, while clearly felonious, was not serious enough or practised widely enough to elicit the type of judicial campaign that was in fact mustered against witches. In order for the intensive hunting of witches to take place, it was necessary for the ruling class to believe that the crime was of the greatest magnitude and that it was being practised on a large scale and in a conspiratorial manner. They had to believe not only that individual witches were harming their neighbours by magical means but that large numbers of them were completely rejecting their Christian faith and undermining Christian civilization. They had to believe that magicians belonged to an organized, conspiratorial sect of Devil-worshippers.

The subscription of many influential and politically powerful Europeans to this set of beliefs regarding witches raises a number of important questions. First, where did all these ideas regarding the pact with the Devil, the sabbath and the ability of witches to fly come from and how were they fused into 'the cumulative concept of witchcraft'? Second, how were these ideas developed and then disseminated among the upper and literate classes of European countries? Third, why did these ideas have such great appeal at this time and why were they not successfully challenged until the late seventeenth century?

THE CUMULATIVE CONCEPT OF WITCHCRAFT

The Devil

At the centre of most learned witch-beliefs was the Devil, the source of the witches' magic, the partner with whom she concluded the pact, and the object of her adoration. Before exploring such matters as the pact, therefore, it is important that we establish who this spiritual power was and what attributes Europeans ascribed to him. As with so many witch-beliefs that involve the Devil, the very conception of him had changed noticeably during the Middle Ages.

Throughout the Middle Ages the Devil was usually referred to as Satan, a name meaning 'the adversary' which appears in the Bible. In the Old Testament Satan did not figure very prominently. Judaism, being a monotheistic religion, originally attributed all creation and the operation of the universe to the one true God, Yahweh. All reality, evil as well as all good, was His responsibility. Only in one of the later books of the Old Testament, the first book of Chronicles, did Satan assume a distinct personality and present himself as the enemy of God and as the embodiment of evil. In the New Testament Satan became much more prominent. Presiding over a host of subordinate demons, he not only tempted Christ himself in the desert but became the powerful opponent of Christianity itself, enticing men to withdraw from Christ and to reject his teaching. A titanic struggle thus arose between the Kingdom of Christ on the one hand and the Kingdom of Satan on the other, a conflict that most believed would continue until the Second Coming.

As Christianity, the Kingdom of Christ, spread throughout the East and the West, it was only natural that the Church fathers would consign the religions with which they were competing, both Jewish and pagan, to the Kingdom of Satan. This process actually contributed to the visual depiction of the Devil in Christian art. One of the most effective tactics of the Christian Church in dealing with converts or potential converts who continued to worship their pagan gods was to demonize those gods – to claim that those deities were actually demons or the Devil himself. Because this equation was made so frequently, Christians began depicting the Devil in the ways that pagans viewed their gods. There was no standard image of the Devil in medieval art, and some of the features that he acquired in these depictions owe more to Christian theology than to pagan imitation. His depiction as black, for example, comes from the traditional association of black with sin rather than from the blackness of any particular pagan god. Likewise the wings derive from the Devil's status as a fallen angel, not from the fact that many pagan gods were themselves winged creatures. Nevertheless, many of the features commonly given to the Devil were originally those of pagan gods. The goatee, the cloven feet, the horns, the wrinkled skin, the nakedness and the semi-animal form bear direct reference to both the Greek and Roman god Pan and to the Celtic god Cernunnos, while the female breasts, which appear often in seventeenth-century English depictions of the Devil, came almost certainly from the fertility goddess Diana.[3]

The resemblance between the medieval Christian Devil and the ancient pagan gods which Christianity replaced and demonized is one of the main pieces of evidence that scholars have used to support the thesis that the witches of the early modern period were in fact practicing an ancient fertility religion. In many witch confessions there were references to the worship of a horned beast as a god.

3 *The Devils Triumph Over Rome's Idol* (London, 1680).

These confessions cannot, however, be taken at face value. Suggested almost certainly by the witch's inquisitor or judge, these descriptions reflect a Christian view of the Devil, whom the inquisitor believed the witch was worshipping as her god. It is only natural that in describing the appearance of this 'god' he would allude to the features most commonly assigned to the Devil, which in turn derived in large part from earlier images of pagan fertility gods.

Although Satan was the most commonly used name to refer to the Devil, it did have some competition. Occasionally the name of Lucifer, which the patristic writers assigned to the great archangel who rebelled against God and was cast down from heaven into hell, was used to describe the Devil. The name, a Roman word for the morning star, does not appear in the Bible, but some of the patristic writers identified it with the star in Isaiah that tried to be like God and which God cast out of the heavens. Lucifer, therefore, became a name that could be used to describe Satan before the fall.

In addition to the Devil, referred to as either Satan, Lucifer or some other title like the Prince of Darkness, the Prince of this World or simply the Demon, medieval and early modern Christians believed that there were large numbers of devils, demons or fiends who assisted the Devil in his work of evil, temptation and destruction. The New Testament indicates that these demons were legion, but it does not give a precise figure, so their exact numerical strength became a topic of speculation among demonologists. The fifteenth-century Spanish theologian Alfonso de Spina came up with a tally of 133,306,668, which was exceeded only by the much less precise calculation of 26 billion in one of the devil-books compiled by Sigmund Feyerabend in 1569.[4] Other estimates were usually much more conservative, in the range of six or seven million. Since these demons were believed to be fallen angels, they were often ranked, like the angels, hierarchically.

Some demons, especially those of the higher orders, were referred to by name, possessed distinct personalities, and presided over certain sins. On such matters there was nothing even approaching a consensus, and the entire matter could become hopelessly confused when demonologists referred to the Devil (i.e., Satan) by the names of one of the chief demons, such as Beelzebub, Leviathan, Asmodeus, Belial or Behemoth, or demoted either Satan or Lucifer (or both) to a status of mere parity with his subordinates. This confusion is not surprising, since the source of these names was either the Bible or the apocryphal books of the pre-Christian period, in which the various

4 Robbins, *Encyclopedia*, p. 130; Lea, *Materials*, III, p. 1084.

names were used interchangeably. The confusion appears not only in the work of demonologists but in the reports of witches' sabbaths, where it frequently cannot be determined whether the Lord of the ceremony, who was often depicted as a horned animal, was supposed to be the Devil or one of his chief demons.

The frequent references throughout the Middle Ages to the physical appearance of the Devil and the equally frequent references to his inhabitation of the bodies of human beings raises the important question of his metaphysical nature and his powers. These subjects remained the source of controversy during the entire medieval period, but in the twelfth and thirteenth centuries a group of scholastic theologians established a view that remained orthodox throughout the period of the witch-hunt. According to the scholastics, demons, like angels, were pure spirits, possessing no flesh or blood. They could, however, take on the appearance of a human or an animal body by mixing the air with various vapours from the earth so as to create a non-corporeal or aerial body. This body, being composed of natural elements, did have a physical reality and it could perform certain bodily functions, such as dancing or the sexual act. According to some demonologists the Devil could even procreate by using semen borrowed from another man, but this view was highly controversial.[5] The peculiar properties of demonic bodies also explain why the Devil and his numerous *incubi* or *succubi* demons are described as being cold during sexual intercourse. We need not postulate that witches were using stone phalluses as part of some sort of fertility rite to explain the frigidity of the Devil's sexual organs; the theological opinion that he had no blood suffices.[6]

In addition to taking on the appearance of a human being or an animal, the Devil or his subordinate demons could actually take possession of or inhabit the body of a human being. Reports of such possession appear in the Bible and continue throughout the early Christian and medieval periods. Very often the persons who became possessed were clerics, who complained about the control that the Devil thereby acquired over certain organs or bodily functions. When the Devil possessed a person he did not have to compress or inspissate air to create an aerial body; he simply occupied the body of the

5 See Rémy, *Demonolatry*, p. 92; H. Kramer and J. Sprenger, *The Malleus Maleficarum*, trans. and ed. M. Summers (London, 1928), pp. 111–12; Lea, *Materials*, II, p. 993.

6 The coldness could also be attributed to the formation of the Devil's body from coagulated water or his use of a cadaver. See R. Masters, *Eros and Evil* (New York, 1966), pp. 20–2.

afflicted person, using his power over matter to direct the functions of the human body. The Devil's possession of individuals could, and eventually did, play a part in witchcraft, since the possession could take place as a result of a witch's actions. The witch could, in other words, command the Devil to possess a victim as part of the pact that the witch had concluded with the Devil. Nevertheless, possession could take place without any involvement of a witch and merely at the whim of the Devil himself, so long as God permitted him to do so.

One of the most important powers that the Devil had was the power to create illusions. Like his power to take on the form of a human being, this derived from his power to move various substances, images and humours. Just as he was able to compress and inspissate air, he could also take the images that were stored in men's minds and impress them upon their mental faculties so that they appeared to see something that was not in fact there. Scholastic theologians emphasized that many of the marvellous effects produced by the Devil were only illusions that he created. This is what they claimed was happening when, for example, he turned men into beasts or deprived a man of his 'virile member'. He did not actually change the substance of a man or alter his physical structure. He merely deluded man into thinking that the change had been made.[7] Either he impressed the image of a beast or a memberless man on a person's imaginative faculty or he confused his perceptive faculties by a similar exercise of his powers of controlling local motion. Much of the magic that the Devil performed was accomplished in this way, although he could also perform magic by moving physical bodies together or apart, in defiance of the normal laws of nature.

It should be clear from this discussion of the Devil's powers that he did not, according to the scholastic point of view, possess anything that came close to unlimited power over the physical world. He could not change the substance of things or perform miracles. Nor could he create new life in any form; he had to work with the universe as it was created by God. God alone had created and presided over the natural and spiritual world. Whatever the Devil did was by the explicit permission of that immanent God, who retained many powers for His exclusive use. To declare that the Devil was in any way equal to God, that he created matter or controlled its operation, was dualist heresy, the doctrine of such sects as the Manichaeans and Cathars. At times orthodox Christians came very close to subscribing to such ideas. Whenever they spoke of the Kingdom of Satan, whenever they

---

7 *Malleus Maleficarum*, pp. 118–24.

expressed doubt that the struggle of Christ against Satan might not result in the victory of the former, whenever they felt that they might not be able to avoid the apparent control that the Devil had over them, they came dangerously close to assigning powers to him that the official doctrine of the Church condemned. Not surprisingly, these expressions of belief in overwhelming demonic power were most common during the period of the great European witch-hunt.[8]

During the fifteenth century, as the power of the Devil in the world appeared to be increasing and as the first witchcraft trials were taking place, the figure of the Devil began to undergo a significant transformation. Throughout the Middle Ages the Devil had been described as the enemy and anti-type of Christ, teaching hatred rather than love. Now, however, he was increasingly depicted as the anti-type of God the Father, the source and object of idolatry and false religion. One of the sources of this transformation was the insistence by late scholastic theologians on the Ten Commandments, rather than the Seven Deadly Sins, as the basis of Christian ethics. The first of the Ten Commandments prohibits the worship of false gods, an offence not readily subsumed under the Seven Deadly Sins. John Bossy has argued that the promotion of this new moral system, which all Catholics and Protestants would eventually adopt at the time of the Reformation, contributed to the transformation of the crime of witchcraft from that of *maleficium* to that of Devil-worship.[9] It is no coincidence that the late medieval theologian who was the main advocate of the new scriptural ethics, Jean Gerson, was the person primarily responsible for the decision of the theology faculty of the University of Paris in 1398 that all magicians, whether maleficent or beneficent, were guilty of idolatry. It is also not surprising that Johannes Nider, the Dominican theologian and inquisitor who wrote one of the first witchcraft treatises, *Formicarius*, between 1435 and 1437, was one of Gerson's German disciples.[10] In that work, Nider described witches as men and women who not only cast spells but

---

8 On the loss of confidence that the Devil was totally subservient to God during the period of the great witch-hunt see F. Cervantes, *The Idea of the Devil and the Problem of the Indian: The Case of Mexico in the Sixteenth Century* (London, 1991), pp. 11–19.

9 J. Bossy, 'Moral Arithmetic: Seven Sins into Ten Commandments', in *Conscience and Casuistry in Early Modern Europe*, ed. E. Leites (Cambridge, 1988), pp. 229–31.

10 Ibid. On Nider's role as a reformer and the connections between *Formicarius* and other catechetical writings of the period, see A. Blauert, *Frühe Hexenverfolgungen*, (Frankfurt, 1990) pp. 32–3.

who also paid homage to the Devil, renounced their Christian faith, and trampled on the cross.[11]

The pact with the Devil

The central idea in the cumulative concept of witchcraft is the belief that witches made pacts with the Devil. Not only did the pact provide the basis of the legal definition of the crime of witchcraft in many jurisdictions but it also served as the main link between the practice of harmful magic and the alleged worship of the Devil. In the fullest sense of the word a witch was both a harmful magician and a worshipper of the Devil, and the pact was the means by which the two forms of activity were most clearly related.

The belief that a human being could make a pact with the Devil can be found in the writings of St Augustine, but it did not become widespread in western Europe until the ninth century, when various legends regarding such pacts were translated into Latin. In these pacts the human party made an agreement resembling a legal contract according to which the Devil provided wealth or some other form of earthly power in exchange for service and, of course, the custody of the human party's soul after death. In some of these accounts the pact involved the practice of magic. In one of the most famous a Jewish magician enticed St Theophilus into signing such an agreement, and as a result of this bargain Theophilus acquired, among other things, magical powers. In another legend, adapted from St Jerome by Archbishop Hincmar of Reims in the ninth century, a boy made a pact with the Devil at the urging of a magician in order to win the affection of a young girl. The boy himself did not acquire magical powers as a result of the pact, nor did the magician make a pact with the Devil, but the boy did obtain the desired object of the love magic, and one can assume that the magician had in fact previously concluded a similar pact. In other stories regarding pacts, such as that told of a ninth-century Italian Bishop who wished to achieve great wealth, there was no allusion to the communication of magical power to the human from the Devil.[12] Nevertheless, the belief that magicians made pacts with the devil was well enough established by the ninth

---

11 See C. Ginzburg, *Ecstasies: Deciphering the Witches' Sabbath* (New York, 1991), pp. 69–71. For an analysis of the different elements in Nider's treatise and the recognition of its novelty see Blauert, *Frühe Hexenverfolgungen*, pp. 56–9.

12 J.B. Russell, *Witchcraft in the Middle Ages* (Ithaca, 1972), pp. 84–5.

century that Hrabanus Maurus could refer to the conclusion of the pact as one reason for condemning the practice of learned magic.[13]

The connection between magic and the demonic pact became much closer in the twelfth and thirteenth centuries, when the translation of many Islamic and Greek books of magic led to a dramatic increase in the actual practice of the art and when ecclesiastical writers became more determined and more explicit in their condemnation of it. The magic that began to be practised at this time involved the invocation and command of demons and was frequently referred to as necromancy, a term that technically means the summoning up of the spirits of the dead. This ceremonial or ritual magic was practised mainly at the courts of European monarchs and even at the papal court. Its practitioners may have appeared to later Renaissance *magi* as 'ignorant necromancers' but they were by no means illiterate and in fact had more in common with both ancient and Renaissance learned magicians than with the witches who later were prosecuted in great numbers. Summoning up demons in order to acquire secret or forbidden knowledge may not have required sophisticated scholarly learning, but it did require more expertise than the mere practice of peasant superstition. The methods of this conjuration varied greatly, but they usually involved adherence to a written formula, the purpose being to entrap the demon in a bottle, ring or mirror and then to command him to provide the desired assistance.

The condemnation of this new type of magic was mainly the work of scholastic theologians, but they gained considerable support from the papacy and from papal inquisitors like Nicholas Eymeric. In condemning such practices these men needed to do more than simply reiterate the traditional patristic attack upon magic; rather they had to answer the objection that the practitioners of this type of demonic magic were pursuing good objectives and were commanding, not serving, the demons that they conjured. The key to the scholastic response to this challenge was the logical argument that demons did not provide services without demanding something in return. The very practices of the magicians suggested that this was so, since they often offered demons either reverence or some sort of physical object, such as a chicken or their own blood, in order to lure them into their service. The conclusion that the scholastics were able to draw from all this was that virtually all magicians made pacts with the Devil. When the magician actually summoned up the demons and

13 Peters, *The Magician, the Witch and the Law*, pp. 16–17.

36

offered them something it was explicit; at other times it was implicit or tacit in the sense that although no direct negotiations took place, the actual practice of magic implied that some reciprocal relationship between the Devil and the magician had to have been established.[14] In either case the magician was to be condemned because by entering into the pact he had given to the Devil something that was due to God alone. The magician was therefore a heretic, in that he was, at least by inference, denying God the exclusive position in the universe that Catholic doctrine claimed He had.[15] Even worse, he was an apostate, for the magician was abdicating his Christian faith by agreeing to worship or otherwise serve the demon.[16]

The designation of magicians as heretics and apostates was not new, and in making this claim the scholastics drew upon earlier patristic condemnations of magic. In a sense the theologians of the fourteenth century were confirming an earlier attitude of the Church towards magic in the face of protestations by ritual magicians that they were not heretics. The novelty of the scholastic position was the emphasis upon the pact as the reason for the heresy and the blanket condemnation of all ritual magic on such grounds. The significance of this thought concerning the pact in the development of learned witch-beliefs is two-fold. First, the condemnation of all ritual magic as heresy could easily be extended to types of magic that did not concern the scholastics, in particular the practice of simple *maleficium* by ignorant peasants. By the logic of scholastic argument they too must have made pacts with the Devil, since only the Devil had the power to work magical effects, and in order to avail themselves of his magical powers they had to give him something in return. Second, the designation of magicians as heretics and apostates made them susceptible to all of the charges that were made against heretics in the later Middle Ages, especially charges of secret, collective worship and totally perverse, antinomian and anti-human behaviour. And since magicians were now also heretics, they could, like heretics, be prosecuted by papal inquisitors.

As the belief that magicians made pacts with the Devil was extended to the perpetrators of simple sorcery or, as one might say,

14 Russell, *Witchcraft in the Middle Ages*, p. 144; Cohn, *Europe's Inner Demons*, p. 176.

15 On the development of this definition of heresy, which does not necessarily involve intellectual error, see Russell, *Witchcraft in the Middle Ages*, p. 174.

16 Many writers insisted that some witches, while clearly apostates, were not heretics. See S. Leutenbauer, *Hexerei- und Zaubereidelikt in der Literatur von 1450 bis 1550* (Berlin, 1972), pp. 48–70; *Malleus Maleficarum*, pp. 194–205.

the magician became a witch, the idea of the pact itself underwent a significant change. The pacts that ritual magicians made with the Devil always involved some sort of worship of the Devil and, at least according to scholastic commentators, the loss of the magician's spiritual integrity and faith, but they also gave the magician certain powers over the Devil. They placed the Devil at the magician's service and compelled the demon to provide him with the assistance he needed. The negotiation of the pact was generally an operation conducted by two equals, each of which tried to outwit the other and entice him into giving more than he received. As the charges of practising magic and making a pact with the Devil were levelled against poor ignorant peasants, however, the official and learned characterization of the pact changed. The magician who was gradually being transformed into the witch became much more the servant than the master of the Devil. As King James VI of Scotland later put it, 'Witches are servants only, and slaves to the Devil; but the Necromancers are his masters and commanders.'[17]

It is true that a bargain was still struck between the two, but the control that the witch exercised over the Devil was restricted to her ability to compel him to perform *maleficium*, while the reverence that the witch paid to the Devil became much more voluntary, obsequious and unconditional. The Devil in many ways gained the upper hand in the process, a position he never had in dealing with the ritual magician. One clear sign of the change is that in the later cases the witch usually agrees to serve the Devil in exchange for very meagre financial or material rewards. Very often he wins the allegiance of the witch with the offer of a small coin which promptly turns to stone after the irrevocable pact is made. The Devil, it should be remembered, is the great deceiver, as the Bible tells us, and once the witch is no longer the equal of the Devil she can easily become his dupe. It is also interesting to note that as the master-magician was transformed into the servile witch, the sex of the malefactor changed from male to female.

The sabbath

The belief that witches made pacts with the Devil was a central witch-belief among the clergy and the secular élite of early modern Europe. The same individuals who held this belief, however, also subscribed to another idea that was of equal and in some respects of

---

17 King James I, *Daemonologie* (1597), ed. G.B. Harrison (London, 1924), p. 9.

greater importance. This was the belief that those witches who made pacts with the Devil also worshipped him collectively and engaged in a number of blasphemous, amoral and obscene rites. This belief was not as widely held as that of the pact, and it was somewhat less uniform in its various expressions. Nevertheless, like the belief in the pact, it served as an essential precondition of the great witch-hunt. Just as the belief in the pact made it imperative that witches be prosecuted, so the belief in the witches' nocturnal gatherings led European authorities to search for their confederates. Without the belief in the sabbath the European witch-hunt would have been a much smaller judicial operation.

Although the two beliefs that witches made pacts with the Devil and attended nocturnal assemblies were closely linked in the minds of many members of the learned élite, and although homage and sometimes even sacrifice to the Devil were elements in both of them, the two ideas had somewhat different sources, and their merger in the cumulative concept of witchcraft did not take place fully until the fifteenth century. Even then, however, the two beliefs were not necessarily associated, even in the literary tradition. For example, the most famous witchcraft treatise ever written, the *Malleus Maleficarum*, has a great deal to say about the pact but makes only passing references to the collective worship of the Devil.[18]

The belief in the sabbath has both general psychological and specific historical sources. The psychological roots, which are, to say the least, inadequately understood, are those which produce nightmares and fantasies about anti-human and amoral activities in many different societies. Every culture has been known to generate myths about persons, sometimes possessing peculiar powers or physical characteristics, who invert the moral and religious norms of society and who therefore present a threat to the very fabric of that society. It can be argued that a belief in the existence of such individuals is necessary in order to establish what those norms are, or at least to reinforce those that are generally accepted. The particular values that these people allegedly invert will vary in accordance with the norms of each society, but since all societies share some similar moral values, the nightmares that they produce possess some common

---

18 The authors simply state that some pacts with the Devil were made 'in a solemn ceremony . . . when witches meet together in conclave on a set day'. *Malleus Maleficarum*, p. 99. They also refer to 'a congress of women in the night-time' at which a man 'saw them kill his child and drink its blood and devour it'. Ibid., p. 66.

features. Thus the practice of cannibalistic infanticide, which most societies consider to be the ultimate moral offence, has been a part of virtually all such nightmares. The same can be said of naked dancing, an activity which many societies, until very recent times, have considered to be socially and morally outrageous.[19]

To some extent the belief in the witches' sabbath, which included both naked dancing and cannibalistic infanticide, represents the late medieval and early modern European version of this standard or even universal nightmare. At the same time, however, the European sabbath had many distinctive characteristics that reflect the influence of medieval Christianity. Certainly the heavy emphasis that was placed on the erotic aspects of the sabbath – the ritual intercourse with the Devil and the prevalence of promiscuous heterosexual and homosexual activity among the witches – derives from the negative attitude of the medieval and early modern Church towards sex. The parody of the Catholic mass, which was by no means common to all descriptions of the sabbath but which appears in the accounts of many French, Spanish and Italian assemblies, also reflects the specifically Christian horror at the mockery of its most sacred ceremony. The parody never involved the saying of a Black Mass, an elaborate ceremony that some modern witches actually perform over the body of a naked woman. But some of the sabbaths that allegedly took place in the sixteenth and seventeenth centuries included the saying of the Nicene Creed backwards while the celebrant stood on his head, the use of such expressions as 'Go in the name of the Devil', the blessing of the congregation with a black aspergillum, the consecration of a host made of offal, turnip or some black substance, and the singing of the choir in 'hoarse, gruff, and tuneless voices'.[20]

The specifically Christian, European depiction of an anti-society that appears in the confessions of witches has its origins mainly in the rhetorical invective that monks developed with respect to heretics in the eleventh and twelfth centuries. Threatened with the frightening spread of heresies like Catharism and Waldensianism, these monks deliberately constructed a picture of an anti-human heretical society in order to prevent the growth of such movements and to encourage their suppression. In constructing this picture the monks, such as

19 See L. Mair, *Witchcraft*, (New York, 1969), p. 40.
20 Russell, *Witchcraft in the Middle Ages*, p. 253; J. Caro Baroja, *The World of the Witches* (Chicago, 1965), pp. 119, 149–50; M. Summers, *The History of Witchcraft* (Secaucus, N.J., 1956), pp. 147–57; Le Roy Ladurie, *Paysans de Languedoc*, p. 413.

Ralph of Coggeshall, drew not only on the universal image of an anti-society but on a number of specific sources.[21] One was the image that Romans had developed of early Christians as members of a secret organization who practiced cannibalistic infanticide and incest – an image that had gained currency both because Christians had in fact met secretly and because the central rite of Christianity, the Eucharist, could easily be misinterpreted as cannibalism. Another source of the sabbath was the image that the patristic writers had developed of the heretic (as well as of the magician and the Jew) as idolators and children of Satan. A third source, partially based on reality but ascribed to all heretics indiscriminately, was the conviction that they, like the early Christians in Roman times, met secretly, a charge that the failure of contemporary authorities to discover heretics only served to encourage.[22] A fourth source was the doctrinal content of heresy itself, or more accurately, the way in which heresy was being interpreted. The Cathars, for example, were dualists, which meant that they exaggerated the powers of the Devil and especially his control over the material world. The purpose of Christianity according to Catharist doctrine, was to teach men how to free their souls, which were spiritual, from the evil matter in which they were entrapped. Christ, who was pure spirit, had provided men with the means by which this could be accomplished. Catharism was therefore emphatically anti-demonic, but it is easy to see how the exaggeration of the Devil's power in the universe and his elevation to a position of near parity with God could lead the defenders of orthodoxy to depict the Cathars, and by extension other heretics, as Devil-worshippers. In the same way the Cathars' contempt for procreation, which to them was the work of the Devil, could lead to the charge that they practised abortion, and this belief in turn nourished fantasies, which had arisen from other sources, regarding the practice of cannibalistic infanticide.

The monks of the late twelfth and early thirteenth centuries, drawing on all of these sources, constructed a stereotype of the heretic as a secret, nocturnal, sexually promiscuous Devil-worshipper. This image, which in many respects acquired a life of its own, could be applied indiscriminately to any heretic or deviant from orthodox Christianity. In the late Middle Ages it was in fact applied to heretics, ritual magicians and simple *malefici* or witches. For our purposes the

---

21 W.L. Wakefield and A.P. Evans (eds), *Heresies of the High Middle Ages* (New York, 1969), pp. 251–4.

22 Cohn, *Europe's Inner Demons*, pp. 1–15.

main question is how and when it came to be applied to the last group, the alleged practitioners of harmful low magic. For some time it was believed that the application first occurred in the trials of a number of Cathars in France in the fourteenth century.[23] These heretics were allegedly practising *maleficia*, and therefore the beliefs that their prosecutors, who were papal inquisitors, had regarding the conduct of Cathars were easily transferred to them as *malefici*. The Cathars were, therefore, being turned into witches. This description of their trials and the confessions made in them have been shown, however, to be forgeries,[24] and therefore we must look elsewhere for the fusion of ideas of magic on the one hand and ideas about the secret and collective practice of heresy on the other.

The most important and celebrated case in which the connection was made was the trial of Dame Alice Kytler and her associates in Kilkenny, Ireland, in 1324–25. Kytler was accused of practicing numerous *maleficia*, some of which involved murder, in order to increase her wealth. During the course of her trial, which took place in the court of the Bishop of Ossory, she and her associates were accused not simply of *maleficia* but also of belonging to a sect of heretics that met secretly at night, renounced the Christian faith, and made sacrifices to demons. Dame Alice, moreover, was accused of copulating with her own personal demon. The members of the sect were not accused of cannibalistic infanticide, but they were charged with having concocted potions out of the clothes of deceased unbaptized babies and the fat extracted from human corpses. The trial shows not only how charges of *maleficium*, which in this case were almost certainly politically motivated, suggested charges of ritual demonic magic, but also how the charges of magic, which had become clearly identified with heresy, in turn suggested charges of secret Devil-worship and copulation with demons.

In the case of Dame Alice Kytler the cumulative concept of witchcraft had not yet been fully formed. For reasons that will be explained below, neither she nor her associates were reported to have flown to their nocturnal gatherings. The sect that they belonged to was much smaller than later witches' covens, consisting of only ten persons. The description of their assemblies, moreover, was not as lurid as the later accounts of the witches' sabbaths, and, as mentioned above, the charge of infanticide was only implicit and

---

23 J. Hansen (ed.), *Quellen und Untersuchungen zur Geschicte des Hexenwahns und der Hexenverfolgung im Mittelalter* (Bonn, 1901), pp. 449–54.

24 Cohn, *Europe's Inner Demons*, pp. 132–8; Kieckhefer, *European Witch Trials*, pp. 16–18.

that of cannibalism absent. Even the pact, which one would expect in a trial involving the alleged practice of ritual magic, does not appear explicitly. Nevertheless, the case is a landmark in the formation of learned notions about witchcraft because it reflects for the first time the belief that *malefici* are organized in a Devil-worshipping heretical sect. It places us, as Norman Cohn has argued, on the threshold of the great witch-hunt.[25]

A second case, in many ways similar to that of Kytler, which took place in Boltigen, Switzerland, between 1397 and 1406, in some respects brings us closer. The trial, that of a man named Stedelen, resembled the Kytler case in that it arose out of charges of *maleficia*. Stedelen was accused of destroying crops, causing sterility among cattle and so forth. Like Kytler, Stedelen confessed under torture not only to the *maleficia* but to summoning up demons and to membership in a heretical sect of Devil-worshippers. The members of this sect renounced their faith in Christ and also killed babies by magical means, using the potions to make magical unguents. Aside from the explicit charge of infanticide, the case differed from Kytler's in two respects. First, all appearances suggest that Stedelen and his associates were not, like Kytler, members of the upper classes but common folk, similar to most of the witches of the sixteenth and seventeenth centuries. Second, the trial took place, like many subsequent witchcraft prosecutions, in a secular court. In this case the court was that of the city of Bern, the judge being Peter of Greyerz, a lay magistrate. This shows that by the beginning of the fifteenth century not only clerics like the Bishop of Ossory but secular magistrates like Greyerz could take originally clerical notions about heretical practices and impose them on individuals accused of *maleficia*. The application is especially noteworthy, since the original crime of which Stedelen was accused was not, like Kytler's crime, heresy but the secular crime of magic.[26]

The image of collective apostasy and Devil-worship that was applied to *malefici* in the trials of Kytler and Stedelen was originally formulated by monks as a description of heretical practices. By the time of these trials, however, the image had lost its connection with heresy and had become associated exclusively with magic. Neither literary accounts of, nor prosecutions for, heresy in the fourteenth century or after depicted heretics in the extreme way that

25 Cohn, *Europe's Inner Demons*, p. 205.
26 Ibid., pp. 204–5. The cases heard by Greyerz form the basis of Nider's description of a sect of *malefici* in the region of Bern and Lausanne.

late twelfth- and early thirteenth-century monks had. The charges of secrecy and collective worship persisted, especially when they had a foundation in reality. But heretics no longer appeared, either in treatises written about them or in court records of their trials, as perpetrators of the same behavioural excesses that the monks had described. In particular, the charge of cannibalistic infanticide against heretics disappeared in the early twelfth century and did not reappear until the 1450s.[27] As more and more became known about the actual activities of heretics, those sensational charges devolved on to ritual magicians and witches. Then in the sixteenth century, as the stereotype of the witch shed most of the remnants of its association with ritual magic – especially the conjuring up of demons – the charges became attached solely to witches. The fantastic stereotype of the heretic-magician became the stereotype of no one but the witch.[28]

Flight

The final major component of the cumulative concept of witchcraft was the belief that witches can fly. In many respects this was a corollary of the belief in the sabbath, in that it provided an explanation for the ability of witches to attend secret nocturnal gatherings in remote areas without their absence from home being detected. When the sabbath was held in very distant lands (such as the assemblies that French peasants from the Pays de Labourd allegedly attended in Newfoundland), and when it was believed that the number of participants was exceptionally large (the top figure was 100,000), the belief in the ability of witches to fly served as a necessary corollary.[29] Nevertheless, the belief in the sabbath could and did exist independently of the belief in night flight, as it did in Scotland. The belief in flying witches, moreover, had sources that contributed only indirectly to the theory of the sabbath itself, and it did not gain acceptance among the educated élite of Europe until they had already come to believe that *malefici* made pacts with the Devil and gathered collectively to worship him.

The belief that witches could fly had much more distinctly popular origins than the belief that they made pacts with the Devil or participated in nocturnal assemblies. There were in fact two originally distinct popular beliefs that lay at the basis of this notion. The first of

27 Ginzburg, *Ecstasies*, pp. 76–7.
28 Peters, *Magician, Witch and the Law* pp. 33–45.
29 Lea, *Materials*, III, p. 1296.

these was the belief, traceable to classical times, that women could transform themselves at night into flying screech owls or *strigae* who would devour infants. This belief in 'night witches' has been shared by many cultures, including many primitive cultures in the modern world, and it was prevalent among the Germanic people even before the period of Roman influence. The *strigae*, which became one of the many Latin words for witches, were also called *lamiae*, a reference to the mythical Queen of Libya, loved by Zeus, who sucked the blood of babies in revenge for Hera's killing of her children. The second belief was that women went out at night on a ride, sometimes referred to as a 'wild hunt', with Diana, the Roman goddess of fertility, who had close associations with the moon and the night and who was often identified with Hecate, the goddess of the underworld and magic. In medieval Germany Diana was often depicted as Holda or Perchta, a goddess who, like Diana, could be terrifying as well as nurturing. Just as Diana, a virgin, could slay would-be lovers and turn them into animals, so Holda could lead a 'Furious Horde' of those who had died prematurely through the sky. When Holda went on her earthly nocturnal journeys, however, she always served beneficent functions. In France and Italy this belief usually took the form of a belief in 'the ladies of the night,' mysterious women under the direction of a queen who visited homes for beneficent purposes.[30]

The beliefs in both the *strigae* and the ladies of the night were so strong among the common people of Europe that some women actually believed that they flew out at night as *strigae*, while others believed that they joined the supernatural queen in her nocturnal meanderings. When the literate élite eventually accepted the reality of such activities, these credulous women were readily suspected and accused of witchcraft. Until the fourteenth century, however, educated men viewed all such beliefs as illusions caused by the Devil. Since the Church had always claimed that Diana and the other pagan gods, especially the chthonic or fertility gods, were in fact demons, it was only natural that the whole spectacle of ladies riding out with Diana should have been viewed as the work of the Devil. Those who imagined that they rode out at night, just like those who believed they were *strigae*, were engaging in pagan superstition, as were those who simply believed that other humans performed these actions. Such beliefs, even if they had no foundation in reality, were not to be taken lightly, since those who held them were heretics.

---

30 See Ginzburg, *Night Battles*, pp. 42–50; Cohn, *Europe's Inner Demons*, pp. 210–19.

The best example of the medieval Church's attitude towards such beliefs was the Canon *Episcopi*, a set of instructions written in the tenth century by Regino of Prüm that became part of the canon law of the Church in the twelfth century. The Canon *Episcopi* is usually referred to as an illustration of the scepticism of the medieval Church towards witchcraft. This is somewhat misleading, for the document deals with a number of practices and beliefs that later became part of the cumulative concept of witchcraft, not with witchcraft as such. In addition to condemning the magical arts as a form of heresy, in the manner of the Church fathers, the Canon specifically singles out

> some wicked women, perverted by the Devil, seduced by illusions and phantasms of demons [who] believe and profess themselves in the hours of the night to ride upon certain beasts with Diana, the goddess of the pagans, and an innumerable multitude of women, and in the silence of the dead of night to traverse great spaces of earth and to obey her commands as of their mistress and to be summoned to her service on certain nights.

These women were accused of infidelity and of leading others into the same error.

During the course of the late Middle Ages the learned attitude towards belief in the *strigae* and the ladies of the night underwent a number of significant changes. First, the two ideas, which in popular culture are quite distinct, were often fused. The ladies of the night became perpetrators of cannibalistic infanticide while their procession or ride on beasts became an airborne flight. The fusion of these ideas can be seen as early as the twelfth century in the work of John of Salisbury,[31] but it was not complete until the fifteenth century. Secondly, the literate élite, which before had argued that the activities described by common folk took place merely in their dreams, began to argue that they had a physical reality. The supernatural visitors were now, in their view, demons who actually took on the appearance of human beings, while the people who had previously only dreamt or imagined that they were following such demons did in fact do so in a fully awakened state. The women who before had dreamt that they flew at night on cannibalistic missions were now actually flying, the power of transportation being provided by the Devil. The reasons for this change in learned attitudes, which one can begin to detect in the fourteenth century, are unclear. The most likely explanation is that it was the product of scholastic demonology.

---

31 A. Kors and E. Peters (eds), *Witchcraft in Europe, 1100–1700* (Philadelphia, 1972), pp. 36–7.

Once the Devil was defined as having extraordinary powers over local motion, then his ability to move people through the air (which was his domain) naturally followed. At the same time the scholastic emphasis on the ability of the Devil to take on human forms and for individuals to make pacts with him encouraged the view that humans could and did attend him in the manner described in stories of the Dianic procession. The third change, partially a product of the other two, was the fusion of the two ideas of the *strigae* and the Dianic procession with the belief in a secret, amoral, Devil-worshipping sect of magicians. That synthesis also took place in the early fifteenth century.

It should be noted that although many members of the European élite subscribed to the belief that the Devil could physically transport human bodies through the air, the older, more sceptical attitude that this happened as a result of diabolical imagination was never completely rejected, even in scholastic circles. The long discussion in the *Malleus Maleficarum* of the ability of devils to transport witches from place to place bears this out. Faced with the unimpeachable authority of the canon law, the authors could not deny the fact that some witches were transported only 'in imagination'. They merely stated, therefore, that one could not deduce from the canon that *all* witches were transported in this way. 'But who is so foolish as to conclude that they cannot *also* be bodily transported?' asked the *Malleus*. The authors then went on to prove, on the basis of scholastic demonology, that the Devil could in fact transport himself from place to place. At the same time, however, they could not deny that transportation by phantasm was just as consistent with scholastic demonology. Much of what the Devil did, according to the schoolmen, was by deliberate delusion. Some, but not all, of the witches' magic was performed in this way, and the alleged metamorphosis of witches into beasts, an idea present in the popular notion of the *strigae*, was clearly the result of the Devil's confusion of the imaginative faculty, not the actual transmutation of substances. It was not at all implausible, therefore, that some individuals would imagine that they were at the sabbath, while others would in fact be transported there bodily. Instead of claiming that the belief in the reality of the witches' flight replaced the belief that the witch imagined such a venture, we should realize that after the fourteenth century both beliefs coexisted. As the *Malleus* concluded, 'they are transported both bodily and phantastically'.[32] The important change, however,

---

32 *Malleus Maleficarum*, p. 108. See also Ginzburg, *Night Battles*, p. 20.

was the admission by a long succession of writers in the late fifteenth and sixteenth centuries that 'sometimes witches are really transported from place to place by the Devil who, in the shape of a goat or some other fantastic animal, both carries them bodily to the sabbath and is present at its obscenities'.[33] Those who continued to maintain the older attitude of the Canon *Episcopi* in all cases were the humanist sceptics of the mid-sixteenth century.

The belief that witches flew to the sabbath and could also use the same power to escape arrest was one that admitted numerous differences in detail. Sometimes witches were described and depicted artistically as riding beasts in the manner of Diana's followers. At other times they rode on sticks, which could be forked in the manner of a divining rod. Less commonly witches appear riding pitchforks or tridents, a symbol frequently associated with the Devil which derives ultimately from the trident of Poseidon (Neptune). Of all the witches' means of aerial transport, however, the most frequently cited, and clearly the most enduring in popular culture, is the broomstick. The broom is primarily a symbol of the female sex, and its use in the fantasy of the witches' sabbath might therefore reflect nothing more than the preponderance of female witches. In this sense the broom serves the same symbolic function as the distaff, which also appears occasionally in descriptions of witchcraft. The broom might have had added significance, however, in that it is often used in fertility rites, thus suggesting associations with ancient pagan goddesses. Last but not least, the broom served as a phallic symbol and therefore was appropriate in a scene that was suffused with sexuality.

Sometimes witches were depicted as having flown without any means of support, either in a gust of wind or simply by their own power. Since in some of these cases they were reported to have anointed themselves with flying unguents, the question has arisen whether the ointments contained hallucinogens that made the witches feel as if they were covering vast distances and perhaps even imagine that they were attending the sabbath. Twentieth-century experiments with the ingredients listed in recipes for such flying unguents have shown that they contained atropines and other poisons which, when rubbed into the skin, can produce high excitement, delusion and life-like dreams.[34] We also know that the excrement from toads, which

33 F.M. Guazzo, *Compendium Maleficarum*, trans. E.A. Ashwin, ed. M. Summers (London, 1929), p. 34.
34 M.J. Harner, 'Hallucinogens' pp. 127–50; L. Gentz, 'Vad förorsakade de stora häxprocesserna', *Arv*, 10 (1954): 37.

Basque witches often kept as familiars, can have a hallucinogenic effect.[35] It is possible, therefore, that some individuals who used these ointments actually imagined that they were flying and attending sabbaths, an argument first advanced by sixteenth-century sceptics like Johann Weyer. But we must not leap to conclusions. Many of the earliest recipes for flying unguents, which come from the fifteenth century, contain nothing but inert elements like bat's blood and soot, and all early accounts of the use of flying unguents show that the ointment was applied to the witch's stick or broom, not directly to her body.[36] The witches' unguents, therefore, should probably be viewed as products of either harmless folklore or demonological theory, and not as effective mind-altering substances.

Metamorphosis

One popular witch-belief closely related to flight that was never fully integrated into the cumulative concept of witchcraft was that of metamorphosis. The belief that humans could change their shape was present in popular culture from earliest recorded times, and it still exists today. Since the process of metamorphosis involves the operation of some magical or supernatural power, it readily became associated with witchcraft, and the claim that witches transformed themselves (or others) into animals, especially wolves, appears in many witchcraft confessions. Like the belief that witches could fly, belief in metamorphosis was considered heretical and illusory by the Canon *Episcopi* and by many other late medieval authorities. Unlike the belief in flight, however, the belief in the physical reality of shape-shifting was generally not accepted by early modern intellectuals.[37] In works by such men as Ulrich Molitor and in the otherwise credulous *Malleus Maleficarum*, the traditional view that metamorphosis was the product of demonic illusion persisted. Even Henri Boguet, after citing the Bible and classical authority to prove that 'the metamorphosis of a man into a beast is possible', admitted that in his opinion the change was always illusory.[38] This interpretation did

---

35 Henningsen, *Witches' Advocate*, pp. 94, 471–2.

36 Kieckhefer, *European Witch Trials*, p. 41. Harner, 'Hallucinogens', p. 131, argues that the stick served as an applicator to the sensitive vaginal membranes but the practical reasons for choosing this method are not made clear.

37 Jean Bodin was one of the few who did. His views, however, were rejected by Pierre Le Loyer, Martin Del Rio and J. de Nynauld. See J. Pearl, 'Humanism and Satanism: Jean Bodin's contribution to the witchcraft crisis', *Canadian Review of Sociology and Anthropology*, 19 (1984): 542–4.

38 Boguet, *Examen of Witches*, p. 143.

not in any way prevent the prosecution of persons who claimed that they could transform themselves into beasts. In certain areas of Europe, especially in heavily forested regions, a number of werewolves were tried and convicted as witches.[39] The charge of metamorphosis, however, did not appear frequently enough in witchcraft trials to become an essential component of the cumulative concept of witchcraft.

THE DISSEMINATION OF BELIEF

By the middle of the fifteenth century the cumulative concept of witchcraft had acquired all of its basic elements. Indeed, in the 1420s and 1430s a number of trials took place in the Alpine regions of France and Switzerland in which certain *malefici* were accused not only of having worshipped the Devil in large nocturnal, orgiastic rites and of having killed and devoured their infants, but also of having flown to these ceremonies.[40] These trials took place in areas where Waldensian heretics were also being prosecuted, and since both they and the witches were accused of meeting secretly, inquisitors probably viewed the two groups as related threats. Magicians were, after all, considered to be heretics and were vulnerable therefore to the same charges that were traditionally made against other heretics. But there is no evidence that the inquisitors of the 1420s and 1430s confused the *malefici* whom they were prosecuting with Waldensians.[41] The charges of practising magic and of flying out at night find no place in the trials of the Waldensians, or for that matter any other heretics, such as Cathars. It had been more than three centuries, moreover, since heretics had been charged with ritual murder and cannibalism. Between the eleventh and fourteenth centuries those charges had been

---

39 Monter, *Witchcraft in France and Switzerland*, pp. 144–51; C. Oates, 'The Trial of a Teenage Werewolf, Bordeaux, 1613', *Criminal Justice History*, 9 (1988): 1–29.

40 See Cohn, *Europe's Inner Demons*, pp. 225–8. Descriptions of metamorphosis also surfaced for the first time in some of these trials. Ginzburg, *Ecstasies*, pp. 72–3. For a trial at Todi in 1428 which had many of the same characteristics of the ones in France and Switzerland see Kieckhefer, *European Witch Trials*, p. 73.

41 See J.J. Marx, *L'Inquisition en Dauphiné* (Paris, 1914), p. 48. Inquisitors during these years often made distinctions between the Waldensians and the 'other pernicious sect'. Nevertheless, a terminological confusion eventually did arise, as the new witches were referred to simply as Waldensians or heretics. See Russell, *Witchcraft in the Middle Ages*, p. 220; Ginzburg, *Ecstasies*, p. 79. In the Jura region, many of the early vernacular words for 'witch' were derived from words for 'heretics'. Monter, *Witchcraft in France and Switzerland*, pp. 22–3.

made only against magicians and Jews, and when they appeared in these trials, as they had in the earlier trials conducted by Peter of Greyerz, it was usually in connection with the production of magical potions.[42] When inquisitors began to prosecute these *malefici*, therefore, they must have been convinced that they had discovered members of a new and very different heretical sect.

The stereotype of witchcraft that first appeared in the trials of the 1420s and 1430s endured for more than two centuries, but it was not yet complete. The belief, for example, that witches received a mark on their bodies from the Devil at the time of the conclusion of the pact did not emerge with any clarity until the early sixteenth century and was developed mainly by Protestant demonologists.[43] In the sixteenth and seventeenth centuries, moreover, the descriptions of the activities that took place at the sabbath were embellished in many different and unusual ways. In some countries, such as Norway and Sweden, the belief in the sabbath was assimilated to a body of folklore regarding flights to distant locations. In the Friuli it was grafted onto a body of peasant belief regarding nocturnal struggles between the members of a fertility cult, the *benandanti*, and the witches.[44] Throughout Europe, moreover, the details of the sabbath varied from place to place and time to time. The Devil or Master of Ceremonies, for example, appears in a wide variety of guises, most commonly as a human being or as a he-goat but also as a bull, cat, dog, horse or sheep. The feast or banquet also reflected local cuisine and could be described in either attractive or unpleasant, tasteless terms. Descriptions of sexual activity at the sabbath also varied, reflecting differences in the erotic imagination of both the accusers and the accused. Sometimes there were reports of sexual commerce between witches and demons, but at others there were allegations of widespread sexual promiscuity among the witches themselves.

42 Ginzburg, *Ecstasies*, pp. 75–6. For the connection with magic see above, n. 26; Kieckhefer, *European Witch Trials*, p. 73; Hansen, *Quellen*, p. 449. The confessions of women to having been *strigae* could easily have reinforced such charges. See Cohn, *Europe's Inner Demons*, p. 228.

43 Monter, *Witchcraft in France and Switzerland*, pp. 159–66. In some cases more than one mark was found. Four marks were located on Janet Bruce of Tranent, Scotland, in 1657. Scottish Record Office, JC26/22, process against Tranent witches, 23 June 1657.

44 Ginzburg, *Night Battles*, pp. 99–145. In *Ecstasies*, pp. 76–8 et passim, Ginzburg argues that a similar body of folkloric culture was one of the main sources of the origin of the idea of the witches' sabbath in the western Alpine region in the late fourteenth and early fifteenth centuries.

Although the specific charges against witches varied from place to place and even from case to case, they still shared a number of common features. These similarities, coupled with the clearly cumulative fashion in which witch-beliefs were developed, suggest strongly that learned notions about witchcraft were transmitted from one area to another and from one generation to the next. It is true, as discussed above, that certain elements of the cumulative concept of witchcraft, such as the belief in a collective, anti-Christian amoral society, can arise *sui generis* at any place and at any time, but this is not true of the entire set of learned European witch-beliefs. These ideas were fused into a quite distinct amalgam by the fifteenth century, a composite product that could not have arisen by itself in the mind of one magistrate or inquisitor. This body of knowledge had to be learned, and hence it had to be transmitted from one time and place to another. The only way that we can deny the fact of that transmission is to claim that organized witchcraft, or some activity closely resembling it, was in fact practised throughout all of Europe. This was the position taken by the French philosopher and judge Jean Bodin, who based his belief in the reality of a European witch-cult on the uniformity of witches' confessions. It was also the position of Margaret Murray, who on the basis of the same confessions concluded that all accused witches were in fact practitioners of the same fertility religion. Neither Bodin's nor Murray's theory can be substantiated, however, and therefore we must explain how learned notions regarding activities that never occurred were actually transmitted.[45]

Both the development and the transmission of learned notions of witchcraft occurred as the result of the interaction between the judicial process on the one hand and a literary tradition on the other. Most learned witch-beliefs were developed and fused with other notions in the actual trials of either magicians or witches. The development or fusion was invariably the work of the judge or inquisitor, who blended the charge against the accused with his own fantasies or obsessions, which were themselves often nourished by either theological and demonological knowledge or the reports of other cases that he or a colleague had adjudicated. By extracting confessions, usually under torture, to the activities that he believed the witch had engaged in, the inquisitor received confirmation of his suspicions, and thus the beliefs acquired validity. The results of these

45 J. Bodin, *Démonomanie*, pp. 135–53; Murray, *Witch-Cult*, p. 13 et passim.

trials became known to other judges, first by word of mouth and then by written manuals for inquisitors, which used the testimony given at the trials to illustrate the various activities of the witches. In this way the set of learned beliefs could become cumulative, since a new inquisitor, in trying a case, would use the information contained in the manual to formulate the questions he would direct to witnesses and the accused. At the same time, however, he might use some of the specific charges against the accused or his own imagination to give a new twist to the standard charges. The confession that he would extract to these somewhat different charges, perhaps embellished by the witch's imagination and folk beliefs, might then be included in another manual or treatise on witchcraft and thus be transmitted to other inquisitors. The entire process of transmission was abetted by the universities, which exposed future judges to the growing body of demonological and inquisitorial literature and which also advised local jurisdictions how to conduct witchcraft prosecutions.[46]

It is difficult if not impossible to determine whether the trials themselves or the large body of literature on witchcraft was more important in the development and transmission of learned witch beliefs. On the one hand judges and inquisitors had often acquired extensive knowledge of witchcraft through their education and reading before actually prosecuting witches. On the other hand, the manuals and treatises which they read tended to reflect rather than to anticipate juridical developments. Without oversimplifying a complex issue, one can argue that as the various notions included in the cumulative concept of witchcraft were being developed and fused, the trials themselves were of primary importance, the literature playing a secondary role in shaping the course of those trials and communicating their results to a wider audience.[47] As the stereotype of the witch became fairly well established, however, the literature became the main vehicle of transmitting knowledge about the crime. The importance of this literature also increased significantly with the introduction of printing in the second half of the fifteenth century. This innovation made it possible for learned beliefs to spread more broadly and more rapidly than in the manuscript age. As this witchcraft literature grew in size and popularity, the trials themselves began to serve only the ancillary functions of validating

46 On the role of the universities in Germany see G. Schormann, *Hexenprozesse in Nordwestdeutschland* (Hildesheim, 1977), pp. 9–44.

47 This was especially true in the fifteenth century. See Russell, *Witchcraft in the Middle Ages*, p. 243.

the beliefs contained in the literature, providing additional examples for new treatises, and making some of these ideas available to the illiterate population in the form of sentences that were read publicly at the time of execution.

The first witchcraft treatise that assumed a major role in making the cumulative concept of witchcraft available to a large audience was the *Malleus Maleficarum*. First published in 1486, and reprinted thirteen times before 1520, it was the work of two Dominican inquisitors, Heinrich Kramer or Institoris (his Latin name) and Jacob Sprenger. Kramer, the principal author, was an elderly and perhaps emotionally disturbed theologian who had been appointed as an inquisitor for southern Germany in 1474. Sprenger, a professor of theology at the University of Cologne, had received a similar appointment as inquisitor for the Rhineland in 1470. The two had cooperated judicially, especially in the prosecution of witches, and when they met resistance from local ecclesiastical and secular authorities in their work, they succeeded in obtaining a Bull from Pope Innocent VIII in 1484 authorizing them to proceed. Two years later, using as examples many of the cases they had adjudicated, they produced the *Malleus*, to which they attached the papal Bull, entitled *Summis desiderantes*, as a preface. They also included an endorsement, which is known to have been at least partially forged, from the theological faculty of the University of Cologne. The book was essentially a manual for inquisitors, similar to the one produced by Nicholas Eymeric, *Directorium Inquisitorum*, in 1376. It took the form of a scholastic disputation, in which a series of questions were asked and answered, and in so doing it relied heavily on scholastic thought, especially that of Thomas Aquinas. In addition to Aquinas, the book drew upon a broad range of theological and legal writers in a rather eclectic fashion.[48]

The *Malleus* did not in any way formulate the cumulative concept of witchcraft. That concept had already been formed fifty years before. In fact, as a statement of the cumulative concept the *Malleus* was somewhat deficient, for it referred to the sabbath only in passing and it did not discuss the obscene kiss or the Devil's mark. Nor did the *Malleus* make a contribution to the further development of witch-beliefs. Its only novel features in this regard were a misogynistic overemphasis on the susceptibility of women to the crime and the

---

48 See S. Anglo, 'Evident Authority and Authoritative Evidence: *The Malleus Maleficarum*', in *The Damned Art: Essays in the Literature of Witchcraft*, ed. S. Anglo, (London, 1977) pp. 1–31.

claim that the most powerful class of witches (those who inflicted every kind of harm and who devoured their children) all 'practise carnal copulation with devils'.[49] Nevertheless, the work did help to strengthen the fusion that had already taken place between many different witch-beliefs by discussing them in a single work and in an ordered, systematic way. It served therefore as an 'encyclopedia of witchcraft' and in that form transmitted an entire set of learned beliefs to a larger audience.

The *Malleus* did much more, however, than simply synthesize a variety of witch-beliefs and package these in a large, well-structured treatise. It also provided theological support for the ideas it was advancing, legal advice on how to bring witches to trial, and perhaps most important of all, a bold claim that those who denied the reality of witchcraft were heretics. The effect that the book had on witch-hunting is difficult to determine. It did not open the door 'to almost indiscriminate prosecutions'[50] or even bring about an immediate increase in the number of trials. In fact its publication in Italy was followed by a noticeable reduction in witchcraft cases.[51] But even if it did not prompt hundreds of inquisitors and magistrates to inaugurate massive witch-hunts in their jurisdictions, it did make them more conscious of the crime of witchcraft and probably more credulous of its reality. We must recognize that the cumulative concept of witchcraft did not command instinctive and immediate belief, either among the educated or the illiterate. People had to be *told* that witches *could* and *did* perform the various acts of which they were accused. The *Malleus* was an appropriate tool in this educative process, since it contained enough information drawn from judicial experience and enough theological citation and argumentation to make it appear to be authoritative. The apparent papal approval that it gained from the inclusion of the Bull of 1484 may have given it even greater authority, although obviously not among those Protestants who used the book in the sixteenth century.[52]

The *Malleus* therefore, while not directly inspiring a frenzy of witchcraft prosecutions, nevertheless did make an important contribution to the development of the entire European witch-hunt. Like the cumulative concept of witchcraft that it helped to transmit, it

49 Anglo, *Malleus Maleficarum*, pp. 41–8, 99.
50 H. Sebald, *Witchcraft*, p. 36.
51 Midelfort, *Witch Hunting*, p. 22, downplays the influence of the book.
52 Hansen, *Witchcraft at Salem*, p. 27, claims that the Puritan minister Increase Mather used the book in late seventeenth-century Massachusetts.

served as a precondition of intensive witch-hunting. It is important to note, however, that the *Malleus* was only one of many important witchcraft treatises that were published during the hunt.[53] Many of those that followed it into print were much more complete in their description of the cumulative concept of witchcraft, especially in dealing with the sabbath, and a few of these works achieved even greater popularity than the *Malleus*. In 1524 Paulus Grillandus, a papal judge who presided at a number of witchcraft trials in the vicinity of Rome, published *Tractatus de Hereticis et Sortilegiis*. This widely read treatise became one of the main sources of information regarding the sabbath, in which Grillandus fully believed.

After the appearance of Grillandus's book there was a forty-year lull in the production of witchcraft literature. Very few treatises were written during that period, nor were new editions of the older works forthcoming. For this surprising gap there are a number of possible explanations, including both a European-wide decline in prosecutions and a preoccupation of the educated élite with the Protestant Reformation. As Protestantism spread, moreover, and as papal inquisitions declined even in Catholic countries, interest in works written mainly by inquisitors naturally waned. After 1570, however, there was a marked upsurge in witchcraft prosecutions, and this development stimulated the printing of the old treatises and the authorship of new ones. Like the *Malleus*, the new treatises of the late sixteenth and seventeenth centuries were the product of judicial action, in that they used evidence from the trials themselves to embellish the stereotype of the witch and to provide officials, especially secular magistrates, with guidance.

In 1595 Nicolas Rémy, a judge from the Duchy of Lorraine who claimed to have executed more than 800 witches in sixteen years, published a treatise, *Demonolatreiae*, which in many ways replaced the *Malleus* as the main source of information regarding the work of Satan on earth. The readers of the *Demonolatreiae* were treated to detailed discussions of the activities that allegedly took place at the sabbath: the obscene kiss, the feasting on horrid foods and human flesh, and the dancing to unpleasant music. A few years later a Belgian Jesuit, Martin Del Rio, published his *Disquisitionum Magicarum Libri Sex*, which like the *Malleus* served as an encyclopedia of magic and also gave specific instruction to judges. Printed twenty times and translated into French in 1611, Del Rio's work became the

---

53 For lists of some of these see Russell, *Witchcraft in the Middle Ages*, pp. 246–50; Leutenbauer, *Hexerei- und Zaubereidelikt*, pp. xiv-xxi.

most popular and authoritative witchcraft treatise in the seventeenth century.

Other late sixteenth- and seventeenth-century works supplemented that of Del Rio and also achieved widespread popularity. A Burgundian judge, Henri Boguet, wrote a treatise on the basis of his judicial experience, *Discours des sorciers* (1602), which went into eight editions. A few years later Pierre de Lancre, a French judge who had conducted a large witch-hunt in the Pays de Labourd, wrote a treatise, *Tableau de l'inconstance des mauvais anges et démons* (1612), which not only described the sabbath in unprecedented detail but also included a now famous engraving by the Polish artist Jan Ziarnko depicting the horrid affair. In 1635 a Lutheran judge from Saxony, Benedict Carpzov, published his *Practica Rerum Criminalium*, a commentary on the laws of Saxony regarding witchcraft and a compendium of decisions by the Leipzig Supreme Court. Carpzov's book, which was reprinted nine times, gained a reputation as the *Malleus Maleficarum* of Protestantism, especially since it provided specific instructions regarding the prosecution of witches. In Italy the most comprehensive guide to witchcraft, the *Compendium Maleficarum*, was written by a Milanese Friar, Francesco Maria Guazzo, in 1608. Guazzo drew heavily on the works of Kramer and Sprenger, Rémy and Del Rio, as well as hundreds of other authorities, thus showing that the work of demonologists was, like the concept of witchcraft that they were elaborating, cumulative. Guazzo included in his book a series of illustrations of witches concluding a pact with the Devil, thereby providing his audience with an important visual supplement to the fantasies he was describing.

Taken together, the witchcraft treatises of the early modern period succeeded in making the literate members of European society aware of witchcraft and convinced of its reality. The readership of these works was, however, limited to a small portion of the population, consisting mainly of members of the upper classes and the ruling élite. This segment of society, which included the lawyers, judges and magistrates, was perfectly capable, on the basis of the knowledge it had acquired regarding witchcraft and the legal power it possessed, of conducting a witch-hunt. In order for intensive witch-hunting to have succeeded, however, it was necessary for the lower classes to have some understanding of the diabolical nature of the crime. Even though many accusations of witchcraft came from 'above' (i.e., from officials and judges), the detection and prosecution of witches required the support of the entire community.

It was the witches' neighbours who were relied upon to identify suspects, facilitate their apprehension and testify against them. If a witch-hunt, especially a large hunt, were to be successful, it was necessary for the lower classes to believe in witchcraft and to assist in the process of hunting. The problem was that most members of the lower classes did not share the learned notions of witchcraft that made the crime so frightening. They believed in magic and *maleficium* and recognized the danger that harmful magic posed to them, but they did not necessarily attribute the power of such activity to the Devil. They believed in *strigae*, the ladies of the night and metamorphosis, and some of them even believed in *incubi* and *succubi*, but they had not fused these disparate ideas in the way that theologians and inquisitors had, with all the frightening implications. Nevertheless, there is evidence that some of the learned notions of witchcraft and certainly the attendant fear of a widespread satanic conspiracy did penetrate the lower levels of European society, at least for brief periods of time. There are enough unforced confessions, for example, to show that many of the fantasies developed by the theologians and inquisitors had percolated down to the lower classes. When we discover that nearly 2,000 illiterate peasants in the Basque country freely confessed to having attended large sabbaths and described the activities that went on at those assemblies, we can be fairly certain that the ideas of the élite had reached them by one route or another.

One method of educating the populace in learned notions of witchcraft was the public reading of the charges against witches at their executions. Another was the deliberate instruction of the people in matters of witchcraft at the time of a large panic. During the Basque witch-hunt of 1610–14 the King of Spain sent letters to all the bishops in the afflicted areas and also to the heads of the preaching orders to have their subordinates preach against witchcraft, just as they had during an earlier hunt in 1527. The purpose of this programme was to prevent people in their ignorance from joining the witches' sect, to secure confessions from those who had already succumbed to the temptation, and to win the support of the people in wiping out the pernicious crime.[54] In the Low Countries ecclesiastical authorities included the activities of witches in the lists of errors that they periodically read to their congregations. Throughout Europe witchcraft sermons were preached during witch-hunts and especially before executions. But perhaps the best example of the role that sermons played in spreading witch-beliefs among an entire

54 See Henningsen, *Witches' Advocate*, pp. 206–7; 'Papers of Salazar', p. 105.

congregation occurred at Salem, Massachusetts, where the minister, Samuel Parris, not only unconsciously prepared his congregation for witch-hunting by depicting a satanic menace both outside and within the village for years before the hunt, but also developed this theme once the actual hunt began.[55]

Although the learned élite did achieve a certain measure of success in educating the lower classes in their demonologically oriented theories of witchcraft, the process of imposing a higher culture on a popular one was not without its difficulties and could result in bitter social conflict. There is perhaps no better example of the gap that existed between learned and popular culture than the prosecution of the *benandanti* in the Friuli in the late sixteenth and early seventeenth centuries. The *benandanti*, as we have seen, believed that they went out 'in spirit' at night during the Ember seasons (quarterly fasting periods) to fight the witches. The officials of the Inquisition, incapable of comprehending this body of peasant folk belief, and suspicious that the *benandanti* were in fact witches going to the sabbath, gradually convinced these members of an old fertility cult that they were maleficent witches. In one sense the entire episode serves as an example of the way in which learned beliefs were able to penetrate social barriers, for the final result was the imposition of a learned notion of the sabbath on a very different set of popular witch beliefs. But the difficulties that the inquisitors encountered in achieving this result are of perhaps greater significance than their ultimate success. Over and over again they interrogated suspects who insisted that they were 'fighting for Christ' against the witches, ensuring the fertility of the crops, and it took the courts more than fifty years to convince them otherwise.[56] When examined in this light, witch-trials can be seen as a form of cultural and social conflict, in which a literate ruling class tried to bring an illiterate peasantry into conformity with its world view and in the process suppressed or at least fundamentally transformed an entire set of popular beliefs.[57]

55 P. Boyer and S. Nissenbaum, *Salem Possessed: The Social Origins of Witchcraft* (Cambridge, Mass., 1974), pp. 168–78.

56 Ginzburg, *Night Battles*.

57 The role played by such popular ideas in the actual formation of the learned stereotype remains a matter of dispute. See Ginzburg, *Ecstasies*, p. 11 et passim, for the argument that the stereotype was 'a hybrid result of a conflict between folk culture and learned culture.' For a different view see R. Muchembled, 'Satanic Myths and Cultural Reality', in *Early Modern European Witchcraft: Centres and Peripheries*, ed. B. Ankarloo and G. Henningsen (Oxford, 1990), pp. 140–1.

THE CHALLENGE OF THE RENAISSANCE

Once the cumulative concept of witchcraft had been formulated and disseminated, it proved to be astonishingly durable for the next two centuries. Its persistence has been a source of mystery to many historians because learned European culture during the period of the witch-hunt came under the influence of an intellectual movement that posed a serious threat to many of these witch-beliefs. That movement was the Renaissance, the rebirth or revival of classical culture which began in Italy in the late fourteenth and fifteenth centuries and gradually spread to northern Europe in the fifteenth and sixteenth centuries. The Renaissance threatened the learned concept of witchcraft in a number of ways. First of all, it encouraged a general contempt for medieval learning, especially scholasticism, which failed to measure up to the high standards of classical civilization. Since witch-beliefs were very much a part of that denigrated medieval culture, they became highly vulnerable to humanist criticism. More specifically, the main philosophical system of the Renaissance, neo-Platonism, posed a direct challenge to the Aristotelian philosophy of scholasticism that underlay the cumulative concept of witchcraft. Instead of attributing apparently magical occurrences to the Devil, in the scholastic manner, neo-Platonists claimed that man could perform magic himself, by exploiting natural forces in the universe. Indeed, many Renaissance humanists were themselves practitioners of natural magic, much of it based on rediscovered classical texts, and they tried to give to their art an intellectual and moral respectability that the Church had always denied it.[58] These men were not, to be sure, very interested in the type of crude magic that witches allegedly practised. This they tended to depreciate as ineffective, peasant superstition. But by defending their own forms of learned magic and by devaluing that of the illiterate, they were attacking many of the presuppositions of the *Malleus Maleficarum*.

The threat that Renaissance humanism presented to the cumulative concept of witchcraft was not illusory. Humanists like Desiderius Erasmus, Pietro Pomponazzi and Andrea Alciati attacked certain witch-beliefs, while Cornelius Agrippa of Nettesheim, the great practitioner of learned magic, criticized both the *Malleus Maleficarum* and

---

58 D.P. Walker, *Spiritual and Demonic Magic: From Ficino to Campanella* (London, 1958); W. Shumaker, *The Occult Sciences in the Renaissance* (Berkeley, 1972), pp. 108–59.

the prosecution of witches.[59] In the late sixteenth century most of the sceptics who challenged the doctrines of the *Malleus Maleficarum*, such as Weyer, Scot and Montaigne, were men of humanist backgrounds and interests. One can also argue that in the long run neo-Platonism succeeded in weakening Aristotelianism and facilitating the acceptance of the mechanical philosophy that eventually displaced it. Nevertheless, despite the seriousness of the Renaissance threat, the cumulative concept of witchcraft survived intact until the end of the seventeenth century.

Why did this happen? Why did the Renaissance, with all of its hostility to scholasticism and its multi-faceted scepticism, fail to destroy learned witch beliefs?[60] One of the reasons for this failure is that neo-Platonism never achieved a dominant position in European intellectual circles and was never able, therefore, to change the mind-set of generations of lawyers and clerics. In fact Aristotelianism experienced something of a revival in the 1590s and reigned supreme in many countries until the middle of the seventeenth century.[61] But even if neo-Platonism had been stronger, it is unlikely that it would have undermined the cumulative concept of witchcraft, for the simple reason that it did not deny two ideas that were central to witchcraft: the existence of the Devil and the efficacy of magic. The demons of neo-Platonism bore little resemblance to the Devil of scholasticism, but Renaissance intellectuals, once they conceded the existence and power of demonic forces, were hardly in the best position to assault the basic principles of medieval demonology. The same is true for Renaissance magic. The learned *magi* of the Renaissance did everything in their power to distinguish the magic they practised and wrote about from the magic of the ignorant necromancers of the Middle Ages and the poor, illiterate witches of their own day. But the distinctions were not always clear, especially when learned *magi* employed demonic magic, and the belief in one type of magic could lead to belief in the other.[62] The connections

---

59 E.W. Monter (ed.), *European Witchcraft* (New York, 1969), pp. 56–7; H.A. Oberman, *Masters of the Reformation* (Cambridge, 1981), p. 174; H.R. Trevor-Roper, 'The European Witch-Craze of the Sixteenth and Seventeenth Centuries', in H.R. Trevor-Roper, *The European Witch-Craze of the Sixteenth and Seventeenth Centuries and Other Essays* (New York, 1969), pp. 132–3.

60 On Renaissance scepticism see C.G. Nauert, *Agrippa and the Crisis of Renaissance Thought* (Urbana, Ill., 1965), pp. 200, 240–1, 292–301.

61 See for example, H. Kearney, *Scholars and Gentlemen* (London, 1970), p. 94.

62 A. Williamson, *Scottish National Consciousness in the Age of James VI* (Edinburgh, 1979), p. 168; R.H. West, *Reginald Scot and Renaissance Writings on Witchcraft* (Boston, 1984), p. 4.

between the two types of magic became even closer in the writings of witch-mongers like Jean Bodin, who combined his attack on witches with an assault on the magic of Agrippa and Pico della Mirandola.[63] In Italy the clerical confusion between magic and witchcraft may actually have contributed to the rise of witch-hunting.[64] Perhaps it is no coincidence that the introduction of humanism in Florence in the late fourteenth century was accompanied by a series of sorcery trials.[65]

Both the strengths and the limits of Renaissance scepticism regarding witchcraft are evident in the work of the most famous of all sixteenth-century critics of witch-hunting, Johann Weyer. Weyer was the disciple of Agrippa and the physician of the tolerant humanist, Duke William V of Cleves. His work reflects the negative attitude of Agrippa towards necromancy as well as the tolerant attitude of Erasmus towards those accused of witchcraft. It also draws upon a tradition that was very strong in Lutheran theological circles which, on the basis of the Canon *Episcopi*, argued that witches did not perform all the activities that were attributed to them. The main purpose of Weyer's books, *De Praestigiis Daemonum* (1563) and *De Lamiis* (1582), was to show that the ignorant women who confessed to witchcraft were suffering from delusion and should not be prosecuted. These books, therefore, constituted a frontal assault upon the views expressed in the *Malleus Maleficarum*. In making his case Weyer used his medical knowledge, claiming both that the alleged *maleficia* of witches could be explained by natural, medical causes and that confessions of witches to diabolical activities were to a large extent the result of a female disease of the uterus, *melancholia*. Weyer also used his knowledge of Roman law to prove that the witch's alleged pact with the devil was not a valid contract and that therefore the crime of having made such a pact was impossible. To Weyer, therefore, witchcraft was an attempt by a mentally disordered person to do something that was both physically and legally impossible.[66]

63 F. Yates, *The Occult Philosophy in the Elizabethan Age* (London, 1979), pp. 67–71.

64 P. Burke, 'Witchcraft and Magic in Renaissance Italy: Gianfrancesco Pico and His *Strix*', in S. Anglo (ed.), *The Damned Art: Essays in the Literature of Witchcraft* (London, 1977), p. 49.

65 G. Brucker, 'Sorcery in Renaissance Florence', *Studies in the Renaissance*, 10 (1963), p. 8.

66 H.C.E. Midelfort, 'Johann Weyer and the Transformation of the Insanity Defense', in *The German People and the German Reformation*, ed. R.P. Hsia (Ithaca, 1988), pp. 234–61.

The weakness in Weyer's argument was that he did not deny the existence of the Devil or his ability to insinuate himself in human affairs. In dealing with the *maleficia* of witches, their pact with the Devil and the ceremonies of ritual magicians he admitted that the Devil could influence the human imagination. The *maleficia* of witches might be attributable to natural causes, but the Devil was responsible for making the witches think that they had caused them. In similar manner the Devil played upon the imagination of the poor, ignorant, melancholic women who claimed that they made pacts with him, and he also deceived evil necromancers into performing the various acts of conjuration for which they were notorious. But if the Devil was capable of this type of activity, why could he not also perform *maleficia* and involve human agents in his work? Without a philosophically and theologically sound discussion of the Devil's powers, Weyer's treatise was incapable of withstanding the assaults that were to be made upon it.

A second weakness of Weyer's argument was that he failed to free the melancholic old women who were accused of witchcraft from moral responsibility for their actions. Even if these persons were imagining that they made pacts with the Devil, they were still guilty of heresy in the same way that the women referred to in the Canon *Episcopi* were. Melancholy had not, according to Weyer, made these women insane and therefore innocent; it had only made them more vulnerable to the Devil's power of delusion. In fact, Weyer did not rule out the prosecution of these women by ecclesiastical authorities, although he did insist that none of them should be put to death. He opposed their prosecution by the secular courts, since they did not actually cause the harm attributed to them, but that had nothing to do with their spiritual crime. And since many Protestants argued that witches could be prosecuted even if there was no evidence of *maleficia*, on the simple grounds that as witches their wills were corrupt, Weyer's plea for tolerance had little force.

Because of the weaknesses of Weyer's arguments, his views were almost entirely discredited by such men as Thomas Erastus and Jean Bodin, both of whom were known mainly for their works of political theory. Weyer found support from writers like Reginald Scot in England, whose views were in fact even more sceptical than Weyer's, but all in all the intellectual establishment throughout Europe rejected Weyer's position and became more certain in the belief that witchcraft was real and that witches should be prosecuted harshly for their crimes.[67] It was not until the middle of the seventeenth century that European intellectuals, displaying a much more fundamental scepticism than Weyer regarding diabolical power, began to undermine the philosophical and theological assumptions upon which the work of Rémy, Boguet, Guazzo, Del Rio and Bodin were based.

WITCHCRAFT AND THE FEAR OF REBELLION

The set of learned beliefs that we refer to as the cumulative concept of witchcraft proved therefore to be highly durable in the sixteenth and early seventeenth centuries. The acceptance of these ideas was sustained by many factors, the most significant being a firm conviction that the Devil had gained extraordinary powers over the course of human affairs. It was in fact this same conviction that originally inspired the formulation of the cumulative concept of witchcraft; without this belief witches would never have been regarded as anything more than superstitious peasants. But why did the men who formulated and then disseminated learned witch-beliefs come to the conclusion that Satan's power was so pervasive and so frightening? What developments in the late medieval and early modern periods led them to believe that the Devil was loose and that he was recruiting large numbers of human accomplices?

There is no simple answer to this question. The apparent manifestations of demonic power during these centuries were many and varied. The numerous calamities of the late fourteenth century, most especially the Black Death, may have encouraged intellectuals to assume greater demonic intervention in the world, whereas the profound economic crises of the early modern period, the trauma of the Reformation, and the frequency of war and plague might easily have reinforced the conviction of men like Rémy, Boguet, Carpzov and Guazzo that the Devil was especially active. As we shall see, these very same factors created anxieties in early modern communities that encouraged magistrates to prosecute witches.[68] But if we wish to identify one factor that underlay both the formulation and the transmission of the cumulative concept of witchcraft, one that most solidly buttressed the belief that the Devil was active in human affairs, then we should focus on the fear of rebellion, sedition and disorder that beset members of the upper classes during these years. It

---

67 Peter Binsfeld also attacked Weyer, claiming that the pact with the Devil was in fact possible. *Tractatus de confessionibus maleficorum et sagarum* (Treves, 1596).

68 See below, Chapter 5.

is no coincidence that the earliest descriptions of the witches' sabbath appeared when Europe was experiencing a wave of social rebellions in the late fourteenth century.[69] Nor is it any coincidence that the learned belief in organized witchcraft spread through Europe during a period of profound instability and chronic rebellion. The era of the great witch-hunt was the great age of popular rebellion in European history, centuries that witnessed countless peasant *jacqueries*, religious civil wars, and ultimately the first national revolutions of the modern world.[70] These disturbances terrified members of the ruling classes throughout Europe, and these fears were reflected in the imagery of the sabbath.

Like the Devil himself, who began his malevolent career with an act of rebellion against God, the witch was the quintessential rebel. Whether the individuals who were accused of witchcraft were in fact rebels is a separate question that we shall address below; the important consideration here is that theologians, magistrates and authors of witchcraft treatises viewed them in this way. As a heretic and apostate the witch was considered guilty of *lèse majesté* or treason against God;[71] as a Devil-worshipper she was part of an enormous political conspiracy; as a lower-class peasant she was striving to turn the world upside-down, inverting the divinely established hierarchical order of society and rejecting all its moral norms.[72] Sometimes the connection between rebellion and witchcraft was made explicit, as when witch-hunters, quoting the Bible, proclaimed that, 'Rebellion is as the sin of witchcraft', or when Scottish royalists, convinced that witches and Covenanters were of the same ilk, proclaimed in 1661 that 'Rebellion is the mother of witchcraft'.[73] Churchmen at the Council of Basel in the early fifteenth century thought that rural rebellion was part of a satanic conspiracy to destroy clerical celibacy

---

69 See Monter, *Witchcraft in France and Switzerland*, p. 18; G. Holmes, *Europe: Hierarchy and Revolt, 1320–1450* (New York, 1975), pp. 125–33. Nider, who offers one of the earliest descriptions of the sabbath, claims that the sect had been active since about 1375. Ginzburg, *Ecstasies*, p. 71.

70 H. Kamen, *European Society 1500–1700* (London, 1984); P. Zagorin, *Rebels and Rulers 1500–1660* (2 vols, Cambridge, 1981).

71 Leutenbauer, *Hexerei- und Zaubereidelikt*, p. 109.

72 On the political nature of such inversion see S. Clark, 'Inversion, Misrule and the Meaning of Witchcraft', *Past and Present*, 87 (1980), especially pp. 110–27.

73 I Samuel 15: 23; J. Kirkton, *The Secret and True History of the Church of Scotland*, ed. C.K. Sharpe (Edinburgh, 1817), p. 126. See also W. Kennett, *The Witchcraft of the Present Rebellion* (London, 1715)

and therefore took steps to facilitate the prosecution of witches.[74] Many witches were in fact accused specifically of treason as well as witchcraft, especially during the early phase of the witch-hunt, when accusations of political sorcery arose frequently. It was not uncommon for Bohemian rebels to be accused of satanism, and during the English Civil War, a radical clergyman, Thomas Larkham, was accused of 'Faction, Heresy, Witchcraft, Rebellion and Treason'.[75]

If witchcraft and rebellion were as closely related as these examples suggest, then the fear of rebellion probably did have an important influence on the formulation and dissemination of the cumulative concept of witchcraft. Lionel Rothkrug has argued that the concern of the authors of the *Malleus Maleficarum* with sorcerers who are archers reflects a widespread fear in German lands of Swiss infantry who had defeated the army of Charles the Bold in 1477 and of South German peasants who were hoping to enlist Swiss support in a rebellion against the Empire.[76] In similar fashion Pierre de Lancre's account of a massive diabolical conspiracy in the Pays de Labourd was conditioned by the fact that the area was a centre of Basque resistance against the French monarchy. Henri Boguet feared that if there were as many male witches as female ones and if they had a 'great Lord' as their leader, 'they would be strong enough to make war upon a King', which some witches had boasted they could do.[77] James VI of Scotland developed the credulous ideas that appear in his *Daemonologie* only after he became convinced that a coven of witches, headed by the earl of Bothwell, was engaged in a political conspiracy against him.[78] Perhaps Jean Bodin, whose absolutistic political views James fully endorsed, was thinking in similar terms when he wrote the *Démonomanie*.[79] Certainly William Perkins, the English Puritan who wrote *A Discourse of the Damned*

---

74 L. Rothkrug, 'Religious Practices and Collective Perceptions: Hidden Homologies in the Renaissance and Reformation', *Historical Reflections*, 7 (1980): 110–11. On the importance of the Council of Basel as the setting for the development of learned notions of witchcraft see Blauert, *Frühe Hexenverfolgungen*, pp. 32–3.

75 R.J.W. Evans, *The Making of the Habsburg Monarchy*, 1500–1700 (Oxford, 1979), p. 413; G.H. Radford, 'Thomas Larkham', *Reports and Transactions of the Devonshire Association*, 24 (1892), p. 97.

76 Rothkrug, 'Religious Practices', p. 108.

77 Boguet, *Examen of Witches*, pp. xxxi, xxxvi.

78 C. Larner, 'James VI and I and Witchcraft', in *The Reign of James VI and I*, ed. A.G.R. Smith (London, 1973), pp. 74–90; S. Clark, 'King James's *Daemonologie*: Witchcraft and Kingship', in *The Damned Art*, pp. 156–81.

79 He certainly considered the witch to be a threat to the good order of the republic. See Bodin, *Démonomanie*, p. 334.

Art of Witchcraft just before the death of Queen Elizabeth, had the image of the rebel-witch in his mind. 'The most notorious traytor and rebell that can be', wrote Perkins, 'is the Witch. For she renounceth God himselfe, the King of Kings, she leaves the societie of his Church and people, she bindeth herself in league with the devil.'[80]

The formulation, transmission and credulous reception of the cumulative concept of witchcraft by members of the learned and ruling élite served as one of the main preconditions of the great European witch-hunt. Without such beliefs there would have been no reason to pursue witches with the determination that judicial authorities manifested during the early modern period. Individual prosecutions for *maleficium*, ritual magic and the pact would certainly have taken place, just as they had in the past, but campaigns against witchcraft and the search for the witches' alleged confederates would be unimaginable. The formulation of the cumulative concept of witchcraft was, however, only one of the two main preconditions of the hunt. The second was the development of legal procedures that facilitated prosecution and conviction of those who were suspected of this crime. To these equally important judicial developments we now turn.

---

80 Perkins, *Damned Art of Witchcraft*, in *Works*, III, p. 651.

3 THE LEGAL FOUNDATIONS

The great European witch-hunt was essentially a judicial operation. The entire process of discovering and eliminating witches, from denunciation to punishment, usually occurred under judicial auspices. Even when witches took their own lives, they usually did so in order to avoid the often gruesome and apparently inevitable processes of the law.[1] Occasionally, agitated villagers took justice into their own hands and executed witches in vigilante style. In 1453 a number of sorcerers from the French village of Marmande perished in this manner, and during the Basque witch-hunt of 1610, large crowds broke into the houses of those who had been named and subjected them to violent torture, killing at least one woman.[2] In 1662 an angry mob at Auxonne in France lynched a group of women who were considered responsible for the demonic possession of an entire convent of nuns.[3] There is no way of determining how many suspected witches died in this illegal manner. In the Polish countryside the numbers may have been fairly high.[4] Central governments, however, were very much opposed to this type of rough country justice, since it constituted a challenge to their authority, and they took steps to prevent its recurrence.[5] We can be fairly certain, therefore, that a large majority of those persons who were executed for witchcraft during the great hunt were formally and legally tried and sentenced.

---

1 Dupont-Bouchat, 'Répression', p. 106; Larner, *Enemies of God*, pp. 114, 116, 119; Naess, 'Norway', p. 376. Rémy interprets suicides as attempts to escape the Devil's powers. *Demonolatry*, p. 161.

2 Hansen, *Quellen*, pp. 559–61; Henningsen, *Witches' Advocate*, p. 209.

3 Robbins, *Encyclopedia*, p. 394; S. Garnier, *Barbe Buvée et la prétendue possession des Ursulines d'Auxonne* (Paris, 1895).

4 Baranowski, *Procesy Czarownic*, p. 178. A.F. Soman suggests that lynchings were prevalent in France because the community could thereby avoid the cost of official justice. 'Parlement of Paris', pp. 42–3.

5 For the prosecution of those responsible for a witch lynching in France in 1587 see Soman, 'Witch Lynching at Juniville', pp. 8–15.

Since witch-hunting usually took a judicial form, it is only reasonable to assume that the legal procedures used in criminal prosecutions and the ways in which European judicial systems operated had a good deal to do with the origins of the great witch-hunt. Indeed, the intensive prosecution of witches in early modern Europe was facilitated by a number of legal developments that occurred between the thirteenth and the sixteenth centuries. First, the secular and ecclesiastical courts of Continental Europe adopted a new, inquisitorial system of criminal procedure that made it far easier for witchcraft cases to be initiated and prosecuted. Second, these courts acquired the right to torture persons accused of witchcraft, thus making it relatively easy to obtain confessions and the names of the witches' alleged accomplices. Third, the secular courts of Europe acquired jurisdiction over witchcraft, thereby supplementing and in many cases replacing the ecclesiastical courts as the judicial engines of the witch-hunt. Finally, local and regional courts were allowed to operate without much interference from central or national judicial control, thus ensuring a relatively high number of convictions and executions.

None of these legal developments, or even all of them taken together, amounted to a sufficient cause of the great witch-hunt, but each of them served as a necessary precondition of that hunt. Just like the intellectual developments discussed in the previous chapter, they helped to make the witch-hunt possible. In fact, the legal and the intellectual foundations of the hunt were closely related, since the adoption of new criminal procedures facilitated the synthesis of the various ideas about the activities that witches allegedly engaged in. Legal developments also help to explain why the great witch-hunt took place when it did. Intensive witch-hunting did not begin until many European courts had adopted inquisitorial procedure and had begun to use torture. On the other hand, intensive witch-hunting did not come to an end until magistrates and judges realized that they were sending innocent people to the stake and consequently instituted a number of significant legal reforms.

CHANGES IN CRIMINAL PROCEDURE

Before the thirteenth century European courts used a system of criminal procedure that made all crimes, and especially concealed crimes, difficult to prosecute. This procedural system, which is generally referred to as accusatorial, existed in its purest form in the secular courts of northwestern Europe, but it was also followed, with some significant modifications, in the secular courts of Mediterranean lands and in the various tribunals of the Church.[6] According to the accusatorial system, a criminal action was both initiated and prosecuted by a private person, who was usually the injured party or his kin. The accusation was a formal, public, sworn statement which resulted in the trial of the accused before a judge. If the accused admitted his guilt, or if the private accuser could provide certain proof, then the judge would decide against the defendant. If there was any doubt, however, the court would appeal to God to provide some sign of the accused person's guilt or innocence. The most common way of doing this was the ordeal, a test that the accused party would have to take to gain acquittal. Either he would have to carry a hot iron a certain distance and then show, after his hand was bandaged for a few days, that God had miraculously healed the seared flesh; or he would have to put his arm into hot water and in similar fashion reveal a healed limb after bandaging; or he would be thrown into a body of cold water and would be considered innocent only if he sank to the bottom; or he would be asked to swallow a morsel in one gulp without choking. As an alternative to the ordeal the accused or his champion might be asked to engage in a duel with the champion of the wronged party, his victory in this 'bilateral ordeal' or trial by combat being construed as a sign of his innocence. He also might be allowed, as an alternative to the ordeal, a trial by compurgation. In this case the accused would swear to his innocence and then obtain a certain number of 'oath-helpers' who would solemnly swear to the honesty (and indirectly, therefore, to the innocence) of the accused. During the trial, in whatever form it took, the judge would remain an impartial arbiter who regulated the procedure of the court but who did not in any way prosecute the accused. The prosecutor was the accuser himself, and if the defendant proved his innocence of the charge, then the accuser became liable to criminal prosecution according to the old Roman tradition of the *lex talionis*.[7]

Regarding this early medieval system of criminal prosecution, two observations are in order. First, it was a fundamentally non-rational process. The determination of guilt or innocence was usually not made by a rational inquiry into the facts of the case but by an appeal to

6 For a brief discussion of the differences between Germanic and Roman forms see Bader, *Die Hexenprozesse in der Schweiz*, pp. 11–12.

7 C.H. Lea, *The Ordeal*, ed. E. Peters (Philadelphia, 1973); J. Gaudemet, 'Les Ordiales au moyen age: doctrine, legislation, et pratique canoniques', in *La Preuve* (Receuils de la Société Jean Bodin, Vol. 17) (Brussels, 1965), pp. 99–136.

divine intervention into human affairs. Man in effect abdicated his own responsibility to investigate crimes and left the matter in the hands of God. Second, the system did not prove to be particularly successful in prosecuting crime. Not only did every prosecution require an accuser who was willing to risk the possibility of a counter-suit on the basis of the talion, but the trial itself could be manipulated in favour of the accused. Callused hands and proper breathing techniques could, for example, help one to pass the ordeal, while men of high reputation (which admittedly many men accused of serious crimes were not) could usually secure acquittal by their mere oath or by compurgation. The system stands as a testament to man's faith in God's immanence but not to his efforts to use the law as an effective instrument of social control.

Beginning in the thirteenth century, however, the ecclesiastical and secular courts of western Europe abandoned this early medieval system of criminal procedure and adopted new techniques that assigned a much greater role to human judgement in the criminal process. The change from the old system to the new was stimulated to some extent by the revival of the formal study of Roman law in the eleventh and twelfth centuries,[8] but the main impetus came from the growing realization that crime – both ecclesiastical and secular – was increasing and had to be reduced. In bringing about this change the Church, which was faced with the spread of heresy, took the lead. The Church also encouraged the new procedures in the secular courts by formally prohibiting clerics from participating in ordeals at the fourth Lateran Council of 1215.[9] Since the ordeals, being appeals to divine guidance in judicial matters, required clerics to bless the entire operation, the action taken by the Council signalled their end.[10]

The new system of criminal procedure that gradually took form during the thirteenth, fourteenth and fifteenth centuries and was employed throughout Continental Europe by the sixteenth century is generally referred to as inquisitorial. Its adoption changed both

8 On this influence see B. Lenman and G. Parker, 'The State, the Community and the Criminal Law in Early Modern Europe', in *Crime and the Law*, ed. V. Gattrell, et al. (London, 1980), pp. 29–30.

9 On the growth of clerical opposition to the ordeal and the crucial role played by the papacy in suppressing it see R. Bartlett, *Trial by Fire and Water: The Medieval Judicial Ordeal* (Oxford, 1986), pp. 70–102.

10 Some municipal jurisdictions nevertheless continued to use the ordeals into the seventeenth century. For the use of the hot water ordeal at Braunsberg in 1637 see Lea, *Materials*, III, p. 1234.

the procedures by which criminal cases could be initiated and the procedures of the trials themselves. Regarding initiation it is important to note that the adoption of inquisitorial procedure did not preclude the commencement of a legal action by private accusation.[11] Many crimes tried according to inquisitorial procedure, including a large number of witchcraft cases, were initiated in this way.[12] The only difference between the new system and the old when suits were begun by accusation was that the accuser was no longer responsible for the actual prosecution of the case, as shall be discussed below. In addition to the initiation of cases by accusation, however, the new procedure allowed the inhabitants of a community to denounce a suspected criminal before the judicial authorities, a procedure that the church courts had used in certain circumstances during episcopal visitations as early as the ninth century.[13] Even more important, the new system allowed an officer of the court – either the public prosecutor, who was sometimes known as the fiscal, or the judge himself – to cite a criminal on the basis of information he had obtained himself, often by rumour.[14] Once again, the Church had employed this procedure in certain cases as early as the ninth century, claiming that the *infamia* or ill-repute of the criminal was the legal equivalent of the private accusation.[15] During the late Middle Ages this practice became widespread in both the ecclesiastical and secular courts. The initiation of cases in this way led to a significant increase in the number of criminal prosecutions, but it also made individuals vulnerable to frivolous, malicious, politically motivated or otherwise arbitrary prosecutions.

Even more important than the adoption of new modes of initiating criminal actions was the officialization of all stages of the judicial process once the charge had been made.[16] Instead of

11 See J. Langbein, *Prosecuting Crime in the Renaissance* (Cambridge, Mass., 1974), pp. 130–1.

12 Some of the witchcraft cases tried in Schleswig-Holstein were initiated by private accusation, but the early modern accusatory process was not the same as that which was used in the Middle Ages, and it often followed the same course as an inquisitorial process. See D. Unverhau, 'Akkusationsprozess–Inquisitionsprozess: Indikatoren für die Intensität der Hexenverfolgung in Schleswig–Holstein', in *Hexenprozesse: Deutsche und skandinavische Beitrage*, ed. C. Degn, H. Lehmann, and D. Unverhau (Neumünster, 1983), pp. 59–143, especially p. 116.

13 On denunciation see *Malleus Maleficarum*, pp. 205–7; Bader, *Die Hexenprozesse in der Schweiz*, p. 15.

14 On the function of the fiscal see F. Merzbacher, *Die Hexenprozesse in Franken* (Munich, 1957), pp. 78–80.

15 H.C. Lea, *Torture*, ed. E. Peters (Philadelphia, 1973), p. xiv.

16 Langbein, *Prosecuting Crime*, pp. 130–1.

presiding over a contest between two private parties in which the outcome was at least theoretically left to God, the officers of the court – the judge and his subordinates – took it upon themselves to investigate the crime and to determine whether or not the defendant was guilty. This they did mainly by conducting secret interrogations of both the accused and all available witnesses, recording their testimony in written depositions. In this way they established the facts of the case, which they then evaluated, on the basis of carefully formulated rules of evidence, to determine whether or not the accused was guilty and to sentence him accordingly. The procedure, therefore, was not only completely officialized but also rationalized. Man was using his own judgement, which was informed by the rational rules of the law, to prosecute crime. It should not surprise us, therefore, to learn that the growth of the new system was closely related, as both cause and effect, to the emergence of a body of scientific legal literature. It also was related to the growth of a large legal profession.

Inquisitorial procedure can be contrasted not only to the accusatorial procedure that it replaced but to the system of criminal procedure that developed at approximately the same time in England. English courts, like their Continental counterparts, abandoned the ordeal and other 'supernatural probations' by the early thirteenth century, and they also entrusted the determination of guilt to human judgement, but they did not allow the criminal process to become as officialized as it did on the Continent. Whereas on the Continent officers of the court acquired the right both to initiate legal pro-ceedings and to determine their outcome, in England lay jurymen – men not trained in the law – performed those functions. A presenting jury, acting in the name of the king, initiated or at least exercised prior review over all 'public' prosecutions, while the determination of guilt was left to a trial jury, whose duty it was to establish the facts of the case. Originally the jurymen had personal knowledge of the crime, but by the beginning of the sixteenth century they were no longer self-informed and sat in court as lay judges of evidence brought before them by local judicial officials. By the middle of the sixteenth century these officials regularly conducted a pre-trial examination of the prisoner and the witnesses, but the system nevertheless did not become inquisitorial because the lay jurors, and not the officials of the court, reached the verdict. In many respects, moreover, the English trial revealed the persistence of the older accusatory process. Technically a private person, the individual who swore out the original complaint, not a legal official, prosecuted the crime. The trial remained public and oral and still resembled a contest between two adversaries, not a secret judicial investigation to establish the truth.[17] And the judge remained at least in theory (though hardly in practice) an impartial arbitrator who presided over the judicial process rather than an official who was entrusted with the detection, investigation, prosecution and conviction of the crime.[18]

By the time intense witch-hunting began, England was the only country in Europe that had not incorporated at least some of the features of inquisitorial procedure into its legal system. The Scottish criminal process represented something of a hybrid between the English and the Continental models. On the one hand the Scots did not have a presenting jury, and as part of the pre-trial procedure Scottish judges compiled large dossiers of written depositions which were used as evidence in criminal trials. On the other hand Scottish trials still resembled English ones, and Scottish trial juries retained considerable independence through most of the early modern period as triers of the fact.[19] England and Scotland were not the only countries of Europe that used juries, but in all other countries they became formal ratifying bodies whose decisions were completely controlled by the officers of the court and by the information that those officers had gathered. Whenever the jury's role became ceremonial, there was a tendency to disregard it, and when that happened the jury itself eventually disappeared or was transformed into a jury of professional judges.

The adoption of inquisitorial procedure facilitated the prosecution of all crime, but it proved to be most useful in the investigation and trial of heresy and witchcraft. Since most heretics were known only by general reputation, and since there were no victims of their crimes demanding retribution, the only effective way of bringing them to justice was through either denunciation or official promotion. It was, in fact, mainly to combat heresy that the Church adopted the new modes of initiation. Witches, who were also known by ill-repute, could likewise be proceeded against *ex officio*, but they could also be accused by those whom they had harmed. In those cases the

17 The English trial was, however, less adversarial than in the modern period. See J. Langbein, 'The Criminal Trial before the Lawyers', *University of Chicago Law Review*, 45 (1978): 307–16.

18 See generally L.W. Levy, 'Accusatorial and Inquisitorial Systems of Criminal Procedure: The Beginnings', in *Freedom and Reform*, ed. H. Hyman and L. Levy (New York, 1967), pp. 16–54.

19 For the weakening of the Scottish jury in the late seventeenth century see I.D. Willock, *The Origins and Development of the Jury in Scotland* (Edinburgh, 1966), pp. 218–21.

main effect of the new system was the elimination of the liability of the accuser.[20] It stands to reason that under the old accusatory system a victim of sorcery would be reluctant to accuse his magical assailant with *maleficium* if there was a chance that he himself might be penalized for making the accusation.[21] Now, however, he could do so with impunity. Once heretics and witches were charged under the new procedures, the likelihood of conviction also increased, since the judge was able to use his powers of investigation to build up a dossier regarding the alleged crime. The direct interrogation of the accused was especially instrumental in this regard, since by this means the judge could elicit the information necessary for conviction.

The only way in which the new procedures threatened to reduce rather than to increase the chances of a successful prosecution was that the standards for proof according to inquisitorial procedure were extraordinarily demanding. Since the adoption of inquisitorial procedure represented a shift from reliance upon divine intervention in human affairs to reliance upon man's rational judgement, jurists agreed that it was absolutely necessary for judges to have conclusive proof of guilt before passing sentence. The standard they adopted, which derived from the Roman law of treason and which we generally refer to as the romano-canonical law of proof, was the testimony of two eye-witnesses or the confession of the accused. No other form of proof, no matter how convincing, would be considered sufficient. Unless two witnesses could testify that they actually saw the crime being committed, or unless the prisoner himself confessed to the deed, the accused could not be convicted. The rigidity of this law of proof can best be appreciated if we compare it with the standards of proof that English juries often used to convict criminals. English juries could and did deliver guilty verdicts on the basis of hearsay, circumstantial evidence or the testimony of only one eye-witness. Now it is true that these same juries did require unanimity in their verdicts after 1367, and they often revealed a great reluctance to find the accused guilty. But when they did decide upon conviction, they often did so on the basis of rather flimsy evidence, even in the eighteenth century, by which time the English law of evidence had begun to take form.

Adherence to the romano-canonical law of proof presented serious problems for judges in situations where eye-witnesses could not be produced. This was especially true in trials for concealed crimes, among which heresy and witchcraft were prominent. Heresy

20 See Kieckhefer, *European Witch Trials*, p. 19.
21 See Cohn, *Europe's Inner Demons*, pp. 160–3.

was essentially a mental crime, although witnesses could testify regarding a heretic's promulgation of his ideas. Witchcraft, which involved heresy, presented similar problems. The number of people who could testify that a witch performed *maleficia* before their very eyes was small indeed, while the only persons who could give eye-witness accounts of diabolism and the sabbath were the alleged accomplices of the witches, who could not be detected until at least one witch confessed and yielded their names. In such circumstances judges had to rely exclusively on confessions in order to obtain convictions. Confessions, however, were not always forthcoming, and consequently judicial authorities began to allow the use of torture in order to obtain them. The use of torture in heresy, witchcraft and other cases was therefore the direct result of the adoption of inquisitorial procedure. The logic of one led to the application of the other.

TORTURE

When we speak of judicial torture we do not mean the use of torture as a punishment for crime. Very often courts would sentence criminals to be tortured before their execution, and the methods used would be the same as those that had been employed during their trial. Some scholars distinguish between this type of *retributive* or *punitive* torture and *interrogatory* torture, but judicial torture, properly defined, refers only to the latter process. Judicial torture was a means employed to obtain either a confession or some concealed information from an accused person or a recalcitrant witness.

The use of judicial torture in the late medieval and early modern periods had ancient and early medieval precedents. In ancient Greece and Rome slaves, who did not possess the same legal rights as free men, were frequently tortured during their trials, while during the Roman Empire even free men were tortured in the prosecution of treason and other heinous crimes. In many barbarian kingdoms torture continued to be used on slaves, but not on free men under any circumstances. Because of these precedents, it is proper to consider the introduction of torture in thirteenth-century Europe as a revival rather than an innovation. Like the inquisitorial procedure with which it is associated, it owed its appearance to some extent to the revival of the study of Roman law, but the main reason for its reintroduction in the West was the need to prosecute crime more effectively and the fact that inquisitorial procedure had been adopted for those purposes.

The first documentary evidence we have of the use of torture in the late Middle Ages comes from the laws of the city of Verona in 1228. Within a few years many other city-states in Italy, the Holy Roman Empire and the kingdom of Castile followed suit.[22] In these secular jurisdictions the main purpose of torture was to obtain evidence from notorious criminals who were suspected of concealed crimes. In 1252 the Church, which had taken the lead in the adoption of inquisitorial procedure, followed the example of the secular courts in allowing the use of torture. At that time Pope Innocent IV authorized papal inquisitors to use torture in the prosecution of heresy, which was in many ways the ultimate concealed crime. It was especially appropriate that suspected heretics should be tortured, since their crime was the ecclesiastical equivalent of treason, and the first free Romans to be subjected to torture had been traitors. The use of torture in heresy trials provided the foundation for its employment against witches in the church courts, while both the example of the ecclesiastical courts and the general practice of using torture in the prosecution of capital crimes led to its employment in secular witchcraft trials.

The use of judicial torture is predicated upon the assumption that when a person is subjected to physical pain during interrogation he will confess the truth. The assumption is not always valid. In many cases, it is true, the application of torture has elicited honest confessions or factual truth from the guilty or otherwise knowledgeable parties. In wartime the torture of military prisoners has often had the same effect. At other times, however, torture has proved to be a highly unreliable means of discovering the truth, for it has produced fabricated or at least partially misleading confessions. The likelihood of such falsification is greatest when (a) the person tortured is innocent of the alleged crime or ignorant of the desired information; (b) the details of the confession are suggested to him by means of leading questions; and (c) the amount of torture is excessive. There is an abundance of evidence from contemporary as well as historical sources to show that if torture is sufficiently painful, even the most tight-lipped, innocent person will perjure himself and confess to virtually anything his torturers wish him to say. The clearest historical evidence we have of this process is the great witch-hunt itself, in which thousands of individuals, when subjected to torture, confessed to crimes they did not commit and which in fact they could not have committed.

22 Lea, *Torture*, p. xiii.

The architects of the system of judicial torture were not unaware of the unreliability of torture as a means of establishing the truth. They knew that although torture could elicit a great deal of otherwise unavailable, accurate, incriminating evidence, it could also seriously prejudice the rights of a defendant and lead to his unwarranted conviction. Before the middle of the thirteenth century the Church had prohibited torture for precisely this reason.[23] When torture was revived in the thirteenth century, therefore, legal writers and other authorities devised a set of rules governing its application. The main objectives of the rules were to minimize the chances that an innocent person would be tortured, to prevent the fabrication of confessions, and to place some limits on the severity and duration of the torture. These rules did not serve as a justification of the use of torture; that lay in the necessity of obtaining confessions to crimes that threatened the state. But the rules did make the entire system more palatable to those who had a genuine interest in the protection of the rights of the accused and who wished to prevent the conviction of innocent persons.

The rules governing the use of torture varied from place to place and they also changed over time. In their original and strictest form they contained, first of all, a prohibition against the use of torture unless the judge could prove that a crime had in fact been committed. Once that was ascertained, the judge still could not sentence a suspect to be tortured unless there was a solid presumption of guilt, which was usually provided by the testimony of one eye-witness (half the proof needed for conviction) or circumstantial evidence (*indicia*) that was the legal equivalent of the testimony of one eye-witness.[24] Even when this requirement was satisfied, the judge was forbidden to use torture unless it was the only way to establish the facts of the case, and before he ordered it he first was required to threaten the suspect with its use.

For both humanitarian and legal reasons rules were also established to restrict the severity and the duration of the torture. The most widely recognized of these was that the torture should not result in the death of the victim, and it was for this reason that most courts used methods of torture that either distended or compressed the extremities. The most common instrument of torture that achieved such an effect was the *strappado*, a pulley that raised the person

---

23 M. Ruthven, *Torture: The Grand Conspiracy* (London, 1980), p. 43.
24 See J. Langbein, *Torture and the Law of Proof* (Chicago, 1978), p. 14 and M. Kunze, *Der Prozess Pappenheimer* (Ebelsbach, 1981), pp. 216–22.

off the floor by his arms, which were tied behind his back. Other instruments of distension, the rack and the ladder, were also used frequently. Of the instruments of compression the most common were the thumb screws, leg screws, head clamps and tourniquets. All of these had the advantage that they could be relaxed as soon as the tortured person agreed to confess or to provide the desired information. They also allowed the torture to be increased gradually. Most jurisdictions had rules governing the intensity of the torture which depended on both the gravity of the crime and the strength of the presumption of guilt. When the *strappado* was used, these rules would determine how long the accused would hang from the ceiling and whether or not he would be jerked abruptly. In the most severe form of the *strappado*, squassation, weights of anywhere from 40 to 660 pounds would be attached to the person's feet and then the ropes would be jerked, a procedure that could dislodge a person's arms from their sockets. All of the grades of torture, however severe, were supposed to be performed on the same day; repetition of torture was forbidden. There were also rules that exempted certain classes of people, such as pregnant women and children, from torture.

Yet another set of rules was designed specifically to prevent the fabrication of confessions. The use of leading questions by the judge, which would of course allow the prisoner to detect what his interrogator wished to hear, was forbidden. Testimony taken in the torture chamber was not admissible, the prisoner being required to repeat his confession 'freely' outside the chamber within a period of twenty-four hours. The judge was, moreover, required to verify the details of confessions extracted under torture.

If the courts of Europe had adhered strictly to these rules regarding the use of torture, then the adoption of this method of criminal investigation would not have led to the innumerable miscarriages of justice with which it is almost always associated. In particular, the European witch-hunt would never have taken place. As it turned out, however, these rules were greatly relaxed and the system was grossly abused. In some jurisdictions the rules were officially changed in order to facilitate the prosecution of all crime. In others the rules were routinely suspended in the prosecution of crimes that were considered to be especially grave and difficult to prosecute. It should be noted that witchcraft was regarded as a *crimen exceptum*, an exceptional crime, and in the prosecution of such an offence certain procedural rules, such as those regarding the qualification of witnesses, did not apply.[25] In still other jurisdictions judges flagrantly ignored or violated the rules, especially in witchcraft cases.

The most significant modification of the rules dealt with the requirement that the judge first establish that a crime had in fact been committed. As John Langbein has argued, if this rule had been strictly enforced, 'the European witch-craze would never have claimed its countless victims'.[26] Unfortunately, however, an exception was made for those occult crimes for which the evidence had vanished at the time of commission. This meant that judges could torture suspects for crimes that were believed to have been committed but for which there was no tangible evidence.[27]

Another official relaxation of the rules regarding torture concerned its repetition. In drafting his manual for inquisitors in 1376, Nicholas Eymeric circumvented the prohibition of repetition by allowing its *continuation* at a later time. Eventually European courts dispensed with this casuistry and permitted judges to repeat the torture at least once and sometimes two or more times if the prisoner proved to be recalcitrant.[28] In some witchcraft cases torture was applied indefinitely. There is at least one recorded instance of its repetition fifty-six times,[29] and in 1631 the hangman of the town of Dreissigacker in Germany revealed in a chilling statement to an accused witch how completely the safeguard against repeating torture had been abandoned. 'I do not take you for one, two, three, not for eight days, nor for a few weeks,' said the hangman, 'but for half a year or a year, for your whole life, until you confess: and if you will not confess, I shall torture you to death, and you shall be burned after all.'[30] It should be noted that the prisoner was pregnant at the time and therefore should not have been tortured at all.

As the duration of the torture was indefinitely extended, so too was its severity. It appears that in many jurisdictions the most brutal tortures were reserved for witches. Certainly one gets that impression from reading the account of the prosecution of Anna Spülerin of Ringingen, who was tortured so gruesomely that her limbs were

25 See J. Bodin, *De la Démonomanie des Sorciers* (Anvers, 1586), Book IV, ch. V; C. Larner, 'Crimen Exceptum?', pp. 49–74.

26 Langbein, *Torture*, p. 14.

27 For the discussion by Caesar Carena of this problem see Lea, *Materials*, II, p. 996.

28 Langbein, *Torture*, pp. 15, 150.

29 Robbins, *Encyclopedia*, p. 256.

30 P. Carus, *The History of the Devil and the Idea of Evil* (New York, 1969), p. 331.

mutilated and her sight and hearing lost. [31] In Scotland Dr Fian, one of the many witches suspected of treason against the king, 'was put to the most severe and cruell paine in the world, called the bootes', with the result that 'his legges were crushte and beaten togeather as small as might bee, and the bones and flesh so bruised, that the bloud and marrowe spouted forth in great abundance'.[32] Some of these tortures were sanctioned by the criminal law of particular states, but others were employed illegally, at the mere command of an over-zealous and perhaps sadistic judge. In Germany many courts used the witches' chair, which was heated by fire from below, while in Scotland there were reports of a witch's fingernails being pulled out by pincers. In Spanish, French and German lands it was not uncommon for courts to force-feed their prisoners with large amounts of water. Among the clearly illegal tortures were filling the nostrils with lime and water, tying the victim to a table covered with hawthorn twigs, rolling a pin with dagger-like points up and down the spine, gouging out the eyes, chopping off the ears, squeezing the male's genital organs, and burning brandy or sulphur over the victim's body.

Many of these especially brutal tortures were used originally or exclusively in witchcraft cases, not simply because witchcraft was the most heinous of all crimes and the most necessary, therefore, to prosecute successfully, but also because many judges feared that witches might employ sorcery to help them withstand pain. In such circumstances the judges may have believed that an especially cruel form of torture would succeed where others had failed. The method that was specifically designed for use in such cases, however, was one that caused no direct physical harm. The torture of forced sleeplessness, or the *tormentum insomniae*, was considered to be the most effective antidote to the sorcery of the victim. Since this method, which kept the victim awake for forty hours or longer, did not actually hurt the body, it had great appeal to humane judges. It also was extremely effective, probably because it resulted in a form of brainwashing. One judge claimed that fewer than 2 per cent of all victims could endure it without confessing.

Just as the limits on the duration and severity of torture were raised or completely ignored, the rules guarding against false confessions were gradually modified or abandoned. Suggestive questioning became routine in witchcraft cases, a practice which the publication of sets of questions to be asked of witches only

---

31 Oberman, *Masters of the Reformation*, pp. 160–1.
32 *Newes from Scotland* (London, 1591), pp. 18, 28.

encouraged. Few attempts were made to verify the details of the confessions, and when an accused witch retracted a confession made under torture, judges allowed a second or even a third or fourth use of torture, thereby violating the rule against repetition.[33] It was not unusual for judges to give non-capital sentences to prisoners who retracted their confessions, but when the crime was that of witchcraft the judges showed great reluctance to follow that course of action. Some witches were not even given the opportunity for retraction, while others who retracted were executed anyway in the manner prescribed for unrepentant heretics.

The question remains, however, whether judges who applied torture with great severity and with apparent disregard of at least the original rules did not worry that they might be forcing innocent parties to incriminate themselves. The answer is almost certainly no. Either they believed that God would protect the innocent and allow them to endure the torture, just as He had allowed them to survive the ordeal, or they did not seriously consider the possibility that the accused might be innocent. Even when the evidence of a person's guilt was insufficient according to the law, judges proceeded with torture on the assumption that the accused was guilty and would therefore speak the truth when pain was threatened or applied. Whatever compunctions the judge might have about subjecting a human being to excruciating torture would be offset by his recognition of the enormity of the crime and the necessity of its effective prosecution. And of course once the torture was begun, judges had an additional motive for completing their task successfully, since the confession itself served as a justification of their use of torture in the first place.

The reintroduction of torture into the legal systems of western Europe and the relaxation of or disregard for the rules regulating its use had a profound effect on the origin and development of the great European witch-hunt. First, torture facilitated the formulation and the dissemination of the cumulative concept of witchcraft. Although the various ideas regarding witchcraft were synthesized and spread mainly by the authors of learned treatises, their fusion first occurred in the courtroom, where inquisitors used torture to confirm their suspicions and to realize their fantasies. In most cases the treatises drew upon and developed ideas that had first emerged in the torture chamber. Once these ideas were put into writing, moreover, the production of confessions under torture confirmed their reality and facilitated their

---

33 Boguet, *Examen of Witches*, p. 225, allows for three administrations of torture in such circumstances.

transmission. The importance of obtaining confessions to ratify beliefs that are otherwise available only in print can best be appreciated by studying the fate of certain witch-beliefs in England. Ideas about witches attending the sabbath and worshipping the Devil were by no means absent from England, at least in literary form, during the sixteenth and seventeenth centuries, but these ideas never gained widespread acceptance among the élite, mainly because torture could not be used in witchcraft cases and confessions to diabolical activities could not, therefore, be easily obtained.

The second effect of the adoption of torture on witch-hunting was that it greatly increased the chances of witches being convicted. The introduction of inquisitorial procedure by itself should have had that effect, but the acceptance of the romano-canonical law of proof threatened to negate its effectiveness in the case of concealed crimes. The use of torture, especially unrestricted torture, not only resolved the problem of insufficient proof but also made possible the conviction of almost anyone who incurred the suspicion of witchcraft. Although we do not have complete statistics, it appears that when torture was used on a regular basis in witchcraft prosecutions, the rate of convictions could be as high as 95 per cent.[34] When it was not used, as in England, the conviction rate was well below 50 per cent. Between the two extremes there were of course many intermediate positions, which could reflect the use of torture in only some cases, a greater or lesser adherence to the rules governing the use of torture, or different degrees of humaneness on the part of the judges.[35] In some jurisdictions torture was ineffective because some prisoners employed certain techniques to help them withstand the pain.[36] There is no question, however, that without torture the conviction of witches would have been less common and the pattern of witchcraft prosecutions and convictions would probably have resembled that of England more closely than that of Germany.

The third and most important effect of the adoption of torture on the European witch-hunt concerns its use in acquiring the names of witches' alleged accomplices. Roman law had declared emphatically that a man who confessed to a crime could not be tortured regarding

---

34 See Midelfort, *Witch-Hunting*, p. 149.

35 For the failure of torture to produce convictions when it was applied by the *parlement* of Paris, see A. Soman, 'Trente procès de sorcellerie dans le Perche (1566–1624)', *L'Orne littéraire*, 8 (1986), 44–5.

36 J. Tedeschi, 'Inquisitorial Law and the Witch', in *Early Modern European Witchcraft*, pp. 102–3.

that of another person, but most European jurisdictions – with the notable exception of the Spanish and papal territories – abandoned this rule during the late medieval or early modern period. Only when this critical change was made, and when authorities began to believe that witchcraft was a conspiracy, did the conduct of large, chain-reaction hunts become possible. The torture of individual witches for their confessions could produce a high percentage of convictions, but only the torture of those witches for the names of their confederates could produce witch-hunts in which scores, if not hundreds of individuals were tried for a collective crime.

WITCHCRAFT AND THE SECULAR COURTS

The third main legal development that made the great European witch-hunt possible was the deployment of the full judicial power of the state in the prosecution of a crime that was primarily spiritual in nature. To the extent that witchcraft involved the worship of the Devil it was a spiritual crime, the crime of apostasy and heresy, and as such it merited punishment by ecclesiastical authorities. Many witches were in fact prosecuted in episcopal courts and in those of papal inquisitors, whose main assignment ever since the early thirteenth century had been to combat the spread of heresy. From the very beginning of the great witch-hunt, however, the secular courts of western European states also took part in witch-hunting, either by cooperating with ecclesiastical courts in their work or by trying witches on their own authority. As the hunt developed, the secular courts assumed an even greater role in the process, while that of the ecclesiastical courts declined. Governments defined witchcraft as a secular crime, and in some countries the temporal courts secured a monopoly over its prosecution. As this change took place the Church continued to have an active interest in the matter of witchcraft, and it often inspired or directed secular authorities to pursue witches aggressively,[37] but the driving judicial force of the witch-hunt became secular rather than ecclesiastical authority. Without the mobilization of this secular power, the great witch-hunt would have been a mere shadow of itself.

The extraordinarily durable notion that the European witch-hunt was essentially a clerical operation, inspired by clerical zeal and

---

37 See for example, S. Clark, 'Protestant Demonology: Sin, Superstition and Society (c.1520–c.1630), in *Early Modern European Witchcraft:*, pp. 49–50; Holmes, 'Popular Culture?', pp. 92–3.

conducted under ecclesiastical auspices, derives both from the size of the contribution that churchmen made to the development of the cumulative concept of witchcraft and from the role that church courts played in the prosecution of the crimes of heresy, magic and witchcraft during the late Middle Ages. That churchmen took the lead in the early formulation of witch-beliefs cannot be denied, although lay theologians like Arnald of Villanova and lay magistrates who adjudicated cases of sorcery played a significant part in the process.[38] The important consideration in this regard, however, is that these ideas, whatever their source, became the property of the lay magistracy as well as of the clerical élite by the time the great witch-hunt began.[39] Once that happened, it was just as likely that the ideas would surface in secular as in ecclesiastical courtrooms.

Regarding the clerical role in the late medieval prosecution of magic, heresy and witchcraft, we must make a number of qualifications. First, the prosecution of magic was undertaken by both secular and ecclesiastical authorities, since it was clearly a crime of 'mixed jurisdiction'.[40] The Church condemned the practice because it involved some sort of commerce with demons, and it prosecuted it as a form of heresy, but secular authorities had a legitimate interest in the crime when it resulted in physical injury, and especially when it was used for political purposes. It was in fact the traditional jurisdiction that secular authorities had over *maleficium*, which can be traced back to Roman times, that provided the major foundation for later statutory prohibitions of witchcraft. Second, secular authorities also played a role, although admittedly a more limited one, in the prosecution of heresy. Almost all heresy trials in the late Middle Ages took place in the courts of episcopal or papal inquisitors, but these officials required and obtained a great deal of assistance in their work from secular authorities. Lay officials helped to locate and arrest suspects, and once they were convicted, executed them on the basis of secular laws. The cooperation of the secular authorities in punishing heretics was essential, since church courts could not inflict bodily

---

38 See Peters, *The Magician, the Witch and the Law*, p. 106.

39 Trevor-Roper, 'European Witch-Craze', p. 171, argues that the ideas of the clergy were extended to lay magistrates (but not to the 'independent laity') by the rather late date of 1600.

40 *Malleus Maleficarum*, pp. 194–205; A. Gari Lacruz, 'Variedad de competencias en el delito de brujería 1600–1650 en Aragón' in *La Inquisición Española*, ed. J. Perez Villanueva (Madrid, 1980), pp. 319–21; Ginzburg, *Night Battles*, pp. 113–14.

harm and were therefore obliged to surrender condemned heretics to the secular arm for punishment. Of course there was very little concern that lay officials would not cooperate, since heresy was widely regarded as a source of civil disorder.[41]

Since secular courts had jurisdiction over magic and *maleficium*, and since they willingly provided indispensable services to the ecclesiastical courts in the prosecution of heretics, they naturally assumed a significant role in the prosecution of witches. When witch-hunting began in the fifteenth century, the trials took place not only in the courts of papal inquisitors and in the episcopal courts but also in various municipal courts. The notorious witch-hunting campaigns of Kramer and Sprenger in Germany during the 1480s, which Pope Innocent VIII directly sanctioned in his Bull of 1484, and the publication of the *Malleus Maleficarum* by these men two years later, have led to a general assumption that most fifteenth-century witch-hunting activities occurred under the auspices of papal inquisitors. This is clearly not the case. It is true that inquisitors were primarily responsible for the numerous witch-hunts that took place in southern France in the early fifteenth century. These trials were to some extent a by-product of the pursuit of Waldensian heretics in that region.[42] In other parts of France and Europe, however, episcopal and secular courts prosecuted witches, sometimes in cooperation with inquisitors or with each other and sometimes independently. In one of the very first witch-hunts, which took place in Bern in the late 1420s, the bishop took a leading role, but in prosecuting the witches he used the secular courts over which he presided as a territorial ruler, not the episcopal courts over which he presided as a prelate.

As the witch-hunt gathered strength in the sixteenth and early seventeenth centuries, a number of developments resulted in the reduction of clerical jurisdiction over witchcraft and a corresponding increase in the amount of secular judicial concern with it. The first was the definition of witchcraft as a secular crime. Both the *Malleus Maleficarum* and a treatise entitled *Layenspiegel*, which was written in 1510 by Ulrich Tengler, the governor of Höchstädt, had established the theoretical foundation of such a definition, but only later in the sixteenth century did secular rulers take official action. Frightened that witchcraft was spreading and that its practitioners were evading

---

41 See R. Kieckhefer, *The Repression of Heresy in Medieval Germany* (Philadelphia, 1980), pp. 75–82.

42 See Cohn, *Europe's Inner Demons*, p. 226.

prosecution, the legislative bodies of many European states either passed specific laws against witchcraft, promulgated edicts to the same effect or included specific prohibitions of witchcraft in their criminal codes. The *Reichstag* of the Holy Roman Empire included an article concerning witchcraft in the famous *Carolina* code of 1532, while many German states within the Empire enacted their own particular laws against the crime. The English Parliament passed witchcraft statutes in 1542, 1563 and 1604, the Scottish Parliament did the same in 1563, and the rulers of Franche-Comté, Sweden, Denmark, Norway and Russia all issued edicts against witchcraft in the late sixteenth and early seventeenth centuries.[43] Most of these witchcraft laws were based upon the traditional jurisdiction that the state claimed over *maleficium,* but in some cases the law allowed prosecution for the exclusively spiritual crime of making a pact with the Devil or, more vaguely, entertaining evil spirits.[44] These laws not only gave secular courts an indisputable right to hear witchcraft cases, but also contributed directly to the growth of the hunt by publicizing the crime and facilitating its prosecution.

A second development that caused a significant shift of witchcraft cases from ecclesiastical to secular tribunals was the decline of both the papal 'inquisition' and other ecclesiastical courts. The general weakening of papal authority in the late fifteenth and early sixteenth centuries and the later Protestant rejection of that authority at the time of the Reformation left the Inquisition, which had never been an organized institution to begin with, in a permanently enfeebled state.[45] Only in Spain, where an Inquisition had been established as a national institution under the authority of the king in the late fifteenth century; in Portugal, which in similar fashion had three inquisitorial tribunals that remained independent of Rome; and in Italy, where a new Roman Inquisition was established on the Spanish model in 1542, did the inquisition continue to show any signs of vitality.[46] The papal inquisition was not, however, the only instrument of ecclesiastical

---

43 France was unusual in having no specific statute against witchcraft. Soman, 'Witch-lynching at Juniville', p. 9.

44 J.C.V. Johansen, 'Denmark: The Sociology of Accusations', in *Early Modern European Witchcraft*, p. 341; Midelfort, *Witch Hunting*, p. 23; S. Fox, *Science and Justice* (Baltimore, 1968), pp. 37–43; Lea, *History of the Inquisition in the Middle Ages*, III, p. 544.

45 On the problem of referring to the papal 'inquisition' as an institution see Kieckhefer, *Repression of Heresy*, pp. 3–8.

46 On the final loss of inquisitorial jurisdiction in Franche-Comté around 1600 see Monter, *Witchcraft in France and Switzerland*, p. 73.

justice that declined at this time. Throughout Europe, especially in Protestant countries but also in those that remained Catholic, church courts lost much of their authority and found themselves clearly subordinated to the secular power of the state.[47] Their coercive and jurisdictional powers were restricted in many countries, and by the middle of the sixteenth century they appear to have become much weaker instruments than the secular courts in the increasingly important task of extirpating witchcraft.

A third reason for the reduction of clerical involvement in the witch-hunt was the growth of a considerable reluctance among church lawyers and judges to tolerate the procedural abuses upon which successful witch-hunting depended. There is no little irony in the fact that papal inquisitors, who earlier had taken the lead in violating many of the procedural rules governing the use of torture, were among the first to recognize that these violations had resulted in numerous miscarriages of justice and to recommend caution in further proceedings. Ecclesiastical officials, moreover, manifested a greater reluctance to mete out harsh sentences in the sixteenth and seventeenth centuries, indicating a return to the traditional penitential and admonitory functions that ecclesiastical justice had originally served. Secular courts, by contrast, being concerned for the maintenance of a public order that was being seriously challenged, generally manifested fewer compunctions.

The assumption of secular control over the crime of witchcraft had a profound impact on the process of witch-hunting in many European countries. In Scotland, for example, large-scale witch-hunts did not begin until after the Scottish parliament defined witchcraft as a secular crime in 1563 and until after the secular courts established a virtual monopoly over witchcraft prosecutions. In Transylvania, where few witches had been executed when the ecclesiastical courts had jurisdiction over the crime in the fifteenth and sixteenth centuries, the assumption of secular control in the seventeenth century was accompanied by a striking increase in executions.[48] In Poland the process of secularization was very slow to develop, and it was only after the fairly tolerant ecclesiastical courts reluctantly allowed municipal courts to prosecute witches that witch-hunting claimed many victims in that country.[49]

47 See for example R. Houlbrooke, 'The Decline of Ecclesiastical Jurisdiction under the Tudors', in *Continuity and Change*, ed. R. O'Day and F. Heal (Leicester, 1976), pp. 239–57.
48 Lea, *Materials*, III, p. 1263.
49 Baranowski, *Procesy Czarownic*, p. 180.

At the same time that the assumption of secular control over witchcraft led to an increase in prosecutions in some countries, the retention of ecclesiastical jurisdiction over the crime helped to keep prosecutions at a minimum in others. The two countries in Europe where ecclesiastical tribunals, and in particular the courts of the Inquisition, maintained primary jurisdiction over witchcraft in the late sixteenth and seventeenth centuries were Spain and Italy. In both areas the number of witchcraft prosecutions and executions during this period remained relatively low by European standards. In Italy this judicial mildness is especially interesting, for during the fifteenth and early sixteenth centuries, when papal inquisitors exercised less restraint in witch-hunting, northern Italy was one of the main centres of prosecution.[50] In Spain the authority of the ecclesiastical courts was so great that they were able, even in the seventeenth century, to mitigate the severity of sentences that secular courts imposed in witchcraft cases.[51]

It is important to note that the decline of ecclesiastical jurisdiction over witchcraft did not involve an abandonment by the clergy of their interest in witch-hunting. The clergy remained just as concerned with the worship of the Devil and the practice of maleficent magic as they had been in the past. The clergy did, however, change their tactics, becoming auxiliaries to judicial authorities in roughly the same way that lay officials had earlier provided assistance to the ecclesiastical judges. In the sixteenth and seventeenth centuries the clergy often put pressure on secular authorities to take stronger action against witches, assisted in the apprehension of suspects, and used the power of the pulpit to maintain witch-hunts. In Salem, Massachusetts, the clergy actively encouraged the prosecution of witches, even though the trials took place in the secular courts.[52] In Scotland the clergy not only interrogated witches after their apprehension but collectively urged the government on several occasions to step up its witch-hunting operations.[53] In the Cambrésis region parish priests were closely involved in the process of identifying and prosecuting witches.[54]

---

50 Kieckhefer, *European Witch Trials*, pp. 21–2.

51 Henningsen, *Witches' Advocate*, pp. 387–8.

52 As the hunt developed, however, the clergy became less enthusiastic. See Boyer and Nissenbaum, *Salem Possessed*, pp. 9–10.

53 Larner, *Enemies of God*, p. 72.

54 Muchembled, 'Witches of Cambrésis', pp. 259–60, 266–7. In Lorraine, however, the local priests generally did not become involved in the trials. See Briggs, *Communities of Belief*, pp. 71–2.

The most direct clerical influence on secular witchcraft prosecutions occurred in those German and Burgundian territories where bishops or monks exercised temporal power.[55] In these quasi-ecclesiastical states the ruling clerics used secular officials and secular authority to prosecute witches, a tactic that gave them more procedural latitude than if they had used the church courts and also freed them from any misgivings they might have had about inflicting corporal punishment through an ecclesiastical tribunal.[56] The witch-hunts that took place in the Catholic ecclesiastical territories of Ellwangen, Mergentheim, Trier, Würzburg and Bamberg were as large as those occurring in any other parts of Germany.[57]

Although witchcraft became a secular crime, triable in the secular courts, and although most secular authorities claimed jurisdiction over it on the grounds that it involved *maleficium* rather than heresy, the form of punishment that the secular courts adopted for this crime reflected its heretical rather than its felonious nature. Except in England and New England, where witches who were sentenced to death were hanged like other felons, witches were usually burned at the stake. This was the punishment that was traditionally inflicted on relapsed heretics, and its use in witchcraft cases served the purpose of identifying the witch with the heretic, both of whom were believed to be servants of the Devil.[58] The practice of burning heretics had a scriptural foundation in the statement that 'if a man not abide in me, he is cast forth as a branch that is withered; and men gather them and cast them into the fire, and they are burned'.[59] Burning witches also was a ritual of purification, which in all mythologies is associated with fire, and it also may have served as an implicit substitute for the ordeal by fire, which the Church abolished just about the time that it started prosecuting and executing people for heresy. Much more practically, death by fire may have provided guarantees for nervous judges that witches would not return from the dead by means of sorcery. But the main reason why secular courts usually decided upon

---

55 L. Rothkrug, 'Religious Practices', pp. 104–5.

56 The Prince-Bishop of Bamberg used a secular council staffed by doctors of civil law to prosecute witches in his diocese. Sebald, *Witchcraft*, pp. 38–9.

57 Midelfort, *Witch Hunting*, pp. 98, 143; Robbins, *Encyclopedia*, p. 35.

58 Witches were treated more severely than heretics, since they were usually executed after the first offence. See Lea, *A History of the Inquisition in the Middle Ages*, III, p. 515.

59 John 15: 16.

this sentence was that witches were guilty of a crime that was similar to, if not identical with, heresy.[60]

Most witches were not burned alive. Although this was the usual practice in Spanish and Italian territories (where relatively few witches were executed), witches in France, Germany, Switzerland and Scotland were usually garrotted at the stake before the flames consumed their bodies. In the German principality of Ellwangen the princely prebend usually changed the sentence of burning to one of death by the sword, but he still had the corpse burned afterwards.[61] In similar fashion an entire group of witches in Ortenau were sentenced to death 'by the sword and burning' in 1630.[62] In Sweden it was standard practice to have condemned witches first beheaded and then their bodies burned.[63] Occasionally other methods of execution, such as drowning, were employed, but in the overwhelming majority of capital sentences either the witch or her corpse was burned.[64]

In some cases secular as well as ecclesiastical courts gave non-capital sentences. These were most common in England, where the witchcraft statutes made provision for such penalties when the crime was the first offence and did not result in the death of the wronged party. In Scotland and in some Continental countries there was a much closer correlation between the number of convictions and the number of executions, but non-capital sentences, usually banishment or imprisonment, were by no means rare.[65] In France the practice of appealing sentences to the provincial *parlements* often resulted in the commutation of death sentences, while in Geneva judges who could not determine guilt with certainty very often banished the accused.[66] Henri Boguet recommended banishment in cases when the prisoner withstood the torture but the judge remained convinced of his guilt.[67] The sentence of banishment does not necessarily imply

60 The Danish witchcraft ordinance of 1617 specified that only those witches convicted of making a pact with the Devil should be burned. Johansen, 'Denmark', p. 341.

61 Midelfort, *Witch Hunting*, p. 99.

62 F. Volk, *Hexen in der Langvogtei Ortenau und der Reichsstadt Offenburg* (Lahr, 1882), p. 27. In 1628 four witches had been burned alive.

63 B. Ankarloo, 'Sweden: The Mass Burnings (1668–1676)', in *Early Modern Witchcraft: Centres and Peripheries*, ed. Bengt Ankarloo and Gustav Henningsen. (Oxford, 1990) p. 295.

64 G. Schormann, *Hexenprozesse in Nordwestdeutschland*, pp. 19, 24, 30–1, 34.

65 See the table in Monter, *Witchcraft in France and Switzerland*, p. 49.

66 Ibid., pp. 51, 66.

67 Boguet, *Examen of Witches*, p. 226.

that the judges viewed the crime of witchcraft as being any less spiritual in nature than heresy; in the few cases when German secular courts prosecuted heretics in the Middle Ages, the judges meted out the very same punishment.[68] But banishment does suggest, at least in cases of 'certain' guilt, that judicial authorities were more concerned with ridding their communities of socially marginal or dangerous individuals than with combating the forces of Satan. This was especially true in countries like Hungary, where there was more emphasis on the magical than on the diabolical aspects of witchcraft.[69]

No matter what its rationale, the use of banishment as a sentence in the secular courts should not be taken to indicate that these tribunals were more lenient than their ecclesiastical counterparts in the prosecution of witchcraft. Generally speaking, that was not the case. The secular courts at Geneva may have been especially reluctant to put witches to death, while the court of oyer and terminer at Salem did not execute anyone who made a confession.[70] But neither of these jurisdictions could match the standard of leniency that the Spanish Inquisition established in the early seventeenth century. In the largest witch-hunt in Spanish history, which involved more than 1,900 persons, only eleven individuals were condemned to the stake, and of these only one, a woman who had recruited other witches, transported toads to the sabbath and had regular intercourse with the Devil, had actually made a confession.[71] In contrast to most secular courts, where a confession usually resulted in conviction and execution, in Spain it usually led to reconciliation with the Church. The original purpose of ecclesiastical justice was precisely such a reconciliation, and in Spain the Inquisition made sure that even in witchcraft cases, only the unrepentant would suffer.

The Spanish example reveals, in a larger context, how absolutely crucial secular participation and eventually secular dominance was to the conduct of the European witch-hunt. If secular courts had not originally supplemented the ecclesiastical courts; if they had not fully cooperated with ecclesiastical authorities in the apprehension and execution of witches; if they had not filled a void that was

---

68 Kieckhefer, *Repression of Heresy*, pp. 76–8.

69 Evans, *Habsburg Monarchy*, pp. 411–12.

70 It is possible that the judges at Salem intended to execute all the confessing witches after they had provided evidence regarding the crimes of others. See P. Boyer and S. Nissenbaum, *Salem Village Witchcraft* (Belmont, Cal., 1972), I, Introduction.

71 Henningsen, *Witches' Advocate*, pp. 143–80, 397.

created when church courts either became more lenient or abandoned the pursuit of witches; and if they had not been available for use in witchcraft cases by the clerics who presided over territorial states, then the great European witch-hunt would not have assumed the dimensions that it did.

WITCHCRAFT AND THE LOCAL COURTS

A final precondition of the great European witch-hunt was the ability of local courts and subordinate tribunals to operate with a certain amount of independence from central political and judicial control. Most witchcraft prosecutions were conducted in courts that had a limited geographical jurisdiction. These were the courts of manors, towns, counties, dioceses, provinces or ecclesiastical territories. This is not to say that central authorities had nothing to do with the prosecution of witches. The Pope, the monarchs of territorial states, royal councils, and national representative assemblies were often directly responsible for passing laws or issuing edicts that sanctioned the prosecution of witches, while it was not uncommon for the highest courts of European states to hold witchcraft trials. It was not unknown for central authorities to inaugurate witch-hunts, and they often gave local or regional officials the authority to hear witchcraft cases.[72] But most witch-hunts were actually conducted by the judicial officers of smaller administrative subdivisions of state or Church.[73] These judges of local or 'inferior' jurisdictions usually demonstrated much more zeal in prosecuting witches than did the central authorities, and when left to their own devices they generally executed more witches than when they were closely supervised by their judicial superiors.

There are two main reasons why local courts usually proved to be less lenient than central courts in the prosecution of witchcraft. The first is that local authorities who presided over witch-trials were far more likely than their central superiors to develop an intense and immediate fear of witchcraft. Central authorities might agree that witches were a threat to society and that they needed to be prosecuted, but they rarely knew the accused witches personally (as many local magistrates did) and they were not faced with the prospect of living in the same community with the witches should they be

---

72 This was particularly true for Finland. See A. Heikkinen, *Paholaisen Liittolaiset* (Helsinki, 1969), p. 381.

73 See for example Evans, *Habsburg Monarchy*, p. 410.

acquitted. They were, moreover, less likely to be affected by the hysterical mood that often engulfed towns and villages when witch-hunts occurred. Central authorities, therefore, would be more likely to proceed against witches on the basis of the evidence against them and to avoid the prejudice that an alarmed judge would naturally develop. The second reason is that central judges were generally more committed to the proper operation of the judicial system and more willing therefore to afford accused witches whatever procedural safeguards the law might allow them.

A comparison between witchcraft prosecutions in Germany and Spain provides a good illustration of the effects that the absence of effective central judicial control had on the pattern of witch-hunting. Germany during the early modern period was an area in which there was very little political and judicial centralization. Although the various German lands were included within the Holy Roman Empire, and although the imperial *Reichstag* passed laws for all of the Emperor's subjects, the country consisted of about three hundred relatively autonomous political units. The extent to which any one of these units followed the law of the Empire and submitted to central control depended on a number of factors. The imperial cities were generally the most obedient, but even they manifested a strong streak of independence and in many ways were self-regulating. The autonomy of the German territories is most clearly evident in judicial affairs. Each territory had its own courts, and although these institutions enforced the imperial law codes to a greater or lesser extent, each had virtual autonomy over its own judicial life. There was no central judicial establishment to send judges on circuit or to supervise the conduct of local justice. There was a supreme imperial court, the *Reichskammergericht*, which sat in Speyer and heard cases on appeal, but there was no regular procedure for doing so.[74] In ecclesiastical affairs the picture was similar, each bishop or ecclesiastical dignitary holding his own court. Before the Reformation, and in those areas that remained Catholic after the Reformation, there was some regulation of local justice by higher authorities, but it was usually minimal. Even the papacy did not have much effective control over the inquisitors it appointed to various regions.[75] These inquisitors received their authority from Rome, but their autonomy

[74] On the *Reichskammergericht* see Merzbacher, *Hexenprozesse*, pp. 63–4; Midelfort, *Witch-Hunting*, p. 114.
[75] See Kieckhefer, *Repression of Heresy*, p. 107.

94

was restricted much more by competition from local secular and episcopal courts than by papal restraints.

The decentralization of judicial life had profound effects on the prosecution of witches in Germany. Without effective control by central authorities, local judges and inquisitors had enormous freedom to hunt witches as they wished. It should not surprise us that the largest single witch-hunts took place within Germany; that the reports of the most barbarous tortures come from Germany; and that the total number of executions for witchcraft within the Empire was greater than in all other areas combined. There are many different reasons for the relatively high intensity of German witch-hunting, but the judicial situation must be considered the most important of these. The significance of these judicial factors becomes even more apparent when we realize that those jurisdictions that adhered strictly to the Imperial code of criminal law, the *Carolina*, executed far fewer witches than those that blatantly ignored it.[76]

Spain, like Germany, was also a politically decentralized country. While not so fragmented as Germany, Spain consisted of a number of kingdoms that were united only by allegiance to a single monarch. There was no more a Spanish state in the early modern period than there was a German one. Spain did, however, have a highly centralized judicial institution, the Spanish Inquisition, which assumed control over most witchcraft prosecutions. The Inquisition in Spain, unlike the medieval inquisition in Germany, was a national institution, the chief officer of which, the inquisitor general, was appointed by the king subject to papal confirmation. The Spanish Inquisition was also a highly centralized institution, in which twenty-one separate regional tribunals throughout the entire Spanish empire were subordinated to a central tribunal, the *Suprema* in Madrid. This council strictly enforced a set of criminal procedural rules that made it much more difficult for witches to be convicted and executed than in other parts of Europe. The council also heard appeals regarding witchcraft cases, and this allowed central authorities to override the judgement of their local or regional subordinates. The operation of this judicial system does not by itself explain why there were relatively few witches prosecuted in Spain, but there is no question that the system prevented witch-hunts, most notably the one that occurred in 1609–11, from getting out of control.

A second illustration of the importance of local judicial autonomy in witch hunting comes from Scotland, where almost all witchcraft

76 Monter, *Witchcraft in France and Switzerland*, p. 106.

Table 2   Execution-rates in Scottish Witchcraft Trials

Type of Court	Persons Tried	Executions (fates known)	% Executed
Justiciary Courts	197	108	55
Circuit Courts	105	17	16
Local Commissions	100	91	91

trials took place in the secular courts under the provisions of the witchcraft statute passed by the Scottish Parliament of 1563. There were three main types of secular courts where Scottish witches could be tried. First there was the Court of Justiciary, which sat in Edinburgh. Cases from all over Scotland could be heard there, but a disproportionate number came from the counties in the immediate vicinity of the capital. Then there were the circuit courts, held in the various shires of the country, over which judges from the central courts presided. These circuit courts did not function with much regularity until the late seventeenth century. Finally, there were local *ad hoc* courts that were commissioned either by the Privy Council or by Parliament to try witches in the areas where they were arrested. These courts, unlike the Court of Justiciary and the circuit courts, were not staffed by professionally trained judges from the central courts but by local landowners and magistrates.

Although we do not have complete statistics, it is quite apparent that the execution-rate in Scotland was dramatically higher when unsupervised local authorities heard witchcraft cases than when judges from the central courts did so, either in Edinburgh or on circuit. As Table 2 indicates, the execution-rate, determined on the basis of only those cases whose outcomes are known, was 91 per cent in the local trials commissioned by the Privy Council or Parliament but only 55 per cent in the Justiciary Court and a very low 16 per cent in the circuit courts.[77] The presence of central judicial authorities, in other words, had a significant, negative impact on the outcome of witchcraft cases. It is not surprising, moreover, to find that in England,

77 The source for Table 2 is Larner et al., *Source-Book of Scottish Witchcraft*, p. 237, Table 2. The figures given here do not include those cases which terminated by the death of the accused in prison, the escape of the accused, or some other 'miscellaneous' outcome.

where virtually all witchcraft prosecutions were conducted by central judges in circuit courts (the assizes), the conviction- and execution-rates were exceptionally low by European standards, although the strict prohibition of torture probably had more to do with that situation than the central supervision of local justice.

A further illustration of the effect of local autonomy on witchcraft prosecutions comes from France, where despite a high degree of political centralization, witchcraft prosecutions usually took place in local or provincial courts. In these tribunals the conviction- and execution-rates were generally somewhere between those that prevailed in Germany on the one hand and those in England on the other. The important consideration in France, however, is that witchcraft cases could be appealed to the regional *parlements*. In the *Parlement* of Paris, which exercised an appellate jurisdiction over most of northern France and was for all intents and purposes a central court, the percentage of appealed cases that resulted in complete dismissal was an astonishingly high 36 per cent, while only 24 per cent of all cases were confirmed.[78] The main reason for the greater leniency of the Parisian tribunal was that it adhered to a more rigid rule of proof than did the lower courts, refusing to sentence witches to death on the basis of a confession extracted under torture. Other considerations, however, including the remoteness of the judges from the actual environment of the witch-hunts and perhaps greater scepticism regarding witchcraft, also played a part. Interestingly enough, the eight provincial *parlements* in France, which were not, like the *Parlement* of Paris, central institutions, had a much less lenient record in prosecuting witches and at the end of the seventeenth century had to be subjected to direct royal control in order to bring the witch-hunt to an end.

The way in which a system of mandatory appeals could restrain the eagerness of local courts to put witches to death can also be seen in Denmark, where legislation passed in 1576 required that a death sentence against a witch from a local or district court had to be reviewed by the County Court. On the basis of evidence from Jutland, where apparently all witchcraft cases were reviewed, the local courts sentenced just under 90 per cent of the accused to death, a figure that corresponds to the percentage of Scottish executions in trials held by local authorities. At the county courts, however, almost 50 per cent of all death sentences were reversed, usually on the grounds of

---

78 Soman, 'Parlement of Paris', p. 36. For an early case see Cohn, *Europe's Inner Demons*, p. 232.

insufficient evidence or the violation of established legal procedures, which included restrictions on the use of torture.[79]

Central authorities did not always have a negative effect upon the process of witch-hunting. High court judges confirmed many sentences on appeal; royal councils occasionally took steps to encourage prosecutions; and sometimes even kings themselves started witch-hunts. In 1590 James VI of Scotland assumed a leading role in one of the largest witch-hunts in Scottish history, while Christian IV of Denmark not only promulgated a witchcraft ordinance in 1617 but actively encouraged the prosecution of witches who were under suspicion in Copenhagen and Elsinore in 1626.[80] Within the Church a number of popes inspired campaigns against magicians and witches in the late Middle Ages. But in most cases central authorities either acted as neutral agents in the process of witch-hunting or imposed some sort of restraints on it. The history of many individual witch-hunts can be written as a story of the way in which local authorities, having decided that witches had to be prosecuted, obtained whatever sanctions were necessary from their superiors and then, armed with those warrants, proceeded against the alleged culprits with much less restraint than the central authorities might have used themselves. The real initiative in the process came from the localities, not the central government.[81]

The essential role that unsupervised and unrestrained local and provincial officials played in the process of witch-hunting makes it difficult to establish a clear causal connection between the growth of the modern state and the great European witch-hunt. In a number of ways the rise of the modern state in western Europe served as a necessary precondition of that hunt.[82] Unless the state had acquired its immense judicial power, which was reflected in the adoption of inquisitorial procedure and which was turned against both traitors and witches with equally devastating effects, the hunt would never have taken place. Moreover, if the states of western Europe had not acquired large judicial bureaucracies, which inquisitorial procedure itself had necessitated, is it unlikely that large numbers of witches would have been prosecuted or convicted. It is no coincidence

---

79 J.C.V. Johansen, 'Denmark', pp. 339–50.

80 Ibid., pp. 341, 345–7; Henningsen, *Witches' Advocate*, p. 18. A period of intense witch-hunting followed the promulgation of the ordinance.

81 Henningsen, *Witches' Advocate*, p. 18; Trevor-Roper, 'European Witch-Craze', p. 114; Briggs, *Communities of Belief*, p. 14; Naess, 'Norway', pp. 379–80.

82 Larner, *Witchcraft and Religion*, p. 89, considers the rise of nation states one of the 'crucial factors' in accounting for the rise of witch-hunting.

that the great witch-hunt occurred during a period of extensive state-building throughout Europe. One can even argue that the process of state-building, which involved an attack upon traditional, communal arrangements, created tensions that found expression in witch-hunting.[83] On the other hand, the European witch-hunt depended in a curious way on the failure of the late medieval and early modern state to realize its full potential.

One of the characteristics of the modern state is a high degree of centralization. Modern states are territorially consolidated structures in which the central government exercises supreme power over even remote geographical areas. Most early modern European states failed to achieve that degree of centralization and continued to cede a certain amount of autonomy to the localities. Indeed, the entire political history of the early modern period can be written in terms of the conflict between the centre and the periphery. Judicially this conflict usually resulted in a situation in which a considerable amount of power was delegated to local and regional authorities. As far as witchcraft was concerned, this delegation of power, or the mere recognition by central governments that local jurisdictions continued to possess it, did as much to make the great witch-hunt possible as the state's acquisition of effective powers of judicial investigation and coercion. In the final analysis, the diffusion of judicial power within the state was just as important as its actual growth.

83 Muchembled, 'Witches of Cambrésis', pp. 261–9.

4 THE IMPACT OF THE REFORMATION

The formation of the cumulative concept of witchcraft and the various legal developments described in the last chapter made the European witch-hunt of the fifteenth, sixteenth and seventeenth centuries possible. If these intellectual and legal developments had not occurred, then the hunt would not have taken place, at least in the form and in the magnitude that it did. These preconditions do not, however, provide a complete causal explanation of the hunt. They were, in other words, necessary but not sufficient causes of the process that claimed the lives of thousands of Europeans. In order to achieve a fuller understanding of the hunt we must explore the religious, social and economic conditions that prevailed in early modern Europe. These conditions created an environment in which the hunting of witches was not merely possible but likely to occur. They encouraged people to believe in witchcraft, created tensions that often found expression in witchcraft accusations, and strengthened the determination of both the ruling élite and the common people to prosecute individuals for this crime. These conditions, therefore, occupy a second level of causation of the European witch-hunt. They were neither necessary preconditions nor efficient causes, but they did serve to intensify the process of witch-hunting. They also help to explain why the hunt occurred when it did.

The purpose of this chapter is to explore the ways in which the profound religious developments that took place in early modern Europe encouraged the growth of witch-hunting. The most important of these changes was the Reformation, the movement that shattered the ostensible unity of medieval Christendom. The main objective of the early Protestant reformers, such as Martin Luther, Jean Calvin, Huldreich Zwingli and Martin Bucer, was to restore the Church to its early Christian purity. In so doing they denied the efficacy of indulgences, redefined the function of the sacraments, eliminated or drastically altered the Roman Catholic mass and changed the role of the clergy. They proclaimed the autonomy of the individual conscience and posited a direct relationship between man and God, removing many of the clerical and angelic intermediaries that medieval Catholicism had established between them. They developed the idea that each believer was a priest who by reading the Bible could acquire the faith which alone could bring him salvation. The incompatibility of these ideas with the doctrines of the Roman Catholic Church, the failure of that Church to reform itself, and the inability of the reformers to find scriptural support for papal authority led them to break with Rome and to establish independent Protestant churches. Millions of Europeans, in many cases encouraged by the establishment of Protestant state churches, left the Roman fold. Protestantism became the dominant religion in many parts of Germany, Switzerland and the Low Countries; in England, Scotland and the Scandinavian kingdoms; and in certain areas of France, Hungary and Poland.

The success of the Protestant Reformation encouraged the growth of a reform movement within Catholicism. This movement, which we refer to as the Counter-Reformation or Catholic Reformation, met a long-standing demand by Catholic clerics and laymen to bring about reform without destroying the structure of the Church. It cannot, therefore, be viewed simply as a negative response to the rise of Protestantism; indeed, its origins can be traced to the pre-Reformation period. The main goals of the Catholic reformers were to eliminate corruption within the Church, to educate the clergy, to inspire and strengthen the faith of the laity, and to reclaim the allegiance of those individuals and communities that had been lost to Protestantism. The Counter-Reformation achieved a significant measure of success. Under the leadership of the papacy, the Church introduced a series of administrative and liturgical changes, many of which were authorized by the Council of Trent (1545–47, 1551–52, 1562–63). Missionaries from the newly formed Society of Jesus and other religious orders helped to reconvert Protestants in many parts of Europe, while ecclesiastical courts maintained theological orthodoxy and moral propriety in nominally Catholic areas. Military forces from Catholic countries waged war against Protestants in a number of internal and international conflicts, the most significant of which were the civil wars in France in the late sixteenth century and the Thirty Years' War in the early seventeenth century. As a result of all this activity parts of Germany, Austria, Bohemia, Poland, Hungary and the Low Countries returned to the Catholic fold, while other areas remained Protestant.

The period during which all of this reforming activity and conflict took place, the age of the Reformation, spanned the years 1520–1650. Since these years include the period when witch-hunting was most intense, historians have always assumed that the Reformation served as a catalyst for witch-hunting. Indeed, some have seen the forces unleashed by both Reformation and Counter-Reformation as the mainspring of the entire witch-hunt. Here we must proceed with caution, since the European witch-hunt actually began almost one hundred years before Luther nailed his ninety-five theses to the castle church at Wittenberg. During the early years of the Reformation, moreover, from 1520 to 1550, there were relatively few witchcraft prosecutions in Europe, so it is difficult to establish any direct causal connection between the two developments. And at the other end of the European witch-hunt, in the first two decades of the eighteenth century, when thousands of witches were still being prosecuted in Poland, it is difficult to speak of either the Reformation or the Counter-Reformation as a contemporary reality. So the most that we can say is that the Reformation and Counter-Reformation served to intensify the process of witch-hunting and perhaps helped the hunt to spread from place to place.[1]

The question of course is exactly *how* the Reformation contributed to the growth of the hunt. In answering this question it is important that we study the effects of both the Protestant and Catholic reformations. The main reason for adopting this comprehensive approach is that extensive witch-hunting took place in both Protestant and Catholic lands. Comparisons between the numbers of witches executed by Catholic and Protestant authorities can easily obscure this fundamental fact. It may be true that Catholics executed more witches in southwestern Germany than did Protestants, just as the opposite may be true in western Switzerland.[2] It may also be true that there are religious explanations for these discrepancies. The important consideration, however, is that large witch-hunts – significantly larger than any that had occurred before 1500 – took place in *all* of these areas during the Reformation era. The mere fact, moreover, that Protestants took the lead in prosecuting witches in some areas while Catholics did so in others recommends that we look at the effects of both reformations. As it is, the two reformations – which were to some extent different manifestations of the same general, European-wide religious revival – had many similar effects on witch-

---

1 For the clearest statement of this argument see Trevor-Roper, 'European Witch-Craze', p. 136 et passim.

2 See Midelfort, *Witch-Hunting*, p. 33; Monter, *Witchcraft in France and Switzerland*, pp. 106–7.

hunting.[3] Protestant and Catholic reformers did, after all, share many of the same witch-beliefs and exhibited a similar desire to extirpate witchcraft.[4]

Approaching the subject in this broad way, we shall pursue three separate lines of enquiry. First, we shall study those changes in religious attitudes and practices during the age of the Reformation that encouraged the growth and persistence of witch-hunting. Some of these changes were more readily apparent in Protestant than in Catholic circles for the simple reason that the Protestant Reformation was more radical than the Catholic, but there is sufficient evidence that the changes were not confined to Protestant areas. Secondly, we shall explore the ways in which religious conflict between Protestantism and Catholicism, and to a lesser extent between the different denominations of Protestantism, inspired witchcraft prosecutions and executions. Finally we shall see how the Reformation, while encouraging witchcraft prosecutions in various ways, also contributed in the long run to its decline.

THE NEW RELIGIOUS OUTLOOK

The fear of the Devil

During the age of the Reformation, Europeans increased their awareness of the Devil's presence in the world and became more determined to wage war against him. One of the main sources of this heightened consciousness of, and militance against, diabolical power was the thinking of the great Protestant reformers Martin Luther and Jean Calvin. These men did not introduce a new and original conception of the Devil; their beliefs in who the Devil was and what powers he possessed were essentially the same as those of late medieval Catholic demonologists. This agreement with the Catholics is in itself somewhat perplexing. Since the reformers challenged so many other aspects of medieval Catholicism, and since they were so critical of scholastic theology, one assumes that they would have developed a distinctly Protestant demonology. Instead they merely adopted the traditional, late-medieval view, modifying it only in some respects and placing it on a firmer scriptural foundation.

3 For the connection between witch-hunting and the Augustinian revival that was common to Protestantism and Catholicism see A.D. Wright, *The Counter-Reformation* (New York, 1982), pp. 1–50.

4 For the influence of Catholic and Protestant writers on each other see N. Paulus, *Hexenwahn und Hexenprozesse vornehmlich im 16. Jahrhundert* (Freiburg, 1910), p. 69.

Although the great reformers did little to change traditional Catholic demonology, they did tend to emphasize the presence of the Devil in the world and exhibit a more profound fear of him. Martin Luther, who reported having active physical bouts with Satan, attributed to him a position in the world that borders on dualist heresy. 'We are all subject to the devil, both in body and goods,' wrote Luther, 'and we be strangers in this world, whereof he is the prince and god.' The Devil, according to Luther, 'liveth, yea and reigneth throughout the whole world'. The danger that Satan presented to man was both physical and spiritual. Not only did he 'rehearseth sorcery among works of the flesh', but he deceived the mind with wicked opinions.[5] A number of late-medieval writers had attributed similar intentions to Satan, but very few of them had described demonic power as being so pervasive. Everyone, even the most holy men, could be deceived and ensnared by the cunning treachery of Satan. Luther was confident that the Kingdom of Christ would ultimately prevail over the forces of darkness, but the struggle against him would be difficult and continuous, and the individual was always vulnerable to deception and harm.[6]

Jean Calvin was no less preoccupied with diabolical power in the world and no less committed to counteracting it. For him the power of Satan was so strong and pervasive that the true Christian saint had to engage in an 'unceasing struggle against him'.[7] The militancy of Calvinism, which often found expression in actual physical battle, had its basis in the continuous campaign that the saint was enjoined to conduct against the Devil. Like Luther, Calvin was completely confident that the Devil would fail in his attempt to triumph over the forces of good. For him, no less than for scholastic theologians, the Devil operated only with the permission of God, whose creature he was. But the number of the Devil's earthly followers was so great that the saint could not afford to relax his efforts.[8]

Neither Luther nor Calvin was preoccupied with witchcraft as such. Although Luther said on one occasion that all witches were the Devil's whores and on another that they should all be burned, his concern was any form of idolatry, which he considered to be a

---

5 Kors and Peters (eds), *Witchcraft in Europe*, p. 197.

6 H.A. Oberman, *Luther: Man between God and the Devil* (New Haven, 1989), p. 104, claims that according to Luther, the omnipotent God was hidden from man; the revealed God, incarnate in Christ, 'laid Himself open to the Devil's fury'.

7 Kors and Peters, *Witchcraft in Europe*, p. 204

8 See M. Walzer, *The Revolution of the Saints* (Cambridge, Mass., 1965), pp. 64–5.

bewitching of God, rather than the traditional forms that witchcraft took.[9] Indeed, he believed that the witchcraft of the sorcerer was not as common as it had been in the past, before the truth of the gospel had been revealed. Calvin said even less than Luther about witchcraft *per se*. On the basis of Exodus 22:18 he insisted that witches 'must be slain', but witchcraft was hardly of paramount importance to him.[10] Nevertheless, the preoccupation that both reformers had with satanic power made many of their followers more determined to take action against witches whenever their presence became apparent. The Lutheran and Calvinist concern with Satan also encouraged an emphasis on the heretical rather than the magical aspects of witchcraft, which in turn inspired a greater determination to extirpate it.

The attitudes of reformers such as Luther and Calvin towards demonic power were capable of having widespread influence because they and their disciples founded an active, preaching ministry, capable of reaching large numbers of people. The impact of the reformers must be measured not simply by the circulation of their published works but by the dissemination of their ideas from the pulpit. Protestants, owing mainly to their reliance upon the Bible as the source of religious truth, placed great emphasis on successful preaching. From the pulpit men of all social classes, not just a small literate élite, acquired, among other things, the sense of the immediacy of diabolical power that was so apparent in the writings of Luther and Calvin. This awareness and fear of the Devil's work in this world might not have stimulated many initial accusations of witchcraft; these continued to originate in peasant fears of *maleficium*. But the heightened consciousness of diabolical activity certainly made early modern European communities – and not just the members of the ruling élite – more eager to prosecute these witches as agents of the Devil whenever accusations of *maleficium* surfaced.

It was not just in Protestant circles that one can detect a greater preoccupation with demonic power in the sixteenth and seventeenth centuries. To many Catholic reformers the Devil became just as frightening and omnipresent as he was to Lutherans and Calvinists. Indeed, the rise of Protestantism itself appeared to many Catholics to be the work of Satan, making them more aware of his capacity for bringing evil of all types into the world. Peter Canisius, the Jesuit missionary, actually mentioned Satan more often than Christ

9 See Monter, *European Witchcraft*, p. 59.

10 On Calvin's statements about witchcraft see J. Teall, 'Witchcraft and Calvinism in Elizabethan England: Divine Power and Human Agency', *Journal of the History of Ideas*, 23 (1962): 27–9.

in the catechism that he prepared.[11] Catholic priests often matched their Protestant colleagues in convincing their parishioners of Satan's omnipresence and in raising their fears of him.[12] They could also be equally effective in encouraging them to campaign ceaselessly against him. In both Catholic and Protestant quarters there arose a zealous commitment, sometimes strengthened by millenarian beliefs, to purify the world by declaring war against Satan. The war was to be waged both internally, by resisting temptation, and externally, by prosecuting witches and heretics.[13]

Personal sanctity, guilt and witchcraft

A second effect of the Reformation on witchcraft arose from the emphasis that both Protestant and Catholic reformers placed on personal piety and sanctity. One of the most salient characteristics of the Reformation era was the evangelical appeal of Protestant and Catholic preachers for all Christians, including the laity, to lead an exemplary moral life and to be responsible for their own salvation. Instead of merely encouraging conformity to certain standards of religious observance (such as attending church), the reformers of the sixteenth and seventeenth centuries instructed the people to lead a more demanding, morally rigorous life. This type of exhortation, which reflected the current preoccupation with the danger of diabolical temptation, helped to Christianize Europe in an unprecedented way. All people, including those in backward, rural areas, were exhorted to become active, morally conscious Christians. The process began with the clergy themselves, whose moral conduct was in many cases not much better than that of their parishioners, and then was spread, through them, to the laity.[14] Among Calvinists there was a special premium placed upon personal sanctity because of their strong belief in predestination. If God had predetermined that certain persons would be saved and others would be damned, then it was especially important that one lead a blameless personal life, for such holiness could easily be construed as a sign of election. Once assured that they were numbered among the elect, moreover, Calvinists would strive to achieve moral perfection both to confirm their status as saints (which was always a source of at least residual doubt) and to thank God for their gift of salvation. The Calvinists' systematic,

11 Thomas, *Religion and the Decline of Magic*, p. 476.
12 See R. Muchembled, 'Witches of Cambrésis', pp. 259–73.
13 See W. Lamont, *Godly Rule* (London, 1969), pp. 98–100.
14 Larner, *Enemies of God*, p. 25

sustained search for salvation contributed to the development of a new personality type, a highly motivated, driven person whose moral energy could be diverted into political and economic activity.

The new emphasis on personal piety and the intense pursuit of salvation took a heavy psychological toll, for it brought with it a deep sense of sin. Whenever conscientious people sinned, whenever they failed to adhere to the demanding standards of behaviour that were being so loudly proclaimed, or whenever they experienced doubts about their own sanctity, they had to deal with what could be profound feelings of guilt and moral unworthiness. These feelings were especially strong among those who faced the frightening prospect that they were not among the elect, but no morally conscious Christian, Protestant or Catholic, could avoid such thoughts completely. When people experienced this type of guilt, they naturally sought to relieve it in any way possible, and one of the methods frequently employed was to transfer it to another person. Even the availability of auricular confession to Catholics and Anglicans did not prevent this process of projection from taking place. And the ideal object of such projection was the witch, a person who personified evil as it was defined in contemporary society. In this indirect way the witch gave both the individual and the community the opportunity to gain reassurance regarding their own moral worth.

The relief of guilt through projection on to another person could easily lead to witchcraft accusations and prosecutions. Alan Macfarlane has shown, for example, that in sixteenth- and seventeenth-century England, many accusations arose when individuals refused to provide economic assistance to people who needed it and who came to one's door asking for it. In denying this aid, which both Catholic and Protestant moral teaching enjoined, the person naturally felt guilty, but by depicting the unaided person as a witch and therefore as a moral aggressor unworthy of support, he could rid himself of the guilt that he was experiencing. In a very real sense the guilty neighbour projected his guilt on to the witch.[15]

Another example of this type of projection comes from the Catholic Low Countries, where the Christianization of the populace, especially the rural populace, took place as part of the Counter-Reformation. In studying witch-hunts in the region of the Cambrésis, Robert Muchembled has observed that the local parish priests, who were the agents of this process, often found themselves backsliding

15 Macfarlane, *Witchcraft in Tudor and Stuart England*, pp. 192–9.

in their adherence to the recently proclaimed stricter rules regarding moral conduct. In the case of the priests, their offence was often sexual incontinence. When the priests experienced the deep sense of moral guilt and weakness, they often projected their guilt on to witches, in whose apprehension and interrogation they took an active part. Since the witches were usually women, who in a certain sense served as symbols of sexuality, the projection was fairly clear. In proceeding against the witches, moreover, the priests did not act alone but in conjunction with many other members of the community, to whom the priests had been transmitting the instructional message of reformed Catholicism. The witches therefore became not only the objects of the priests' projected guilt but 'expiatory victims' of an entire community that was striving to establish a new moral order.[16]

In the case of Salem, Massachusetts, there is further evidence of projected guilt in witchcraft accusations. Paul Boyer and Stephen Nissenbaum have shown that the people who made accusations against witches in Salem village clung desperately to a strict Puritan set of social and moral values, while those who were accused represented a new, secular, commercial ethic. The situation was, therefore, somewhat different from that which prevailed in Essex, England, where the accusers appeared to be the ones affected by the values of a commercial society and the witches acted as the guardians of the old morality. Nevertheless, the accusers at Salem were not that different from their English counterparts, since they too were lured by the materialism of the new society and experienced guilt for such acquisitiveness. The witchcraft accusations that they made, therefore, were not only attempts to preserve the moral fabric of a model Christian community against corrupting influences, but also projections of their own guilt on to others. Once again, of course, the process was collective as well as individual.[17]

The religiously inspired guilt that lay at the root of many witchcraft prosecutions was not always projected. Sometimes witches themselves manifested a deep sense of sin and guilt. This was most obvious among those individuals who considered themselves to be witches or gradually came to that realization, but even when accused witches did not reach such a conclusion they sometimes seemed to be very much aware of their sinful enmity towards others. William Monter has claimed that in the Jura region witches were dominated by

16 Muchembled, 'Witches of Cambrésis', pp. 266–7, 259–60.
17 Boyer and Nissenbaum, *Salem Possessed*, pp. 179–216.

such feelings, so much so that one can draw a clear contrast between the morally superior British witch whose guilt is projected on to her by others and whose act of revenge can in a certain sense be justified, and the Jura witch whose guilt is internal and whose acts of vengeance were gratuitous.[18]

The attack upon superstition, paganism and magic

The Christianization of the European populace involved not only a demand that all Christians lead exemplary lives but that they learn the elements of the true Christian faith and the proper forms of worship. The process was, in other words, doctrinal and liturgical as well as moral, and the preaching and catechetical instruction of the reformed clergy served all of these related objectives. One of the main purposes of this instruction was to purify the faith by eradicating superstitious beliefs and practices, eliminating vestiges of paganism, and suppressing magic (the great rival of true religion) in all its forms. The activities that came under attack included simple popular blessings and exorcisms that were modelled on medieval liturgical practice, the use of holy water, charms and amulets to protect oneself and one's possessions from evil power, and the practice of healing, divination and love magic, all of which could involve incantations and the recitation of prayers.[19]

The nature of this campaign against popular superstition and magic can be seen in a large body of demonological writings by Protestant pastors, most of whose writings originated as sermons to their congregations. Unlike the theologians and jurists who wrote learned treatises on witchcraft and demonology, these pastors were just as concerned with charms, divination and healing as they were with maleficent witchcraft. Indeed, English Protestant writers like William Perkins considered 'good witches' even more dangerous than their maleficent counterparts.[20] Since these Protestant pastors wished to alert their congregations to the moral and spiritual implications of magic and witchcraft, they emphasized the commerce with demons

---

18 E.W. Monter, *Witchcraft in France and Switzerland*, p. 137.

19 For some of these practices see Thomas, *Religion and the Decline of Magic*, pp. 27–50; R. Scribner, 'Ritual and Popular Religion in Catholic Germany at the Time of the Reformation', *Journal of Ecclesiastical History*, 35 (1984), 47–77, and E. Duffy, *The Stripping of the Altars* (New Haven, 1992), pp. 277–87. On the process of the 'folklorization' of Christianity see J. Delumeau, *La Peur en Occident XIVe–XVIIIe siècles* (Paris, 1978), pp. 166–70.

20 Perkins, *Damned Art of Witchcraft*, pp. 638–8.

that all such activities involved, rather than the actual effects of magical actions. As good Protestants, they also drew on the Bible, especially the books of the Old Testament, to establish the different types of 'witchcraft' they were condemning.[21]

The determination of Protestant clergy to wipe out superstitious popular practices and thereby purify the faith finds its counterpart in the Catholic clergy of the Counter-Reformation, especially those who served as inquisitors in Mediterranean lands. Recognizing that the external practices reflected inner beliefs, inquisitors worked with local clergy to eradicate superstition and error and to standardize all devotional practices. Catholic reformers obviously did not label the official liturgy of the medieval Church as magical in the way that Protestants did, but they did try to eliminate many of the prayers, blessings and practices that had derived from that liturgy, as well as the various forms of white magic that were in popular use, especially healing and love magic.[22]

The campaign of reformers against these various forms of superstition and white magic led to an increase in witchcraft prosecutions in two very different ways. First, those individuals whom Protestant and Catholic reformers identified as practitioners of white witchcraft could easily incur the suspicion of having also engaged in maleficent witchcraft. It is true that white magicians and those guilty of superstitious practices were generally treated more leniently than maleficent witches, but that did not prevent the charges against white witches from being rewritten to include harmful deeds. Indeed, it was not uncommon for healers to be charged with maleficent witchcraft, since it was widely believed that those who could cure could also harm.[23] Even when the two types of charges were kept fairly distinct, the campaign against magic in general led to an increase in witchcraft prosecutions. In the 1580s, for example, the Roman Inquisition, acting in the spirit of the Counter-Reformation, turned its attention increasingly to cases of superstition, magic and sorcery. It prosecuted numerous cases of divination, love magic, therapeutic magic and spells, and at the same time it tried people for witchcraft.[24]

21 Clark, 'Protestant Demonology', pp. 45–81.

22 R. Martin, *Witchcraft and the Inquisition in Venice, 1550–1650* (Oxford, 1989), pp. 246–50; M. O'Neil, 'Magical Healing, Love Magic and the Inquisition in Late Sixteenth-Century Modena', in *Inquisition and Society in Early Modern Europe*, ed. S. Haliczer (Totowa, N.J., 1987), pp. 88–114.

23 See below, Chapter 5.

24 Parker, 'Some Recent Work', p. 529; W Monter, *Ritual, Myth and Magic in Early Modern Europe* (Athens, Ohio, 1983), pp. 66–8.

The second way in which the attack upon superstition and magic contributed to the intensification of witch-hunting was that it deprived the victims of sorcery of some of the weapons they customarily used to protect themselves from witches. Those who felt threatened or harmed by a witch, at least in Protestant lands, could no longer make the sign of the cross, sprinkle holy water on their houses, hang up medals of the saints or perform many of the protective rituals that Europeans had traditionally employed when threatened with diabolical power. It is true that Protestant reformers never completely succeeded in eliminating popular forms of counter-magic, but they did manage to discourage their use in many godly communities. When that happened, the victims of witchcraft could easily have been led to the conclusion that the only way to deal with witches was to take legal action against them, thus leading to an increase in the number of prosecutions.[25]

It is interesting to note that both Protestants and Catholics continued to take action against various forms of white magic and superstition long after trials for maleficent witchcraft had ended. These prosecutions took place only in ecclesiastical courts, and they never resulted in executions, but they did proceed on the assumption that the accused had had commerce with the Devil. Thus in the Netherlands, which ended its trials for witchcraft in the early seventeenth century, trials for magic continued well into the eighteenth century.[26] The same was true in Scotland, where Presbyterian courts took action against 'charming' many years after the last witch had been executed. In 1728, for example, the synod of Merse and Teviotdale warned those within its jurisdiction that a particular type of charming known as 'scoring the brow', which was done when people imagined that they or their relatives had been 'ill done', was 'justly reckoned a sort and degree of witchcraft, not to be tolerated in a Reformed land'. It was also observed that such scorings, since they involved the 'effusion of human blood, may be called sacrifices to the Devil'.[27] In Catholic Spain and Italy the Inquisition continued to prosecute people for various forms of magic and superstition throughout the eighteenth century on the grounds that such practices involved either the adoration of the Devil or the abuse of the sacraments and thus were classified as 'manifest heresy'.

---

25 See Thomas, *Religion and the Decline of Magic*, p. 498.

26 M. Gijswijt-Hofstra, 'Witchcraft in the Northern Netherlands', in *Current Issues in Women's History*, ed. A. Angerman et al. (London, 1989), p. 77.

27 Scottish Record Office, CH2/265/2, p. 165.

Witchcraft and the godly state

Another effect of the Reformation on witchcraft prosecutions was evident in the legislative process itself. As mentioned above, the entire process of religious reform was characterized by a zealous concern for purifying society and promoting individual morality. Preaching and catechetical training were the main methods used to achieve these ends, but reformers did not hesitate to use the legislative power of the state to facilitate the process. One sign of this new tactic was the passage of a considerable amount of legislation against moral offences. These crimes traditionally had been the exclusive preserve of the ecclesiastical courts, but the general decline of ecclesiastical jurisdiction, especially in Protestant countries, encouraged secular authorities to use the legislative and judicial authority of the state to achieve the same ends. Witchcraft was just one of the moral offences that came under attack; secular authorities also passed laws against sodomy, fornication, prostitution and adultery. But for our purposes it is significant that many of the laws against witchcraft, which as mentioned above constitute one of the main preconditions of the European witch-hunt, originated in a mentality that the Reformation helped to breed. This same mentality also found expression in a new emphasis upon the responsibility of the secular magistrate to prosecute moral offences more determinedly. The end product of all this zeal was the creation of the godly state, a secular institution that assumed the obligation to preserve the moral purity of society. To some extent the medieval state had pursued this objective, especially in dealing with heresy, but the strength of the Church as an independent institution had made it unnecessary for the state to devote its energies to such a task. In the age of the Reformation, however, the state, often acting under clerical pressure, became a guardian of individual morality. The change was most evident in Scotland, where the clergy applied a number of pressures on the state to realize its new mission; in New England, where the clergy exercised exceptionally strong influence in civil government; and in Sweden, where the government took the advice of the clergy in deciding how to handle infractions of the Mosaic law. In all these areas civil authorities authorized and conducted large witch-hunts.[28]

28 Larner, *Enemies of God*, pp. 67–8, 71–5; B. Ankarloo, *Trolldomsprocesserna in Sverige* (Stockholm, 1971), p. 328.

The Bible and witchcraft

This brief survey of the different ways in which the Reformation contributed to witch-hunting would not be complete without mentioning the effect of Protestant biblicism on the process. The Protestant Reformation not only established the Bible as the sole source of religious truth but also led to the translation of the scriptures into every major European language. At the same time there was a new insistence upon the literal interpretation of those scriptures. The net effect of all this is that as the Reformation spread, increasingly large numbers of Europeans were able to read the Bible and to take those passages that refer to witchcraft literally. Of prime importance among those was Exodus 22: 18, 'Thou shalt not suffer a witch to live.' It did not matter that the original Hebrew word translated as 'witch' in this passage meant a poisoner or 'someone who works in darkness and mutters things' rather than a sorcerer who makes a pact with the Devil and worships him. In this regard the efforts of scholars like Erasmus and Weyer to prove that the Bible had little to say about sixteenth-century witchcraft fell on deaf ears.[29] Nor did it matter that some theologians could not accept the injunction as positive law, on the grounds that Christ had abrogated the judicial law of the Old Testament.[30] The important consideration is that the word was translated as 'witch' in all western European languages and that the text was used by preachers and judges to sanction an uncompromising campaign against witches. 'We have here,' claimed Reverend James Hutcheson of Killallan in Scotland in a sermon preached on this text, 'a precept of the law of God in reference to a certain sort of malefactor to be found within the visible church.'[31]

David Meder, the pastor of Nebra in Thuringia, gave no fewer than eight sermons on Exodus 22:18 in order to encourage secular magistrates to take action against witches.[32] Even Jean Bodin, a Catholic, relied upon the text of Exodus to support witch-hunting, although he did so not because of any sort of biblicism but because

29 Johann Weyer, *Witches, Devils, and Doctors in the Renaissance*: Johann Weyer's *De Praestigiis Daemonum*, ed. George Mora (Binghamton, 1991), pp. 93–8. See also Sir Robert Filmer, *A Difference betweene an English and Hebrew Witch* (London, 1653).

30 For a survey of Protestant opinion on this difficult question see P.D.L. Avis, 'Moses and the Magistrate: a Study in the Rise of Protestant Legalism', *Journal of Ecclesiastical History*, 26 (1975): 149–72.

31 A.L. Drummond and J. Bulloch, *The Scottish Church 1688–1843* (Edinburgh, 1973), pp. 12–13. See also J. Stearne, *A Confirmation and Discovery of Witchcraft* (London, 1648), p. 9.

32 Paulus, *Hexenwahn*, p. 82.

he anchored his condemnation of witchcraft in the Jewish tradition.[33] Interestingly enough the Bible also served to corroborate many people's belief in the reality of witchcraft. Even in the late eighteenth century, when the belief in witchcraft was highly unfashionable in most intellectual circles, John Wesley wrote that 'the giving up of witchcraft is, in effect, giving up the Bible'.[34] The celebrated English jurist William Blackstone, writing at about the same time as Wesley, claimed no less credulously that 'To deny the possibility, nay, actual existence of witchcraft and sorcery is at once flatly to contradict the revealed word of God.'[35]

RELIGIOUS CONFLICT

The Reformation and the Counter-Reformation not only changed many aspects of the religious outlook of both Protestants and Catholics but also led to bitter conflicts between them. Protestant efforts to establish the reformed religion throughout Europe encountered increasingly strong Catholic resistance and led eventually to attempts at reconversion. Conflicts also arose between the different Protestant denominations, such as the Lutherans and the Calvinists. All of this confessional strife, which often erupted into domestic or even international warfare, played an important role in European witch-hunting. The role was, however, much more indirect than some scholars have argued.[36]

The uneven geographical distribution of witchcraft prosecutions throughout Europe suggests, in a very tentative way, that religious conflict had some connection with witch-hunting. A very rough correlation can be established between the intensity of witchcraft prosecutions on the one hand and the extent of religious divisions on the other. Witch-hunting was most severe in countries or regions where either large religious minorities lived within the boundaries of a state or where the people of one state or territory adhered to one religion and the residents of a neighbouring state adhered to another.

Witch-hunting was most intense in Germany, Switzerland, France, Poland and Scotland, all of which were religiously heterogeneous countries. In Germany, which consisted of hundreds of political units within

---

33 U. Lange, *Untersuchungen zu Bodins Démonomanie* (Frankfurt, 1970), pp. 159–60.

34 *Journal of the Rev. John Wesley* (New York, 1906), III, p. 330.

35 W. Blackstone, *Commentaries on the Laws of England* (Oxford, 1769), IV, p. 60.

36 For the classic statement of the argument see Trevor-Roper, 'European Witch-Craze', p. 161. For the opposite point of view see Schormann, *Hexenprozesse in Nordwestdeutschland*, p. 159.

the weak Holy Roman Empire, the official religion of a particular area was in most cases determined by the religion of the local prince. Consequently, some areas, especially those in the north, became Lutheran, while others remained Catholic or became Calvinist. In Switzerland, which comprised thirteen loosely confederated cantons, six cantons became Protestant while the other seven remained Catholic.

In France the situation was somewhat different, since the country remained nominally Catholic throughout this period. Calvinism, however, gained great strength in many areas, especially where the local nobility had converted. After the bitter religious wars of the late sixteenth century King Henry IV, who converted from Protestantism to Catholicism, issued the Edict of Nantes (1598), which granted freedom of conscience to all Frenchmen, freedom of worship in all towns where Protestantism had been established, and a significant measure of political independence to those same towns. The Edict, which was not repealed until 1685, ensured the preservation of a large Calvinist minority, the Huguenots, throughout the seventeenth century. In Scotland the situation was even more confusing. The Protestant national Church, which was established by law in 1567, was essentially a Calvinist Church that acquired a Presbyterian form of church government by the 1590s. At the same time, however, the episcopal structure of the Church, which derived from Catholic times and resembled the Protestant episcopal structure of the Church of England, survived in attenuated form and was strengthened and restored on a number of separate occasions by the king, who after 1603 was also the king of England. The Scottish Church was therefore divided between rival Protestant factions, while outside the Church a large number of Catholics survived, especially in the north.

In all of these areas religious divisions and conflicts fostered political instability and violence. In Germany a long struggle between the Catholic emperor and the Protestant princes led ultimately to the Thirty Years' War and the virtual collapse of the Empire in 1648. Switzerland avoided that devastating conflict but nevertheless suffered politically from religious disunity. Not only did the growth of Protestantism lead to open warfare between Protestant and Catholic cantons in the 1530s, but religious divisions made national unity virtually impossible to attain for the next two hundred years. In France the religious wars of 1560–98 created political chaos, and even after the promulgation of the Edict of Nantes, Catholic rulers like Cardinal Richelieu waged intensive campaigns against Huguenot political autonomy and craftily undermined many of the protections offered to Huguenots by the Edict. In Scotland religious differences between Presbyterians and Episcopalians (whom the Presbyterians considered to be popish) led to revolution in the 1640s and prolonged conflict afterwards.

If witch-hunting was more widespread and intense in areas that were religiously divided, then the converse was also true. Religiously homogeneous or monolithic states generally experienced only occasional witch-hunts and relatively low numbers of executions. The two best illustrations of this correlation are Spain and Italy, both of which remained solidly Catholic throughout the Reformation era. Neither country avoided witch-hunting completely. Spain experienced large hunts in the Basque country in the 1520s and in 1609–11, while northern Italy provided the setting for a number of trials in the fifteenth and early sixteenth centuries. But neither country had a rash of local panics such as those that afflicted Germany, France and Switzerland in the late sixteenth and early seventeenth centuries, and the total number of executions in both countries, while impossible to measure precisely, was extremely low. A similar situation prevailed in Ireland, which, despite the arrival of Protestant English and Scottish settlers, remained predominantly Catholic. In the Scandinavian kingdoms, which were solidly Lutheran, there were, once again, relatively few witchcraft prosecutions and executions.

We can therefore establish a very general correlation between religious disunity and conflict on the one hand and intense witch-hunting on the other. Such a correlation, however, does not necessarily indicate that there was any causal connection between the two phenomena. The reasons why more witches were prosecuted in some areas than in others are many and varied, some of them being of a legal or judicial nature, as we have seen. It is *possible* that religious tensions had very little or nothing to do with the prosecution of witches. Historians have, for example, discredited the idea that the relatively high concentration of witchcraft prosecutions in the English counties of Essex and Lancashire reflected conflicts between Anglicans and a large Puritan minority in the former county and a Catholic minority in the latter.[37] Nevertheless, the general geographical correlation between religious conflict and intense witch-hunting is so close that *some* causal connection almost certainly exists between them.

But what is that connection? In answering that question we must rule out a number of possibilities. First, the adherents to the dominant faith in a religiously divided area generally did not use

---

37 Thomas, *Religion and the Decline of Magic*, p. 499n.

witchcraft prosecutions to dispose of their religious antagonists. This may have happened at Freudenberg, where Bishop Julius Echter von Mespelbrunn of Würzburg allegedly accused Protestants of witchcraft in order to consolidate the return to Catholicism that he had engineered.[38] But Erik Midelfort and Gerhard Schormann have shown that such patterns rarely occurred.[39] For the most part, individuals who were prosecuted for witchcraft belonged at least formally to the same faith as their prosecutors. Since witches usually came from the same communities or regions as their judges, one would expect that to be the case. Now it is true that witches were usually considered to be heretics, a label that Catholics would just as readily apply to a Protestant in their midst and Protestants might even use to describe Catholics. But the heresy of the witch was something quite different from the heresy of the Catholic or Protestant non-conformist. The witch was a heretic because she had completely abandoned her Christian faith and made a pact with the Devil; the religious non-conformist was a heretic because she rejected one or more doctrines of the established religion. The two might be prosecuted by the same authorities, and both could serve as scapegoats for the ills of society, but their crimes would rarely be confused. This was true back in the fifteenth century, when the crime of witchcraft was in the process of definition, and it was even more true in the sixteenth and seventeenth centuries, by which time the stereotype of the witch was widely known.[40]

Occasionally a Protestant reformer, such as Bishop Palladius of Denmark, would threaten to prosecute those who were 'backward' in religion as witches.[41] The threat illustrates the close connection that Protestants made between Catholic superstition and magic, but there is no evidence that Danish authorities actually used witchcraft trials to solve this religious problem. In Scotland the charges against many witches suggested that they were still practising the old religion. Women like Agnes Sampson, for example, were accused of using Catholic prayers in their magical practices and also of praying in ruined churches.[42] These charges tell us much more about the

38 Midelfort, *Witch Hunting*, p. 138.

39 Ibid.; Schormann, *Hexenprozesse in Nordwestdeutschland*, p. 159.

40 Marx, *L'Inquisition en Dauphiné*, p. 48; Burr, 'Fate of Dietrich Flade', p. 229. There may have been some confusion between witches and secret Protestants who gathered in conventicles in Habsburg lands. See Evans, *Habsburg Monarchy*, p. 406.

41 See E. Cowan, 'The Darker Vision of the Scottish Renaissance', in *The Renaissance and Reformation in Scotland*, ed. I.B. Cowan and D. Shaw (Edinburgh, 1983), p. 128

42 Ibid.

concerns of Sampson's prosecutors than about her actual religious behaviour. There is no evidence that Sampson was actually a recusant, but even if she was, it is unlikely that Scottish authorities would have resorted to a witchcraft trial to prosecute her. Reginald Scot claimed that some English witches were papists, but he did not thereby suggest that witchcraft prosecutions were a means of solving the recusant problem.[43] The most that can be said about the connection between Protestant or Catholic non-conformity and witchcraft is that those persons who were suspected of or had been prosecuted for some form of religious non-conformity, just like those who had been prosecuted for immorality or petty crime, were more liable to subsequent witchcraft accusations than others. In Massachusetts, for example, Anne Hutchinson was suspected of witchcraft after she had already been identified as an antinomian 'heretic'.[44] But this process is very different from the deliberate use of witchcraft accusations to prosecute religious non-conformists.[45]

We must also discount the possibility that religious wars between Protestants and Catholics inspired witch-hunting.[46] This simply is not true. The entire European witch-hunt may have coincided with the age of religious warfare, but the outbreak of hostilities in a particular locality usually had a negative impact on the process of witch-hunting. Luxembourg, for example, stopped the prosecution of witches just about the time that France entered the Thirty Years' War, and both Franche-Comté and Württemberg experienced reductions in witchcraft prosecutions from the moment they went to war. Conversely, the most intense periods of witch-hunting in northern France and in Paris itself were times of religious peace.[47]

There are a number of reasons for this inverse relationship between religious warfare and witchcraft prosecutions. First, warfare very often impeded the operation of the regular judicial machinery that was used to prosecute witches. When foreign armies occupied a given area, they sometimes even took over the operation of that machinery, and since witchcraft did not present an immediate threat to the newly arrived authorities, they usually did not assign a high priority to its prosecution. The presence of soldiers in an area also

---

43 R. Scot, *The Discoverie of Witchcraft*, ed. M. Summers (London, 1930), p. 4.

44 J. Demos, *Entertaining Satan* (New York, 1982), p. 64.

45 For a different critique of witchcraft prosecutions as 'camouflaged heretic hunts' see Henningsen, *Witches' Advocate*, p. 16.

46 Trevor-Roper, 'European Witch-Craze', pp. 143–5.

47 Delumeau, *La Peur*, pp. 356–8.

gave local residents an alternative means of explaining misfortune. In more peaceful times members of a community often attributed the misfortunes of everyday life to witches, who thereby became scapegoats of society. In wartime, however, misfortunes – which usually became more severe – could readily and persuasively be attributed to soldiers or, more generally, to the enemy. War, in other words, focused the hostilities of a community on people other than witches. It is true of course that in the long run war aggravated a number of social and economic problems that eventually encouraged witchcraft accusations. Warfare could upset the economic life of a community, drastically affect the size and composition of the population, and introduce disease. Eventually these effects of war helped to create situations in which witchcraft accusations and prosecutions became more likely. Even then, however, we must keep in mind that these long-term effects of war were in no way peculiar to religiously inspired conflicts. It is, in other words, difficult to attribute an increase in witch-hunting to religious warfare as such.

What effect, then, did religious conflict and division have on witchcraft prosecutions? In the most general terms it made communities more fearful of religious and moral subversion, more aware of the presence of Satan in the world, and more eager therefore to rid their communities of corrupting, subversive influences, the most obvious and vulnerable of whom were witches. It stands to reason that the fear of moral and religious subversion would be stronger in those areas where the adherents of rival religions lived in relatively close proximity to each other than in those which were religiously homogeneous.[48] The knowledge that a neighbouring community or territory had been converted or reconverted to a rival faith naturally encouraged the fear that the same thing might happen in one's own area. The possibility that an army might enforce such a conversion only strengthened the fear. In such an atmosphere it is not difficult to imagine how the fear of religious conversion could be generalized into a fear of any type of moral or religious subversion. If Satan was responsible for conversion to Protestantism or reconversion to Catholicism, he was obviously active in society and dangerous in a number of ways. Witchcraft was only one of these signs of Satanic activity, but it is one that could be directly counteracted. Trying witches might not be a direct means of dealing with the threat of

---

48 In Lorraine and the three archiepiscopal electorates in the Rhineland, all of which were close to Protestant lands, there was a 'combative' religious attitude and there were also many witch-hunts. Monter, *Ritual, Myth and Magic*, p. 84.

Protestantism or Catholicism, for the witch was probably not of that rival faith. But the prosecution of witches did help to protect a community from general corrupting influences and sinister forces, and it also strengthened the conviction of the community that they were among the godly. Just as the hunting of witches allowed individuals to project their guilt on to other members of the community and thus vindicate their own godliness, so it also allowed Protestant or Catholic communities in religiously divided areas to prove that God was on their side, or, more properly speaking, that they were on His.

The prosecution of witches in a religiously divided area served, therefore, as an *alternative* to the prosecution of heretics or religious non-conformists. Both represented attempts to counteract the religious subversion that Satan was inspiring and abetting. The clearest evidence for their common cause and purpose comes from France, where trials for witchcraft often began at precisely the same time that trials for heresy stopped. In similar fashion the Catholic Bishop of Cologne stopped trials of Anabaptists and started trials of witches in 1605.[49] In Italy the Inquisition began trying witches in the late sixteenth century at the very same time that the percentage of heresy cases dropped more than 75 per cent.[50] Such neat patterns do not appear in all parts of Europe. In some areas witchcraft trials took place before heresy trials began, while in others they occurred at the same time.[51] In many areas, moreover, especially when the predominant religion was Protestantism, there were no heresy trials at all. The important consideration, however, is that in all these areas witchcraft trials served a function that was very similar to that of heresy trials: eliminating individuals who were believed to be in league with Satan and corrupting society. And the belief that such corruption was taking place was generally stronger in areas where the 'heretical' activities of either a Protestant or Catholic minority were close, visible and threatening.

THE REFORMATION AND THE DECLINE OF WITCHCRAFT

The Protestant Reformation, the Catholic Reformation, and the bitter conflict between Protestants and Catholics during the sixteenth and

49 Monter, *European Witchcraft*, pp. 35–6.

50 Parker, 'Some Recent Work', p. 529.

51 At Trier the prosecution of heretics was still going on at the time of the great witch prosecutions of the late 1580s and early 1590s. See Burr, 'Fate of Dietrich Flade', pp. 228–9.

seventeenth centuries did, therefore, have an effect upon the growth of the European witch-hunt. At the same time, however, these very same developments laid the foundation for its eventual decline. The Protestant emphasis on the sovereignty of God, the success of the Christianization of the laity, the growth of biblical literalism and the scepticism engendered by Catholic and Protestant exorcisms in cases involving witchcraft all had this ultimately negative effect.

Christianity, being a monotheistic religion, has always insisted upon the sovereignty of God. It has accepted the existence of a supernatural evil power, the Devil, in the universe, but it has rejected as heretical the theological view of the Devil as a power co-equal to that of God. As mentioned above, some Protestant reformers, most notably Luther, seemed to exaggerate the extent of diabolical activity in the world, almost to the point of flirting with Manichaean or dualist heresy. The appearances, however, are deceptive, for Luther insisted that in the bitter struggle between God and Satan, the former would always prevail. Calvin emphasized even more strongly the majesty of God, arguing that the Devil could do nothing without God's permission and was little more than His servant or executioner. The insistence upon God's sovereignty led a number of Protestant writers and preachers to deny the Devil's ability to produce certain types of marvels, such as hailstorms, and this fostered a scepticism toward *maleficia* that involved such wonders. Consequently Protestants were less likely than Catholics to accuse a witch of raising a hailstorm to destroy crops, a common form of *maleficium*.[52] During the main period of the European witch-hunt this Protestant tendency did not result in an overall reduction of witchcraft prosecutions and executions in Protestant lands, because it was to a large extent offset by a greater Protestant willingness to prosecute witches simply on the basis of the demonic pact. Eventually, however, the Protestant emphasis on God's sovereignty led to a general scepticism regarding the reality of *maleficia*, and that in turn developed into a more general scepticism regarding all aspects of witchcraft.

The way in which the Protestant conception of the sovereignty of God could undermine witch-beliefs even at a fairly early date can be seen in the work of George Gifford, a Puritan clergyman in the English county of Essex who wrote two treatises on witchcraft in the late sixteenth century.[53] Gifford was by no means a complete sceptic

---

52 Monter, *Witchcraft in France and Switzerland*, pp. 151–7.
53 *A Discourse of the Subtle Practice of Devils by Witches* (1587); *A Dialogue Concerning Witches and Witchcraft* (1593).

when it came to witchcraft, and in typically Protestant fashion he cited Exodus 22:18 to justify the prosecution of witches who had made a pact with the Devil. But Gifford's main purpose was to bring an end to the recent rash of witchcraft prosecutions, which he thought were distracting men from the real danger of Satan winning men's souls. The problem, as he saw it, was that people had lost their faith in God; hence the connection between witchcraft and the stubborn persistence of Catholicism. If people could only become fully aware of God's sovereignty, if only they would recognize that Satan operates as an agent of God and that *maleficia* occur only with his permission, then the punishment of witches for doing such things as destroying cattle would cease. And once men had faith in God, then He would no longer give permission to Satan and witches to exercise power in the world.[54]

A second contribution that the Reformation made to the eventual decline of witchcraft prosecutions resulted from the Christianization of the populace, especially in rural areas. This process of Christianization, which was characteristic of both the Protestant and Catholic Reformations, had played an important role in the growth of the hunt. It had instilled a deep sense of sin and personal guilt in both parish priests and laity, which in turn had been projected on to witches, and it had also encouraged the agents of Christianization – the newly educated clergy and members of the ruling élite – to attack magic in its various forms. In the long run, however, the process of Christianization had the effect of reducing the belief in, and the practice of magic among the rural populace and thereby giving witch-hunters less cause for concern. It also encouraged the growth of a strictly spiritual concept of the Devil – something that was implicit in much Protestant thought – and de-emphasized the common view of him as a physical creature, the black man or animal who appeared at the sabbath. These changes did not come about quickly, but by the 1660s they began to have a demonstrable effect.[55]

Biblical literalism had a similar effect of first abetting and then reducing witch-hunting. Since the Old Testament contained the lethal injunction, 'Thou shalt not suffer a witch to live,' the close adherence to the letter of scripture could and often did encourage authorities to put witches to death. In the long run, however, the increased reliance

---

54 J. Hitchcock, 'George Gifford and Puritan Witch Beliefs', *Archiv für Reformationsgeschichte*, 58 (1967): 90–9; Teall, 'Witchcraft and Calvinism', pp. 21–36.

55 Delumeau, *Catholicism*, pp. 172–4; Larner, *Enemies of God*, pp. 160–2.

upon scripture could give serious pause to witch-hunters. Not only did scripture contain very few references to witchcraft, and none to Devil-worship, but it also gave an abundance of evidence regarding the restraints that God placed on diabolical power in the world. Calvin's firm belief in the sovereignty of God and his assurance that God would prevail over the Devil was, after all, based on a firm scriptural foundation. Calvinism may have encouraged men to engage in an incessant war with Satan, but it also encouraged them eventually to define exactly what he could do and to adopt the purely spiritual view of him that we have discussed above. It is not surprising therefore that in the late seventeenth century the attack upon witchcraft prosecutions came as much from conservative Protestants like Bathalsar Bekker as from sceptical deists.[56]

Even the conflict between Catholics and Protestants played a significant, albeit indirect role in bringing an end to witchcraft prosecutions. One of the interesting forms that this conflict took was the attempt by authorities to prove that they adhered to the true religion by exorcising demons from possessed persons. By using the Eucharist as one of the methods of such exorcism, for example, Catholics attempted to prove that Christ was really present in the Eucharist, a doctrine that Calvinists denied. Protestants, on the other hand, employing distinctly non-Catholic methods, tried to drive out demons to prove that God favoured the cause of Protestant reform. These efforts were closely related to witch-hunting, for in the late sixteenth and seventeenth centuries many of those demoniacs who were exorcised accused witches of causing their possession. The problem, however, was that the possessions and the efforts of the exorcists, which attracted widespread publicity, engendered a great deal of scepticism. Many people became convinced that the possessions were fraudulent and that the exorcisms were shams. By extension, therefore, the accusations of witchcraft, which the exorcists had often encouraged, were discredited, as were the prosecutions that resulted from them. It was therefore partly as a result of simple Catholic–Protestant rivalry in cases of possession that critics of witch-hunting acquired evidence to bolster their case.[57]

We must of course keep the negative effects of the Reformation on witch-hunting in perspective. The decline of witch-hunting was, like its rise, a complex phenomenon. Many other factors that had very

---

56 In Finland, the opposition came from bishops. See Heikkinen, *Paholaisen Liittolaiset*, p. 394.

57 R. Mandrou, *Magistrats et sorciers*; D. Walker, *Unclean Spirits* (London, 1982).

little to do with the Reformation or even with religion in general played a part in bringing an end to the European witch-hunt. These factors will be discussed fully below. We also must not lose sight of the fact that the Reformation had more to do with the rise of witchcraft than with its decline. But the fact that the Reformation had a negative as well as a positive effect on European witch-hunting should make us pause before we blame the entire European witch-hunt on the Protestant Reformation, the Catholic Counter-Reformation, or both.

5 THE SOCIAL CONTEXT

In order to provide a satisfactory explanation of the European witch-hunt, we must consider not only the religious changes and conflicts of the early modern period but also the broader social environment in which accusations arose. In studying any crime, of course, we can profit from this type of investigation, for by acquiring a knowledge of the social setting of the crime and the relationship between the criminal and his victim we can more fully understand the motivation of the criminal. In the case of witchcraft, however, which was to a great extent an imagined crime, a social investigation can be even more revealing, since it can help to explain why the alleged victims of the crime, or their kin, singled out innocent persons for prosecution. The social history of this crime, therefore, becomes more than a study of deviant behaviour. In dealing with witchcraft the historian must explain not only why the witch acted in a certain way but also why the witch's neighbours suspected and accused her. The witch may have been responding to social or economic pressures when she cursed at her enemies or used sorcery against them, but her neighbours, by denouncing the witch and testifying against her, were being no less responsive to the social conditions in which they lived. Witchcraft accusations allowed members of early modern European communities to resolve conflicts between themselves and their neighbours and to explain misfortunes that had occurred in their daily lives.

In establishing the social context of the European witch-hunt historians confront a number of problems. The first of these is a dearth of information regarding the lives and activities of those who were accused of witchcraft and those who accused them. Although trial records usually give the names of those who were tried for witchcraft and, less commonly, the names of those who testified against them, they very often do not tell us much more. They carefully catalogue the various *maleficia* that the witches allegedly committed, and they often describe in lurid detail the various acts of diabolism that they engaged in. But the records only rarely tell us how old the witches were, what their marital statuses were, what occupations they or their spouses engaged in, and what kind of dealings they had with their neighbours. Sometimes the court records contain the depositions of witnesses against the accused, and since these statements mention conflicts that had arisen between the deponents and the witch, we can learn from them a limited amount of information about the social status of the individuals involved and the circumstances surrounding the prosecution. All too often, however, these depositions have been lost or, in some cases, never even taken. Especially during large witch-hunts, when many witches were implicated by persons who had already been convicted, the legal record contains nothing but the mere allegation of Devil-worship. Faced with such lacunae in the sources, historians of witchcraft must base their interpretation of the social dynamics of witchcraft accusations on a very small sample of cases.

A further problem arises in trying to generalize about the social context of witchcraft prosecutions throughout Europe over an extended period of time. Although many cases of witchcraft arose out of similar socio-economic circumstances, conditions obviously varied from place to place and from time to time. Even when we concentrate our attention on a particular geographical area during a relatively brief period of time, we find that witchcraft accusations and prosecutions often reflected a wide variety of social tensions. For this reason it is impossible to provide a single socio-economic interpretation of the European witch-hunt. The best that we can do is to describe the most typical environments in which witchcraft accusations arose, establish the most common social characteristics of the individuals who were singled out for prosecution, and explore some of the reasons why these individuals were particularly vulnerable to the charge of witchcraft. This technique will allow us to draw some general conclusions about the identity of the 'typical' European witch without failing to appreciate the variety of circumstances that could have led to her accusation and prosecution.

In addition to these problems of insufficient evidence and geographical and temporal diversity, the social investigation of witchcraft raises two substantive issues. The first deals with the relative importance of social and economic factors in explaining the great witch-hunt. It should be clear from the preceding chapters that the hunt had long-term intellectual and legal causes and more immediate religious ones. It is possible that in some witch-hunts these factors, taken together, provide a sufficient explanation of the prosecutions that took place. This was most commonly the case when witch-hunts were initiated from above, i.e., by magistrates or inquisitors, when torture was used to obtain the names of accomplices, and when charges of diabolism took clear precedence over those of *maleficia*. In these situations religious ideology very often became the driving force of the hunt, the only social dynamic being the interaction between the upper-class official and the lower-class witch. When witch-hunting was initiated from below, however, when the initial reason for bringing charges against a person was the determination of her neighbours to punish her for *maleficia*, then social and economic considerations assumed paramount importance. In most cases, of course, there was extensive involvement of both magistrates and villagers in witch-hunting. When prosecutions were initiated from above, neighbours were called upon to testify regarding alleged *maleficia*; when they originated from below, magistrates eventually assumed control of the proceedings and emphasized the diabolical nature of the crime. For this reason one can rarely neglect the social context of witch-hunting. At the same time, however, one must be careful not to exaggerate the importance of that context. There were many reasons for accusing a person of witchcraft, and not all of these were conditioned by general social and economic factors.

The second substantive issue concerns the importance of social and economic *change* in explaining the rise of witch-hunting. Since the European witch-hunt was a time-bound phenomenon, beginning in the fifteenth century and ending by the early eighteenth, it is tempting to see it as the product of the profound social and economic changes that occurred during those very same centuries. During the early modern period the population of Europe increased dramatically after a long period of stagnation and decline; prices of all commodities rose at an unprecedented pace; towns grew in size and number; and both mercantile and agricultural capitalism were introduced in many areas. To add to all the confusion there were periodic outbreaks of the plague and other epidemic diseases and many years of bad harvests and famine. During the same period of time family life was also transformed and new moral values were proclaimed to accommodate a changing world. There is no question that all of these changes influenced witchcraft prosecutions. They engendered conflict within communities and, perhaps even more importantly, contributed to a general mood of anxiety that encouraged witch-hunting. Historians such as Keith Thomas, Alan Macfarlane, Robert Muchembled, Paul Boyer and Stephen Nissenbaum have all shown how witchcraft accusations reflected the tensions that were generated by these changes. The problem, however, is that many of the specific social and economic conditions that lay at the basis of witch-hunting were not all that new. Many of the social conflicts that gave rise to witchcraft accusations were common to pre-capitalistic, medieval communities and do not appear to have been exacerbated by novel developments. Witchcraft accusations may have taken place in communities that were in a state of transition, but many others arose in villages that were still part of a relatively static, traditional world.[1] In these areas the interpersonal conflicts that led people to accuse others of witchcraft were not any more intense in the early modern period than they had been during the Middle Ages. The reasons why these conflicts resulted in witchcraft prosecutions in the early modern period, whereas they had failed to do so before, had much more to do with changes in the nature of witch-beliefs, the growing awareness of witchcraft in all segments of society, the possibility of successful legal prosecution and the impact of the Reformation than with the realities of social change.

In dealing with the social and economic context of witchcraft prosecutions, therefore, we must recognize that the environment we are describing was not necessarily new and that the social conflicts which led to or reinforced prosecutions were not always the product of broad social change. It may be true that some witch-hunts occurred at critical periods in early modern European history, when a new set of values and a new way of life clashed with the old. It may also be true that all witch-hunting was to some extent a by-product of the anxiety engendered by rapid social change. But if we assume that every witchcraft accusation and every prosecution can be directly attributed to a process of social change, we run the risk of reading too much into the documents and of failing to recognize that the personal conflicts that often found expression in witchcraft accusations could occur in a relatively static as well as in a rapidly changing world.

THE GEOGRAPHICAL AND SOCIAL SETTING

In establishing the social context of witchcraft prosecutions it is important first to determine the type of communities in which the hunts took place. The general impression we have is that witchcraft

---

1 In this regard a contrast between England and such areas as southeastern Scotland, Lorraine and Franche-Comté is instructive. See B.P. Levack, 'The Great Scottish Witch Hunt of 1661–1662', *Journal of British Studies*, 20 (1980): 102; Delumeau, *La Peur*, p. 375.

during this period was essentially a rural phenomenon.[2] The over-whelming majority of witches appear to have come from small agricultural villages that were part of a peasant economy. This localization of witchcraft in the countryside is usually attributed to two characteristics of rural life: the strength of superstitious beliefs among an uneducated and conservative peasantry and the small size of these communities. We know from anthropological studies of primitive societies today not only that magical beliefs are especially durable among an uneducated peasantry but also that accusations of sorcery tend to arise when people live in a close-knit, face-to-face community, where everyone knows everyone else and where undesirable people cannot easily be ignored.[3] Since similar conditions prevailed in the rural villages of early modern Europe, witchcraft has come to be regarded as a peculiarly rural phenomenon. Some historians have gone so far as to argue that a witch-believing peasantry was a necessary precondition of the great European witch-hunt.[4]

Although it is incontestable that a great majority of early modern European witches came from the countryside, the occurrence of witchcraft accusations and prosecutions in the towns and cities of early modern Europe cannot be ignored. Indeed, some of the largest and most famous witch-hunts during the craze took place within an urban environment. No account of European witchcraft can ignore the witch-hunting that occurred at Loudun, Trier, Würzburg and Bamberg. In some cases, of course, the urban setting of witchcraft is deceptive, since the witches were brought from the countryside to the towns for trial. In the records of Scottish witchcraft, for example, there are occasional references to witches coming from Edinburgh, Aberdeen or Dalkeith, but on close examination it appears that they actually lived in rural villages near those cities or towns. In Geneva, where a number of witch-hunts took place in the sixteenth and seventeenth centuries, roughly half of the victims came from the rural hamlets which surrounded the city but which supplied only about 20 per cent of that tiny republic's population.[5]

2 Caro Baroja, *World of the Witches*, p. 100; Schormann, *Hexenprozesse in Deutschland*, p. 72; Muchembled, 'Satan ou les hommes? La Chasse aux sorcières et ses causes', in M. Dupont-Bouchat et al., *Prophètes et sorciers dans les Pays-Bas, XVIe–XVIIIe siècle* (Paris, 1978), p. 19; Monter, *Witchcraft in France and Switzerland*, p. 128; Larner, *Enemies of God*, p. 199.

3 See L. Mair, *Witchcraft*, pp. 9–10.

4 See, for example, Larner, *Enemies of God*, p. 193.

5 Monter, *Witchcraft in France and Switzerland*, p. 65. See also Blauert, *Frühe Hexenverfolgungen*, p. 14.

Even if we discount all of the urban trials in which the accused witches came from the surrounding countryside, we still are left with a substantial number of strictly urban cases, especially in Germany. Exactly what percentage of the total these cases constitute is impossible to determine. There is good reason to believe, however, that the percentage was higher than that of the urban component of the entire population. In other words, the number of urban witchcraft cases may have been disproportionately high. In Poland, for example, 19 per cent of those accused of witchcraft lived in urban areas, a small proportion to be sure, but far greater than the relative size of the urban population of that country, which was almost certainly less than 5 per cent.[6] In Finland, which was no less rural than Poland, the proportion of urban witches was an even higher 26 per cent.[7] We must not forget that despite their enormous economic and political importance, towns did not contain a very large percentage of the early modern European population. Even if we use the low figure of 2,000 inhabitants to define the minimum size of a town, the urban population of neither Germany nor England was more than 10 per cent at the beginning of the sixteenth century.[8]

In some cases of urban witchcraft the social environment was not much different from that of the rural villages. Towns served different economic functions from those of villages, and they also had a distinct identity, but their size was often only marginally greater. Some of the smaller towns in the early modern period had a population of little more than 2,000 souls and were, therefore, just as much face-to-face communities or 'small-scale societies' as their rural counterparts.[9] It should not surprise us, therefore, to learn that the overwhelming majority of urban Polish witches came from small towns and that in Essex, England, where witchcraft was largely a rural affair, the few urban witches came from market towns like Chelmsford or cloth towns like Braintree, Coggeshall and Dedham. In these small

6 Baranowski, *Procesy Czarownic*, p. 180. Peters, *Magician, Witch and the Law*, p. 206, suggests that witchcraft may be as much an urban as a rural phenomenon.

7 Heikkinen, *Paholaisen*, p. 386.

8 See F. Braudel, *The Structures of Everyday Life* (New York, 1981), pp. 482–4. If we use the figure of 10,000, the percentage drops to just over 3 per cent. J. De Vries, *European Urbanization* (Cambridge, Mass., 1984).

9 Schormann, *Hexenprozesse in Deutschland*, p. 72, uses 2,000 as the minimum population of a medium-sized town and 500 as the minimum size of a small town. D. Herlihy and C. Klapisch-Zuber, *Tuscans and their Families* (New Haven, 1985), p. 54, use 700–800 inhabitants as the dividing line between a village and a small city.

communities it would be difficult to establish the existence of any peculiarly urban characteristics of witchcraft accusations.[10]

In larger towns and cities, however, we are dealing with a completely different type of environment. In these communities, which had more than 5,000 inhabitants, one could usually ignore, or at least avoid, one's neighbours. The prevalence of witchcraft accusations in these urban areas, therefore, must be attributed to factors other than inevitable social interaction or, for that matter, peasant superstition. There were in fact a number of reasons why a relatively large urban environment might have proven to be fertile ground for witchcraft accusations and prosecutions. The first is that the practice of politically inspired sorcery, which figured in some of the earlier hunts, usually took place in the cities, where most significant political activity tended to occur. The prevalence of political sorcery in the cities might help to explain why the majority of trials for sorcery, diabolism and invocation during the period from 1300 to 1500 took place in the towns, not the countryside.[11]

In addition to serving as an arena for the practice of political sorcery, towns were the only places where plague-spreaders (*engraisseurs*) were prosecuted as witches. Plague-spreaders were persons who allegedly had succeeded in distilling the essence of the plague in the form of an unguent, which they then used to infect various parts of towns. Like other sorcerers, plague-spreaders were accused of worshipping the Devil and of acting collectively; thus they became indistinguishable from witches. Their prosecution also resembled that of witches, for a visitation of the plague could trigger a plague-spreader panic, in which a large number of *engraisseurs* were accused and tried. Geneva experienced no fewer than three of these hunts in the sixteenth century and another one took place at Milan in 1630.[12] Because outbreaks of the plague in the sixteenth and seventeenth centuries were almost entirely restricted to the towns, plague-spreader panics represented a peculiarly urban form of witchcraft prosecution.

Another predominantly although not exclusively urban form of witchcraft was the use of magical powers to cause collective demonic possession. Although cases of possession and even of group possession were reported in rural areas during the period of the great witch-hunt, the largest and most famous cases of multiple or collective possession involving witchcraft occurred in towns, especially in France. The

10 Macfarlane, *Witchcraft in Tudor and Stuart England*, pp. 149, 325–30.
11 Kieckhefer, *European Witch Trials*, p. 95.
12 See Monter, *Witchcraft in France and Switzerland*, p. 207.

main reason for this concentration may have been the simple fact that collective demonic possession often took place in convents and hospitals, which very often were located in cities and towns. Cities were also capable of supplying the large crowds of observers upon which such episodes thrived, as we know from the numbers that flocked to witness the exorcism of the Ursuline nuns at Loudun in 1634.[13]

There are two other reasons why towns proved to be surprisingly fertile ground for witchcraft prosecutions. The first is that a hunt, once started, was more likely to take a heavier toll in the more densely populated towns than in the countryside, especially since the number of persons in any community who could be successfully prosecuted for witchcraft without raising some sort of opposition was limited. It is for this reason that rural witchcraft panics tended to move from village to village by means of rumour and occasional accusations of non-villagers, whereas urban panics developed more quickly and took a heavier toll. The second reason is that urban life generated a number of tensions that could find expression in witchcraft accusations. It may have been easier to ignore one's neighbours in the cities and become convinced that they had no magical power over you, but at the same time the problems of urban residents in adjusting to urban life may have led them to suspect their neighbours of witchcraft more readily than if they had been living in the countryside.

We may conclude, therefore, that there was more than one 'world of the witches' in early modern Europe. There was, to be sure, a peasant world in which witchcraft suspicions and accusations formed a staple of everyday life and periodically resulted in isolated trials or large panics. This was a world in which peasant beliefs combined in an often lethal manner with the interpersonal conflicts that arose regularly in a face-to-face society. But there was also an urban world of witchcraft in which the political sorcerer, the ritual magician, the possessed nun and the plague-spreader also played a part and in which accusations and chain-reaction hunts could spread rapidly. This urban world was also the destination of many rural witches, the place where the illiterate peasant who had been accused by her neighbours confronted an urban, literate magistrate or cleric as her inquisitor. When this confrontation occurred, the witch found herself accused not only by neighbours who believed she had harmed them magically but by a judiciary determined to place the testimony they heard in a demonological context. The trial, therefore, became the place where

13 See A. Huxley, *The Devils of Loudun* (New York, 1952).

élite and popular culture interacted and where the countryside actually came in contact with the town.

WHO WERE THE WITCHES?

In order to understand the social tensions that underlay witchcraft prosecutions, it is necessary to determine which groups of people were most commonly tried as witches during the period of the great witch-hunt and to discover why these groups were more vulnerable to such charges than others. As mentioned above, the dearth of evidence that is available regarding both the witches and the motivation of their accusers makes this type of investigation somewhat speculative. Even when a fair amount of information can be collected, it is still difficult to determine which characteristics of the witch's personality and which conflicts between her and her neighbour led to her accusation. There is, however, enough data available to establish some general patterns of accusation and to offer some possible reasons why these persons were accused.

Sex

The most well-documented characteristic of those persons who were prosecuted for witchcraft is that they were predominantly, if not overwhelmingly, female. As Table 3 indicates, the percentage of female witches exceeded 75 per cent in most regions of Europe, and in a few localities, such as Essex county, England, the Bishopric of Basel, and the county of Namur (in present-day Belgium), it was more than 90 per cent.[14]

These figures suggest that witchcraft was a sex-related but not a sex-specific crime. Women, in other words, were more readily suspected of and prosecuted for witchcraft by virtue of their sex,

14 Sources for Table 3: Midelfort, *Witch-Hunting*, p. 281; Monter, *Witchcraft in France and Switzerland*, pp. 119–20; Peter Kamber, 'La Chasse aux sorcieres et sorcières dans le Pays de Vaud: aspects quantitatifs (1581–1620)', *Revue Historique Vaudoise*, 90 (1982): 22–3; Dupont-Bouchat, 'La Répression', p. 138; A. Denis, *La Sorcellerie à Toul aux XVIe et XVIIe siècles* (Toul, 1888), pp. 177–8; Gari Lacruz, *Variedad de competencias*, p. 236; R. Martin, *Witchcraft and the Inquisition in Venice, 1550–1650* (Oxford, 1989), p. 226; Heikkinen and Kervinen, 'Finland', p. 321; M. Madar, 'Estonia I', pp. 266–7; V. Kivelson, 'Through the Prism of Witchcraft: Gender and Social Change in Seventeenth-Century Muscovy', in *Russia's Women*, ed. B.E. Evans et al. (Berkeley, 1991), p. 83; G. Klaniczay, 'Hungary', p. 222; Macfarlane, *Witchcraft in Tudor and Stuart England*, p. 160; C. Karlsen, *The Devil in the Shape of a Woman: Witchcraft in Colonial New England* (New York, 1987), p. 47; Larner et al., *Source-Book of Scottish Witchcraft*, p. 240, Table 6.

Table 3   Sex of Accused Witches

Region	Years	Male	Female	% Female
Southwestern Germany	1562–1684	238	1,050	82
Bishopric of Basel	1571–1670	9	181	95
Franche-Comté	1559–1667	49	153	76
Geneva	1537–1662	74	240	76
Pays de Vaud	1581–1620	325	624	66
County of Namur	1509–1646	29	337	92
Luxembourg	1519–1623	130	417	76
City of Toul	1584–1623	14	53	79
Dept. of the Nord, France	1542–1679	54	232	81
Castile	1540–1685	132	324	71
Aragon	1600–1650	69	90	57
Venice	1550–1650	224	490	69
Finland	1520–1699	316	325	51
Estonia	1520–1729	116	77	40
Russia	1622–1700	93	43	32
Hungary	1520–1777	160	1,482	90
County of Essex, England	1560–1675	23	290	93
New England	1620–1725	75	267	78

but they had no natural monopoly of the crime.[15] There was nothing in the definition of a witch that excluded males. Men could, just like women, practice harmful magic, make pacts with the Devil, and attend the sabbath. In some of the woodcuts and engravings produced during the sixteenth and seventeenth centuries, especially those illustrating the pact with the Devil, male and female witches are shown in equal numbers.[16] In two countries, Russia and Estonia, men constituted a solid majority of all accused witches, while in most Scandinavian countries the sex distribution was close to even.

There were only a few situations in which men tended to arouse as much suspicion of witchcraft as women. One of these arose when witch-trials were closely linked to prosecutions for other forms of heresy. William Monter has shown that in the Jura region in the fifteenth century, when prosecutions for witchcraft occurred in conjunction with those for Waldensian heresy, far more males were prosecuted than females.[17] The reason for the large percentage of males in these trials is that heresy, unlike witchcraft, was not generally sex-related. Women were, to be sure, well-represented in medieval heretical sects, and their prominence in these groups might have reinforced their later identification as witches, but men were even more active in these heretical sects and for that reason could easily be suspected in connection with the new 'heresy' of witchcraft.[18] It is significant that in these early witchcraft trials, most of which were conducted in ecclesiastical courts, the judges were much more concerned with the diabolical or heretical aspects of witchcraft than with *maleficium*.[19]

15 For the argument that witchcraft is universally specific to women see R. Briffault, *The Mothers* (New York, 1927), II, p. 556. See also M. Hester, *Lewd Women and Wicked Witches* (London, 1992), pp. 109–23.

16 See, for example, the illustrations in Guazzo, *Compendium Maleficarum*, passim.

17 Monter, *Witchcraft in France and Switzerland*, pp. 23–4. See also S. Burghartz, 'The Equation of Women and Witches: A Case Study of Witchcraft Trials in Lucerne and Lausanne in the Fifteenth and Sixteenth Centuries', in *The German Underworld*, ed. Richard J. Evans (London, 1988), p. 64. The witches described in Nider's *Formicarius* (1435–37) were both male and female. Ginzburg, *Ecstasies*, p. 70.

18 Russell, *Witchcraft in the Middle Ages*, p. 281; B. Easlea, *Witch-Hunting, Magic and the New Philosophy: An Introduction to the Debates of the Scientific Revolution 1450–1750* (Brighton, 1980), pp. 35–6.

19 Burghartz, 'Equation of Women and Witches', p. 64. The percentage of female witches was much higher in the trials conducted in the secular courts, such as at Lucerne, during the same period of time. In these trials, in which the demonological stereotype of the female witch was not very well established, more attention was given to *maleficium* than diabolism. Ibid., pp. 62–4.

The fact that heresy was not sex-linked may also explain why the Spanish and Roman Inquisitions tried a higher percentage of male witches than most other European courts. As Table 3 indicates, the percentage of male witches tried by the Inquisition in both Castile and Venice was well above the European average. In the kingdom of Aragon, where almost all the witches prosecuted in the secular courts were female, 72 per cent of the witches tried by the Inquisition during the first half of the seventeenth century were male.[20] Just like the ecclesiastical courts in the Jura in the late fifteenth century, the Inquisition in Italy and Spain prosecuted witchcraft mainly as a form of heresy and displayed little or no concern with *maleficium*.[21] With the crime defined in this way, men were likely to be prosecuted in large numbers.

Another situation in which men tended to be prosecuted for witchcraft was when the crime involved political sorcery. During the Middle Ages a number of men had actually practised sorcery in order to advance their political fortunes, using ritual magic as their tool.[22] It was in connection with such practices that many witch-beliefs were developed. As the magician was gradually transformed into the witch, the sex and social status of the malefactor changed, but during the early period of the great witch-hunt this transition was not complete. Many early trials for witchcraft, therefore, involved treasonous activities, and consequently a higher number of men were prosecuted during the early stages of the hunt than at its peak. A third situation that led to the prosecution of substantial numbers of male witches occurred when witch-hunts got out of control. In these episodes, which did not occur very frequently, the development of chain-reaction accusations and the hysterical mood of the populace led to the almost indiscriminate naming of witches. In such circumstances the stereotype of the witch broke down and many persons who did not conform to the model of the typical witch, including men of high social standing, found themselves accused.

Recognizing these three main exceptions to the general rule, we are still left with the task of explaining why in most situations, and certainly in all prosecutions taken together, witches were overwhelmingly female. It will not suffice to say that the stereotype of the

---

20 See Gari Lacruz, 'Variedad de competencias', p. 326.

21 On the preoccupation of the Venetian Inquisition with forms of magic that savoured of manifest heresy and their lack of interest in *maleficium*, see Martin, *Witchcraft and the Inquisition in Venice*, pp. 254–7.

22 See Peters, *Magician, Witch and the Law*, pp. 120–5.

witch had always been female and that consequently those who feared
that witchcraft was being used against them instinctively suspected
and accused women rather than men. To some extent, of course, this
was true. Since the prototype of the witch in ancient and medieval
culture and in both literature and art was always female, women were
naturally suspected of this crime more readily than men.[23] The image
of the witch was, however, as much the product as it was the source
of witchcraft accusations and prosecutions. If women had not been
much more readily suspected of and prosecuted for witchcraft than
men, then the image of the witch would not have been exclusively
female.

To some extent women were suspected of witchcraft because
they were believed to be morally weaker than men and more likely,
therefore, to succumb to diabolical temptation. This idea, which
dates from the earliest days of Christianity, appears often in the
witchcraft treatises of the early modern period, especially in the
intensely misogynistic *Malleus Maleficarum*.[24] The *Malleus* relates
this weakness not only to women's intellectual inferiority and super-
stitiousness but also to their sexual passion, and concludes that 'all
witchcraft comes from carnal lust, which is in women insatiable'.[25]

The image of women as the more carnal and sexually indulgent
members of the species was pervasive in medieval and early modern
European culture; only in the eighteenth century did it begin to
give way to the alternative depiction of her as sexually passive.[26]
The image received its strongest endorsement from clerics, especially
monks, who viewed women as sexual temptresses, but it was by no
means restricted to clerical circles. Bodin, a lay jurist and magistrate,
referred to the 'bestial cupidity' of women in a manner similar to that
of Sprenger and Kramer, while Boguet, also a secular judge, claimed
that the Devil had sexual relations with all witches because he knew
that 'women love carnal pleasures'.[27] The view that women were
driven by lust was especially pertinent to the crime of witchcraft, for

23 Holmes, 'Popular Culture?', p. 95, argues that the association of maleficent
power with women was 'a perdurable component of popular belief'.

24 *Malleus Maleficarum*, pp. 41–7; Lea, *Materials*, II, p. 449; P. de Lancre, *Tableau
de l'inconstance des mauvais anges et démons*, ed. N. Jacques-Chaquin (Paris, 1982),
pp. 89–93; Rémy, *Demonolatry*, p. 56; James VI, *Daemonologie*, pp. 43–4.

25 *Malleus Maleficarum*, p. 47.

26 For the strength of the old image in the late seventeenth century see
R. Thompson, *Unfit for Modest Ears* (London, 1979), p. 97.

27 Bodin, *Démonomanie*, p. 386; Boguet, *Examen of Witches*, p. 29.

it was believed that the witch often made a pact with the Devil as a result of sexual temptation and then engaged in promiscuous sexual activity at the sabbath. Male witches also took part in these orgies, but the assumption that women were more eager to satisfy their lust in this way simply reinforced the image of the female witch. That image received strong visual reinforcement in the engravings of Hans Balgrung Grien, who depicted witches as the embodiment of female sexual power.[28]

The image of the witch as morally weak and sexually inclined may very well have encouraged members of the educated and ruling classes to suspect and prosecute women as witches, especially when they were engaged in religiously inspired campaigns to reform popular morality.[29] Among the common people, who very often were the first to accuse or denounce witches and who testified against them, that image was of somewhat less importance. These people may have shared some of the clerically inspired views of women, but being more concerned with the magical than with the diabolical aspects of witchcraft, they tended to suspect women because their customary roles in society gave them more opportunities to practise harmful magic. Women in early modern European communities generally served as the cooks, healers and midwives, and each of these functions made them vulnerable to the charge that they practised sorcery. As cooks they not only had the opportunity to gather herbs for magical purposes, but they also had the skill to turn them into potions and unguents. It is no accident that witches are often portrayed standing over cauldrons, for it was in such vessels that many of the agents of sorcery were in fact concocted. The image of a man engaged in this type of activity is at the very least implausible.

Women also acted as healers in early modern European villages. Often known as 'wise women', these persons used a variety of folk remedies – mainly herbs and ointments – in their work. Many of these treatments should be regarded as magical, if only because natural ingredients were usually supplemented with magical formulas or superstitious prayers. Since wise women served a useful function in their communities, they were generally tolerated by their neighbours. They were, however, vulnerable to the charge of practising white magic, and when villagers contracted a disease or died unexpectedly,

28 C. Zika, 'Fears of Flying: Representations of Witchcraft and Sexuality in Early Sixteenth-Century Germany', *Australian Journal of Art*, 8 (1989): 19–48.
29 J. Klaits, *Servants of Satan*, pp. 65–85, argues that the novelty of the 'new misogyny' was its connection to ideologically based movements for reform.

they could easily be accused of using their magical arts for maleficent purposes. The *Malleus Maleficarum* makes specific reference to those witches who could cure as well as injure, and in 1499 a woman from Modena reassured the Inquisition that 'who knows how to heal knows how to destroy'.[30] Studies of witchcraft depositions in France, Switzerland, Austria, Hungary, Schleswig-Holstein, England, Scotland and New England reveal that many of those who were prosecuted for witchcraft were in fact wise women.[31] The same was true in France, where roughly one-half of the witchcraft cases that reached the *Parlement* of Paris on appeal involved accusations of magical healing.[32]

Like cooks and healers, midwives were also vulnerable to charges of sorcery. Until the eighteenth century, when male midwives and doctors began to assist in the process of childbirth, the delivery of infants was entrusted entirely to women. A number of these midwives – although probably not as many as was once believed – were prosecuted for witchcraft.[33] The main reason for their susceptibility to charges of this nature was that they could easily be blamed for the death of infants. In an age when as many as one-fifth of all children died either at birth or during the first few months of life, and when infanticide was by no means a rare occurrence, the charge that a midwife had killed a child by sorcery was both functional and

---

30 *Malleus Maleficarum*, p. 99; Ginzburg, *Night Battles*, p. 78. See also Monter, *Witchcraft in France and Switzerland*, p. 179; T. Dömötör, 'The Cunning Folk in English and Hungarian Witch Trials', in *Folklore Studies in the Twentieth Century*, ed. V.J. Newall (Woodbridge, 1978), p. 183. In Russia healers who treated male impotence were sometimes suspected of having actually caused it. V.A. Kivelson, 'Through the Prism of Witchcraft: Gender and Social Change in Seventeenth-Century Muscovy', in *Russia's Women: Accommodation, Resistance Transformation*, ed. B.E. Evans et al. (Berkeley, 1991)', p. 89.

31 Horsley, 'Who were the Witches?', pp. 700–12; Dömötör, 'Cunning Folk', pp. 183–6; R.C. Sawyer, '"Strangely Handled in All Her Lyms": Witchcraft and Healing in Jacobean England', *Journal of Social History*, 22 (1989): 461–85; Larner, *Enemies of God*, pp. 138–42; J.P. Demos, *Entertaining Satan: Witchcraft and the Culture of Early New England* (New York, 1982), pp. 81–4.

32 Soman, 'Parlement of Paris', p. 43. See also Briggs, *Communities of Belief*, p. 16.

33 At Lucerne only one of forty-five women tried for witchcraft can be identified as a midwife. Burghartz, 'Equation of Women and Witches', p. 67. D. Harley, 'Historians as Demonologists: The Myth of the Midwife-witch', *Social History of Medicine*, 3 (1990): 1–26, establishes that midwives, contrary to widespread belief, were not widely prosecuted as witches, especially in England. But midwives remain virtually the only female occupational group that receives any mention at all in the records.

plausible, and it offered the bereaved parents a means of revenge. In some cases the midwife became the victim of years of accumulated suspicion. In the German town of Dillingen a licensed midwife by the name of Walpurga Hausmännin was accused in 1587 of having caused the death of forty children, some of them as early as twelve years before, by witchcraft.[34]

Once the midwife had been accused of various *maleficia*, demonological theory, which was admittedly of greater importance to judges than to the common people, gave added plausibility to her crime. Witches, it will be recalled, were eager to obtain unbaptized babies so that they could sacrifice them to the Devil, feast upon their flesh at the sabbath meal, and use their remains in the production of magical ointments. As midwives, witches were ideally situated to procure the necessary infants, and they also had a perfect opportunity to baptize them into the Devil's service. In 1728 a Hungarian midwife from Szeged who was burned at the stake for witchcraft was charged with baptizing 2,000 children in the Devil's name.[35]

More numerous than midwives among the accused were women who were engaged in caring for other women's children. Lyndal Roper has shown that many witchcraft accusations in Augsburg in the late sixteenth and early seventeenth century arose out of conflicts between mothers and the lying-in maids who provided care for them and their infants for a number of weeks after birth.[36] It was not unnatural for the mothers to project their anxieties about their own health, as well as the precarious health of their infants, on to these women. When some misfortune did occur, therefore, the lying-in maids were highly vulnerable to charges of having deprived the baby of nourishment or of having killed it. What is interesting about these accusations is that they originated in tensions among women rather than between men and women. The same can be said regarding many other accusations made against women for harming young children.[37]

---

34 E.W. Monter, *European Witchcraft* (New York, 1969), pp. 75–81. In Hungary, competing midwives from different localities often accused each other of witchcraft, leading to the execution of both women. Klaniczay, 'Hungary', p. 254.

35 *Malleus Maleficarum*, p. 66; Lea, *Materials*, III, p. 1255. See generally T.R. Forbes, *The Midwife and the Witch* (New Haven, 1966).

36 L. Roper, 'Witchcraft and Fantasy in Early Modern Germany', *History Workshop Journal*, 32 (1991): 19–43, especially pp. 30–1.

37 Ibid., p. 23; J. Sharpe, 'Witchcraft and Women in Seventeenth-Century England: Some Northern Evidence', *Continuity and Change*, 6 (1991): 179–99.

The origin of these tensions in female circles helps to explain why a large number of witnesses in witchcraft trials were in fact women.[38]

A final explanation of the preponderance of female witches is that women, who generally had neither men's physical nor political power, were believed to be able to use sorcery as an instrument of protection and revenge. The power to bring about harm by magical means was one of the few forms of power that were available to women in early modern Europe. Even if women did not actually have recourse to the magical arts for such purposes, they were naturally suspected of doing so. This popular view of the witch as a powerful woman reminds us that although the witch was often a scapegoat for the ills of society and a victim, many of her neighbours viewed her as both powerful and threatening.[39] By having her tried and executed her neighbours were not simply picking on a helpless old woman but counteracting a form of female power that had placed them, their children and their domestic animals in considerable danger.

Age

The most common stereotype of the witch, that of an old woman, had a firm foundation in the prosecutions of the early modern period. The limited data that we have regarding the ages of witches, which are summarized in Table 4,[40] show that a solid majority of witches were older than fifty, which in the early modern period was considered to be a much more advanced age than it is today.[41] It appears, moreover, that the typical witch was significantly older than fifty. In two locations, Geneva and the county of Essex, the median age of witches was an even sixty. Reginald Scot was on solid ground, therefore, when he claimed that 'Witches are women which be commonly old.'[42]

---

38 C. Holmes, 'Women: Witnesses and Witches', *Past and Present*, 140 (1993): 45–78.

39 On the power of witches see Sharpe, 'Witchcraft and Women', pp. 185–6.

40 Sources for Table 4: E. Bever, 'Old Age and Witchcraft in Early Modern Europe', in *Old Age in Pre-industrial Society*, ed. P. Stearns (New York, 1982), p. 181; J.P. Demos, 'Underlying Themes in the Witchcraft of Seventeenth-Century New England', *American Historical Review*, 75 (1970): 1315.

41 Historians have set the age at which old age begins anywhere from forty, the age of menopause in early modern Europe, to sixty-five. See Bever, 'Old Age and Witchcraft', p. 165. For the use of the age of sixty in New England see Demos, *Entertaining Satan*, p. 67.

42 Monter, *Witchcraft in France and Switzerland*, p. 123; R. Scot, *The Discoverie of Witchcraft*, ed. M. Summers (London, 1930; repr. New York, 1972), pp. 4, 19.

Table 4   Ages of accused witches

Region	Years	Witches of known age	Number over 50	% over 50
Geneva	1537–1662	95	71	75
Dept. of the Nord, France	1542–1679	47	24	51
County of Essex, England	1645 only	15	13	87
Württemberg	1560–1701	29	16	55
Salem, Mass.	1692–1693	118	49	42

There are a number of reasons why witches tended to be advanced in years. To begin with, witches generally were prosecuted after suspicion of them had mounted over the years – a situation which naturally kept the average age of those tried fairly high. As we have seen, some witches were also wise women and folk healers, persons who were old almost by definition. A further explanation lies in the fact that older people, especially if they were senile, often manifested signs of eccentric or anti-social behaviour which tended to make neighbours uncomfortable and to invite accusations of witchcraft.[43] The same type of older person would also be more likely to confess freely to diabolical activities as a result of her senility. As the sceptical Cyrano de Bergerac wrote in the mid-seventeenth century: 'She was old: age had weakened her reason. Age makes one gossipy: she invented the story to amuse her neighbors. Age weakens the sight: she mistook a Hare for a Cat. Age makes one afraid: she thought she saw fifty instead of one.'[44] A final reason for the large number of old witches is that older persons were physically less powerful than younger ones and more likely, therefore, to use sorcery as a means of protection or revenge. Younger women, who are often depicted in Renaissance art as capable of violence, might have been able to

43 S.R. Burstein, 'Aspects of the Psychopathology of Old Age Revealed in the Witchcraft Cases of the Sixteenth and Seventeenth Centuries', *British Medical Bulletin*, 6 (1949): 63–72.
44 Quoted in Monter, *European Witchcraft*, p. 115.

defend themselves against some of their enemies,[45] but older women were forced to rely upon the tenuous authority they had acquired by virtue of either their longevity or the alleged control that they exercised over the occult forces of nature.[46]

The stereotype of the old, unattractive female witch was by no means incompatible with the prevailing view of the witch as a woman driven by sexual desire. It might strike us that beautiful, young women, who often appear as witches in contemporary paintings and engravings,[47] would have been considered more sexually voracious than old crones, but contemporaries did not always see it that way. It is true that the authors of the *Malleus* distinguished between the 'honest matrons who are little given to carnal vice' and young girls, who were 'more given to bodily lusts and pleasures', but other writers did not agree with them.[48] The Englishman Robert Burton, in his popular book, *Anatomy of Melancholy* (1621), while complaining that girls sought sex as soon as they reached puberty, emphasized that older women were just as lustful. 'Yet whilst she is so old a crone', wrote Burton, 'she caterwauls and must have a stallion, a champion; she must and will marry again, and betroth herself to some young man.'[49] Even today, in the Spanish province of Andalusia, widows are 'commonly believed, even in cases of apparent implausibility, to be sexually predatory upon young men'.[50]

Underlying the depiction of the old, sexually voracious hag was a deep male fear of the sexually experienced, sexually independent woman. The young maiden, lustful though she may have been, was at least still assumed to be sexually inexperienced until she married, at which time she became strictly subordinated to her husband. There was much more to be feared from the sexually experienced, mature woman, whose passion had not subsided, especially if she was no longer married and no longer able to conceive a child. Perhaps it was this fear that lay at the basis of the frequent condemnation and

45 C. Merchant, *The Death of Nature: Women, Ecology and the Scientific Revolution* (New York, 1980), pp. 132–6.

46 On the power of older New England women see Demos, *Entertaining Satan*, p. 68.

47 Hans Baldung Grien, *Prints and Drawings*, ed. J.H. Marrow and A. Shestack (Chicago, 1981), pp. 116–19.

48 *Malleus Maleficarum*, p. 97.

49 R. Burton, *Anatomy of Melancholy* (New York, 1932), III, pp. 55–6.

50 J. Pitt-Rivers, 'Honour and Social Status', in *Honour and Shame: The Values of Mediterranean Society*, ed. J.G. Peristiany (Chicago, 1966), p. 69.

ridicule of female, post-menopausal lust.[51] An added source of male anxiety in this regard was the widespread recognition that men were not only less ardent but less sexually capable than women as they entered old age.[52]

It was the old witch, therefore, and especially the old widow, who became the primary object of male sexual fear, male hostility and male accusations of witchcraft. The designation of such women as witches also made sense in the context of demonological theory, since the Devil, who was known for his sexual prowess, was believed to appear to prospective witches in the form of an attractive young man and make sexual advances to them. Since older women were considered to be driven by lust and yet were often unable to find sexual partners, they would be ideal prey for the Prince of Darkness. In a witchcraft treatise written in about 1540 Arnaldo Albertini, the Bishop of Patti in Sicily, argued that witches were mostly old women who could not find lovers and who therefore became *strigae*.[53]

Although the great majority of witches were old or middle-aged, younger persons were by no means immune to prosecution. Those witches who were originally accused of performing love magic, for example, tended to be in their twenties or early thirties, since it was customary for relatively young women to practise that particular trade. This probably explains why the Venetian Inquisition, which was particularly concerned with the practice of love magic and not with *maleficium*, tried more witches who were in their twenties and thirties than in their forties and fifties.[54]

Occasionally children and adolescents were tried and executed for witchcraft.[55] Children are probably more famous as the source than as the object of witchcraft accusations, but in some hunts they were prosecuted in large numbers, especially in the late seventeenth and early eighteenth centuries.[56] One set of circumstances in which they

51 For some of these statements see Bever, 'Old Age and Witchcraft', p. 175 n. 112. The sexual appetites of post-menopausal women were related to their dryness and desire for seminal fluid. See Roper, 'Witchcraft and Fantasy', pp. 28–9.

52 See Easlea's discussion of Montaigne's views on this subject in *Witch Hunting*, p. 28.

53 Lea, *Materials*, II, p. 449.

54 Martin, *Witchcraft and the Inquisition in Venice*, p. 228.

55 See, for example, F. Byloff, *Hexenglaube und Hexenverfolgung in den österreichischen Alpenländern* (Berlin/Leipzig, 1934), p. 117; E.W. Monter, *Ritual, Myth and Magic in Early Modern Europe* (Athens, Ohio, 1983) p. 104.

56 W. Behringer, 'Kinderhexenprozesse: zur Rolle von Kindern in der Geschichte der Hexenverfolgung', *Zeitschrift für Historische Forschung*, 16 (1988): 31–47.

appeared in fairly large numbers was when the process of making accusations got out of control. At Würzburg, for example, more than 25 per cent of the 160 witches executed between 1627 and 1629 were children, all of them having been implicated in the later stages of the hunt.[57] Occasionally the children of witches were suspected of and charged with witchcraft, for it was widely believed that witches could acquire their powers from their parents, usually by instruction but sometimes by heredity.[58] In one case in Saxony in 1660 the two children of a magician were summarily executed upon the conviction of their father.[59] Children also figured prominently in witch-hunts when the fertile imaginations of youth were given encouragement and credence. In the famous witch-hunt in the Basque country in 1610–14, when witches were given freedom to confess with impunity, more than 1,300 of the some 1,800 individuals who confessed were minors. In another well-known hunt, which began at Mora in Sweden in 1669, a combination of youthful imagination and the naming of accomplices resulted in the production of a disproportionately high number of child witches. The hunt began when a fifteen-year-old boy accused a young girl and several others of stealing children for the Devil. In the trials that followed, a number of children were condemned to death, while many others were given non-capital punishments on the basis of testimony by confessing witches that the children had accompanied them to the sabbath.[60]

Marital status

The marital status of accused witches varied greatly from place to place and from time to time, as the scant evidence summarized in

57 See H.C.E. Midelfort, 'Witch Hunting and the Domino Theory', in *Religion and the People, 800–1700*, ed. James Obelkevich (Chapel Hill, NC, 1979), p. 283.

58 Henningsen, *Witches' Advocate*, p. 34; Bader, *Hexenprozesse in der Schweiz*, p. 209; C. Karlsen, *The Devil in the Shape of a Woman: Witchcraft in Colonial New England* (New York, 1987), pp. 3, 71; Perkins, *Damned Art of Witchcraft*, p. 643; R. Mandrou, *Magistrats et sorciers en France au XVII siècle* (Paris, 1968), pp. 115–16; W.G. Soldan and H. Heppe, *Geschichte der Hexenprozesse*, ed. M. Bauer (Munich, 1912), I, pp. 483–5; Rémy, *Demonolatry*, p. 92; D.W. Sabean, *Power in the Blood: Popular Culture and Village Discourse in Early Modern Germany* (Cambridge, 1984), p. 107.

59 Lea, *Materials*, II, p. 902.

60 Robbins, *Encyclopedia*, pp. 348–50.

Table 5   Marital status of accused female witches

Region	Dates	Married	Widowed	Single	% Married
City of Toul	1584–1623	17	29	7	36
Basel	1571–1670	110	60	11	61
Montbéliard	1555–1661	31	25	11	50
County of Essex, England	1645 only	22	21	8	43
County of Kent, England	1560–1700	11	24	19	25
Scotland	1560–1727	245	67	7	70
Salem, Mass.	1692–1693	68	22	40	52
Sweden	1668–1676	49	19	32	49
Geneva	1537–1662	104	81	50	44
Venice	1550–1650	170	71	32	62

Table 5 indicates.[61] In most regions, however, the percentage of unmarried witches (i.e., those who were either widowed or who had never married) was higher than the percentage of such people in the general female population. In six of the ten regions represented in the table, married witches did not even form a majority of those accused, and in some areas, such as the English county of Kent and the City of Toul in Lorraine, the percentage of married witches was astonishingly low. Among the unmarried witches the widows were the most numerous, but we cannot ignore the single witches, for without them we would not be able to claim that the typical European witch was unmarried.

61 Sources for Table 5: Denis, *Toul*, p. 177; Macfarlane, *Witchcraft*, p. 164; A. Pollock, 'Social and Economic Characteristics of Witchcraft Accusations in Sixteenth- and Seventeenth-Century Kent', *Archaeologia Cantiana*, 95 (1979): 41, Table 3 (excluding those listed as 'married and spinster' in the indictments); Larner et al., *Source-Book of Scottish Witchcraft*, p. 241, Table 8; Karlsen, *Devil in the Shape of a Woman*, p. 72; Ankarloo, 'Sweden', p. 311; Monter, *Witchcraft in France and Switzerland*, p. 121; Martin, *Witchcraft and the Inquisition in Venice*, p. 229.

It is difficult to determine how much the unmarried status of witches made them vulnerable to witchcraft accusations. Villagers and townspeople may have suspected widows and elderly spinsters of witchcraft mainly because they were old and poor rather than because they were unmarried.[62] There is reason to believe, however, that the single status of many witches contributed at least indirectly to their plight. In a patriarchal society, the existence of women who were subject neither to father nor husband was a source of concern, if not fear, and it is not unreasonable to assume that both the neighbours who accused such women and the authorities who prosecuted them were responding to such fears.[63] These same accusers might also have come to the conclusion that unmarried women, regardless of age, were more likely than their married counterparts to have been seduced by a demon impersonating a man.

The fears of authorities regarding unmarried women acquired greater urgency during the early modern period both because their numbers were increasing and because their position in towns and villages was changing. The percentage of widows in the female population, which usually ranged from 10 to 20 per cent, rose at certain times and in certain places to 30 per cent.[64] These increases usually occurred after visitations of the plague, which often caused more deaths among men than women, and after periods of warfare, when men suffered greater casualties than women.[65] At the same time the number of women who never married increased from about 5 per cent in the late Middle Ages to 10 per cent and in some places to as much as 20 per cent by the seventeenth century, a development that coincided with an increase in the age of first marriage.[66] As this change was taking place, the institutions that had accommodated a large proportion of the single female population in the Middle

---

62 Burghartz, 'Equation of Women and Witches', pp. 65–6, argues that in Lucerne age was a more important distinguishing characteristic of witches than widowhood.

63 Women who had left their husbands were particularly vulnerable to suspicion of witchcraft. Martin, *Witchcraft and the Inquisition in Venice*, pp. 229–30. See also Karlsen, *Devil in the Shape of a Woman*, p. 73.

64 In Tuscany in the early fifteenth century the proportion of widows ranged from 16 per cent in the country to 25 per cent in the towns. D. Herlihy and C. Klapisch-Zuber, *Tuscans and their Families* (New Haven, 1985), pp. 216–17.

65 In some communities, such as Mora, Sweden, where a large witch-hunt took place in 1668, the number of adult men was less than half the number of adult women, mainly as a result of warfare. See Ankarloo, 'Sweden', p. 316.

66 See S.C. Watkins, 'Spinsters', *Journal of Family History*, 9 (1984): 315–16; P. Laslett, *The World We Have Lost* (3rd edn, New York, 1984), p. 111.

Ages – the convents – either experienced a decline in membership or were dissolved as a result of the Reformation. This meant that early modern European communities not only contained more unmarried women than they had during the Middle Ages but also had greater difficulty accommodating them. Many unmarried women, to be sure, found places in the patriarchal households of masters, brothers or adult children, but others opted for an independent existence. To make matters worse, most of these unmarried women were fairly poor, and thus they represented a serious social problem. If men already harboured deep fears of unattached women, their fears were aggravated by a process of social and demographic change.

Unlike the single and widowed witches, married witches generally did not become vulnerable to charges of witchcraft by virtue of their marital status. Other factors relating either to their sex or economic position appear to have been much more important in arousing suspicion of them. There were, however, two situations in which the marriage of a witch contributed at least indirectly to the charges against her. The first was when conflicts between her and her spouse or children gave rise to accusations of witchcraft. One of the attractions of accusing someone of witchcraft was that it allowed a person to express hostile feelings that did not have any other socially approved means of expression. Generally speaking, hostilities among family members were not allowed to result in violence or legal action. We might expect, therefore, that witchcraft accusations would occasionally surface within family units, and with the notable exception of England, they often did.[67] Since witchcraft was generally viewed as a crime practised by adult females, wives and mothers were more vulnerable to such charges than other members of the family. Not only did husbands occasionally name their wives as witches, but children sometimes accused their mothers.[68] In a number of cases children and their spouses used witchcraft accusations to retaliate against a mother who disapproved of their marriage. Indeed, witchcraft accusations became one of the many weapons that were used to attack the custom of arranged marriage – a practice that underwent a gradual loss of popularity during the early modern

---

67 For England see M. MacDonald, *Mystical Bedlam* (Cambridge, 1979), p. 110; Thomas, *Religion and the Decline of Magic*, p. 561.

68 See, for example, Midelfort, *Witch Hunting*, pp. 101–2. E. Delcambre, 'La Psychologie des inculpes Lorrains de sorcellerie', *Revue historique de droit français et étranger*, ser. 4, 32 (1954): 517.

Plate 1 A disease of the eyes attributed to sorcery. From Georg Bartisan, *Ophthalmologeia* (Dresden, 1583).

Plate 2 The hanging of the Chelmsford witches. The small animals in the foreground are familiar spirits who received nourishment from the witches and aided them in performing their magic. From a contemporary sixteenth-century broadside.

Plate 3 The Devil seducing a woman into making a pact with him. From Ulrich Molitor, *De Lamiis* (1489).

Plate 4 Witches, having changed themselves into animals, cast their spells at the door of a neighbour. One of the woodcut illustrations to Guazzo's *Compendium maleficarum* (1610 edń).

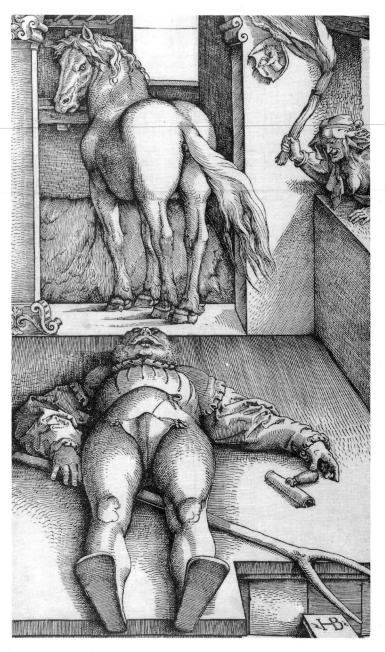

Plate 5 Hans Baldung Grien's early sixteenth-century depiction of the death of a stable hand by witchcraft.

Plate 6 Witches burning and boiling infants. From Guazzo (1610 edn).

Plate 7 Witches showing their subjection to their master, the Devil, by kissing him on the buttocks. From Guazzo (1610 edn).

Plate 8   The Devil re-baptizing a witch. From Guazzo (1610 edn).

Plate 9   Witches trampling on the cross at the Devil's command, an act symbolizing their apostasy. From Guazzo (1610 edn).

Plate 10 Hans Bladung Grien's depiction of witches, young and old, playing leapfrog.

Plate 11 Ritual magician summoning up a demon. From the title page of Christopher Marlowe, *Dr. Faustus* (1636).

Plate 12 The execution of Urbain Grandier at London 1634.

Plate 13   The swimming of Ruth Osborne by a mob at Tring, Hertfordshire, in 1751.

period, as religious reformers insisted upon marital fidelity and as the age of first marriage increased.[69]

The second situation in which a woman's marital status led to her accusation as a witch was when she became involved in conflicts over her husband's property. Although married women had no independent wealth or property at this time, they very often assisted their husbands in their work. All too often, therefore, they found themselves involved in disputes over rents, labour, or even the possession of land, and we know that many of these disputes led to witchcraft accusations. From the point of view of the accuser, the naming of an antagonist's wife as a witch would appear to be most attractive when there was no legal mechanism available to resolve the conflict between them.

Social and economic status

Although very little hard evidence regarding the social, occupational and economic status of witches has survived, we can be fairly certain that the great majority of those prosecuted came from the lower levels of society. The general comments made by the authors of witchcraft treatises, the allegation that witches made pacts with the Devil in exchange for very little material gain, the motives attributed to witches for taking action against their neighbours, and the mere fact that so many witches were unattached women of no apparent social distinction all point to this conclusion. Witches were not necessarily the very poorest members of society. The wandering poor, for example, do not appear to have figured very prominently in the trials, except in certain Habsburg lands,[70] and many witches owned some property.[71] Witches did, however, often live on the margin of subsistence, and some of them did in fact have to resort to begging to survive.[72] Indeed, the Italian physician Girolamo Cardano described witches as 'miserable old women, beggars, existing in the valleys on chestnuts and field herbs', while Nicolas Rémy, in his treatise of 1595, claimed that witches were 'for the most part beggars, who support

---

69 See S. Ozment, *When Fathers Ruled* (Cambridge, Mass., 1983), pp. 27–8, for a discussion of parental control of marriage.

70 Evans, *Habsburg Monarchy*, pp. 412–13.

71 See, for example, A. Pollock, 'Kent', p. 45.

72 Heikkinen, *Paholaisen*, pp. 388, 390, shows that even some of those Ostro-bothnian witches who were not classified as beggars often found it necessary to beg.

life on the alms they receive'.[73] In New England, the great majority of women accused of witchcraft before the Salem episode of 1692 were dependent members of the community who qualified for poor relief.[74] In Norway, where large numbers of accused witches were described in the trial records as extremely poor, most of those who were actually convicted were beggars.[75]

There are a number of reasons why the people who filled the lowest ranks of society incurred accusations of witchcraft. Poor people, especially poor women, were the weakest and most vulnerable members of society. 'Witches', wrote Johann Weyer, 'are poor ignorant creatures, old and powerless.'[76] Because of this impotence, they were most readily chosen as scapegoats for the ills of society. As individuals in dire financial straits, moreover, they were the persons most likely to resort to the selling of magical cures in order to survive, or to use sorcery as a means of revenge against those who threatened to deprive them of their already meagre resources. Even if they did not actually practise maleficent magic, they would be the ones most readily suspected by their neighbours of doing so. In a similar vein, poor people were the most likely members of society to try to make pacts with the Devil in order to improve their economic situation, and even though very few of them did so, a charge to that effect was eminently plausible. Finally, and perhaps most important, poor people, being dependent upon the community, easily aroused feelings of resentment and (when assistance was not forthcoming) guilt among their neighbours. The naming of poor people as witches in these circumstances represented attempts either to retaliate in a legitimate fashion against those who imposed on them or to project their own guilt on to the same persons.

Since the poverty of witches appears to have been of no little importance in encouraging people to accuse them of this crime, it is reasonable to assume that some of the economic changes of the early modern period played some part in causing the great witch-hunt.[77]

---

73 G. Cardano, *De Rerum Varietate* (Basel, 1557), cited in Lea, *Materials*, II, p. 446; Rémy, *Demonolatry*, p. 159. On Rémy's exaggeration in this regard see Briggs, *Communities of Belief*, p. 75.

74 Wiseman, *Witchcraft, Magic and Religion*, pp. 76–91. See also Thomas, *Religion and the Decline of Magic*, pp. 562–3.

75 Naess, 'Norway', p. 377.

76 Quoted in Lea, *Materials*, II, p. 491.

77 W. Behringer, *Hexenverfolgung in Bayern* (Munich, 1987), pp. 96–112, relates the agrarian crisis of the late sixteenth century as well as the social changes of the period to the increased prosecution of witches.

There is no doubt that the hunt occurred at a time when poverty was becoming more severe and widespread. The main reason for this unkind development was a dramatic increase in the European population from the late fifteenth to the early seventeenth century. Because labour was in abundant supply, real wages declined sharply. At the same time, an unprecedented inflation, caused mainly by the pressure of an expanding population on a limited supply of resources, had a more serious impact on the poor than the rich. The net result was a decline in the standard of living – a process that began in the late fifteenth century and continued well into the eighteenth.[78] This decline was widely felt, but it most seriously affected the most marginal elements of society, the very people who became the main victims of the great witch-hunt.

If economic change deepened the predicament of the poor, making them more willing to contemplate sorcery as a solution to their problems, it also made their accusers more willing to make witchcraft accusations. Since almost all people were at least frightened by the prospect of economic decline, they became less accommodating and tolerant in their dealings with the poor and more willing to use witchcraft accusations to maintain their tenuous position in society. In some cases, as in many English witchcraft prosecutions studied by Alan Macfarlane, they became less willing to give the poor the assistance that medieval social and religious theory demanded. In other cases, the accusers of witches became more intolerant of the poor and more willing to take legal action against them because they reminded them all too clearly of what they themselves might have become in such times.

Although the great majority of witches lived in straitened economic circumstances, a few were relatively well off. Sometimes these wealthier witches were accused in the later stages of chain-reaction hunts, just as men and children were, as the stereotype of the witch broke down. At other times, however, prominent and wealthy men (or, more safely, their wives) became the early targets of witchcraft accusations. This happened most frequently at the beginning of the European witch-hunt, when a number of witches in high places were accused, usually in connection with some sort of real or imagined political conspiracy. When charges of this nature arose, they bore a close resemblance to the charges of politically inspired

---

sorcery that occurred frequently in the fourteenth and fifteenth centuries. Even in seventeenth-century accusations, however, political motives could come into play, such as when members of town councils accused their rivals or their wives of witchcraft.

Another motive for accusing wealthy and prominent persons was the desire of either relatives or magistrates to acquire the witches' property upon conviction. In colonial New England inheritance played a particularly important role in the accusation of witches. Carol Karlsen has shown that most of the New England women named as witches had either inherited property or stood to inherit it. The wealth of these women varied greatly, but as mothers without sons or as women without brothers they all 'stood in the way of the orderly transmission of property from one generation of males to another'.[79] Thus conflicts between men and women over economic resources played a central role in determining the pattern of New England witchcraft accusations.

The personality of the witch

As we turn to the personal as opposed to the social and economic characteristics of the witch, we encounter a picture of broad diversity. As one might expect, witches did not all conform to one single personality profile. They did, nevertheless, often exhibit certain behavioural characteristics that explain why they, rather than others, were singled out for accusation and prosecution. First and most commonly, witches were often described as sharp-tongued, bad-tempered and quarrelsome – traits that naturally involved them in disputes with their neighbours and directed non-specific, communal resentment against them.[80] Witches were very often the village scolds who, among other things, were prone to cursing – a habit that could easily be interpreted as an act of sorcery and the cause of a neighbour's misfortune. In colonial New England those women accused of witchcraft had a reputation for their threatening and 'disorderly' speech.[81] Witches were, in other words, people one did not enjoy having as neighbours.

---

79 Karlsen, *Devil in the Shape of a Woman*, pp. 111–16.

80 Thomas, *Religion and the Decline of Magic*, p. 530. Macfarlane, *Witchcraft in Tudor and Stuart England*, pp. 158–60; Monter, *Witchcraft in France and Switzerland*, pp. 136–7; Demos, *Entertaining Satan*, pp. 54–6.; J. Kamensky, 'Words, Witches and Woman Trouble: Witchcraft, Disorderly Speech and Gender Boundaries in Puritan New England', *Essex Institute Historical Collections*, 128 (1992): 286–307.

81 Kamensky, 'Words, Witches and Women Trouble', p. 288.

Since witches were a group of predominantly old persons, they often manifested signs of senility. It is of course senile persons who very often exhibit the signs of contentiousness and irritability that we have just referred to. The senility of witches, moreover, best explains the widespread but erroneous belief that witches were mentally unbalanced.[82] Witches certainly had vivid imaginations, as the details of free confessions clearly reveal, and some of them may have been mythomaniacs.[83] Whether any significant number of them suffered from hysteria, as many demoniacs probably did, is much more doubtful.[84] The sixteenth-century sceptic, Johann Weyer, thought that the 'silly and miserable' women who believed they had made pacts with the Devil and rode out at night with Diana had contracted the female uterine disease of melancholy, and it is possible that some witches were in fact depressed. But on the basis of what we know today regarding the mental effects of old age, the women about whom Weyer was writing, as well as the great majority of 'mentally unbalanced' witches, were probably exhibiting the signs of nothing more than senility.[85]

Another personal characteristic of many witches was their reputation for various forms of religious or moral deviance. Witches were, by definition, intrinsically evil creatures, and consequently their neighbours assumed that their acts of sorcery and Devil-worship formed only part of a poor moral record. Conversely, the reputation of witches for other moral transgressions made them more vulnerable to the charge of witchcraft. In determining the moral reputation of those persons accused of witchcraft we cannot rely upon the references to their recurrent sinfulness that often appear in the formal charges against them, since magistrates might have deliberately inserted such statements, regardless of their veracity, into the record in order to present the witch in the worst possible light. But there is independent judicial evidence, usually contained in church court records, that many witches had in fact been suspected of, and occasionally prosecuted for other manifestations of immoral behaviour. Witches were surely not hardened criminals, and no more than a small percentage of them had ever been prosecuted for serious crimes

---

82 G. Zilboorg, *The Medical Man and the Witch during the Renaissance* (New York, 1941), pp. 204–20.

83 E. Delcambre, 'La Psychologie', pp. 391–2.

84 For this argument see I. Veith, *Hysteria: The History of a Disease* (Chicago, 1965), pp. 58–61.

85 See Burstein, 'Old Age', pp. 65–8.

like theft.[86] A number of witches, however, had been named in ecclesiastical courts for such crimes as non-attendance at church, Sabbath-breaking, cursing, fornication, prostitution, abortion, and even adultery, while some male witches had been suspected, if not formally accused, of homosexuality.[87] An English woman tried for witchcraft in 1613 had given birth to three illegitimate children, while some of the women accused of witchcraft in Lucerne were known to have spoken openly about sexual matters or to have displayed their sexuality publicly.[88] It is also clear that women who were suspected of religious nonconformity or who had no religion at all were vulnerable to charges of witchcraft.[89] On the basis of all this evidence it may be too strong to suggest that witches were deviants,[90] a word that often connotes criminality, but they certainly had displayed 'inappropriate female behaviour' and had failed to protect their reputations.[91]

Witches as rebels

The witch was viewed by authorities as a rebel – an apostate rebel against God and a conspirator against the political, social and moral order of man. As we have seen, the fear of rebellion in late medieval and early modern European society played a significant role in creating the fantasy of the witches' sabbath and in arousing fear

---

86 In New England 10 out of 118 witches had been prosecuted for theft. See Demos, *Entertaining Satan*, p. 77. In Norway, 40 persons accused of witchcraft are known to have been previously brought before local courts for other crimes. See Naess, 'Norway', p. 378. See also Monter, *Witchcraft in France and Switzerland*, p. 136.

87 Delcambre, 'La Psychologie', p. 105; Levack, 'The Great Scottish Witch Hunt', p. 101; Karlsen, *Devil in the Shape of a Woman*, p. 138; Byloff, *Hexenglaube*, p. 117; A. Evans, *Witchcraft and the Gay Counterculture* (Boston, 1978), pp. 76–7; E.W. Monter, 'La Sodomie à l'époque moderne en Suisse romande', *Annales*, 29 (1974): 1031–2.

88 *Witches Apprehended, Examined and Executed* (London, 1613), sig. B; Burghartz, 'Equation of Women and Witches', pp. 68–9.

89 Scot, *The Discoverie of Witchcraft*, ed. M. Summers (London 1930; repr. New York 1972), p. 4; Delcambre, 'La Psychologie', p. 105.

90 Muchembled, 'Witches of Cambrésis', p. 222, rejects the use of the term. On deviance see K. Erikson, *Wayward Puritans* (New York, 1966), and C. McCaghy, *Deviant Behavior* (New York, 1976), pp. 2–4; N. Ben-Yehuda, *Deviance and Moral Boundaries* (Chicago, 1985).

91 C. Garrett, 'Women and Witches: Patterns of Analysis', *Signs*, 3 (1977): 466. Karlsen, *Devil in the Shape of a Woman*, pp. 119, 127, argues that in New England witches were women who refused to accept the place in society assigned to them by men.

and hatred of the witch. It remains to be determined, however, to what extent witches conformed in reality to this learned stereotype. Since an actual sect of witches almost certainly did not exist, it is difficult to depict them, in the tradition of nineteenth-century French historiography, as rebellious peasants who gathered secretly to protest the economic and social injustices of their world.[92] It is possible to interpret some of their confessions, in which they described a world turned upside down, as symbolic protests against the established order, as Emmanuel Le Roy Ladurie has claimed.[93] But since many of these confessions were adduced under torture, the symbols contained in them usually reflect the projected fears of magistrates more than they do the protests of the poor. As long as we see witches as scapegoats and victims, which in the great majority of cases they were, it is difficult to depict them as protesters or rebels, even if it can be shown that some of them came from rebel families.[94] Only in colonial Peru, where witches became identified as the defenders of native Andean culture against the Spanish regime, could witches be considered actual political subversives, encouraging disobedience to both the parish priests and local political authorities.[95]

In a certain sense, however, European witches did play the part of rebels. All too often the witch, in her determination to survive in a hostile environment, registered a protest against her male social and political superiors. Sometimes it took the form of a curse or an act of sorcery, the witch's only weapons against the villagers and authorities who victimized her. At other times it took the form of a heroic protest against the courts that investigated her. Some witches, to be sure, submitted meekly to the pricker and the torturer in the naive confidence that they would be vindicated. Sometimes, almost inconceivably, they expressed gratitude to their torturers.[96] At other times, however, they submitted reluctantly, voicing threats against their inquisitors. At Salem, for example, the witches who were punished most severely were those who refused to recognize the authority of the court that was trying them.[97] Such individual

92 See for example, J. Michelet, *Satanism and Witchcraft*, trans. A.R. Allison (New York, 1939).

93 Le Roy Ladurie, *Paysans de Languedoc*, pp. 407–13.

94 Muchembled, 'Witches of Cambrésis', p. 264, insists that the witches of that region were not rebels but passive victims.

95 I. Silverblatt, *Moon, Sun, and Witches: Gender Ideologies and Class in Inca and Colonial Peru* (Princeton, 1987), pp. 195–6.

96 Delcambre, 'La Psychologie', pp. 87–8.

97 D. Konig, *Law and Society in Colonial Massachusetts* (Chapel Hill, NC, 1980), pp. 173–4.

protests did not turn the witch into a conspiratorial rebel, but they do suggest that the image of her as a totally passive victim must be seriously qualified. In the Duchy of Württemberg, witches displayed an aggressiveness that was regarded as inappropriate for their sex, while in the Pays de Labourd they were known for their 'effrontery'.[98]

If we need one word to describe the witch of the early modern period, we might refer to her as a non-conformist. The witch was usually not a foreigner or stranger in her community, but she was hardly a typical villager. Older and poorer than average, and more often than not unmarried, she did not adhere to the traditional behavioural standards of her community or of her sex. By her actions and her words she defied contemporary standards of docility and domesticity and inverted the ideal of the good Christian wife and mother.[99] Cranky, acerbic and often angry about her plight, she attracted attention, hostility, suspicion and fear. Sometimes, but by no means always, she possessed physical characteristics that made her appear even more different from the norm. For Reginald Scot, witches were 'commonly old, lame, blear-eyed, pale, foul and full of wrinkles ... lean and deformed, showing melancholy in their faces to the horror of all that see them'.[100] By prosecuting such persons members of the ruling élite may not have been eliminating deviants or rebels in the traditional sense of the word, but they were, perhaps unconsciously, making their communities more homogeneous and possibly even more harmonious. They also were upholding conventional standards of female conduct.

SOCIAL CHANGE AND THE GREAT WITCH-HUNT

Although social and economic factors certainly played an important role in prompting witchcraft accusations and in determining which individuals were blamed for personal misfortune, it is much more debatable whether the European witch-hunt, taken as a whole, should

98 E.W.M. Bever, 'Witchcraft in Early Modern Württemberg' (Princeton Ph.D. thesis, 1983); N.Z. Davis, *The Return of Martin Guerre* (Cambridge, Mass., 1983), p. 32.

99 S. Brauner, 'Martin Luther on Witchcraft: A True Reformer?', in *The Politics of Gender in Early Modern Europe*, ed. J.R. Brink et al., *Sixteenth-Century Essays and Studies* 12 (1989): 29–42; A.P. Coudert, 'The Myth of the Improved Status of Protestant Women: The Case of the Witchcraze', in *The Politics of Gender in Early Modern Europe*, ed. J.R. Brink et al., pp. 61–94.

100 Macfarlane, *Witchcraft in Tudor and Stuart England*, p. 158; Scot, *Discoverie*, p. 320.

be considered the product of social and economic *change*. There is no question that some of the economic, social and demographic developments that occurred in early modern Europe aggravated the tensions that underlay many witchcraft accusations. As mentioned above, inflation, an increase in poverty, pressure by a growing population on a limited supply of resources, the growth of the unattached female population and changes in the structure of the family all played some part in encouraging witchcraft accusations. Some women may have been accused of witchcraft because they were most adversely affected by such change or, with respect to the advent of capitalism, most resistant to it.[101] In addition, specific economic crises, such as famine, outbreaks of epidemic disease, and dislocations caused by war, may have helped to trigger many individual witch-hunts, as shall be discussed below. In more than a few cases, however, there does not appear to have been any connection between witch-hunting and these specific developments. Many of the personal conflicts that led to witchcraft accusations, as well as the misfortunes that triggered them, were a constant feature of village life and could just as easily have developed in good times as in bad.[102] In many cases the charges against witches provide little evidence that they or their neighbours were responding to social or economic change, and when magistrates or inquisitors initiated and directed the prosecutions, the connections often become even more elusive.

There was, however, a more general and indirect way in which social change contributed to witch-hunting. When combined with the religious and political changes of this period, social and economic change created a mood of anxiety in all segments of society that made men more aware of the danger of witchcraft in the world and more eager to counteract it. It can of course be claimed that all historical ages are periods of monumental change and transformation and that the process of change invariably creates fear and anxiety among those who either experience or witness it. That may very well be true, but the period of the witch-hunt, which was the time when Europe experienced the birth-pangs of the modern world, was a special case. During these years Europe not only experienced an unprecedented inflation and a decline in the standard of living but also the growth of capitalism, the emergence of the modern state, a rash of rebellions

101 Macfarlane, *Witchcraft in Tudor and Stuart England*, p. 161; Thomas, *Religion and the Decline of Magic*, p. 562.
102 Briggs, *Communities of Belief*, p. 74.

and civil wars, international conflict on an unprecedented scale, and the destruction of the ostensible unity of medieval Christendom. The changes that took place were more fundamental, rapid and extensive than at any other time in European history before the advent of the industrial revolution. These changes took a heavy psychic toll. For a population that believed in the fixed order of the cosmos, the transformation of almost every aspect of their lives was a disconcerting experience. It may have produced the mood of gloom, pessimism and sadness that both contemporaries and later historians have detected in late medieval and early modern Europe, and it certainly created deep fear among those who were unable to cope with the instability and uncertainty of the new world. It was the prevalence of such fear throughout Europe and in all social classes that has led to the designation of this period as the 'Age of Anxiety' and as one of the 'most psychically disturbed periods in human history'.[103]

The prevalence of this anxiety created a mood both among the élite and the common people that greatly encouraged the process of witch-hunting. Among the learned and ruling classes it encouraged a tendency to attribute the turmoil, instability and confusion that they saw everywhere around them to the influence of Satan in the world, a process which in turn suggested the activity of witches. Many of the concrete signs of social disintegration – religious dissent, popular rebellion, the apparent spread of poverty, and even the emergence of the spirit of capitalism – were in fact often attributed to Satan and his allies. Convinced that the Devil was loose, members of the administrative élite could easily come to the conclusion that one of the best ways to counteract him and his destructive influence was to prosecute those individuals who had made pacts with him. In this way the world could be purified of its diabolical contaminants and the order of society restored. By conducting a witch-hunt, moreover, administrative authorities could heal, at least temporarily, potentially dangerous divisions in society by focusing the attention of the entire community on a common enemy, and so distract it from more serious (and more real) concerns.[104]

Among the common people an attack on witches also helped to relieve anxiety. The individuals who brought the initial charges

---

103 L. White Jr, 'Death and the Devil', in *The Darker Vision of the Renaissance*, ed. R.S. Kinsman (Berkeley, 1974), p. 26.

104 For the extreme view that the ruling class deliberately used witch-hunting to create insecurity among the lower classes and to divert latent revolutionary energy see M. Harris, *Cows, Pigs, Wars and Witches* (New York, 1974), pp. 225–40.

against witches were of course doing this in a very specific way, since by denouncing witches they were explaining misfortunes that had befallen them and gaining revenge against those who had harmed them. But in a more general way the entire community, by assisting in the apprehension of witches, testifying against them and flocking to their execution, was responding to an emotional need. Faced with inflation, increased competition for a limited amount of land, periodic famine and visitations of the plague, and an often bewildering set of religious and political changes, peasants and labourers found in witch-hunting a release from the psychic turmoil they were experiencing. Witch-hunting, in other words, became one of the ways that people could maintain their equilibrium at a time of great stress. Witches became the scapegoats not simply of those who had experienced misfortune but of entire communities.

The role played by witch-hunts in relieving anxiety becomes even more obvious when we consider the moral or spiritual anxiety that many villagers were experiencing at the time of the Reformation. As a result of the moral instruction and exhortation of religious reformers – both Protestant and Catholic – European villagers and townsmen of the sixteenth and seventeenth centuries were made highly conscious of their need to attain salvation. This process was naturally accompanied by widespread feelings of guilt for moral transgressions and anxiety regarding one's eternal destiny, especially since the standards of moral behaviour were themselves being transformed. In such circumstances the prosecution of individuals who by definition were intrinsically evil and who were allegedly undermining the entire moral order provided a certain amount of reassurance to troubled souls. Support for witchcraft trials provided a means by which the members of European communities could acquire confidence in their own moral sanctity and ultimate salvation.

The moral dimension of early modern European anxiety reveals how difficult it is to separate the effects of social and economic change from that of religious change. The malaise that early modern Europeans experienced may be vague and difficult to analyse, but it certainly resulted as much from the process of religious change as from the transformation of society and the economy. In the final analysis it was the process of change itself rather than any one particular change that laid the psychological foundation for witch-hunting. Once a general mood conducive to witch-hunting had been established, then much more specific social and economic concerns came into play and led to the identification of certain individuals – usually poor, old women – as witches.

6 THE DYNAMICS OF WITCH-HUNTING

The prosecution of witches in early modern Europe is usually viewed in monolithic terms. We commonly refer to *the* European witch-hunt or witch-craze of the fifteenth, sixteenth and seventeenth centuries. There are legitimate reasons for viewing the pursuit of witches in this general, comprehensive fashion. The various ecclesiastical and secular authorities who prosecuted witches from Spain to the Baltic and from Scotland to Transylvania were in a sense participating in a common enterprise: the destruction of a particularly dangerous heresy and form of rebellion that had spread throughout Europe. The intensity of their campaign varied greatly from place to place and from time to time, but their reasons for prosecuting witches, the charges they brought against them and the methods they used to discover them had a great deal in common. In a certain sense, therefore, there *was* a large hunt or campaign that began in the fifteenth century, became much more intense in the second half of the sixteenth century, reached a peak around 1620 and then slowly declined in the late seventeenth and eighteenth centuries. It is this large, pan-European hunt that has been the main focus of this book so far.

However valid the concept of a single European witch-hunt may be, it can be misleading. Not only can it encourage the formulation of general statements about European witchcraft that ignore national and regional variations (which will be the subject of the next chapter), but it can also obscure the fact that the hunt was an amalgam of hundreds, if not thousands of separate hunts that occurred at different places and at different times. Each of these hunts, like the larger composite phenomenon, has its own history, and each is capable of detailed analysis. Some of these individual hunts, such as the series of trials at Trier in the 1580s and 1590s, the campaign against witchcraft in the Basque country in 1609–14, the hunt conducted by Matthew Hopkins and John Stearne in England during 1645–46, the great Scottish witch-hunt of 1661–62 and the episode that occurred at Salem, Massachusetts in 1692 have been the subjects of detailed research. Many others, of varying size, still await scholarly investigation. We have enough information, however, to explore the many different ways these hunts got started, the different forms they took as they developed, and the different ways they came to an end. The picture that emerges is of such wide diversity that it becomes difficult to describe a 'typical' witch-hunt.

THE PRECONDITIONS

Before any witch-hunt could take place it was necessary for certain preconditions to have been satisfied. These preconditions, which roughly parallel those of the broader, European hunt, concern the witch-beliefs of the local population, the laws and judicial institutions of the area, and the mood of the entire community. Concerning witch-beliefs, it was necessary that both the ruling élite and the common people had some knowledge of the various activities that witches allegedly engaged in. This does not mean that all the residents of those communities that experienced witch-hunts had a full knowledge of the cumulative concept of witchcraft. It does mean, however, that the people in general believed in the reality of harmful magic and that the magistrates and clergy were at least vaguely familiar with the demonological theory that intellectuals had been developing since the late Middle Ages to explain that magic. If the common people did not believe in the reality of *maleficia* and the existence of witches, they would not have been inclined to testify that their misfortunes were attributable to witchcraft. Reluctance of this sort could thwart the efforts of even the most determined prosecutor and might even lead to popular opposition to the trials. It was essential, therefore, to have a witch-believing populace before a witch-hunt could start. In most instances this precondition was easily satisfied. Popular witch-beliefs predated the formation of the cumulative concept of witchcraft and were easily rekindled by preachers when they became convinced that witches were loose in the community. On the other hand, there were areas of Europe, notably southern Spain, where such beliefs were weak, and the virtual absence of witchcraft prosecutions there can be attributed at least in part to that fact.[1]

Much more important than popular beliefs were those of the ruling and administrative élite. Because these men controlled the judicial process, their belief in witchcraft was essential to the conduct of a witch-hunt. As we know from the events of the late seventeenth

---

1 G.L. Kittredge, *Witchcraft in Old and New England* (Cambridge, Mass., 1929), p. 357; Henningsen, *Witches' Advocate*, p. 389.

century, by which time scepticism had begun to penetrate the upper levels of society, popular beliefs were incapable of generating a witch-hunt if they met with bureaucratic disbelief and judicial inaction. In order for a witch-hunt to take place, therefore, it was necessary for this group of officials to believe in the reality of witchcraft and to harbour deep fears of it. It was also necessary for these men to be sufficiently familiar with the contemporary demonological theory of witchcraft, according to which the essence of the crime was the pact with the Devil. And if a large hunt was to take place, in which accomplices would be sought, it was necessary for these men to believe in witchcraft as a collective, conspiratorial activity. As the ruling élite in Europe became more educated, as more literature (including witchcraft treatises) began to reach small communities, and as news of witchcraft spread by word of mouth among provincial élites, witch-hunts became much more likely to occur. In the Cambrésis region the rise of witchcraft prosecutions accompanied the spread of literacy among the local élites, and in the outlying regions of Europe, such as in Scandinavia and Transylvania, witch-hunting never took place until after the introduction of learned witch-beliefs.[2]

A second set of preconditions for specific witch-hunts concerns the laws and the judicial machinery that operated in the area where the hunts took place. In order for such hunts to begin it was necessary for the courts which exercised jurisdiction in that particular locality to have possessed both a clearly defined jurisdiction over the crime of witchcraft and the procedural tools necessary to prosecute witches successfully. The need for clear definition, which usually was obtained through the passage of a witchcraft statute, the promulgation of a witchcraft edict, or the issuance of a new legal code that made reference to witchcraft, was most clearly evident in England, where virtually no trials took place until the passage of the witchcraft statute of 1542. In similar fashion the promulgation of the Imperial criminal code, the *Carolina* of 1532, which contained specific references to the crime of witchcraft, facilitated the conduct of witch-hunts throughout the Holy Roman Empire. Looking back to an earlier period, one can argue that the prosecution of witchcraft by papal inquisitors was not possible until sorcery was specifically classified as heresy.[3] Even then,

---

2 Muchembled, 'Witches of Cambrésis', pp. 256–7.

3 The first step was taken by Pope Alexander IV in 1258. See Kors and Peters, *Witchcraft in Europe*, pp. 77, 79.

however, it was necessary for Pope Innocent VIII to issue his famous Bull, *Summis desiderantes*, to give his two inquisitors, Kramer and Sprenger, authority to proceed against witches in Germany in 1484.

In addition to possessing clear jurisdiction over witchcraft, European courts had to have adopted certain procedures in order to prosecute witches successfully. At the very least they had to have abandoned the rule by which the accuser was liable to a charge of false accusation, the *lex talionis*, in the event that the accused proved his innocence. If a large hunt were to develop, it was also necessary for the judicial authorities to have the right to accuse and interrogate individuals on their own authority and to use coercive measures – usually torture – to obtain confessions. In most cases courts acquired these rights when inquisitorial procedure was introduced, a process that had taken place in most European jurisdictions by the middle of the sixteenth century. In England, of course, inquisitorial procedure was not adopted, and torture could not be used in witchcraft cases. This meant, in effect, that large witch-hunts were unlikely to occur in that country, and indeed very few did. Nevertheless, the use of public prosecutions that were initiated by grand juries acting in the name of the community after a private complaint was entered, coupled with a certain amount of judicial coercion, could result in successful witchcraft prosecutions, with or without confessions. And although torture could not be employed in England, the ability of the jury to reach verdicts on the basis of circumstantial evidence meant that the English judicial system was quite capable of facilitating a witch-hunt.

The final precondition of witch-hunting in European communities was the presence of an atmosphere that heightened the fear of witchcraft and encouraged people to take action against it. We have already seen how a general mood of anxiety throughout Europe provided the emotional setting for the entire witch-hunt. In the towns and villages where witch-hunts occurred this mood became readily apparent, either among a small group of villagers or magistrates or, more commonly, among the entire populace. The anxiety that these people shared could arise either from the discussion of witchcraft or, somewhat more indirectly, from economic, political or religious developments.

Probably the most common source of an atmosphere that was conducive to witch-hunting was the public discussion of witchcraft itself. In many cases the sermons of a witch-hunting preacher prepared the minds of his parishioners to look for witches among their daily associates. The role of the reformed clergy, both Protestant and Catholic, in spreading the witch-craze from the pulpit has long been recognized,[4] and the sermons of Samuel Parris at Salem prior to the witch-hunting that began there in 1692 provide a good case in point. Occasionally contemporaries made observations about the role that preaching played in starting witch-hunts. As part of his criticism of the great Basque witch-hunt of 1610, the inquisitor Alonso de Salazar claimed that 'the matter started there after Fray Domingo de Sardo came there to preach about these things', and in an astonishingly perceptive commentary on the entire process of witch-hunting he asserted that 'there were neither witches nor bewitched until they were talked about and written about'.[5]

Preachers were not the only individuals who were responsible for the talking and the writing. The news of witch-hunts and executions in other parts of a country could easily fan popular and élite fears and create a mood that was conducive to witch-hunting in a village or town. It was because of such communications that many hunts spread from village to village, even when confessing witches did not implicate accomplices outside their communities or when witch-hunters did not move from place to place. Sometimes the dissemination of pamphlets or treatises discussing witchcraft cases served the same purpose, while official pronouncements regarding the danger of witchcraft could also raise fears that might otherwise have been dormant. One witch-hunt in Franche-Comté in the first decade of the seventeenth century began shortly after the publication of Henri Boguet's *Discours des sorciers* (1602), while another in the same province in 1657 started only after inquisitors proclaimed a *monitoire* in each province requiring anyone with information about acts of witchcraft to make it known to inquisitors.[6]

In a somewhat more indirect way, the experience of economic, religious or political crisis often produced a mood in which the hunting of witches could easily begin. In a number of instances a succession of bad harvests and near famines appears to have encouraged the growth of witch-hunting. At Trier, for example, a combination of many different natural calamities succeeded in destroying all but two harvests between 1580 and 1599, during which time a ferocious epidemic of witch-trials took place.[7] In

---

4 See, for example, Trevor-Roper, 'European Witch-Craze', pp. 137–9; Clark, 'Protestant Demonology', passim; Naess, 'Norway', p. 374.

5 Kors and Peters, *Witchcraft in Europe*, p. 341.

6 Monter, *Witchcraft in France and Switzerland*, pp. 72–3, 81. For an illustration of the effects of rumours on witch-hunting see B. Ankarloo, *Trolldomsprocesserna i Sverige* (Stockholm, 1971), pp. 338–9.

7 See Robbins, *Encyclopedia*, p. 202.

similar fashion a couple of bad harvests in the northern portions of Franche-Comté set the stage for the witch-hunt that took place there in 1628–29.[8] Epidemics of disease, including the plague, often had a similar effect, such as at Ellwangen in 1611.[9] In certain areas of Europe there appears to have been a rough correlation between periods of dearth, famine and pestilence on the one hand and periods of intense witch-hunting on the other. In Germany, for example, the years witnessing the most serious agrarian crises between 1562 and 1630 were also the years in which large witch-hunts began.[10] Similar patterns can be seen in Switzerland throughout the fifteenth century and in the Pays de Vaud between 1581 and 1620.[11] It would be misleading to explain individual witch-hunts entirely in such terms, but agrarian crises and epidemics of disease did apparently contribute to the creation of an atmosphere in which accusations of witchcraft were likely to arise.

Religious crises, especially the experience of recent, current or impending religious change, also had great potential for creating the type of communal anxiety that led to witchcraft accusations, and, as we have seen, this might explain why witch-hunting most commonly occurred in religiously volatile areas. Another religious sentiment that could have a similar effect was millenarianism, the belief that the anti-Christ had appeared and that the rule of Christ was imminent. Witches were not identified with the anti-Christ, but the desire to cleanse the world to prepare the way of the Lord could easily encourage the pursuit of them, for they were, after all, the agents of the Devil.[12] The prevalence of millenarian sentiment in East Anglia in 1645 might very well have made communities there receptive to the witch-hunting activities of Matthew Hopkins.[13]

The role that political crises played in preparing the ground for witch-hunting is more subtle than that of famine, disease or religious change. Political crises usually had a greater impact on the ruling élite than the general population, and for that reason

---

8 Monter, *Witchcraft in France and Switzerland*, pp. 77, 86.

9 Midelfort, *Witch-Hunting*, p. 122.

10 Behringer, 'Erhob sich das ganze Land', pp. 141–3. The plague did not always have such an effect. See Midelfort, *Witch-Hunting*, p. 122.

11 Blauert, *Frühe Hexenverfolgungen*, pp. 20–3; Kamber, 'La Chasse', pp. 26–8.

12 John Stearne, *A Confirmation and Discovery of Witchcraft* (London, 1648), p. 60, argues that when the millennium arrived, there would be no witches. See also Trevor-Roper, 'European Witch-Craze', pp. 172–3.

13 Macfarlane, *Witchcraft in Tudor and Stuart England*, pp. 141, 223; W. Lamont, *Godly Rule* (London, 1969), pp. 14, 99.

probably created profound anxieties only within the upper levels of society. Political crises could, moreover, have an immediate negative impact on witch-hunting by disrupting the operation of the judicial machinery. Nevertheless, the experience of political turmoil could create an unease among magistrates that might lead them to begin a witch-hunt, especially in the immediate aftermath of the crisis. In those circumstances witch-hunting would offer the élite an opportunity to suppress what they considered to be a dangerous challenge to the order of society and perhaps even to punish malefactors who might have eluded the arm of the law in the midst of more pressing political change or as the result of judicial paralysis. It was partly for such reasons that large witch-hunts took place in Scotland in 1661–62 after the end of English rule and two years of judicial inactivity; in Lorraine in 1658 after the end of French rule; and at Salem in 1692 after years of constitutional turmoil and judicial uncertainty.[14]

The final factor that played a significant role in preparing people psychologically for witch-hunting was war, which because of its profound and far-reaching effects had an enormous capacity for generating communal anxiety. Here again, however, we must not make unwarranted assumptions. The direct and immediate effect of armed conflict on witch-hunting, just like the effect of the political crises that often accompanied war, was usually negative. The experience of war was so disruptive, the effects so pervasive, that communities where battles were fought or where troops were quartered had little time to be concerned with the activities of maleficent sorcerers or even apostates. In the towns and villages of France, Germany, Switzerland, Austria and the Low Countries witchcraft trials were relatively rare during periods of actual warfare and even during the period of exhaustion that followed. Witch-hunting was for all intents and purposes a peace-time pursuit.[15] Nevertheless, the actual experience of war, which entailed a disruption of social life for years after hostilities had ceased, could contribute to the communal anxiety that was central to the process of witch-hunting. It was no coincidence that a priest at Besançon in 1657 thought witchcraft had reached epidemic proportions 'because the troubles of the late wars had been so great and had caused such disorders in the province'.[16] The same circumstances may explain

---

14 Levack, 'Great Scottish Witch Hunt', pp. 90–5, 107–8; Trevor-Roper, 'European Witch-Craze', p. 160.

15 Monter, *Witchcraft in France and Switzerland*, p. 81; Kamber, 'La Chasse', p. 27; Byloff, *Hexenglaube*, p. 160.

16 Monter, *Witchcraft in France and Switzerland*, p. 81.

why witchcraft prosecutions in Hungary tended to increase a few years after a war or internal uprising had come to an end and after the country had begun to experience its long-term effects.[17] It is also possible to make a fairly clear connection between the long-term effects of war in Poland and the beginning of intense witch-hunting there in the late seventeenth century.[18]

In dealing with the psychological foundations of witch-hunting it is important to note that in most cases no single factor produced a mood that made people eager to pursue witches. Usually a combination of circumstances, such as war, plague and famine or bad harvests, coupled with the promulgation of an official edict against witchcraft, was responsible. There was, moreover, no necessary causal connection between a mood that is conducive to witch-hunting and the actual occurrence of such a hunt. We should not be surprised, therefore, when one combination of factors seems to have 'caused' a witch-hunt in one locality while a virtually identical situation produced not one official prosecution in another. The mood of a community was merely one precondition of witchcraft, and those preconditions simply made witch-hunting possible, not inevitable.

THE TRIGGERS

Witch-hunts did not start spontaneously in those communities that were intellectually, legally and psychologically prepared to experience them. Someone – either a private citizen, a group of villagers, or a magistrate – had to start the ball rolling by accusing or denouncing someone or by citing a person who was rumoured to be a witch. That being the case, we must ask what specific events prompted these initial accusations. In most cases the catalyst was a personal misfortune that a person and his neighbours interpreted as an act of maleficent magic. The sudden death of a child or family member, the contraction of a disease (especially one for which there was no known cause), the loss of a farm animal, sexual impotence or romantic failure, fire or even theft led the victim of such misfortune, in an effort both to explain what had happened and to wreak vengeance upon the alleged malefactors, to attribute the harm to witchcraft and to bring the witch to justice. In some cases, especially in larger hunts, a number of individuals, each seeking satisfaction for his own personal misfortune, brought their complaints to the proper authorities.

17 Klaniczay, 'Hungary', p. 224.
18 Baranowski, *Procesy Czarownic*, p. 178.

Most of the misfortunes that triggered witch-hunts were individual in nature, but occasionally they were communal, and in those cases the initial action against the witches was taken by the magistrates as representatives of the community. Hail storms, which could destroy an entire crop within a few minutes, were probably the most frequent of such communal misfortunes, and in many instances, most notably at Wiesensteig in Germany in 1562, they provided the initial impetus for a round-up of all the local witches.[19] Less frequently fire (which was very difficult to control in early modern times) could lead its victims to think of witchcraft as its source, while in coastal communities storms at sea (which often destroyed life as well as property) could have the same effect. A storm in the North Sea in the spring of 1590 that destroyed one of the ships in the entourage of James VI of Scotland and his new bride, Anne of Denmark, was the first of many events that led to witch-hunts in both kingdoms.[20]

Somewhat surprisingly the plague, which ravaged entire communities during the entire period of the European witch-hunt, did not very often serve as the catalyst of specific witch-hunts. Like many of the other epidemics that affected Europe at this time, the plague did aggravate social tensions and, as mentioned above, it probably contributed to a mood that encouraged witch-hunting, but it did not lead directly to many accusations. This may have been because the disease was known to spread from place to place and was not therefore likely to be the work of local witches. In a few cases, however, individuals were accused of spreading the plague by capturing its essence in an ointment that they smeared on houses. These plague-spreaders were accused of both magic and Devil-worship, and were prosecuted as witches. Plague-spreading panics took place at Geneva in 1530, 1545, 1567–68, 1571 and 1615; at Chambéry in 1577; at Vevey in 1613; and at Milan in 1630.[21]

The process of scapegoating in response to misfortune was probably the most common trigger of European witch-hunts, but it was by no means the only one. Sometimes, for example, individuals deliberately and maliciously brought charges of witchcraft against their antagonists – political rivals, economic competitors, and sometimes even family members with whom they were in conflict – in order to resolve their differences and bring vengeance upon them. At

---

19 Midelfort, *Witch Hunting*, pp. 88–90.

20 See C. Larner, 'James VI and I and Witchcraft', in *The Reign of James VI and I*, ed. A.G.R. Smith (London, 1973), pp. 80–1.

21 Monter, *Witchcraft in France and Switzerland*, pp. 44–7.

other times they actually saw the accused party practise some sort of magical ritual or cast a spell on someone and therefore brought the action to the attention of the authorities.

Although alleged *maleficia* were responsible for precipitating most witch-hunts, accusations of Devil-worship could also provide the stimulus to prosecution. Since it is unlikely that sabbaths ever took place, we do not hear of witch-hunts beginning when unsuspecting travellers chanced upon cannibalistic orgies or saw witches flying to or from such gatherings. Less dramatic meetings of small numbers of women did, however, occasionally start witch-hunts. In Neuchâtel, for example, a woman named Jehanne Berna was arrested for witchcraft after she was seen dancing around a fire with several other women; one assumes that the gathering was thought to be the sabbath.[22] In the county of Essex, in England, the notorious witch-hunt of Matthew Hopkins and John Stearne began when Hopkins concluded that Elizabeth Clarke and other women were gathering at regular assemblies in a home near Hopkins's residence in Manningtree.[23] A charge of diabolism also sparked the great Swedish witch-hunt of 1669. That episode began when a fifteen year-old boy accused a number of other children and a seventy-year-old woman of stealing children for the Devil.

Some witch-hunts began when individuals made free confessions to diabolical activity, either with the coaxing of their confessors or in the context of an investigation for another crime. It appears that some of the earliest witch-hunts occurred when inquisitors who were investigating Waldensian heresy in France and Switzerland came across some women who confessed to riding out at night with Diana. More commonly, some women did actually attempt to make pacts with the Devil, and their free confessions to such arrangements served as prima-facie evidence of witchcraft. In similar fashion the 'dream epidemic' that apparently ran wild in the Basque villages of northern Spain in 1610 provided the original stimulus to the witch-hunt of that year.

One trigger of a number of witch-hunts, demonic possession, deserves special consideration. In a certain sense possession was a personal misfortune, since it entailed fits, skin lesions, and other unusual physical afflictions. On the other hand, possession was by no means simple *maleficium*, since according to demonological theory the Devil actually entered the body of the afflicted person

---

22 Ibid., pp. 92–3.
23 M. Hopkins, *The Discovery of Witches* (London, 1928), p. 50.

rather than acting upon it externally. The affliction, moreover, was often communal, being experienced by a large number of individuals, such as nuns and children. No matter how we wish to classify it, demonic possession did serve as the trigger of some famous witch-hunts in France (at Aix-en-Provence in 1611, Lille in 1613, Loudun in 1634 and Louviers in 1647), and of some smaller hunts in England and Franche-Comté. At Salem in 1692 the afflictions that the girls suffered, which led ultimately to the execution of nineteen witches, were gradually perceived by contemporaries as the signs of demonic possession.

Whenever one deals with the origins of witch-hunts, the question arises whether the prosecutions came from 'above' or 'below', i.e., from the judges and other members of the ruling élite or from the common people. Everyone agrees that in England, where judges could not initiate cases by themselves, the pressure to prosecute came from the witches' neighbours.[24] Justices of the Peace might occasionally encourage people to make accusations, but the nature of the judicial process prevented them from taking the first steps. On the Continent, however, and to a lesser extent in Scotland, judicial authorities could take the initiative, and this has led to the assumption that most witchcraft prosecutions outside England came from above. One historian has suggested that the common people were so tolerant of witchcraft suspects that they had to be prodded by officials into testifying against them.[25] That some magistrates decided on their own initiative to start a witch-hunt – and not simply when they themselves were the witches' alleged victims – cannot be denied. In these cases the judges drafted the charges against the witches and then summoned villagers to court to testify against them. But in most cases the original pressure to prosecute came, just as in England, from the common people.[26] This pressure from below often took a long time to materialize. As a rule, villagers were not eager to take legal action against their neighbours, and did so only after

24 Thomas, *Religion and the Decline of Magic*, pp. 457–8; A. Gregory, 'Witchcraft, Politics and "Good Neighbourhood" in Early Seventeenth-Century Rye', *Past and Present*, 133 (1991): 31–66.

25 Horsley, 'Who were the Witches?', p. 713.

26 C. Baxter, 'Jean Bodin's *De la Démonomanie des Sorciers:* The Logic of Persecution', in S. Anglo (ed.), *The Damned Art*, p. 78; Muchembled, 'Witches of Cambrésis', p. 241; Soman, 'Parlement of Paris', pp. 42–3; Schormann, *Hexenprozesse in Deutschland*, pp. 109–10; Henningsen, *Witches' Advocate*, p. 1; Ankarloo, 'Sweden', pp. 308–9.

all the alternatives, including reconciliation with the witch and the employment of counter-magic, had been exhausted.[27]

Once villagers did decide that the witch should be prosecuted, they would denounce the suspect before a local court or ask the members of the governing body of the village, such as the elders of the church or the local magistrates, to take action against her. These men generally belonged to what we might call the village élite, a social group that lay between the peasantry on the one hand and the aristocracy and the central court justices on the other.[28] Only occasionally would villagers apply pressure directly on the members of that higher group. One such instance occurred in Scotland in 1661, when the tenants of the earl of Haddington threatened to leave his lands in Samuelston if the local witches were not prosecuted. Haddington, an influential nobleman, then petitioned Parliament to delegate a commission to try the malefactors, thus beginning the largest witch-hunt in Scottish history.[29]

The members of the local élite who responded to popular pressure were usually responsible for the arrest and initial interrogation of the accused. These men were often familiar with demonological theory, so it was at this stage of the judicial process that notions of the pact and the sabbath were often introduced.[30] The members of the local élite were also the ones who pricked the witch to see if she had the Devil's mark, and they sometimes applied judicial torture, thereby facilitating the imposition of their demonological notions. In most circumstances, however, these men did not actually try the accused witch. In order to do that it was usually necessary to obtain approval from higher levels of government. In Scotland, for example, the elders in the kirk session often referred the witchcraft cases they heard to the civil magistrate, or they requested that the Privy Council authorize certain men to try the witch locally. Securing the cooperation of higher judicial officials was not always as easy as it may seem. At Mora in Sweden in 1669, the parents of numerous bewitched children, the elders of the parish, and the vicar all put pressure on the local bailiff in order to get him to start legal proceedings against the accused witches when the county sheriff would not visit the area. Later in the hunt the same parties

---

27 Larner, *Witchcraft and Religion*, p. 134; Briggs, *Communities of Belief*, p. 63; Macfarlane, *Witchcraft in Tudor and Stuart England*, p. 103.

28 Briggs, *Communities of Belief*, p. 36; Soman, 'Witch Lynching at Juniville', p. 15.

29 *Register of the Privy Council of Scotland*, 3rd ser., I, pp. 11–12.

30 Briggs, *Communities of Belief*, p. 136.

found it necessary to appeal to the royal government in Stockholm in order to bring the witches to trial.[31]

THE DEVELOPMENT OF HUNTS

Once judicial officials agreed to hear witchcraft cases, they assumed complete control of the witch-hunting process. Judges have been referred to as the gate-keepers of witch-hunts, in that they decided which cases to prosecute and which ones to ignore. They decided which witnesses to call, which persons should be tortured, and which alleged accomplices of the witches should be pursued. In most cases they determined the guilt or innocence of the accused, and they also determined what sentences the witches were to receive. Even when the original impetus to prosecute had come from below, the way in which hunts developed was determined mainly from above. The common people played only a supporting role, by testifying against those implicated in the process and maintaining a popular mood that was conducive to witch-hunting.

Individual prosecutions and small hunts

Once the first suspects were brought to trial, the hunt would develop according to one of three different models. The first, which was by far the most common, involved the prosecution of usually one and not more than three persons. To use the word 'hunt' to describe such a process is in a sense inappropriate, since that term usually connotes the search for, and the prosecution of, a large group of persons who share similar beliefs and personal characteristics.[32] But since even this type of operation involved the search for witches and the attempt to impose fantasies upon innocent persons, it merits classification as a hunt. The main feature of the small hunt is that the search for malefactors is limited to the individuals who were originally accused. It was most common in England, where charges for witchcraft usually had a solid foundation in *maleficia* and where judges could not use torture to obtain the names of accomplices. Throughout Europe, however, the prosecution of individuals for isolated acts of sorcery was not at all uncommon. Even in Germany, which is notorious for its large chain-reaction hunts, there was a

---

31 Ankarloo, 'Sweden', p. 308.

32 On the modern connotations of the word see Larner, *Witchcraft and Religion*, p. 88.

steady stream of individual prosecutions.[33] Most of these operations had the potential for developing into larger hunts, since charges of attending the sabbath could easily have arisen in almost any continental trial, and those charges could in turn have led to a search for accomplices. Very often, however, a chain-reaction hunt of this sort did not develop, perhaps because of judicial preoccupation with other matters or because of the failure of the mood of the community to reach a state of panic. Many continental hunts may have failed to grow because the populace or the authorities were determined only to rid themselves of specific individuals, and once that was achieved, they felt no pressing need to pursue the matter further.

Medium-sized hunts

When authorities were not content to restrict their investigation of witchcraft to those persons who had initially been accused, then witch-hunts that conformed more closely to the stereotype of such operations could develop. One of the forms that such hunts took was that of the medium-sized hunt, a process that claimed somewhere between five and ten victims. William Monter has found that this type of hunt, which he calls a 'small panic', often occurred in French-speaking Switzerland, and other examples can be adduced from Germany and Scotland. The main characteristic of the medium-sized hunt is that torture was employed and a second round of accusations took place but the process did not get out of hand. In some of these hunts, such as the prosecutions that occurred in the county of Neuchâtel in 1583 and in Fribourg in 1634, restraint was achieved through the spare use of torture and the grant of non-capital sentences. Other hunts may have ended after the naming of the first set of accomplices because the supply of stereotypical witches had dried up. Technically, of course, anyone could be a witch, and in some of the larger hunts virtually everyone was vulnerable. But in most communities there was a fairly small number of individuals whom people instinctively suspected of witchcraft. Witches were those people whom 'everybody knew to be witches by common reputation'.[34] When such persons were disposed of, it was necessary to have recourse to less discriminating standards of witchcraft if the hunt was going to continue. In communities where medium-sized hunts occurred, there may not have been a sufficient amount of popular hysteria for the less rigorous standards to be invoked. In

33 Roper, 'Witchcraft and Fantasy', p. 21.
34 Garrett, 'Women and Witches', p. 464.

the final analysis, therefore, the reason for the limited development of the medium-sized hunt might very well have been the absence of full-scale panic among either the judicial authorities or the people in general.

Large hunts

The large witch-hunts of the sixteenth and seventeenth centuries, those that claimed anywhere from ten to hundreds of victims and were characterized by a high degree of panic or hysteria, were the prototypes of the classic 'witch-hunt'. These hunts were most common in Germany, but almost all European countries, including England, Spain and Sweden, experienced at least one such episode.[35] Many of these mass prosecutions were chain-reaction hunts, in which the first witches who were tried gave the names of accomplices, who in turn were arrested, tried, convicted and forced to denounce others. The largest of these hunts took place in Trier, where a total of 306 witches named about 1,500 different accomplices, each accused witch offering an average of twenty names.[36] Other well-known chain-reaction hunts took place at Ellwangen in 1611, Würzburg in 1627–29, Bamberg in 1630, and the Pays de Labourd in Guienne in 1609. The chain reaction was not, however, the only means by which large hunts developed. In some cases a single accuser or group of accusers served as the main source of names throughout the hunt. Demoniacs, such as the afflicted girls at Salem, could do this relatively easily since they, not being guilty of witchcraft themselves, were not executed during the course of the hunt. Even when there was no demonic possession, a small number of accusers could be responsible for the entire progress of the hunt. At Rouen, for example, a group of nine persons provided a total of 525 indictments in 1670.[37] Another variation in the mechanics of the large hunt occurred when a small group of magistrates summoned large numbers of suspects before them on the basis of information they had gathered by various means. When this scenario unfolded, the hunt took the form of a general round-up of witches, very often from a few small villages, rather than a series of accusations that spread gradually from one village to the next.

35 In Bavaria there were fourteen large hunts, each claiming twenty or more lives, between 1586 and 1631. These hunts accounted for more than half of the 929 witchcraft executions in that region. Behringer, *Hexenverfolgung in Bayern*, pp. 65–8.

36 Robbins, *Encyclopedia*, p. 515.

37 Ibid, p. 318.

Our picture of large-scale witch-hunting becomes even more variegated when we realize that many large witch-hunts were in fact composites of a number of small hunts. This was especially true when the defined area of the hunt was very large or when the period during which the hunt took place was very long. In Scotland, for example, we speak of the great witch-hunt of 1661–62, since during those years there were hundreds of accusations, trials and executions throughout the country, especially in the southeastern counties. These prosecutions were not completely divorced from each other. The Privy Council or Parliament approved all of the trials; a solid number of the cases were heard before the same judges; some of the villages hired the same men to search suspects for the Devil's marks; and in a few instances the witches from one village implicated accomplices from another. But for the most part the individual hunts that comprised this larger campaign were discrete operations, separate manifestations of a general, national panic regarding witchcraft. The same could be said about the Swedish hunt of 1669–75 and the English hunt of 1645–46, although in the latter case the travels of Matthew Hopkins and John Stearne to various towns and villages in Essex and Suffolk provided more structural unity than the Scottish hunt possessed. In a curious way the English witch-finding movement of 1645–46 resembled the campaigns that papal inquisitors often conducted on the Continent, moving from town to town to try cases of witchcraft.

Even when officials or witch-hunters remained stationary and heard cases brought before them, large witch-hunts could lack the cohesion that they appear to have had. Not only did judges often hear cases from many different areas within their jurisdiction but they did so over a long period of time. Witch-hunts very often occurred in waves, each rash of trials having its own dynamic. When a witch-hunt spanned a two- or three-year period, marked by intervals when there were no trials at all, it becomes problematic whether there was one large campaign or a succession of smaller operations conducted by the same court or the same judge. A close examination of the witch-hunt that took place in the imperial city of Offenburg during the period 1627–30 reveals the complexity of what may be described as a single large hunt. The campaign began in 1627 as an offshoot of a hunt that took place in the *Langvogtei* of Ortenau, the larger territorial unit in which Offenburg was situated. On the basis of denunciations made by witches in the Ortenau, the members of the Offenburg council began a hunt that took the lives of twelve witches between November 1627 and January 1628. After a respite of five months the council, receiving further information regarding the children of one of the witches executed in January, started a new round of trials that resulted in the execution of seven more witches and the death of another during torture. Then, after another interval of four months the council began a long series of trials that lasted until January 1630 and claimed an additional forty lives. The hunt, in other words, really comprised three distinct operations, each of which had its own dynamic.[38]

Although many large hunts were in fact composites of smaller hunts, the intensity of fears regarding witchcraft provided a unity to all of the trials that occurred in places like Offenburg. Indeed, one of the main characteristics of the large witch-hunt was the prevalence of a mood of profound fear or panic while the hunt was going on. It is this mood that gives substance to the use of the word 'mania' or 'craze' that is used to describe the process of witch-hunting. Appearances suggest that communities involved in witch-hunting sometimes experienced a form of mass hysteria. We must be careful, however, to distinguish this psychic development from the pathological hysteria that groups of demoniacs contracted. Certainly the officials and villagers or townsmen who became panic-stricken by the realization that witches were infesting their neighbourhoods did not manifest the signs of clinical hysteria, which involved paroxysms, lesions and partial paralysis.[39] The hysteria of the witch-hunters was rather one form of what we would call today 'collective obsessional behaviour', a general term that can be applied to various group phenomena ranging from fads or booms to the frenzy of the riot. In the case of witch-hunting it was the product of the general anxiety that served as a precondition of virtually all witch-hunting. Like the terrified Londoners who learned about the Popish Plot in 1678 and the people who experienced the Red Scares of 1919–20 and 1947–54, these villagers and townspeople, learning that more and more of their neighbours and even some of their rulers were being denounced as witches, became terrified – terrified that their closest friends and neighbours were witches, terrified that their communities would be made totally captive of diabolical power, perhaps even terrified that they themselves might be falsely accused. This terror led them to support the trials, to bring suspects to the attention of the proper authorities and even to imagine that they witnessed people flying through the air or attending sabbaths. In the same mood people

---

38 F. Volk, *Hexen in der Langvogtei Ortenau und der Reichsstadt Offenburg* (Lahr, 1882), pp. 58–88; Midelfort, *Witch Hunting*, p. 128.
39 I. Veith, *Hysteria: The History of a Disease* (Chicago, 1965).

who harboured deep feelings of guilt may have even been led to confess freely to acts of witchcraft. There is no question that the 'dream epidemic' in which hundreds of persons admitted that they had attended sabbaths in the Basque country in 1610–11 reflected the hysterical mood that prevailed during that massive witch-hunt. In a similar vein, the depositions of French peasants from Rouen in 1670 that they had seen naked people flying through the air for a period of thirty minutes was stimulated by the diagnosis of an epidemic disease as having been caused by witchcraft.[40]

In all of this we must be careful to distinguish between the mass hysteria of some witch-hunts and the individual psychological problems of some of the participants in these hunts. The occasional sadistic judge or hangman, the compulsive witch-finder, the insane or 'melancholic' witch all manifested abnormal forms of behaviour, but these should not be confused with the general, collective mood or group psychosis with which we are concerned. We must also be careful not to apply a simple label such as the 'witch-craze' or the 'witch-mania' or 'mass delusion' to the entire European witch-hunt. But within the context of specific witch-hunts we can legitimately – although at the same time hypothetically – talk about mass hysteria. Without such collective behaviour the history of European witchcraft would have been a much more restrained affair.[41]

THE END OF WITCH-HUNTS

Witch-hunts usually did not last for very long periods of time. The large witch-hunts often spanned a period of two, three or four years, and occasionally they lasted even longer, but they never went on indefinitely. In most cases, moreover, they ended rather abruptly and their termination usually signalled the end of witch-hunting in that area for many years, sometimes for generations. The end of small and medium-sized hunts does not require detailed analysis. The small hunts were isolated prosecutions that ended when the accused was either executed, given a non-capital sentence or acquitted. The medium-sized hunts came to an end for pretty much the same reasons that they had been restricted in their scope: the tight control that magistrates retained over the process of investigation, the restriction of accusations to stereotypical witches, and the absence of a mood of panic. The end of large hunts, however, is more problematic, for

---

40 Robbins, *Encyclopedia*, p. 317.

41 G. Rosen, 'Psychopathology of the Social Process', *Journal of Health and Human Behavior*, 1 (1960): 200–11.

they had the potential for indefinite extension. The mass hysteria that underlay them, the willingness of authorities to use torture freely and the determination of those same authorities to elicit the names of accomplices meant that the trials could go on and on. Contemporaries were fully aware of the open-ended character of the large hunts. In the German town of Rottenburg, for example, authorities worried that the witch-hunt of 1585 would eliminate all the women in the town. Their fears were not exaggerated; in that very year two villages had been left with only one female inhabitant apiece in the aftermath of witch-hunts.[42] In most cases, however, witch-hunts ended before they took such a heavy toll. Indeed, one of the most perplexing features of the larger witch-hunts is the number of individuals who were implicated by confessing witches but were never tried. In the Scottish witch-hunt of 1661–62, for example, a total of 664 persons were named as witches, but apparently not even half that number were actually prosecuted. At Salem some 162 individuals were accused, but only seventy-six were actually tried and only thirty were convicted. At Trier only a few of the 1,500 witches named by accomplices were ever prosecuted.

The reasons for the suspension of the judicial process in these large hunts are many and varied, and responsibility for the suspension could be attributed either to the officials who conducted the trials, the general populace or officials in the central government. In most cases the hunts ended when some or all of these people came to the conclusion that innocent people were being accused and executed or that the social effects of the hunt were more detrimental than beneficial. In all of these hunts there was a loss of confidence in the process of witch-hunting, and in many cases this was a result of the breakdown of the stereotype of the witch. As mentioned above, the great majority of witches were old, poor women, and the frequency of their prosecution led to the creation of a stereotype of the witch that was accepted both by villagers and members of the élite. In many large witch-hunts, especially in Germany but also in Massachusetts, the stereotype broke down as accusations and implications became more indiscriminate and as motives of political and economic advantage came increasingly into play. In the early stages of most large witch-hunts the victims conformed to the stereotype, but as the hunts progressed a higher percentage of wealthy and powerful individuals, children and males were named.

---

42 Midelfort, *Witch Hunting* p. 91; Lea, *Materials*, III, p. 1075.

At Würzburg in 1629 the chain of accusations led to the naming of numerous children, law students, clerics and eventually the Bishop's chancellor and the Bishop himself. At Trier a similar pattern emerged, while at Bamberg a former burgomaster was named. This breakdown had the effect of arousing suspicions that innocent persons were being accused and of making men aware that the procedure of torturing confessed witches to obtain the names of accomplices could not be trusted. When the accusations reached into very high places the breakdown of the stereotype had the added effect of prompting the implicated officials to put an end to the trials. This is exactly what the Bishop of Würzburg did in 1629, and a similar motive may have been at work when Governor Phips helped to end the Salem trials after his own wife had been accused.[43]

Although the breakdown of the stereotype sowed the seeds of doubt in some large hunts, it did not occur very frequently. In the five major Scottish witch-hunts of the late sixteenth and seventeenth centuries, the great majority of witches conformed fairly closely to the stereotype throughout the period of the trials. The same pattern prevailed in most French and Swiss hunts and even in some German ones. How then did these hunts come to an end? In some cases judges became sceptical as they tried an ever-increasing number of suspects. We must remember that although judicial officials placed great credence in confessions adduced under torture, they did not always conduct careful analyses of all the evidence brought before them. As witch-hunts developed, this evidence became sparser and weaker, if only because specific evidence of *maleficia* was usually not forthcoming when witches were named by their accomplices. This dearth of evidence might help to explain the acquittals that occurred in the midst of even the most intense hunts. Another reason for acquittals was the occasional endurance of torture. Whatever their reasons, acquittals could have a profound effect on the development of the hunts themselves, since they strengthened the conviction that at least some of the accusations were false and possibly even malicious, thereby encouraging greater judicial caution. Acquittals also broke the chain of accusations and may even have contributed to a popular scepticism regarding the trials.

Perhaps the most dramatic end to witch-hunts occurred when conscious fraud or deceit was discovered. The most famous of these was the Pendle Swindle of 1633 at Hoarstones, England. In that episode a young boy, Edmund Robinson, deposed that a woman had taken him to a witches' sabbath where some sixty participants

---

43 Midelfort, 'Domino Theory', pp. 177–88.

were producing meat, butter and milk by pulling on ropes that were attached to the top of a barn. Upon his father's suggestion the boy named a number of witches, seventeen of whom were convicted. Doubts about the guilty verdicts led the justices of the peace to request an investigation by the Privy Council, and during an interrogation conducted by the Bishop of Chester the boy admitted that his story had been fabricated and that the names had been suggested by his father 'for envy, revenge and hope of gain'.[44] Upon this admission all of those who had been convicted were acquitted, and one of the few large witch-hunts in English history came to an abrupt end. A number of smaller English hunts ended in similar fashion, and the suspicion of fraud may even have led to the end of the great witch-hunt conducted by Hopkins and Stearne.[45] In Scotland the large national hunt of 1661–62 collapsed when two witch-hunters, John Kincaid and John Dick, were prosecuted by the Privy Council for fraud and deceit in their work of pricking witches for the Devil's mark.[46]

Occasionally financial considerations were responsible for bringing witch-hunts to an end. The role of private gain in witchcraft trials has probably been exaggerated by historians.[47] There is no question that throughout Europe at this time lawyers and officials welcomed and may have even encouraged business in order to make money, which in most cases came from fees that were either paid directly to lawyers or indirectly to the officials of the court. In criminal cases the confiscation of the guilty party's property often paid these fees and provided additional revenue for the prince. Among the various types of cases that they might have to argue or adjudicate, however, witchcraft cases were probably the least lucrative, if only because the economic status of witches was usually so low. In some cases, however, especially those in which wealthy and powerful people were accused, the chance to profit from witch-hunting contributed to the zeal of the prosecutors. It is perhaps for this reason that in Germany, where confiscation was the accepted procedure in witchcraft cases, and where prosecutions often reached high up the social ladder, the financial motive for prosecutions was most powerful.

Another group that could profit from witchcraft prosecutions were the prickers and finders who offered their services to local

---

44 R. Seth, *Children against Witches* (New York, 1969), pp. 164–9; W. Notestein, *A History of Witchcraft in England* (Washington, 1911), pp. 146–63.

45 Ibid., pp. 140–3; Hopkins, *Discovery of Witches*, pp. 47, 49–62.

46 *Register of the Privy Council of Scotland*, 3rd ser., I, pp. 187, 210.

47 See for example E.P. Currie, 'Crimes without Criminals: Witchcraft and its Control in Renaissance Europe', *Law and Society Review*, 3 (1968): 21–8.

communities to help them to identify witches in their midst. When such financial motives were operative, a reduction of fees resulting either from the general impoverishment of the community or from the reluctance of communities to pay for the services of a witch-hunter could help to bring a hunt to an end. It was reported that the mass witch-trials at Trier in the 1580s and 1590s, which brought considerable wealth to the judicial establishment, came to an end when the population, drained of its resources, could no longer support this costly judicial extravagance and when the fees that officials collected were reduced.[48] Another financial motive for ending witch-hunts, which may have led directly to the general impoverishment reported at Trier, was the cost of keeping suspects in prison. If witches were not able to pay the cost of their maintenance in gaol, then the town or village had to foot the bill until the trial. Sometimes those trials did not take place for weeks or months after arrest. In the case of one Scottish witch in 1661, who languished in prison for eight months at public charge, a local laird petitioned the Privy Council to have her either tried or set at liberty.[49] When one considers the number of suspects who were held in gaol at any one time during large witch-hunts, the burden of prison maintenance becomes a plausible explanation for opposition to the continuation of the hunt.

The responsibility for ending witch-hunts varied from place to place, as did the methods of termination. Sometimes popular pressure, arising from a recognition that innocent persons were being accused, appreciation of the costs of the hunt, or a realization that the witch-hunt was destroying the equilibrium of daily life, served as the main stimulus to ending the affair. In this situation the common people had surprising power. Not only could they refuse to denounce or testify against their neighbours, but they could also express their disapproval by boycotting executions and making protests to the appropriate authorities. In England and Scotland they had the decisive power of returning not-guilty verdicts, a tactic that clearly helped to bring the Scottish hunt of 1661–62 to a close. Finally, the more articulate members of society, especially the clergy, could formulate a critique of the trials, a risky though not unusual tactic. The largest witch-hunt in Scandinavian history ended when a young doctor demonstrated that the entire panic was the result of imagination, insanity or malice.[50]

---

48 Kors and Peters, *Witchcraft in Europe*, p. 217.
49 *Register of the Privy Council of Scotland*, 3rd ser., I, p. 78.
50 Robbins, *Encyclopedia*, p. 350.

The men who had the greatest opportunity to bring witch-hunts to an end were the magistrates and inquisitors. They might have done so because they themselves or their wives had been accused, because they had developed serious doubts about the guilt of many of the accused, or, more practically, because they realized that the hunt was causing popular discontent or social chaos. Whatever their motivation, they had control of the judicial machinery and therefore were capable of terminating the hunt at any stage of the proceedings. They could acquit the witches whose cases were still pending or, more commonly, simply refuse to interrogate those who were implicated by others or any other persons whose names might be brought before them.

When hunts were not terminated by the action of either the general populace or the men entrusted with local judicial power, higher political or judicial authorities often intervened in the process. As we saw in Chapter 3, men who held positions of prominence in the higher levels of government tended to be more restrained, if not more sceptical, in dealing with witchcraft, both because they were usually not involved in the local tension that produced witch-hunts and because they tended to be more committed to the maintenance of official standards of criminal procedure. We also saw that whenever such authorities played a regular role in the prosecution of witches, either as officials of a central court or as circuit judges, witch-hunting was more restrained. It stands to reason, therefore, that the same men might be more disposed than local officials to admit that some large witch-hunts had got out of control and to bring them to an end. Their intervention could take one of two forms: either they could overturn negative witchcraft verdicts on appeal or they could issue edicts that forbade further prosecutions or established more rigid procedures for conducting them.

The effect of appeals in stopping witch-hunts can most readily be observed in the Pendle Swindle discussed above and in a number of French witch-hunts. In France it was customary, and eventually obligatory, for witchcraft verdicts to be appealed to one of the nine *parlements*.[51] Although these *parlements* often confirmed the verdicts of the lower courts, they also did not hesitate to overturn or reduce the sentences of many witches.[52] Even when these reconsiderations

---

51 On the resistance of lower courts to the appeal procedure in witchcraft cases and the insistence on automatic appeal to the Parlement of Paris in 1624 see Mandrou, *Magistrats et sorciers*, pp. 343–8.

52 Soman, 'Parlement of Paris', p. 36.

did not bring about an abrupt end of one of these hunts, they certainly helped to reduce their intensity and may have even encouraged the judges of the lower courts to proceed more cautiously in handling witchcraft cases in the future. In the *Parlement* of Paris the sceptical attitude of the jurists was so influential that they not only interrupted a series of small hunts but actually contributed to a long-term decline in all witchcraft prosecutions.[53]

The promulgation of edicts or the establishment of tougher standards of judicial interrogation could have a much more dramatic and sudden impact on witch-hunts. One example of this effect comes from Scotland in 1597, when the country was engaged in one of its largest national hunts. In some respects this hunt was the continuation of the one that had taken place in 1591–92, since at that time and in the following years the Privy Council had issued standing commissions to local authorities to try witches. In some communities, such as Aberdeen, an almost uncontrolled epidemic of witch-hunting had resulted. Once it became aware of the fact that innocent persons had been executed in this panic, the Privy Council recalled all of the standing commissions and inaugurated a policy of granting individual commissions upon application to the Privy Council. The policy had the immediate effect of terminating the hunt of 1597, although it still had the potential (which was later realized) of allowing witch-hunts to occur with governmental support.[54]

A second example of the effects of edicts on witch-hunting comes from Spain, where the supreme council of the Inquisition played a key role in ending the Basque hunt of 1610–14. The turning point in that hunt came when Salazar, the inquisitor at Logroño, investigated the thousands of confessions that had been made and concluded that no act of witchcraft had ever taken place. Salazar's reconsideration of the evidence in this hunt is a good example of the loss of confidence that prosecuting judges themselves often experienced, but his investigation was not decisive in ending the hunt, since any action on the basis of his conclusions had to come from Madrid. After a long delay Madrid acted, adopting Salazar's recommendations for a set of new, stricter guidelines for the prosecution of witches. This action, like that of the *Parlement* of Paris, not only ended the great Basque hunt but had the added effect of greatly reducing the intensity of witch-hunting in Spain.[55]

53 Mandrou, *Magistrats et sorciers*, pp. 313–63.
54 Larner, *Enemies of God*, pp. 71–2.
55 Henningsen, *Witches' Advocate*, pp. 357–93.

A third example comes from France, where in 1669–70 a very large hunt took place in Normandy. Unlike the *Parlement* of Paris, the *Parlement* of Normandy at Rouen had confirmed the first twelve death sentences and was still to consider an additional twenty-four when the families of the twelve convicted witches appealed directly to King Louis XIV for a pardon. Partially motivated by a determination to curb regional judicial autonomy, Louis issued the pardon, and despite subsequent pleas from the officials at Rouen, he refused to rescind his decree. Twelve years later, in fact, Louis took a more decisive action by issuing an edict banning all witchcraft cases in France. Like the other cases discussed, therefore, the action of Louis had an impact not only on the particular hunt at Rouen but on the entire process of witch-hunting in France.[56]

On the basis of all this we may draw a number of simple if not self-evident conclusions. First, witch-hunts were highly contingent operations. Their beginning, development and continuation depended on a number of variables and therefore they could be limited or terminated – sometimes very abruptly – by any one of many factors. Second, witch-hunts were enormously complex historical phenomena, involving the interaction of intellectual, legal, social and psychological trends. Third, witch-hunts varied greatly in their size and dynamics, so much so that we really cannot speak of a typical witch-hunt. Nevertheless, witch-hunts possessed enough common features that a stereotype has in fact emerged, and that stereotype has been used to define various campaigns against deviants in the modern world. All witch-hunts, then and now, involve the pursuit of a secret enemy of society, an assumption that this enemy was not alone but part of a broader movement (if not an actual conspiracy), and the use of extraordinary legal measures to uncover what is not only a secret but also an ideological or religious crime. All witch-hunts, therefore, involve a high degree of judicial and communal anxiety, and it is this mood that both justifies the exceptional legal procedures and reinforces the fear that accomplices or other malefactors lie undiscovered. When, therefore, in the modern world various courts, commissions or investigatory panels conduct open-ended inquiries into allegedly subversive political, ideological or religious movements on the assumption that such an investigation will reveal the names and activities of the enemies of society, we are witnessing a phenomenon that bears a striking resemblance to the hundreds of witch-hunts that took place in early modern Europe.

56 Mandrou, *Magistrats et sorciers*, pp. 425–86.

7 THE CHRONOLOGY AND GEOGRAPHY OF WITCH-HUNTING

One of the most difficult tasks facing historians of European witch-craft is to account for the variations in the intensity of witch-hunting at different times and places. Why, for example, did more European prosecutions take place between 1580 and 1630 than between 1530 and 1580? And why was witch-hunting so much more intense in Germany than in Spain, or in Scotland than in England? To answer such questions we must pursue two separate lines of enquiry. On the one hand we must establish the general chronological patterns of witch-hunting throughout Europe, suggesting various reasons for the waxing and waning of prosecutions over the 300-year period from 1450 to 1750. Then we must survey the history of witchcraft prosecutions in the various states and regions of Europe, an enterprise that will also take into account chronological changes within those particular areas. Both investigations will provide further illustration of the complexity and the diversity of the general phenomenon with which we are concerned.

CHRONOLOGICAL PATTERNS

Prior to 1430 it is difficult to refer to prosecutions for witchcraft in the full sense of the word, since the cumulative concept of witchcraft was still in a process of formation. The cases for which we have records during these years are either for simple *maleficium* or for ritual magic. With these reservations in mind we can nonetheless detect some significant chronological patterns in these prosecutions. Richard Kieckhefer has divided the period from 1300 to 1435 into three components, the first of which, from 1300 to 1330, was characterized mainly by the trial of political sorcerers. From 1330 to 1375 the trial of politically related cases virtually ceased, but there were a substantial number of sorcery cases. Whether these were for simple *maleficium* or for ritual magic is difficult to determine, but in either case the most noteworthy feature of the trials is the absence of charges of diabolism. During the third period, from 1375 to 1435, not only did the number of prosecutions increase but charges of diabolism became more common, mainly in Italy. This development, which was facilitated by the adoption of inquisitorial procedure in local courts, reflected the gradual assimilation of charges of diabolism to those of sorcery.[1] Beginning in 1435 the history of European witchcraft prosecutions entered a new and radically different phase. Not only did trials for sorcery increase in number but charges of diabolism were more and more frequently grafted on to them, and witch-hunting began to assume the various characteristics that we have described in this book. The period from 1435 to 1500, which is the last with which Kieckhefer is concerned, foreshadowed the mass hunts of the late sixteenth and seventeenth centuries. It was during this period, moreover, that a large number of witchcraft treatises appeared, a development that both reflected and stimulated the increase in the number of prosecutions. For all intents and purposes, these fifteenth-century trials denote the beginning of the European witch-hunt.[2]

It is at this point that the history of European witch-hunting begins to follow a somewhat surprising course. Instead of slowly gathering strength and leading into the large panics of the late sixteenth and early seventeenth centuries, the number of trials levelled off during the first half of the sixteenth century and in certain areas actually declined.[3] The decline did not escape the notice of contemporaries. Martin Luther, writing in 1516, claimed that although there had been many witches and sorcerers in his youth, they were 'not so commonly heard of' anymore.[4] As might be expected, there were some areas where Luther might have heard much more about witches during these years. There were a number of trials in the Basque country between 1507 and 1539; in Catalonia in 1549; in the diocese of Como and in other parts of northern Italy in the 1510s and 1520s; in the northern parts of Languedoc between 1519 and 1530; and in Luxembourg, Namur, Douai and other parts of the Low

---

1 Kieckhefer, *European Witch Trials*, pp. 10–26.

2 For a detailed treatment of these fifteenth-century trials in Switzerland and a discussion of some of the treatises see Blauert, *Frühe Hexenverfolgungen*.

3 Compare the numbers of trials and executions for 1450–1500 and 1500–50 in Hansen, *Quellen*, pp. 68–262; in M. Foucault, *Les Procès de sorcellerie dans l'ancienne France devant les jurisdictions séculières* (Paris, 1907), pp. 297–306; and in Midelfort, *Witch-Hunting*, pp. 201–2.

4 Kors and Peters, *Witchcraft in Europe*, p. 201.

Countries throughout the first half of the sixteenth century.[5] There also were occasional prosecutions in places like Nuremberg,[6] but it is difficult to avoid the conclusion that the early sixteenth century was a period of relative tranquillity as far as witchcraft was concerned.[7]

The reduction in the intensity of witch-hunting during the first half of the sixteenth century was reflected in, and to some extent even caused by, an interruption in the publication of witchcraft treatises and manuals. The *Malleus Maleficarum*, for example, while enormously popular between 1486 and 1520 and again between 1580 and 1650, was not reprinted at all between 1521 and 1576. In similar fashion, none of the other fifteenth-century witchcraft treatises found a market during these years. And after the publication of Grillandus's *Tractatus de Hereticis et Sortilegiis* in 1524 there was very little written in support of witch-hunting until the 1570s. In other words, if we take the production of witchcraft literature as a gauge of the intensity of witch-hunting, there was definitely an early sixteenth-century gap, lagging a little behind the actual reduction in the number of trials. Instead of one continuous European witch-hunt, there were really two separate campaigns: an early, geographically limited assault in the late fifteenth century and a much more intense and widespread hunt in the late sixteenth and seventeenth centuries.

The lull in witch-hunting during the early sixteenth century was caused in part by the combined effects of learned scepticism and the initial shock of the Reformation. This period witnessed the spread of Renaissance humanism throughout Europe, and although the humanists failed to undermine the cumulative concept of witchcraft, they did attack parts of it as well as the scholastic mentality that proved receptive to it. For a brief period of time the critiques of witch-beliefs and prosecutions that one finds in the writings of men like Erasmus, Alciati, Pomponazzi and Agrippa may have shaken the resolve of various authorities to pursue witches in great numbers.[8]

---

5 H. Kamen, *Inquisition and Society in Spain in the Sixteenth and Seventeenth Centuries* (Bloomington, 1985), pp. 210–12; Monter, *Frontiers of Heresy*, pp. 255–67; G. Bonomo, *Caccia alle Streghe* (Palermo, 1959), p. 143; Lea, *Materials*, III, pp. 1112–13; Le Roy Ladurie, *Paysans de Languedoc*, p. 408. J. Delumeau, *Catholicism between Luther and Voltaire: A New View of the Counter-Reformation* (London, 1977), pp. 170–1.

6 H.H. Kunstmann, *Zauberwahn und Hexenprozess in der Reichsstadt Nürnberg* (Nuremberg, 1970), pp. 39–73.

7 Trevor-Roper, 'European Witch-Craze', p. 136.

8 Evans, *Habsburg Monarchy*, p. 402, attributes the absence of Austrian witch prosecutions at this time to 'an atmosphere of Humanism, tolerance and comparative urbanity'.

Their insistence that magic could be performed naturally, without the aid of demons, and that witches were harmless creatures victimized by delusion had at least the effect of raising doubts about the practice of the crime. At the same time there developed in Germany, especially in the work of the preacher Martin Plantsch of Tübingen, a belief that God was directly responsible for many of the natural disasters like hail storms that were often attributed to witchcraft.[9] This early sixteenth-century scepticism was articulated most clearly by the tolerant humanistic physician, Johann Weyer.

The role that the Protestant Reformation played in the early sixteenth-century reduction of witchcraft prosecutions is more complex and problematic. There is little doubt that the combined efforts of the Protestant and Catholic Reformations did much to encourage witchcraft prosecutions in the late sixteenth and seventeenth centuries. During the early years of the Reformation, however, the disintegration of medieval Christianity and the intense controversy surrounding that process may have served to distract European élites from the task of witch-hunting, not unlike the way in which the conduct of physical warfare could prevent witch-hunts from taking place. More specifically, the Protestant rejection of Roman Catholicism naturally led to a desire on the part of reformers to formulate their own theories of witchcraft rather than to rely on the work of fifteenth-century Catholic demonologists and inquisitors. The Protestant theory that eventually emerged was in fact very similar and in many respects indistinguishable from its Catholic ancestor, but the process of formulating a nominally Protestant theory did take time. At the very least the ostensible rejection of Catholic witchcraft theory contributed to a decline in the demand for the older, fifteenth-century treatises. Finally, and most important, the Protestant rejection of the Inquisition, its drastic overhaul of all ecclesiastical jurisdiction and its transfer of much ecclesiastical jurisdiction from the ecclesiastical to the secular courts involved extensive alterations in the judicial machinery that was used to prosecute witches. Even within Catholic areas the assumption of secular jurisdiction over witchcraft required both the passage of specific legislation to facilitate it and the acceptance by secular magistrates of the necessity to use it.

During the 1550s, 1560s and 1570s there were many signs that Europe was poised on the threshold of a new outbreak of witch-hunting, one that was much more intense and widespread than the initial assault of the late fifteenth century. During those decades there

9 Oberman, *Masters of the Reformation*, pp. 158–83.

were few mass panics, but there was a notable increase in the number of individual trials and small hunts. During this time, moreover, a number of witchcraft laws were passed in England, Scotland and the German territories. Even more significantly, theologians, lawyers and other intellectuals overcame their doubts regarding witchcraft during these decades, resulting finally in the refutation of Weyer by Thomas Erastus and Jean Bodin.[10] The resumption of the printing of the *Malleus Maleficarum* as well as the initial publication of some fifteenth-century treatises that had survived only in manuscript (such as Nicholas Jacquier's *Flagellum haereticorum fascinariorum*) served notice that the period of scepticism had passed, while waiting in the wings were a whole new corps of witchcraft writers like Boguet, de Lancre, Guazzo and Del Rio, who would use the evidence of late sixteenth-century trials to confirm the reality of witchcraft, increase the fear of it, and provide guidance for its effective prosecution.

The revival of witchcraft prosecutions and their unprecedented intensification in the late sixteenth century reflected not only the resolution of learned doubt and the settlement of jurisdictional uncertainty but also the impact of both the Protestant and Catholic Reformations on the lives of thousands of Europeans. By this time the Bible, with its literal death sentence for witches, was being widely circulated in the vernacular; preachers had heightened people's awareness of the immediacy of Satan; reformers had declared war on magic in all its forms; and the process of Christianization had helped to cultivate the feelings of both moral superiority and guilt that played such an important part in witch-hunting. To make matters worse the conflict between Protestantism and Catholicism on the one hand and between various forms of Protestantism on the other began to reach its peak, a development that reinforced a fear of the Devil and a hostility towards witchcraft.[11]

A final and perhaps decisive factor in the intensification of witch-hunting in the late sixteenth century was the onset of one of the most economically volatile and politically unstable hundred-year periods of European history. During the years from 1550 to 1650 Europe experienced continued inflation, a transition to commercial agriculture, a series of famines (the worst being in the 1590s), a number of depressions in trade, and a process that has been

---

10 Monter, *European Witchcraft*, pp. 55–71. For the disappearance of scepticism in Luxembourg see Dupont-Bouchat, 'Répression', p. 87.

11 Trevor-Roper, 'European Witch-Craze', pp. 137–40.

described as a crisis of production.[12] Political turmoil took the form of a series of provincial revolts, civil wars, religious wars and even national revolutions. In many parts of Europe, moreover, there were serious epidemics of the plague and of other diseases on a scale that had been unknown to the early sixteenth century. To some extent these developments aggravated the personal conflicts that often found expression in witchcraft accusations. Their main effect, however, was to foster a mood of anxiety that encouraged the rise of witch-hunting.

Although the 1550s, 1560s and 1570s witnessed an increase in the number of prosecutions, it was not until the 1580s and 1590s that Europe entered the period of mass trials and large hunts, although these did not begin in some countries until a few decades later. Without complete statistics it is difficult to determine which decade between 1580 and 1650 was the time of the most intense witch-hunting. The 1580s were especially bad in Switzerland and the Low Countries; the 1590s in France, the Low Countries and Scotland; the 1600s in the Jura region and in many German states; the 1610s in Spain; and the 1620s and 1630s in Germany. In terms of sheer numbers, the years from 1610 to 1630, which witnessed hundreds of executions in places like Würzburg, Bamberg and Ellwangen, were probably the worst.

The period from 1580 to 1650 was certainly the height of the European witch-hunt. The entire episode did not end for another hundred years, but even in the midst of the peak period there were signs that the process would soon begin to work itself out. In Spain the turning point came during the 1610s and in France during the 1620s, while the mass trials in Germany, especially those between 1627 and 1632, generated a crisis of confidence that brought about dramatic reductions in the intensity of prosecutions.[13] England had its largest hunt in the 1640s, Scotland in the 1660s and Sweden and Finland in the late 1660s and early 1670s, but after these traumas all of these countries experienced dramatic reductions in witch-hunting. By 1675 the only countries that had not yet borne the full brunt of witch-hunting were Austria, Hungary, Transylvania, Poland and New England.[14] For most of Europe, the period from 1675 to 1750 was a

---

12 See E. Hobsbawm, 'The Crisis of the Seventeenth Century', in *Crisis in Europe, 1560–1660*, ed. T. Aston (New York, 1967), pp. 5–62.

13 See Midelfort, *Witch-Hunting*, pp. 121–63.

14 Byloff, *Hexenglaube*, p. 160; Evans, *Habsburg Monarchy*, pp. 404–5. Baranowski, *Procesy Czarownic*, p. 179.

time of contraction in the prosecution of witches, and those trials that did take place usually involved only one or two defendants.

GEOGRAPHICAL PATTERNS

Any attempt to establish the broad chronological patterns of European witch-hunting is complicated by regional variations. Some clear patterns are evident, but witch-hunting began, peaked and declined at different times and in different places. To make matters even more complex, the sum total of prosecutions, convictions and executions varied greatly in the different states and regions of Europe. A full study of these regional patterns, broken down by individual provinces, counties and towns would be impossible to undertake in a study of this nature. We can, however, establish some of the broader geographical patterns. Choosing the most appropriate geographical units for such comparison presents some difficulty. If we were to use the political boundaries of sovereign states we would have to deal separately with each of the individual states of Germany and Italy and with the various kingdoms of Spain, and we would also have to take into account the changes in sovereignty that occurred in many European areas during the early modern period.

If we use the criterion of language, we would be unable to discuss Switzerland or, for that matter Scotland, as distinct units. Medium-sized geographical regions are perhaps the most sensible units of analysis, and in this category we have some very fine studies by Midelfort on southwestern Germany, Schormann on northwestern Germany, Behringer on Bavaria, Muchembled and Dupont-Bouchat on the Low Countries, Monter on the Jura region, and Demos on New England. It is often difficult, however, to find other regions with which these regions can be conveniently and legitimately compared, and even when such areas can be defined, there is often not sufficient data available to make meaningful comparisons. For the purposes of this study we shall discuss five very large areas of Europe: (1) western and west-central Europe: Germany, France, Switzerland and the Low Countries; (2) the British Isles and Britain's overseas possessions: England, Scotland, Ireland and colonial America; (3) Scandinavia: Denmark, Norway, Sweden and Finland; (4) east-central and eastern Europe: Poland, Hungary, Transylvania and Russia; and (5) southern Europe: Italy, the Iberian peninsula and the Spanish and Portuguese overseas empires. We shall exclude the area effectively controlled by the Ottoman Empire, with the exception of the relatively autonomous provinces of Moldavia and Wallachia, since no witchcraft prosecutions occurred in that area. Within each of these large areas there were some pronounced regional and national differences with regard to witch-hunting. There were, for example, significant differences between France and Germany, England and Scotland, Norway and Sweden, Poland and Russia, and Spain and Italy. But these large geographical zones, in addition to being fairly cohesive geographically, exhibit enough similarities regarding witch-hunting to make the broader comparisons worthwhile. These similarities are rooted in various religious, legal and political characteristics that the countries in these large zones shared.

Western and west-central Europe

The overwhelming majority of witchcraft prosecutions – perhaps as many as 75 per cent – occurred in Germany, France, Switzerland and the Low Countries, an area which comprised roughly one-half of the entire population of Europe. Not surprisingly, this was also the area where most large hunts and panics took place, and it is mainly because of these panics that the total number of prosecutions and executions was disproportionately high. During the early years of the hunt most prosecutions took place in France, especially in those areas in the eastern part of the country which bordered on Swiss and Burgundian lands. By the late sixteenth century, however, when the hunt had entered its most intense stage, Germany had become the centre of prosecutions. Trials continued in France, especially in the southern borderlands, and there were a number of urban cases of demonic possession that led to witchcraft prosecutions. But the largest panics of the late sixteenth and seventeenth centuries took place in German-speaking lands.

More than half of the territory in the western and west-central zone lay within the Holy Roman Empire. In 1559 the Empire extended so far in the west and the south that it included all of the Netherlands and Franche Comté (which were under Spanish control), the Swiss Confederation, and even parts of northern Italy, while to the east it embraced Bohemia, Austria and Silesia. By 1648 its boundaries had shrunk considerably, as both the northern provinces of the Netherlands and the Swiss Confederation had established their identity as sovereign states, while the duchies of Savoy, Milan, Genoa and Tuscany were no longer included within the Empire. The shifting boundaries of the Empire make it difficult even to attempt any sort of estimate of the total number of witch-trials held there, but it is not unreasonable to assert that the number was significantly greater than for all other parts of Europe combined.[15] If we restrict ourselves to German-speaking lands within the Empire, the number of prosecutions was at least 30,000 and possibly three times that figure.[16]

The political weakness of the Empire may have been the single most important reason for the high concentration of witchcraft trials in this part of Europe. The Empire was a very loose confederation of numerous small kingdoms, principalities, duchies and territories which acted either as sovereign or near-sovereign states. Some of these territories, such as the Spanish Netherlands, were possessions of foreign rulers. Others were dependencies of larger units within the Empire, such as Montbéliard, which was technically under the sovereignty of the Duke of Württemberg. Still others were ecclesiastical territories under the control of a prince-bishop or abbot. There were, moreover, a number of imperial cities which, while having a direct relationship to the imperial structure, operated with relative autonomy. The judicial effect of all this political diversity and decentralization was to give virtual judicial autonomy to relatively small political units. The Empire itself provided very little legal unity and exercised very little judicial control over the activities of the various tribunals that heard witchcraft cases. It supplied a legal code, the *Carolina* of 1532, for the entire Empire, but it did not provide effective mechanisms for enforcing it. There were no itinerant imperial judges to ensure that the code was upheld and no procedure for regular appeals to the imperial supreme court at Speyer. Even the larger political units within the Empire, being either weak patrimonial estates or themselves confederations of smaller entities, often failed to exercise effective judicial control over the various courts within their territories. In most cases, therefore, the trial of witches in Germany was entrusted to courts which exercised jurisdiction over a relatively small geographical area.

The prevailing pattern of jurisdictional particularism in Germany meant that witch-hunting could easily go unchecked. It would be an exaggeration to claim that this situation gave every lord, parson or magistrate the freedom to 'burn to his heart's content', but German judges did have a latitude in handling witchcraft cases

---

15 Monter, 'The Pedestal and the Stake', p. 130, claims that more than one half of the executions took place there.

16 See Schormann, *Hexenprozesse in Deutschland*, p. 71. Behringer, 'Erhob sich das ganze Land', estimates 20,000 executions for all of Germany.

that zealous witch-hunters in other parts of Europe would certainly have envied.[17] One of the most striking examples of this type of jurisdictional independence was the *Fürstpropstei* of Ellwangen, a fairly small Catholic territory in southwestern Germany which was almost completely independent of all outside political and ecclesiastical control and which never permitted appeals to higher courts. Not surprisingly, Ellwangen was the location of one of the most severe witch-hunts in German history, an operation that took the lives of almost 400 individuals between 1611 and 1618.[18]

The distribution of witchcraft prosecutions within the Empire provides additional support for the thesis that the size of German jurisdictional units had a great deal to do with the intensity of witch-hunting. Without oversimplifying an immensely complex situation, we can divide Germany into two regions, one of which experienced much more intense witch-hunting than the other. The lands that exercised relative restraint for the most part lay to the north and to the east, the one notable exception to this rule being the northeastern duchy of Mecklenburg, which was a particularly black spot in the history of German witchcraft. The main centres for witch-hunting, however, lay to the south and to the west, a large area that included Würzburg, Bamberg, Eichstätt, Württemberg and Ellwangen, to name only a few sites of famous witch-hunts. As Gerhard Schormann has shown, there are a number of differences between these two regions, but one of the most significant is that the northern and eastern areas consisted of much larger, less fragmented political units than in the south and the west.[19] In keeping with this thesis Schormann classifies the large southeastern principality of Bavaria with the northern and eastern lands, for it executed a relatively small number of witches for a political unit of its size.[20] If we include the even larger countries

---

17 Lea, *Materials*, III, p. 1231.

18 Midelfort, *Witch-Hunting*, pp. 98–100.

19 Schormann, *Hexenprozesse in Deutschland*, pp. 65–6. The topography of the two regions is also different. The north and east are mainly lowlands, whereas the south and west are characterized by medium altitude mountains.

20 Behringer, *Hexenverfolgung in Bayern*, p. 69, estimates there were 1,000–1,500 executions in the entire region of southeastern Germany. Within the old duchy of Bavaria (after 1623 a principality and then an electorate) there were perhaps only about 300 executions. Outside the principality, the region was characterized by extensive political fragmentation. These smaller jurisdictions played a disproportionately large role in the panic of 1590. See pp. 139–40. For comparisons between the entire southeastern region and other parts of Germany see Behringer, 'Erhob sich das ganze Land', pp. 163–5.

of Austria and Bohemia (both of which were in the Empire) in this scheme, the relationship between the size of autonomous political units and the intensity of witch-hunting becomes even clearer. The total number of executions in Austria was probably about 900 and in Bohemia about 1,000. The great majority of these prosecutions took place in the late seventeenth and eighteenth centuries, somewhat later than the bulk of German prosecutions.[21]

Although local German courts usually did not have to deal with appeals to imperial tribunals or with supervision by imperial judicial authorities, they were required to consult with the universities in witchcraft cases. This requirement, which was included in Article 109 of the *Carolina*, was intended to help local judges deal with the complexities of criminal procedure in an area of the law with which they were often unfamiliar. Before proceeding with torture and before sentencing they would send reports to the law faculty of the neighbouring university (there were twenty-three within the Empire by the early seventeenth century) to request advice. Instead of leading to greater restraint and caution in witchcraft prosecutions, such as often resulted from the intervention of central authorities, this practice usually had the opposite effect. Indeed, since the universities were the centres for the development and dissemination of demonological theory, consultation with learned jurists helped to introduce diabolical ideas to local magistrates whose beliefs were sometimes no different from those of simple peasants.[22] In this case, therefore, local determination to eliminate witchcraft was strengthened rather than weakened by the intervention of 'higher' judicial authorities.

Once we leave the Holy Roman Empire we can still witness the importance of jurisdictional factors in determining the intensity of witch-hunting within the 'heartland' of witchcraft. In Switzerland, where it has been estimated that as many as 10,000 witches were executed[23] the picture is extremely complex, since the Confederation

21 Behringer, *Hexenverfolgung in Bayern*, p. 414; Evans, *Habsburg Monarchy*, pp. 402–17. Byloff, *Hexenglaube*, pp. 159–60, estimates that 1,700 individuals were accused in Austria but admits that the number may have been as high as 5,000.

22 See Midelfort, 'Heartland of the Witchcraze', p. 30; Lea, *Materials*, III, pp. 1229, 1246, 1251; Schormann, *Hexenprozesse in Nordwestdeutschland*, pp. 158–9; S. Lorenz, *Aktenversendung und Hexenprozess: Dargestellt am Beispiel der Juristenfakultäten Rostock und Greifswald (1570/82–1630)*, 2 vols (Frankfurt, 1982–83).

23 The figures of 8,888 accusations and 5,417 executions in Bader, *Hexenprozesse in der Schweiz*, pp. 211ff, are definitely too low. See Behringer, 'Erhob sich das ganze Land', pp. 162–3.

was religiously, culturally and linguistically pluralistic. The cantons were also jurisdictionally autonomous, a situation which not only encouraged a diversity in witch-hunting patterns but also made uncontrolled witch-hunting possible. The severity of Swiss witch-hunting is best illustrated in the Pays de Vaud, where more than 90 per cent of those tried for witchcraft were executed and where the total number of victims exceeded 3,000. On the other hand Geneva, while experiencing a few severe plague-spreading panics from time to time, had a very mild record of witch persecutions.[24]

As we move north from Switzerland we encounter a whole string of territories which, while technically within the Empire, were virtually autonomous, such as Franche Comté, Lorraine and the Low Countries. In all of these areas witch-hunting was encouraged by *de facto* jurisdictional independence, although in the case of the Spanish possessions it was aggravated by the attempts of royal agents to define witchcraft as a crime and encourage its prosecution. In these areas there was in fact a lethal combination of central and local involvement in witch-hunting, with the King of Spain, the Holy Roman Emperor or the Archduke of Burgundy providing the legislation and sometimes the initial inspiration to witch-hunting and the small duchies or states possessing the freedom to proceed as they wished.[25] As might be expected, prosecutions for witchcraft took a heavy toll in these small territories. In Lorraine, where Nicolas Rémy sent more than 800 witches to their deaths between 1586 and 1595 and more than 2,000 during his entire career, travellers could see 'thousands and thousands of the stakes to which witches are bound'.[26] Of the 3,000 individuals tried for witchcraft in Lorraine between 1580 and 1630, about 90 per cent were convicted.[27] In Luxembourg there were 358 executions between 1509 and 1687 and in the other parts of the Spanish Netherlands many more.[28]

24 Monter, *Ritual, Myth and Magic*, p. 47.

25 For the efforts of Philip II and the Council of Luxembourg to introduce new legal procedures and to encourage general inquisitions for witchcraft see Dupont-Bouchat, 'Répression', pp. 86–99.

26 Boguet, *Examen of Witches*, p. xxxiii; Rémy, *Demonolatry*, p. 56, refers to no fewer than 800 executions and 'nearly as many more' who have fled or endured torture. For the estimate of 2,000–3,000 total executions, see C. Pfister, 'Nicolas Rémy et la sorcellerie en Lorraine la fin du XVI siècle', *Revue historique*, 93 (1907): 239.

27 R. Briggs, 'Witchcraft and Popular Mentality in Lorraine, 1580–1630', in *Occult and Scientific Mentalities in the Renaissance*, ed. Brian Vickers (Cambridge, 1984), p. 338.

The only political units in this part of Europe that did not conform to this general pattern of intense prosecution were the Northern Netherlands. In this region, later known as the Republic of the United Provinces, which had more than one million inhabitants, fewer than 150 witches were executed. Executions for witchcraft also ended earlier in this region than in any other part of Europe. The Netherlands did experience a few large hunts in the provinces of Groningen, Utrecht and North Brabant, but none of these areas executed as many witches as the region of Limburg, which at that time had not yet been incorporated into the country.[29]

It is unlikely that jurisdictional factors, which account for the intense persecutions in so many parts of Germany, can be used to explain the pattern in the Netherlands. The entire judicial system was highly decentralized – a situation which elsewhere often facilitated prosecutions – and the degree of central control within each province varied widely.[30] It is noteworthy, however, that in the province of Friesland, where justice was centralized, there were virtually no prosecutions, while in the province of Groningen, where local courts were given considerable freedom of action, two fairly large witch-hunts took place in the sixteenth century.[31]

The main explanation for the tameness of Dutch witch-hunting appears to be more ideological than judicial. Although Dutch judges had all the procedural tools for conducting massive witch-hunts, including the right to use torture, they never believed that witches were engaged in the activities described in the demonological literature. The cumulative concept of witchcraft developed slowly in the Netherlands, and even when it finally appeared, it never found fertile ground.[32] Magistrates accepted the reality of the pact with the Devil, but they never subscribed to the notion of a vast diabolical conspiracy. Without that frightening belief, they were more likely

28 Dupont-Bouchat, 'Répression', p. 127
29 M. Gijswijt-Hofstra, 'Six Centuries of Witchcraft in the Netherlands', in *Witchcraft in the Netherlands: From the Fourteenth to the Twentieth Century*, ed. M. Gijswijt-Hofstra and W. Frijhoff (Rotterdam, 1991), pp. 25–30.
30 A.F. Soman, 'Decriminalizing Witchcraft: Does the French Experience Furnish a European Model?', *Criminal Justice History*, 10 (1989): 17, sees the Netherlands, where a decentralized judiciary achieved a very early decline of witch-hunting, as an exception to the rule that prevailed in most European jurisdictions.
31 Gijswijt-Hofstra, 'Six Centuries', pp. 31–2.
32 M. Gielis, 'The Netherlandic Theologians' Views of Witchcraft and the Devil's Pact', in *Witchcraft in the Netherlands*, pp. 37–52.

to respect the rules for judicial caution that were readily available to them.

In accounting for the weakness of Dutch witch-hunting, two other possible explanations deserve consideration. The first was the intense preoccupation of the country with the struggle for independence from Spain, a conflict which was all-consuming between 1568 and 1609 and not formally resolved until 1648. As mentioned above, witchcraft prosecutions did not generally occur during periods of war or domestic political crisis, and in this case the conflict with Spain covered the entire period of witch-hunting. The second explanation was the reluctance of either Catholic or Protestant ecclesiastical authorities to engage in campaigns against magic and superstition. Those same authorities were also reluctant to assist secular authorities in the detection and prosecution of witches.

Turning finally to France, the question arises whether political and jurisdictional factors played as much of a role in determining the intensity of witch-hunting as in the Empire. The overall pattern of witchcraft prosecutions, especially after secular courts assumed the main burden of prosecution in the sixteenth century, suggests that they did. The areas within France that were most heavily affected by witchcraft were situated on the frontiers of the kingdom: the north, the east, Languedoc, the southwest, and (belatedly) Normandy. All of these areas were resistant to the efforts of the French monarchy to establish a centralized, absolutist state.[33] It is possible that this situation led royal judges to prosecute witches as part of a general programme of disciplining and Christianizing the population and of curbing rebellion in these outlying regions. As we have seen, contemporaries made associations between witchcraft and rebellion in Languedoc, and they may have been at least partially correct. But the main reason for intense witch-hunting in the peripheral regions of France is that courts in these regions operated with greater independence from central governmental control than did those in the centre of the country. And as we know from the late seventeenth-century trials in Rouen, the right of particular localities to prosecute witches without interference from the central government was one of many issues that pitted Louis XIV against the various provinces in his kingdom.[34]

The struggle between the centre and the periphery in France did, therefore, have a great deal to do with witchcraft prosecution in that

---

33 Muchembled, 'Satan ou les hommes?', p. 18.
34 Mandrou, *Magistrats et sorciers*, pp. 449–62.

kingdom, and the greater success that France had in establishing a powerful central monarchy in the sixteenth and seventeenth centuries goes a long way towards explaining why far fewer witches were executed within its boundaries than in Germany. Another factor, not unrelated to this process of centralization, was the regular system of appeals from local courts to the eight provincial *parlements*. In some cases, as in Normandy in the 1590s, when the provincial *parlement* at Rouen fully supported the trials and confirmed sentences that were appealed to it, this system of provincial control did little to discourage prosecutions by local authorities. But the reversal of many sentences by the *parlement* of Paris, which exercised an appellate jurisdiction over most of northern France, and which set the standards for the other provincial *parlements*, did have a negative effect on the entire process of witch-hunting in France. More than any one factor it explains why France, with a population only marginally smaller than that of the Empire, prosecuted far fewer witches. Until more work is done on the records of the provincial *parlements* most estimates will remain a matter of guesswork, but it would not be unreasonable to suggest a figure of 4,000 for the areas that actually came within the king's jurisdiction.[35] The numbers of illegal executions, such as the 300 that occurred in the Ardennes in the early seventeenth century, might swell this figure some more.[36] Even so, this larger figure would not denote a persecution much more intense than took place in England, provided we take into account the relative size of the population of the two countries.

The concentration of the great majority of witchcraft prosecutions in the west-central core of Europe had religious as well as political and judicial causes. There is no question that this was the most ecclesiastically volatile region in all of Europe. It was a hotbed of heresy in the late Middle Ages and the very centre of the Protestant

35 For the area within the jurisdiction of the *parlement* of Paris we have records of 1,288 appeals and 554 cases that never reached that stage. A. Soman, 'Trente procès', pp. 42–7. Briggs, *Communities of Belief*, p. 12, suggests that France as a whole did not suffer from a significantly higher level of persecution than England, if we take the relative size of the two populations into account.

36 Soman, 'Parlement of Paris', p. 40. Muchembled, 'Witches of Cambrésis', notes that with the exception of Lorraine, which was not in France at this time, the numbers of French witches were counted in the hundreds rather than the thousands. The *parlement* of Paris confirmed only 115 death sentences between 1565 and 1640. See Soman, 'Parlement of Paris', p. 26. There were, however, some fairly severe hunts in the outlying regions of the country. For de Lancre's report of 400 executions at Toulouse in 1577 see Mandrou, *Magistrats et sorciers*, p. 92.

Reformation. After the Reformation the region became ecclesiastically unstable, with certain areas changing their religious affiliation more than once and others becoming religiously pluralistic. In Germany each prince determined the religion of his lands after 1556, while in France a period of qualified religious toleration occurred from 1598 to 1685. Throughout France, therefore, there were many religiously divided areas, and in both France and Germany there was extensive religious conflict. All of this religious dissent, instability and diversity encouraged the prosecution of witches. The mere tradition of dissent, of course, made authorities conscious of the possibility of witchcraft, since witchcraft was, after all, a new and particularly virulent strain of heresy. The close proximity of adherents to a rival faith may also have strengthened the consciousness of the Devil in these areas, while the frequency and intensity of outright religious conflict contributed to the mood of anxiety that lay at the foundation of witchcraft prosecutions.

The British Isles

Once we leave the west-central area of Europe and survey witchcraft prosecutions on its periphery, we confront a general pattern of witch-hunting that is relatively mild and restrained. All of these peripheral areas had their witch panics, but they were far more limited in size and in number than in the European heartland. Looking first at England, Scotland and England's overseas possessions, we find a pattern that varies considerably but which as a whole stands in stark contrast to that which prevailed in west-central Europe. England, to be sure, experienced a major witch-hunt in the 1640s, while Scotland had a number of national panics in the late sixteenth and seventeenth centuries, and Salem, Massachusetts, was the site of the famous hunt of 1692, but few of these hunts can compare in size or intensity to the holocausts that occurred at Ellwangen, Würzburg or Bamberg. The total number of British trials, moreover, probably did not exceed 5,000, and the number of executions was less than 2,500 and may have been as low as 1,500.

The main reason for the relative tameness of witch-hunting in Britain was the belated and incomplete reception of the cumulative concept of witchcraft. The failure of the great medieval heresies to cross the Channel and the absence of papal inquisitors to extirpate them made both Englishmen and Scots less paranoid about the introduction of a new heresy like witchcraft in the fifteenth century, and when the cumulative concept of witchcraft began to spread throughout all of Europe in the sixteenth century, it did not find very fertile ground in Britain. It received only reluctant and half-hearted support from the administrative and ruling élite in England, and even in Scotland, where the new ideas were more eagerly embraced, the concept was never fully developed. The witch-belief that was most responsible for the development of large witch-hunts – the belief in the sabbath – worked its way into a number of English trials in the seventeenth century and also into the major Scottish hunts, but it was never embellished as it was on the Continent. English and even Scottish sabbaths were relatively tame affairs where witches dined with the Devil but did not usually engage in cannibalistic infanticide, participate in orgies or fly to and from their gatherings. The belief in the sabbath, when it found acceptance, was sufficient to provoke a search for accomplices, but the number of participants was invariably small and the general picture did not inspire the type of terror that the standard Continental nightmare did.

The slow and incomplete acceptance of the cumulative concept of witchcraft in Britain had a great deal to do with the second main reason for the mildness of witch-hunting in this region: the spare use of torture in witchcraft cases. In both England and Scotland torture could be used only at the specific command of the Privy Council and only when matters of state were involved.[37] In England this prohibition was strictly enforced, with the result that only once, during the disruptive period of the Civil War, was torture used illegally in witch-hunting. In Scotland, where central control of local justice was less effective than in England, torture was used without warrant more frequently, very often during pre-trial investigations.[38] It was also used by official order in one very important witch-hunt, when King James VI was considered to be the intended victim of witchcraft.[39]

The relatively spare use of torture in Britain had a two-fold effect on witch-hunting. On the one hand it weakened the reception of Continental witch-beliefs, for it was mainly through confessions

---

37 For the English warrants, which number eighty-one for the period 1540–1640, see Langbein, *Torture*, pp. 94–123. There were thirty-four Scottish warrants issued between 1590 and 1689. See *Register of the Privy Council of Scotland*, passim.

38 See, for example, B. Whitelocke, *Memorials of the English Affairs* (London, 1682), p. 522. One of the reasons for the use of torture was that the Privy Council required a confession in order to approve a local witchcraft trial. Mackenzie, *Laws and Customes*, p. 88.

39 *Register of the Privy Council of Scotland*, IV, p. 680.

to such activities as attending the sabbath and flying through the air that such beliefs were accepted by the administrative classes, let alone by the common people. It is certainly worthy of notice that the British hunts in which the idea of the sabbath was most fully developed were those in which torture was in fact employed, legally or illegally. On the other hand, the infrequent use of torture prevented the development of chain-reaction hunts. There were only two of these in Britain, the Scottish hunts of 1590–92 and 1661–62, and in both cases torture was used extensively. Even in these hunts, however, the majority of prosecutions originated independently of the others and could not be considered part of any sort of judicial chain.

A further legal reason for the relative mildness of British witch-hunting was the practice of trying witches by jury both in England and Scotland. Although juries were not bound by the strict laws of evidence that prevailed on the Continent, and although they could convict a witch on the basis of either reputation or circumstantial evidence, in practice they proved to be relatively lenient, returning a number of acquittals in both countries. The presence of juries, moreover, reflected another characteristic of British justice: the absence of inquisitorial procedure, which of course is the system that led to the use of torture. Scottish justice, being influenced by Roman law, did incorporate some features of inquisitorial procedure, but until the late seventeenth century it remained essentially English in its character. Not only did juries retain their independence, but another feature of inquisitorial procedure, the initiation of witch-hunts by official promotion, occurred only rarely in Scotland, and never in England.

Although witch-hunting throughout Britain was much tamer than in Germany, France and Switzerland, prosecutions in Scotland were much more intense than in England. When we consider the fact that as many as three Scottish witches were executed for every one in England and that England had a population four times that of Scotland, we can appreciate how great the differences between the two countries were in this regard. The main reasons for these differences were the more complete reception of the cumulative concept of witchcraft in the northern kingdom and the more frequent illegal use of torture. Another Scottish practice, of possibly even greater consequence, was the custom of granting witchcraft commissions to local magistrates to try witches without the supervision of itinerant judges. In those cases the conviction-rate and the execution-rate were higher than when cases were heard before the central judges in Edinburgh or on circuit. In England virtually all witchcraft cases were heard before circuit judges at the county assizes.

A number of other legal and religious factors contributed to the greater intensity of Scottish witch-hunting. Scottish juries required only a majority to convict a criminal, whereas English juries required unanimity. It is hard to determine the precise effect of this difference on the total number of convictions, but we do know that many Scottish convictions were majority decisions. The differences in the sentencing provisions of the witchcraft statutes of the two countries may also have led to a higher number of Scottish executions (although not convictions). Whereas the English statutes of 1542, 1563 and 1604 provided for non-capital sentences in certain types of cases on the first offence, the Scottish statute of 1563 called for death in all cases – a grim example of the notorious severity of Scottish justice. In fact, many Scottish witches were given non-capital sentences, but the number was far lower than in England.

Religious factors may also have played a part in the different results of English and Scottish witch-hunting. Both countries were Protestant after 1560 and both countries had their fair share of religious conflict, but there were significant religious differences between them. The greater strength of Calvinist thought in Scotland does not appear to have encouraged witch-hunting, but the Scottish clergy did play a more active part in the religious life of their country than their English counterparts. Not only did Scottish ministers and elders assist in the initial interrogation of witches by virtue of their status as members of the kirk sessions of their parishes, but as members of the General Assembly they applied constant pressure on the government to establish a godly state by prosecuting witches. This type of pressure stands as one of the clearest examples of the way in which religious reformers influenced secular governments to redouble their efforts at hunting witches.[40]

Witchcraft in England's overseas possessions deserves special comment. In Ireland, where the fourteenth-century case of Dame Alice Kytler had marked an important stage in the formulation of the cumulative concept of witchcraft, witch trials were surprisingly rare. Although the land was believed to abound in sorcerers and warlocks, and although the Irish Parliament passed a witchcraft statute in 1586, the total number of trials does not appear to have been very large. It is possible that the low number reflects the incompleteness of

---

40 Larner, *Enemies of God*, pp. 67–8, 71–5.

the judicial record, but the absence of other evidence regarding witch-hunts suggests that Irish authorities did not take legal action against witchcraft very often. The unsettled state of Irish justice and the conflict between English law and native Gaelic or Brehon law may have had something to do with this situation. It is quite possible that native Irish refused to bring charges against witches in courts operating under English law, thereby preventing the initiation of prosecutions.

In any event, the evidence that we have regarding witchcraft accusations and prosecutions makes it clear that Continental ideas of diabolism did not penetrate Ireland to any appreciable extent. The statute of 1586, which was passed at least to some extent to remedy the legal difficulty encountered in 1578 when judges had to resort to the natural law to convict two witches, resembled the English statute of 1563 rather closely, and the charges brought against Irish witches resembled those raised against their typical English counterparts rather than German or French witches. One of the few cases that we know about, that of the Protestant clergyman John Aston in 1606, involved charges of digging for treasure, an activity with which English witchcraft cases were frequently concerned. The most famous case of the seventeenth century, that of Florence Newton, 'The Witch of Youghal', in 1661, also conforms closely to an English model. Newton's problems began when she demanded a piece of beef from the household of John Pyne and upon being refused went away cursing. Shortly thereafter she kissed one of Pyne's servants, Mary Longdon, and when Longdon subsequently experienced fits, trances and vomiting, she named Newton as the cause of her ordeal. Newton's predicament worsened while in prison, for she allegedly kissed one David Jones through the gate and thereby caused his death. The ultimate outcome of this case is not known, but as far as we can tell, the charges did not reflect Continental ideas of collective diabolical activity. Nor should we expect such charges to have been made, since torture was not used in this or in any other Irish cases. Witchcraft in Ireland, as in England, was essentially the crime of *maleficium*, not Devil-worship.[41]

Turning to the English colonies in America, we find a somewhat different situation from that which existed in Ireland. In the middle and southern colonies, to be sure, witch-hunting was either restrained or non-existent. There were only occasional trials in New York, New

---

41 St John Seymour, *Irish Witchcraft and Demonology* (Dublin, 1913), pp. 105–13.

Jersey, Delaware, Maryland and Virginia, and only one of these, a prosecution in Maryland in 1685, ended with an execution.[42] In New England, however, the picture was quite different. All told, some 234 New Englanders were indicted or presented for this crime in the seventeenth century, and of these thirty-six were executed. When we realize that the population of New England was on average only about 100,000 persons at this time, we can appreciate the intensity that witch-hunting reached in that locale. It was significantly more intense than in the county of Essex, in England, and perhaps even more intense than in Scotland. New England, moreover, exhibited many of the signs of a witch-craze. Continental European witch-beliefs were current there, and a large witch-hunt, claiming more than half of the total number of victims for all of New England, occurred at Salem in 1692.[43]

The presence of 'Continental' witch beliefs in New England should not strike us as highly unusual, for such notions did exist, at least in literary form, in England by the early seventeenth century and were readily available in New England by the time of the Salem hunt. Nor should the conduct of a large witch-hunt in an 'English' world prove incapable of explanation. Not only did an extraordinary combination of political and social tensions provide a foundation for the panic that developed at Salem, but the court's decision to allow spectral evidence in what was originally a case of demonic possession allowed the afflicted girls to implicate a larger number of suspects than might normally be expected in an English hunt. In one case, moreover, a mild form of torture was used in order to obtain the names of accomplices.[44]

The real problem connected with New England witchcraft is why the entire population was more fearful of witchcraft and more eager to prosecute it than in the southern colonies, Ireland or even England itself. The explanation is almost certainly religious rather than social or economic. The New England colonies were, at least in their inception, theocratic institutions whose purpose was to create a New Jerusalem. The same urge to create a godly state that was evident in Scotland also existed in New England, and in both cases the mission entailed the prosecution of witches as God's enemies. Witchcraft in Massachusetts, just as in England, was a secular crime tried in a civil

---

42 F.N. Parke, 'Witchcraft in Maryland', *Maryland Historical Magazine*, 31 (1936): 284, 290.

43 Demos, *Entertaining Satan*, pp. 11–13.

44 Hansen, *Witchcraft at Salem*, p. 284.

court, and most of the charges brought by villagers against their neighbours were mainly for *maleficia*. The clergy, however, and the magistrates whom they advised, viewed witchcraft exclusively in terms of a demonic compact and interpreted the Massachusetts witchcraft law of 1642 in those terms.[45] For these influential men, who directed the witch-hunt at Salem, the prosecution of witches was part of a general assault upon diabolical power, not an attempt to punish the perpetrators of *maleficia*.[46]

Scandinavia

Witch-hunting in Scandinavia was somewhat more intense than it was in the British Isles. The total number of prosecutions in Denmark–Norway and Sweden–Finland was roughly 5,000, of which somewhere between 1,700 and 2,000 resulted in executions. These figures are roughly equivalent to those for the British Isles, but they denote a more intense prosecution since the population of Scandinavia was only about 40 per cent of Britain's.[47] In other respects Scandinavian witch-hunting bore a close resemblance to its British counterpart. In both areas the cumulative concept of witchcraft met with an incomplete and belated acceptance, entering Sweden and Finland only in the middle of the seventeenth century. Throughout Scandinavia, moreover, there was a general reluctance to use torture in order to obtain the confessions of accused witches or the names of their accomplices. The combined effect of ideological weakness and judicial restraint explain the relative mildness of Scandinavian witch-hunting, but as in Britain, these characteristics were not universal and large witch-hunts took place in certain areas at specific times.

Denmark was the first of the Scandinavian countries to engage in witch-hunting. As early as the 1540s Peter Palladius, the Lutheran bishop of Sealand, urged the prosecution of witches, arguing that those who exhibited Catholic tendencies were culpable of the crime.

---

45 Wiseman, *Witchcraft, Magic and Religion*, pp. 12–13. The wording of the law was based on Mosaic language.

46 One of the reasons for the extraordinarily low conviction rate in Massachusetts before the Salem trials was that charges brought by the witches' neighbours usually referred only to *maleficia*, whereas the judges required evidence of diabolical compact. See Richard Godbeer, *The Devil's Dominion: Magic and Religion in Early New England* (Cambridge, 1992); Wiseman, *Witchcraft, Magic and Religion*, Ch. 7.

47 In 1600 the population of Britain was approximately 5.4 million persons, that of Scandinavia approximately two million. J. De Vries, *European Urbanization* (Cambridge, Mass., 1984), p. 36.

Palladius reported in 1544 that a fairly large chain-reaction hunt had claimed the lives of fifty-two persons. In 1547, however, the government declared that the testimony of those who had been convicted of infamous crimes, including sorcery, could not be used to convict another person. It also forbade the application of torture until after a death sentence had been pronounced.[48] These two laws, taken together, prevented the development of large witch-hunts, kept the total number of convictions at a fairly low level, and also prevented notions of the sabbath from being fully received. This is not to suggest that beliefs in diabolism were absent in Denmark. A number of Danish witches were in fact accused of making pacts with the Devil and of worshipping him collectively.[49] In 1617 a royal ordinance defined witchcraft for the first time in terms of diabolical compact and specified that those convicted of such charges would be burned.[50] But the legal reforms of 1547, together with the mandatory appeal of all death sentences to the county courts after 1576, kept Denmark from going the way of many German states. According to the most reliable estimates, there were approximately 2,000 witchcraft trials in Denmark and about 1,000 executions.[51] These totals are roughly proportional to those of Scotland, which had a population almost twice as large as that of Denmark.[52]

Witchcraft prosecutions in Norway, which during this period was governed by Denmark, were slightly less intense than those in the southern kingdom. With a population of about three-quarters the size of Denmark's in 1650, a total of approximately 1,400 prosecutions was fairly proportional to the Danish total, but only about 25 per cent of those tried were executed.[53] As in other countries where witch-

---

48 J.C.V. Johansen, 'Denmark: The Sociology of Accusations', in *Early Modern Witchcraft: Centres and Peripheries*, ed. Bengt Ankarloo and Gustav Henningsen. Oxford, 1990. p. 340.

49 G. Henningsen, 'Witchcraft in Denmark', *Folklore*, 93 (1982): 134, argues that neither the sabbath nor the pact ever figured prominently in the charges against Danish witches. See also Johansen, 'Denmark', p. 343.

50 Johansen, 'Denmark', pp. 341–7. Most of the executions after this time, however, were still based upon charges of *maleficium*.

51 Henningsen, 'Witchcraft in Denmark', p. 135. See also Johansen, 'Denmark', pp. 344–5.

52 The population of Denmark in 1650 was 580,000, whereas that of Scotland was approximately one million. A. Lassen, 'The Population of Denmark in 1660', *Scandinavian Economic History Review*, 13 (1965): 29.

53 Naess, 'Norway', p. 371, calculates an execution rate of 38 per cent on the basis of those cases in which the fates of the accused are known. His estimate for all trials, p. 372, is only 25 per cent. B.G. Alver, *Heksetro og Trolddom* (Oslo, 1971), p. 63, also estimates an execution rate of 25 per cent.

hunting was relatively mild, a combination of legal and ideological factors provides an explanation. The main form of criminal procedure in Norway was accusatorial, according to which the testimony of two eye-witnesses to any crime was required for conviction. Public prosecutions based on rumour could, however, be used in witchcraft cases, since witchcraft was a *crimen exceptum*. Torture was allowed in Norwegian trials, but it was used only occasionally, and this probably explains why charges of diabolism figured in less than one-fifth of all cases.[54] Notions of diabolical conspiracy did penetrate Norway, mainly from Danish sources, and were apparent as early as the 1590s, but they did not predominate in the trials whose records are extant. There was, to be sure, a widespread belief in Norway, both among the common people and the élite, that witches frequently assembled with the Devil in the northern parts of the country. Because of the remoteness of such assemblies a belief in the ability of witches to fly also gained currency, and this belief was closely connected to a belief in metamorphosis. In the actual trials, however, charges of attending the sabbath appeared only occasionally, and they usually did not become central to the case against the accused.[55] The belief remained much more a part of popular legend than of demonological theory. The related beliefs in metamorphosis and flight, however, often did become central to the trials and were grafted on to traditional charges of *maleficium*. Those persons who, for example, were accused of causing storms at sea – a frequent charge in all seafaring countries – were often accused of working their craft while airborne, and others were accused of having performed *maleficia* after having taken the form of a wolf, raven, dog or cat.

The most famous case of Norwegian witchcraft was that of Anna Pedersdotter Absalon, who was executed at Bergen in 1590. The case owes its fame to a Norwegian play by Hans Wiers-Jenssen, an English translation by John Masefield, and a brilliant film by Carl Theodore Dreyer, *Day of Wrath*.[56] Although the play and film possess little historical accuracy, the actual trial throws a great deal of light on the nature of Norwegian witchcraft. Anna Pedersdotter Absalon was the wife of Norway's most famous humanist scholar, the Lutheran minister Absalon Pedersen Beyer. The charges against

54 Although torture was applied in forty trials, it was used before sentencing in only ten of these. Naess, 'Norway', pp. 375, 373.

55 See Robbins, *Encyclopedia*, pp. 361–2. The case of 1680 appears to have been an exception to this rule.

56 H. Wiers-Jenssen, *Anne Pedersdotter: A Drama in Four Acts*, trans. John Masefield (Boston, 1917).

Anna arose out of the opposition that had developed in Bergen to the efforts of Absalon and the clergy to destroy the holy images that had been so characteristic of the pre-Reformation Church. The impetus for witch-hunting was therefore different from that in Denmark fifty years earlier, where the Lutheran clergy apparently took the initiative in spreading the fear of witchcraft and perhaps even in formulating accusations. In this Norwegian case the reforming clergy were the object rather than the source of the accusations. The changes, moreover, were directed against the wife of one of the leading clerics, since the clergy themselves were too highly placed to be attacked successfully. This was a pattern of witchcraft accusations that occurred frequently in German towns, where members of political factions used charges of witchcraft against their rivals' wives in order to advance their own political careers. It is also important to note that the court in which Anna was tried was a civil tribunal and not, as both the play and the film suggest, a Lutheran church court.

Although Anna was exonerated when the charges were first brought against her in 1575, the year of Absalon's death, the case was reopened in 1590. The most interesting aspect of this second trial was the set of charges brought against Anna. Most of them were traditional charges of *maleficia*: putting into a coma a man who had refused her prior payment for a weaving frame; inflicting sickness on a man who had refused to give her wine, beer and vinegar; and causing the death of a four-year-old boy by giving him a bewitched biscuit. As so often happened in cases that began with accusations of *maleficia*, charges of diabolism were introduced. Anna's servant testified that Anna had turned her into a horse and had ridden her to the sabbath at a mountain called Lyderhorn, where a number of witches plotted a storm to wreck all ships arriving at Bergen and then, on subsequent occasions, to burn the town and cause it to be flooded. The sabbath, however, was dispersed by a man in white who said that God would not allow it. On the basis of the testimony of her servant and others, Anna was burnt as a witch.[57]

The trial of Anna reveals how charges of collective Devil-worship influenced but did not dominate Norwegian witchcraft trials. The sabbath that allegedly took place at Lyderhorn derived mainly from Norwegian belief, not demonological theory, and it lacked most of the distinctive features of German, French and Swiss sabbaths. There was, for example, no infanticide or cannibalism, and although Anna

---

[57] R. Bainton, *Women of the Reformation: From Spain to Scandinavia* (Minneapolis, 1977), pp. 128–33.

and her servant allegedly took the sacrament on their journey home, there was no alleged demonic administration of that sacrament at the sabbath. The sabbath was in fact a more restrained affair than those that allegedly occurred in Scotland or even in England. In fact, Anna was convicted mainly on the basis of her individual and collective *maleficia*, the occurrence of a storm in Bergen at the time of the sabbath proving to be the conclusive evidence. Anna was burned as a witch, a penalty that reflects a belief that witchcraft was a crime of heresy rather than sorcery, but the charges upon which she was convicted reflected her putative status as a magician, not a person who made a pact with the Devil and worshipped him.

Two other features of Anna's trial provide us with insights into the nature of Norwegian witchcraft. First, although the testimony of two women previously executed for witchcraft was introduced at her trial – a procedure that would not have occurred in Denmark – this testimony did not have a decisive impact on the outcome of the trial. Second, Anna was apparently not tortured during her trial, and her confession was not required for conviction. Nor was she tortured to secure the names of accomplices. While torture was not unknown to Norwegian law, it was apparently used as sparingly as in Denmark, and this restraint prevented both the full imposition of demonological theory upon a body of native folklore and the development of large chain-reaction hunts. It also probably explains the relatively low number of Norwegian executions, which on a proportionate basis was as low as in England.

Sweden originally followed a pattern of witch-hunting which resembled that of Norway, but in the late seventeenth century it experienced a large panic that was, by Scandinavian standards, quite exceptional. Prosecutions for witchcraft had begun in the 1580s, but most of those early trials were for simple *maleficium*, and very few of them resulted in executions. A law of 1593 requiring either the testimony of six witnesses or a confession for a capital conviction, together with a requirement that all death sentences be appealed to a royal court in Stockholm after 1614, were in large part responsible for holding witch-hunting in check. Charges of diabolism were not absent from these trials, however, and since torture was often allowed in witchcraft cases, the potential for large-scale witch-hunting clearly existed. Soldiers returning from Germany from the Thirty Years' War may have introduced more extreme diabolical ideas during the 1640s.[58]

58 Ankarloo, *Trolldomsprocesserna*, pp. 326–8; K. Baschwitz, *Hexen und Hexen-prozesse* (Munich, 1963), p. 321.

Queen Christina, who put an end to the witch-trials that were being conducted in Sweden's German territory of Verden during the Thirty Years' War, claimed many years after her abdication that in 1649 she had forbidden the death penalty in all Swedish witchcraft cases except those involving murder. She also said that she had attributed the confessions of witches to female disorders or diabolical illusions. There is reason to doubt the queen's honesty in this claim to early enlightenment, but whatever action she did take was insufficient to prevent a major hunt from occurring during the reign of Charles XI. The hunt began in 1668 in the northern Swedish province of Dalecarlia (now Dalarna) and eventually spread throughout the entire northern part of the country and even spilled over into the Swedish-speaking sections of Finland. The hunt was unusual in that a large number of both the accusers and the accused were children. Drawing on a body of Swedish legend about witches visiting a mythical place called Blakulla, where they allegedly feasted, danced and married devils, several children accused parents, neighbours and older children of having taken them to this Swedish version of the sabbath.

Charles appointed a number of royal commissions to investigate the matter in the localities and to try the accused witches. To make matters worse, the first wave of trials, which took place in the vicinity of Mora, encouraged parents and magistrates in many small villages to demand the prosecution of witches in their communities, a task that was entrusted to newly appointed commissions. The commissioners were forbidden to use torture, but it appears that in the hysterical mood that prevailed they did not always follow that policy. These royal commissions pronounced a number of death sentences, including more than a hundred in 1675, the year marking the height of the panic. The hunt did not end until after it had spread to the south and affected Stockholm. Two new commissions, appointed in 1676, acted more cautiously than their predecessors and exercised a moderating influence on a panic-stricken population. At the same time the Court of Appeal, which had confirmed many of the sentences during the past eight years, began interrogating witnesses directly. When many of the children began to confess that their charges were groundless, the court reviewed all the evidence and set the most recently condemned witches free.[59]

59 Ankarloo, 'Sweden: The Mass Burnings', in *Early Modern European Witchcraft*, pp. 285–317; Lea, *Materials*, III, pp. 1282–5; Heikkinen, *Paholaisen*, pp. 375–7.

More than 200 persons were executed during the north Swedish hunt of 1668–76. Like Matthew Hopkins's hunt in England in the 1640s, the entire episode reveals that even countries not known for their severe treatment of witches could occasionally experience large panics. All that was required was a belief in the sabbath, a relaxation of judicial restraint and the creation of a popular mood that pressured authorities to take action.

Finland at this time was a part of Sweden, and the two provinces in which the largest number of Finnish witch trials took place were Swedish-speaking. For these reasons witch-hunting in Finland must be considered in connection with the Swedish experience. Indeed, a large number of Finnish prosecutions occurred as a part of the panic that began in Dalecarlia. On the other hand, the history of witchcraft in Finland followed a course that differed in large measure from that of Sweden. Among all the Scandinavian countries, Finland was the last to begin its prosecutions for witchcraft. Witch-beliefs, including reports of Devil-worship, were not unknown in Finland in the late sixteenth and seventeenth centuries. They entered the country both from the northern, Swedish-speaking provinces and from the lower Baltic countries of Estonia and Livonia, which were part of the Swedish state and had extensive cultural contacts with both Finland and Germany.[60] Despite these influences, however, Finland did not concern itself with witchcraft until 1640, when the Swedish bishop, Isaac Rothovius, became the vice-chancellor of the first Finnish university, Turku Academy. Rothovius, who was a champion of the Lutheran cause against both Catholics and Calvinists, did not express concern over witches attending the sabbath, but he did encourage the extirpation of sorcery (which he regarded in an old-fashioned way as a form of residual pagan superstition) and he also inaugurated a campaign, which was joined by other officials and his successor, against the practice of demonic magic in Turku Academy. In this respect Finland was beginning an operation in 1640 that other European countries had started more than two centuries earlier.

It was not until the 1660s that the full concept of witchcraft appeared in Finnish trials, and the person most responsible for the introduction of these ideas was Nils Psilander, a judge of the civil court in the Swedish-speaking province of Ahvenanmaa. Psilander had been educated in the Baltic area at Tartu Academy, where he

---

60 On Estonian witchcraft, see Madar, 'Estonia I', and J. Kahk, 'Estonia II: The Crusade against Idolatry', in *Early Modern European Witchcraft*, pp. 257–84.

had become familiar with current German juridical thought regarding witchcraft. Between 1666 and 1674 he conducted a protracted chain-reaction hunt in which original accusations of soothsaying and sorcery were overlaid with demonological theory and were also fused with Swedish legend concerning trips to Blakulla. In many of these trials the Devil's mark was located and torture was used, but sceptical juries and a somewhat less sceptical court of appeal at Turku kept the hunt from getting out of control. Although the first suspect, Karin Persdotter, denounced thirteen accomplices, only four of them, together with Karin and one later suspect, were executed.

In Finland's other predominantly Swedish-speaking province of Ostrobothnia, a large number of witch trials took place between 1665 and 1684. This hunt, in which at least 152 persons were accused of witchcraft, resulted in twenty death sentences (most of which were probably confirmed on appeal) and the execution of another eight persons for whom trial records are missing. These trials were inspired by the great northern Swedish witch-hunt of 1668–75. Somewhat surprisingly, however, these trials did not centre on charges of Devil-worship. With the charges of witchcraft coming mainly from below, and in the absence of a counterpart to Psilander to introduce learned theories of witchcraft, the charges against the accused remained essentially those of *maleficia*. Only when children and one servant denounced their elders for taking them to Blakulla, a charge that occurred only in a small percentage of cases, did charges of Devil-worship surface, and even then they did not form the basis of the case against the accused.

All in all, the Ostrobothnian witch-hunt of 1665–84 was a relatively tame affair. Since only about one-third of the witches were denounced by others, it was not primarily a chain-reaction hunt. The denunciations, moreover, were not extracted under torture. Those denunciations that did not spring from juvenile imagination either arose out of malice or were elicited by zealous clergymen. Nor were the sentences especially harsh. More than half (57 per cent) of those accused were acquitted or released, while a smaller number were given ecclesiastical punishments, fined or sentenced to prison or hard labour. The death-sentence was imposed in only 13 per cent of all cases, and some of those sentences may have been reduced on appeal.[61]

Looking at Finland as a whole, one is led to the conclusion that witchcraft prosecutions never got out of control. The total number of

61 Heikkinen, *Paholaisen*, pp. 386–9.

trials probably did not exceed a thousand;[62] notions of Devil-worship were never fully received and only occasionally became the focal point of witch-trials; torture was used sparingly; juries tempered the zeal of witch-hunters; and the execution-rate was lower than in other Scandinavian countries. Among Finnish-speaking people the process of witch-hunting was even more restrained. At least one half of the Finnish trials took place in the province of Ostrobothnia and only one execution is known to have taken place outside of the two Swedish-speaking provinces of Ostrobothnia and Ahvenanmaa.

East-central and eastern Europe

It is difficult to make many broad generalizations about witchcraft prosecutions in eastern European lands – those that lay to the east of the Holy Roman Empire and north of the uncontested boundaries of the Ottoman Empire. In all of these areas witch-hunting began much later than in western Europe and it also lasted much longer, until the middle of the eighteenth century. The intensity of this witch-hunting, however, varied greatly from region to region. In certain parts of Poland, where the cumulative concept of witchcraft found fertile ground, prosecutions were as intense as in all but the most panic-stricken German territories. In Hungary, where learned notions of witchcraft were only partially and reluctantly received, there was a substantial but by no means extraordinarily large number of trials and only a few large hunts. In Transylvania, Wallachia and Moldavia, where demonological ideas were weak or non-existent, prosecutions were much less common. In the most general terms we can say that those areas that were closest to Germany, had cultural contacts with Germany or were populated by German-speaking people prosecuted far more witches than those which were more exclusively Slavic. It is also readily apparent that those regions which followed the rites of Orthodox Christianity did not engage in intensive witch-hunting. We can no longer claim that witchcraft prosecutions were entirely absent from these areas, since there were a number of Russian trials and also some in the Orthodox and Uniate sections of Lithuania.[63] But there is little question that the lands in the easternmost parts of Europe did not participate in the European witch-hunt with anywhere near the same degree of enthusiasm as their western and Latinized neighbours.

---

62 Heikkinen and Kervinen, 'Finland', p. 320.

63 See Schormann, *Hexenprozesse in Deutschland*, p. 6, and Cohn, *Europe's Inner Demons*, p. 253, for the traditional view.

The only eastern or east-central European country that prosecuted witches in great numbers was Poland. Because of the incompleteness of the judicial record, the total number of trials and executions cannot be determined with any degree of accuracy. Baranowski's estimate of 10,000 legal executions may be too high, but a total merely half that size would still exceed those of both the British Isles (which had a slightly larger population) and Scandinavia. Poland cannot, therefore, be relegated to the status of a peripheral and reluctant participant in the European witch-hunt. It was however, a belated participant. Large-scale prosecutions did not begin until after 1650, and more than half of the executions took place between 1676 and 1725, the worst years being those of the early eighteenth century.[64]

The severity of Polish witch-hunting can be attributed to three related factors: the presence of theories of diabolism, the absence of effective central control over prosecutions, and the unrestricted use of torture. The theories of diabolism were essentially a foreign import, just as they were to a large extent in Britain and Scandinavia. Poles had long believed in *maleficium,* but the belief in formal pacts with the Devil and the sabbath came from Germany in the late sixteenth and early seventeenth centuries. Learned witch-beliefs were received first in those parts of Poland that were close to Germany, which had a large German-speaking population and which had close commercial or cultural links with German lands. From there these ideas spread to the other provinces of the country, a process that was greatly facilitated by the translation of the *Malleus Maleficarum* into Polish at the beginning of the seventeenth century. The only areas where these beliefs did not take root were the far eastern section of Lithuania (which became fully integrated into the Polish state in the sixteenth century) and Galicia to the south. It should come as no surprise that these sections of Poland did not experience the full force of the European witch-hunt.

The great majority of Polish witchcraft cases took place in the municipal courts, despite the fact that a law of 1543 had entrusted jurisdiction over witchcraft to the ecclesiastical courts. Although Bishop Czartoriski of Leslau made an effort to enforce the Church's jurisdictional monopoly in 1669 and demanded that all prosecutions be authorized by him, the municipal courts continued the trials. Royal edicts of 1672 and 1713, themselves evidence of the failure of the bishop's efforts, also failed to control the jurisdictional appetite of the local courts. Since the Polish state was exceptionally weak at this

---

64 See Baranowski, *Procesy Czarownic,* p. 179.

time, it is in no way surprising that these efforts did not succeed. In any event, the success of the municipal courts in ignoring central edicts had a profound effect upon the progress of the witch-hunts, since the municipal courts, which used inquisitorial procedure, repeatedly violated all of the procedural rules that were designed to protect the accused. We know from the instructions of Bishop Czartoriski himself that these courts were withholding the proofs from the accused, denying them counsel and, most importantly, torturing them without restraint to obtain both their own confessions and the names of accomplices. In Poland, therefore, all of the conditions that encouraged large-scale witch-hunting – diabolical theories, local autonomy and the unrestricted use of torture – were present, and consequently the number of victims was high. In its basic essentials the Polish hunt resembled the German one, and since Polish witch beliefs were originally German and the heaviest prosecutions took place in the western half of the kingdom (Royal Poland and Royal Prussia) we can consider the entire Polish hunt as an extension of the German phenomenon.

The problem still remains why witch-hunting in Poland began so much later than in Germany. Theories of a slow transmission of ideas, which might be used to explain Sweden's belated adoption of demonological theory, are less applicable in a country where German influence was more direct and immediate. It seems as if Poland, despite the availability of advanced witchcraft theories, was simply not disposed to engage in witch-hunting in the early seventeenth century but then rather suddenly began a major legal campaign in the later period. One reason for this delayed inauguration of a national witch-hunt was the sudden and unprecedented devastation caused by the wars of the mid-century. During the sixteenth and early seventeenth centuries, Poland experienced neither civil war nor invasion. In the middle of the seventeenth century, however, a Cossack rebellion (1648) and the first northern war against Sweden and Russia (1655–60) signalled the beginning of 'the deluge', during which hostile forces ravaged the country and paralysed the government. As in other parts of Europe, the wars did not lead to an immediate intensification of witch-hunting, but the long-term effects of the deluge created the necessary social, economic and psychological preconditions for witch-hunting, which had not been present before.[65]

A second, less tangible cause of the belated seventeenth-century inauguration of witch-hunting in Poland was a change in the religious

---

[65] Ibid., p. 178

atmosphere. The Reformation ran an unusual course in Poland. The growth of Protestantism and the successful efforts of the Counter-Reformation to reclaim its converts led neither to religious warfare nor suppression but to the establishment of a policy of toleration that had no parallel in Europe.[66] For a variety of practical reasons (including the weakness of the central government and the attitude of an unzealous and religiously divided nobility) Poland became a 'state without stakes' in which a Protestant minority coexisted with a Catholic majority. In the seventeenth century, however, especially after 1648, Catholic intolerance increased and led to a number of restrictions of Protestant freedom. It is possible that this new spirit of intolerance towards religious dissent encouraged witchcraft prosecutions. Religious dissent and witchcraft were of course different phenomenona, but since they were both forms of religious rebellion they also shared many similarities, and intolerance towards one *could* lead to harsher treatment of the other. It is probably no coincidence that the burning of Polish witches coincided with the rise of a more militant, uncompromising Catholicism and the ostensible decline of toleration, even if this did not involve the actual burning of heretics. One might even speculate that the burning of witches was one of the means by which an intolerant Catholic majority expressed its will to impose religious uniformity on a country which, even in the late seventeenth and early eighteenth centuries, remained religiously pluralistic.

A final reason for the slow development of the witch-hunt in Poland was the prolonged maintenance of ecclesiastical jurisdiction over the crime of witchcraft. As we have seen, the intensification of witch-hunting in Europe was encouraged by the decline of ecclesiastical jurisdiction and the transfer of jurisdiction over witchcraft to much more ruthless secular courts. In the late sixteenth century Polish ecclesiastical courts were, like so many of their European counterparts, restricted in their jurisdiction, but they were not deprived of their traditional jurisdiction over *maleficium*.[67] Throughout the late sixteenth and early seventeenth centuries, therefore, the church courts, which adopted a rather tolerant attitude towards witchcraft, prevented the secular courts from turning their potentially lethal attention to this crime. Only in the second half of the seventeenth century did the local courts become strong enough

---

66 J. Tazbir, *A State without Stakes*, trans. A.T. Jordan (Wydawniczy, 1973), p. 92.

67 Ibid., pp. 169, 208.

to ignore the official ecclesiastical monopoly and assume jurisdiction over witchcraft as a civil crime. And of course at this time the royal government was so weak that it could not uphold the clerical monopoly. In this way the rise of Polish witchcraft prosecutions did in fact reflect a decline in ecclesiastical jurisdiction, even if the decline occurred much later than in other parts of Europe.

Witch-hunting in Hungary was much less intense and took a lower toll than in Poland, although the total number of trials and executions was by no means insignificant. Between 1520 and 1777, just under 1,500 individuals were tried for witchcraft, of whom some 450 are known to have been executed (most by burning), while at least 225 suffered non-capital punishments.[68] Most of the trials took place in the kingdom of Hungary, the only part of the country to remain independent of the Ottoman Empire after King Louis II was defeated at the battle of Mohács in 1526. There were also a number of prosecutions in the southeastern province of Transylvania, which remained an autonomous province within the Ottoman Empire between 1526 and 1699, and which did not become fully reintegrated into the kingdom of Hungary (which was ruled by the Habsburgs) until 1711.

Although there was a history of witchcraft in Hungary, it took a long time for intense witch-hunting to develop. As early as the fifteenth century sorcery was defined as a form of heresy, and in 1421 the Stadtrecht of Buda decided that sorcerers were obliged to wear the Jew's hat. Western demonological ideas, however, took a long time to penetrate the country, except in areas inhabited by Germans, and they were never fully developed. A few copies of the *Malleus Maleficarum* circulated in the sixteenth century, but there was no significant volume of witchcraft literature, and the few Hungarian intellectuals who addressed such questions tended to take a sceptical position.[69] It was not until Benedict Carpzov's *Practica Rerum Criminalium* was codified for Austria in 1656 and incorporated into the body of Hungarian law in 1696 that Western demonological ideas were made readily available to Hungarian judges. Those judges succeeded in extracting confessions to most of the charges of diabolism that were commonplace in the West. The way in which this process worked can be seen in a series of trials in 1728–29 in Szeged, where thirteen witches were executed and another twenty-eight were spared by the intervention of Emperor Charles VI. This hunt began

---

68 Klaniczay, 'Hungary', p. 222. The fates of only 932 are known.
69 Ibid., pp. 233–4, 249–50.

with accusations of destroying vineyards with hail storms, but these charges easily led to the further charges of making explicit pacts with the Devil, receiving his mark (usually in the shape of a chicken's foot), and attending the sabbath.[70]

In addition to these standard demonological ideas, a variety of native Hungarian folk beliefs found expression at the trials. One of the most interesting of these beliefs, which dates back at least to 1656 and which was present in the Szeged trials, was that the witches were organized in military fashion, with the Devil being the commander-in-chief. There may be some connection between this belief and that of the *benandanti* in the Friuli, who were likewise organized militarily to fight against the witches.[71] Many native Hungarian beliefs dealt with the *táltosok*, shaman-like magicians and healers whose souls left their bodies in a trance and went out to fight with other *táltosok*.

The slow reception of learned witch-beliefs in Hungary was matched by a belated adoption of inquisitorial procedure, which was not introduced into the kingdom of Hungary until the 1580s. Predictably, the first significant trials and convictions did not take place until that decade. In the province of Transylvania, which had a separate legal system, inquisitorial procedure arrived even later. Until 1725 all accusations in Transylvania were made publicly and under the threat of the talion; witnesses were presented on behalf of both parties; and the main means of probation was the water-ordeal, the purpose of which was to produce a confession. Torture was used only if there was strong suspicion of witchcraft and if the water-ordeal failed. It was also used on one occasion to secure the names of accomplices.[72] This system was in large part responsible for keeping the number of convictions in Transylvania at a minimum. Most of the Transylvanian trials about which we have information occurred in Siebenburgen, an area originally settled by Germans in the twelfth century. The witch-trials that took place in this region were all conducted by secular authorities, although local pastors often played an important part in the process.[73]

The chronological pattern of witch-hunting in Hungary resembles that of Poland. Beginning in the 1580s there was an irregular

---

70 Ibid., p. 230, n. 30.

71 Ginzburg, *Night Battles*, pp. 7, 13. For beliefs similar to those of the *Benandanti* in Hungary see G. Klaniczay, 'Benandante—kresnik—zduhac—táltos', *Ethnographia*, 94 (1983).

72 Lea, *Materials*, III, pp. 1264–5.

73 Ibid., III, pp. 171–3.

succession of isolated trials and an occasional small panic, such as in 1615, when a number of witches allegedly attempted to destroy all of Hungary and Transylvania with hail storms, a danger that somewhat ironically emerged when the country was suffering from a drought.[74] The great majority of witchcraft prosecutions, however, did not occur until the eighteenth century. This belated intensification of witch-hunting in Hungary cannot be explained simply in terms of heightened German and Austrian political and legal influence after 1699. It is much more likely attributable to a more general historical pattern by which the social, economic and cultural conditions that facilitated witch-hunting in the west did not develop until much later in eastern regions.[75]

In Russia the most distinctive feature of witch-hunting, apart from the high proportion of men among the accused,[76] was the absence of western demonological theory. Prosecutions for *maleficium* have a long history in Russia. During the eleventh, twelfth and thirteenth centuries, when prosecutions in the west for simple *maleficium* were rare and executions even rarer, Russian men and women who allegedly used magic to cause droughts were executed in sufficient numbers to attract the notice of chroniclers and foreign travellers. The clerical interpretation of these acts of sorcery was not much different from that which prevailed in the west at that time: they were vestiges of pagan superstition. But whereas in the west this interpretation gradually gave way to a belief that sorcerers were allies of Satan and adherents of a new form of heresy, in Russia the old interpretation prevailed. Prosecution for the crime increased somewhat in the fifteenth and sixteenth centuries, including a mass burning of twelve witches at Pskov in 1411, but the theory upon which the prosecutions were based did not change.

In the middle of the sixteenth century the tsar, being concerned about the practice of sorcery at the royal court, secured the support of the Church in classifying witchcraft as a secular crime. As so often happened in the west, this assumption of secular control over witchcraft facilitated the prosecution of the crime and led to an increase in the number of prosecutions. We know for certain that between 1622 and 1700 the reports of forty-seven trials, involving ninety-nine defendants, were referred to Moscow for confirmation and sentencing. Of the ninety-nine defendants at least ten were

---

74 Ibid., III, p. 1254.
75 Klaniczay, 'Hungary', pp. 221–35.
76 See above, Chapter 5

sentenced to death, three died during interrogation, and twenty-one were acquitted. Other scattered pieces of evidence suggest that there were other local trials which for one reason or another did not reach Moscow on referral. In 1667, for example, six women from Gadiach were executed for having allegedly bewitched a nobleman and his wife.[77] Another series of trials in the small town of Lukh between 1656 and 1660 resulted in the accusation of twenty-five persons, five of whom were executed. Most of the charges brought against the witches of Lukh were for having caused the possession of some thirty-five townspeople.[78] All of this indicates that there was something resembling a 'witch-scare' in seventeenth-century Russia, but no 'witch-craze'. Witch-hunting was probably more common in Russia than in the province of Transylvania, but it did not even approach the dimensions that it reached in Poland, which for reasons of proximity and comparable size is the most appropriate standard of comparison.[79]

It is unlikely that the Russian system of criminal procedure had very much to do with the relatively low number of convictions and executions in that country. It is true that all criminal prosecutions in Russia were supposed to come from the local community rather than the officers of Church or state. This requirement, however, did not prevent local officials from bringing charges against suspected witches when private parties failed to do so. Once the original accusation was lodged, the state took over all prosecutions, thus making the Russian system essentially inquisitorial. Torture, sometimes in the most severe form, was freely used, both to secure confessions and to obtain the names of accomplices.[80] Judgement could be reached without the participation of lay jurors. Indeed, the only procedural rule that served as a restraint on unlimited witch-hunting in Russia was the requirement of referring cases to Moscow, and it may very well be that this rule could be ignored.

The main reason why Russian witch-hunting never developed into a major witch-craze was the absence of western demonological theory. If the witch-beliefs that flourished in German intellectual circles had penetrated Russia and had been embraced by local and

77 R. Zguta, 'Was There a Witch Craze in Muscovite Russia?', *Southern Folklore Quarterly*, 40 (1977): 125.

78 Kivelson, 'Through the Prism of Witchcraft', pp. 74–94.

79 R. Zguta, 'Witchcraft Trials in Seventeenth-Century Russia', *American Historical Review*, 82 (1977): 1187–207.

80 J. Baissac, *Les Grands jours de la sorcellerie* (Paris, 1980), pp. 154–5; Kivelson, 'Through the Prism of Witchcraft', p. 81.

central authorities, Russia would probably have had a witch-hunt similar to Poland's. But the ideas simply were not available. The only evidence from the Moscow trials that reflects such beliefs was an alleged renunciation of Christ and an oath of allegiance to Satan by a male witch tried in 1663.[81] Whether this charge reflects a late seventeenth-century Polish influence or the survival of an older, Augustinian idea that sorcerers were servants of Satan, it is clear that there was no Russian belief in the sabbath, cannibalistic infanticide or flight. Russian witchcraft, even more than English witchcraft, remained a crime of harmful magic, not Devil-worship. *Maleficium*, moreover, even when tried in secular tribunals, remained a sign of paganism, not demonic heresy, and as such it was incapable of inspiring a massive witch-hunt among either the ruling class or the peasantry (which was tolerant of paganism to begin with). The reason for the relative mildness of Russian witch-hunting, therefore, lies ultimately in the failure of Orthodox Christianity to develop the same demonological world-view as the Latin Church did in the late Middle Ages.

Southern Europe

It may seem inappropriate to consider the Mediterranean region last in this survey of European witchcraft, for it was in Spain, Portugal and Italy that the most durable symbol of witchcraft prosecutions – the Inquisition – maintained its strength longer than in any other parts of Europe. It was in Italian lands, moreover, that some of the earliest witchcraft prosecutions took place.[82] Yet if we use the total number of executions as a standard for evaluating the relative intensity of witchcraft prosecutions, then these southern countries deserve to be treated last. Indeed, if we exclude the Italian-speaking Alpine regions, it would be difficult to find evidence for more than 500 executions in the entire Mediterranean region. Most of these were ordered by secular courts rather than the various tribunals of the Inquisition.[83] In the Spanish American colonies there were apparently no executions

---

81 Ibid., p. 1204.

82 Kieckhefer, *European Witch Trials*, p. 21; Baissac, *Les Grands jours*, pp. 34–43; Trevor-Roper, 'European Witch-Craze', p. 135.

83 Henningsen, 'Papers of Salazar', p. 104, estimates a few hundred executions for all of Spain. For a report of some of the local prosecutions see Kamen, *Inquisition and Society*, pp. 210–15. In Portugal secular courts were responsible for all but one execution for witchcraft. F. Bethencourt, 'Portugal: A Scrupulous Inquisition', in *Early Modern European Witchcraft: Centres and Peripheries*, ed. B. Ankarloo and G. Henningsen (Oxford, 1990), p. 405.

at all.[84] We must not conclude from this, however, that witchcraft was of little concern to Italian, Spanish and Portuguese authorities. The total number of prosecutions in these countries was in fact fairly substantial. For example, in Spain during the period 1580–1650 the Inquisition tried more than 3,500 persons for various types of magic and witchcraft.[85] In Italy, where the records of the Inquisition are still being researched, the numbers were even higher: the tribunal in Venice alone dealt with more than 700 persons.[86] In Portugal, where work on the records is also incomplete, a total of 291 witches were tried in the southern part of the kingdom alone.[87] The mildness of Iberian and Italian witchcraft, therefore, derives mainly from the reluctance of Spanish, Portuguese and Italian courts to put witches to death. This reluctance can in turn be explained by the way in which inquisitors viewed the crime they were prosecuting, the procedures that they followed, and the careful supervision of their work by central authorities.

One of the most striking features of Italian and Iberian witchcraft prosecutions was the rarity of charges of collective Devil-worship. The belief in such assemblies was not unknown in either peninsula, and in a few large hunts it appeared in a rather dramatic form. The confessions of the Basque witches of 1610 provide us with some of the richest descriptions of the witches' sabbath in all of Europe.[88] But in the large majority of cases heard by Spanish and Roman inquisitors, especially in the southern parts of both peninsulas, these charges are completely absent. Peasants and town-dwellers were accused of performing various types of magic, including love magic and healing, and their magic was considered to be heretical, but this was not taken to mean that they had made face-to-face pacts with the Devil or had worshipped him collectively. Nor were the magical practices of these people generally considered to be maleficent. They were to be prosecuted, of course, but the purpose was to correct error and purify

84 Monter, *Ritual, Myth and Magics*, pp. 98–107; R.E. Greenleaf, *Zumárraga and the Mexican Inquisition, 1536–1543* (Washington, 1962), pp. 111–21; idem, *The Mexican Inquisition of the Sixteenth Century* (Albuquerque, 1969), p. 173. For Brazil see L. de Mello e Souza, *O Diabo e a Terra de Santa Cruz* (São Paulo, 1987), pp. 277–378.

85 Parker, 'Some Recent Work', p. 529.

86 Martin, *Witchcraft and the Inquisition in Venice*, p. 226.

87 F. Bethencourt, 'Portugal: A Scrupulous Inquisition', in *Early Modern Witchcraft: Centres and Peripheries*, ed. B. Ankarloo and G. Henningsen (Oxford, 1990); p. 405.

88 Henningsen, *Witches' Advocate*, pp. 69–94.

the faith, not to protect society from a conspiratorial menace.[89] The end result, therefore, was the frequent administration of non-capital sentences by the Inquisition in the traditional manner of ecclesiastical justice.[90]

There is no single explanation for the prevalence of this view of witchcraft in Spain and Italy. One important factor was the widespread belief in classical forms of witchcraft. Both the Spanish and the Italian witch were very often viewed in the manner of Horace's Canidia or the even more widely known sorceress Celestina, a woman depicted in Fernando de Rojas's play, *Tragicomedy of Calisto and Melibea* (1499), who engages in love magic, fortune telling and divination. Such women were believed to use the flesh of children to make their spells and to acquire the power to summon up the Devil, but they had little in common with the German and Swiss witches who flew to the sabbath. As Julio Caro Baroja has shown, this type of witch tended to flourish in urban rather than rural environments, not only because such women actually plied their trade there but also because the Renaissance culture that supported the belief in such figures was predominantly urban to begin with.[91] It is no coincidence that the areas of both Italy and Spain in which the cumulative concept of witchcraft was widely known and in which a majority of the prosecutions took place were both rural and northern, subject to northern (i.e., either German or French) influences.

A survey of Italian and Spanish witchcraft literature reinforces the conclusion that the stereotypical view of the witch never gained widespread acceptance in the Mediterranean world. It is true that in the late Middle Ages Italian and, to a lesser extent, Spanish intellectuals had made important contributions to the cumulative concept of witchcraft, while the Papacy itself was largely responsible for equating magic and heresy. Once the concept of witchcraft had been formulated, however, very few Spanish or Italian writers provided explicit support for the definition of witchcraft that had emerged or contributed to its further development. The overly credulous judge Paulus Grillandus did subscribe to most of the learned

89 M. O'Neil, 'Magical Healing, Love Magic and the Inquisition in Late Sixteenth-Century Modena', in S. Haliczer (ed.), *Inquisition and Society in Early Modern Europe*, (Totowa, NJ, 1987), pp. 88–114. Martin, *Witchcraft and the Inquisition in Venice*, pp. 292, 254.

90 J. Tedeschi, 'Inquisitorial Law and the Witch', in *Early Modern European Witchcraft*, p. 94.

91 Caro Baroja, *World of Witches*, pp. 99–102.

notions of witchcraft in his *Tractatus de Hereticis et Sortilegiis*, drawing upon cases that he had adjudicated in Rome and southern Italy, but after that time the only Italian author who fully subscribed to the cumulative concept of witchcraft was Francesco Maria Guazzo, a Milanese friar who based his popular *Compendium Maleficarum* not only on numerous French and German sources but also on his own experience as a witchcraft prosecutor in the Rhineland.[92] It can be argued, therefore, that at the height of the great hunt the most extreme and credulous Italian witch-beliefs had northern rather than native sources. The same can be said for Spain, where the demonological ideas that prevailed during the great Basque trials can be traced to southern France and the work of the demonologist Pierre de Lancre.[93] Overall, the cumulative concept of witchcraft did not become firmly established in Spain, especially in the south.[94]

The failure of the cumulative concept of witchcraft to take hold in Italy during the height of the witch-craze can be explained partly by the strength of a sceptical tradition within Italian intellectual circles. Much of this scepticism can be linked either directly or indirectly to humanism, which had its oldest and deepest roots in Italy. Humanism, as discussed above, was not intrinsically incompatible with witchcraft doctrine, for it did not deny the existence of diabolical power in the world and it accepted the efficacy of magic. The practice of learned magic by neo-Platonists might also have contributed, in an indirect way, to the rise of witch-hunting in Italy.[95] But humanism did encourage a sceptical attitude towards scholastic thinking, and many humanists did in fact criticize certain aspects of the cumulative concept as well as witchcraft prosecutions themselves. It was largely due to this Renaissance scepticism that the views of the *Malleus Maleficarum* met with especially strong criticism in Italy in the early sixteenth century, and it may well have been the persistence of such attitudes during the later period that prevented French and German ideas from finding enthusiastic support.[96]

The failure of many learned witch-beliefs to take hold among Italian inquisitors may have had something to do with the popularity of Nicholas Eymeric's *Directorium Inquisitorum* (1376), the in-

92 Robbins, *Encyclopedia*, pp. 236–7; Monter, 'Witchcraft in France and Italy', *History Today*, 30 (1980): 33.

93 Henningsen, 'Papers of Salazar', pp. 88–96.

94 Henningsen, *Witches' Advocate*, pp. 22–3.

95 P. Burke, 'Witchcraft and Magic in Renaissance Italy: Gianfrancesco Pico and his *Strix*', in S. Anglo (ed.), *The Damned Art*, p. 49.

96 See Caro Baroja, *World of Witches*, pp. 104–5.

quisitorial manual most widely used in Italy throughout the period of the great witch-hunt. The form of witchcraft described in Eymeric's manual was ritual magic, which Eymeric considered in true scholastic fashion to be a form of heresy, since it involved a pact with the Devil. There was a dramatic difference between this conception of witchcraft and that which was later enshrined in works like the *Malleus Maleficarum* and Del Rio's *Disquisitionum*. Eymeric had nothing to say about the sabbath or, for that matter, *maleficium*. By relying on Eymeric's definition of witchcraft, therefore, Italian inquisitors perpetuated an earlier view of the crime which excluded many of the elements that had been added to the cumulative concept of witchcraft after he wrote the manual.[97]

Another reason for the relative tameness of witchcraft prosecutions in Italy and Spain was the adherence of the Inquisition in each country to fairly strict procedural rules. In the Middle Ages papal inquisitors had become notorious for their unrestrained use of torture and the many other ways in which they had prejudiced the case against the accused. By the time the European witch-hunt began, however, inquisitors had produced a large body of cautionary literature, and the two early modern institutions that succeeded the medieval inquisition – the Spanish and the Roman Inquisitions – demonstrated exceptional concern for procedural propriety. Indeed, the Roman Holy Office has been referred to as 'a pioneer in judicial reform'.[98] Unlike many secular courts, it made provision for legal counsel; it furnished the defendant with a copy of the charges and evidence against him; and it assigned very little weight to the testimony of a suspected witch against her alleged confederates.[99] One of the most noteworthy features of both Spanish and Roman inquisitorial procedure is that torture was rarely employed. In Spain it was used only when there was strong circumstantial evidence but no proof, and it was applied towards the end of the trial, just before judgement was pronounced.[100] Even in the great Basque witch-hunt of 1610–14, which involved thousands of suspects, the Inquisition tortured only two of the accused, and since the torture actually allowed their sentences to be commuted from death to banishment,

---

97 Martin, *Witchcraft and the Inquisition in Venice*, pp. 50–66, 253–5.

98 J. Tedeschi, 'Preliminary Observations on Writing a History of the Roman Inquisition', in *Continuity and Discontinuity in Church History*, ed. F.F. Church and T. George (Leiden, 1979), p. 42.

99 Ibid., pp. 242–3.

100 Henningsen, *Witches' Advocate*, pp. 44, 170.

it can be legitimately considered an act of mercy.[101] The only pressure to use torture as a deliberate means to extract confessions came from local secular authorities and local mobs, groups whose extra-legal tactics the Inquisition sought to restrain. In Italy there was no less of a reluctance to use torture.[102] Even the *benandanti*, the members of an ancient fertility cult who were gradually convinced that they were witches, were never put to torture.[103]

The restraint shown by both the Spanish and the Roman Inquisitions in the use of torture had a predictable effect upon witch-hunting in the Mediterranean world. It did not completely prevent large witch-hunts from taking place, since local panics and dream epidemics were by themselves capable of supplying large numbers of suspects. But without the unrestricted use of torture the hunts that developed did not produce as many convictions or result in as many executions as the large hunts that occurred in Germany and Switzerland. Even more important, the reluctance to use torture prevented the development of extreme, diabolical witch-beliefs. Without torture the potential for transforming simple acts of superstition into crimes of diabolical conspiracy was greatly limited, since only through confessions adduced under torture could diabolical beliefs gain the widespread legitimacy that was necessary to sustain further witch-hunting. Without torture it was certain that the learned as well as the popular view of witchcraft would remain essentially an individual moral transgression, not a large-scale attack upon Christian civilization.

In explaining the relative tameness of Spanish and Italian witch hunting one additional factor – the strength of central control – must also be mentioned. Although medieval inquisitors had always received their commissions from Rome, they had never been subject to central regulation or coordination. In the sixteenth and seventeenth centuries, however, inquisitors lost this autonomy. The loss was most apparent in Spain, where a new national institution under the king was established in 1478, superseding the medieval inquisition that had operated only in Aragon. The main organ of this new institution was the supreme council at Madrid, which exercised strict control over a large number of regional tribunals (eventually twenty-one)

---

101 Ibid., pp. 170–1. Salazar proposed that the same procedure be used with the other accused witches, pp. 179–80.

102 Tedeschi, 'Inquisitorial Law and the Witch', pp. 97–104; Martin, *Witchcraft and the Inquisition in Venice*, pp. 26–8.

103 For the threat of torture against one of the *benandanti* see Ginzburg, *Night Battles*, p. 105.

throughout Spain and its overseas possessions. In the early sixteenth century some of these courts had managed to exercise a large measure of local autonomy, but by 1550 the supreme council had established its superiority over all local tribunals.[104] The effect of this assertion of central control on the process of witch-hunting became evident in Barcelona in the 1530s, when the supreme council put an end to a witch-hunt by establishing its right to confirm all sentences.[105] Even more dramatically, the supreme council put an end to the great Basque witch-hunt of 1610–14 and dealt the entire witch-craze a serious blow when, upon the recommendation of Salazar, it issued a very strict set of procedural rules for the prosecution of witches throughout the country. The authority and influence of the supreme council was even evident in secular witchcraft prosecutions. In a number of seventeenth-century cases, most notably in northern Vizcaya in 1621, the council managed to bring about modifications of very severe sentences.[106]

The various inquisitorial tribunals that operated in Italy outside the Papal States were not subject to the same degree of central control as those in Spain. Some of the regional bodies, such as the Inquisition in Venice, which included lay members representing the secular government, operated with a certain measure of independence from the Congregation of the Holy Office in Rome.[107] Nevertheless, the Roman Inquisition achieved some success in its efforts to standardize procedure and sentencing practices throughout Italy. It gave prior approval to all sentences and, even more important, occasionally demanded that provincial inquisitors conduct further investigation of cases that it believed required such action.[108] Even the Venetian Inquisition, which jealously defended its independence, often consulted with Rome on matters of procedure and sometimes extradited suspects to Rome for trial.[109]

Before leaving the subject of Mediterranean witchcraft we must consider Trevor-Roper's thesis that witchcraft prosecutions in Spain were relatively mild because the Spanish directed all their hostility towards Jews instead of witches. This thesis is based upon the

---

104 E. Peters, *Inquisition* (Berkeley, 1989), pp. 90, 101. For conflict with local tribunals in Saragossa in 1535 and Barcelona in 1548–49 see Monter, *Frontiers of Heresy*, pp. 264–6.
105 H. Kamen, *The Spanish Inquisition* (New York, 1965), p. 145.
106 Henningsen, *Witches' Advocate*, pp. 387–9.
107 Peters, *Inquisition*, pp. 109–19.
108 Ginzburg, *Night Battles*, pp. 125–6.
109 Peters, *Inquisition*, p. 117.

assumption that the prosecution of witches was just one manifestation of a more general need of society to find scapegoats for its problems and to release social tension by prosecuting them. Witches and Jews (and for that matter heretics and any other minority groups) were in a certain sense interchangeable. Either of them could serve as an object of social fear and discrimination; it was simply a question of which group appeared more threatening. One of the corollaries of this argument is the elimination of the fear of one group can lead to the prosecution of the other, as society finds new scapegoats after the old ones are dispensed with. Another corollary is that judicial officials have only so much time to devote to the prosecution of deviant groups and that it is likely therefore that only one such group would be prosecuted at one time.[110]

This thesis has only limited value in explaining the mildness of Spanish witch-hunting. It can help us to understand why relatively few Spanish witches were prosecuted in the late fifteenth and early sixteenth centuries. Although Spanish inquisitors had been concerned with ritual magic in the fourteenth and fifteenth centuries, they did not maintain their vigilance as such magicians in France and the Rhineland were transformed into witches. Instead they turned their attention almost exclusively to Jews, who were the main reason for the establishment of the Inquisition in 1478 and who bore the full brunt of its force until about 1540. It is difficult, however, to attribute the mildness of Spanish witch-hunting *after* 1540 to the presence of Jewish scapegoats, since by that time the problem had been largely resolved and the Inquisition had turned its attention to other matters. Now one might argue that the increase in the number of Spanish witches after 1580 was in fact a result of the decline of the Jewish threat; that would be consistent with the general tenor of Trevor-Roper's argument. But it is impossible to explain the *mildness* of Spanish witch-hunting – which as we have seen is not to be measured by the number of trials but by the number of executions – in this way. There is simply no way we can attribute the 'moderate wisdom' of Spain in handling witches after 1540 to the presence of Jewish scapegoats in Spanish society. The fact of the matter is that Jews were *not* being prosecuted during this period and witches were. The reasons for the lenient treatment of witches had a great deal to do with the nature of the Inquisition and the way in which the crime of witchcraft was perceived at the time, and precious little to do with the Jews.

110 Trevor-Roper, 'European Witch-Craze', pp. 110–12.

CONCLUSION

In describing the general patterns of European witch-hunting, historians frequently compare the European continent with England, showing how the prohibition of torture and the incomplete reception of demonological theory in England prevented witchcraft prosecutions from becoming as intemperate and extensive as they were in places like Germany and Switzerland. The comparison is both valid and instructive, but its frequent use can lead to an oversimplified view of the geography of European witchcraft. On the one hand it can lead to the unwarranted conclusion that England was the only European country in which authorities prosecuted witches in moderate numbers. On the other hand it can lead to the equally false assumption that there was a common 'continental' European pattern of witchcraft prosecutions. The foregoing regional survey of witchcraft should make the invalidity of those assumptions readily apparent. England, with its distinctive body of national law and its failure to adopt either civil law or inquisitorial procedure, may have been very different from France and the various states of Germany in the way it dealt with witches (just as it was different from them in many other ways), but it was by no means the only exception to the prevailing European norm. One can just as easily claim that witchcraft prosecutions in Denmark, Norway, Russia and Spain were 'exceptional' by German or Swiss standards.

There were in fact so many regions in Europe where demonological ideas were only partially received, where the application of torture was effectively restricted, where the conviction- and execution-rates in witchcraft cases were kept fairly low, and where mass witch-hunts occurred only on rare occasions, that one must seriously question whether there really was a general European witch-craze. There was certainly a general European witch-*hunt* in which various countries participated to a larger or somewhat smaller extent. But a witch-craze, characterized by an unrestrained and often panicky pursuit of large numbers of witches, really only took place in western and west-central Europe. Although we shall never have complete statistics, those that are available suggest that as many as 75 per cent of all witchcraft prosecutions occurred in that large and populous area. Within that zone we can define the boundaries of the witch-craze even more narrowly, since the number of trials in the kingdom of France was relatively small. The real centre of the witch-craze was the area that encompassed the Holy Roman Empire, Switzerland and the various French-speaking duchies and principalities that bordered on

German and Swiss lands. In comparison to this area, all other regions – except perhaps Poland – were temperate in their pursuit of witches and mild in their treatment of them.

There are of course no simple explanations for the rather uneven geographical pattern of prosecutions we have traced in its broader outline. Generally speaking, however, four separate but related variables had the greatest effect. The first was the nature of witch-beliefs in a particular region and the strength with which they were held. Wherever witchcraft was defined primarily as *maleficium* and not as Devil-worship, witch-hunts tended to remain limited in scope, mainly because the suspicion that one person practised sorcery did not usually lead to a search for accomplices. The contrast between Germany, where the belief in diabolism was widespread, and a country like Russia, where it was virtually absent, could not be more pronounced. In many areas, however, the crime of witchcraft could be defined in either way, with theories of diabolism receiving only occasional expression and commanding only limited subscription. This was certainly the situation in England, the Scandinavian countries, and Spain, and in each of these countries the pattern of witchcraft prosecutions included both a number of individual trials for *maleficium* and a few larger hunts for Devil-worship.

The second major factor in determining the relative intensity of witchcraft prosecutions was the system of criminal procedure that was used in the courts. Although we tend to assume that all European courts, with the exception of those in England, followed 'inquisitorial' procedure and used torture freely, we have seen that witchcraft trials were conducted in a wide variety of ways. Methods of initiating cases, rules regarding the use of torture, customs regarding the appointment of advocates, and procedures for appealing sentences all differed from place to place. Differences in procedures had profound effects on the process of witch-hunting, since they greatly influenced the chances of conviction and execution. Legal procedures also had an effect upon the reception of witch-beliefs among the judicial class, for it was often only under torture that certain witch-beliefs could be legitimized through confessions.

The third major determinant of the intensity of witchcraft prosecutions was the degree of central judicial control over the trials. Central control did not necessarily serve as a restraining force in witchcraft cases, since some rulers were often very eager to see witchcraft eliminated, and occasionally even initiated witch-hunts. But as a rule local authorities (the magistrates of a particular town or village or the judicial officers of a small region) were more determined to detect, prosecute and execute witches than those who occupied higher positions of authority in Church or state, and more likely to violate the procedural rules formulated by central governments while doing so. The relative mildness of English, Swedish, Russian and Spanish witch-hunting, as well as that which took place in the central areas of France, can be attributed at least in part to the success of central secular or ecclesiastical authorities in restraining the enthusiasm of local authorities for waging a full-scale war against Satan's allies.

The final factor that must be taken into account in explaining regional patterns is the degree of religious zeal manifested by the people of a particular region. It is of course difficult to measure religious zeal, and it is even more difficult to demonstrate its effects upon witchcraft prosecutions. But it clearly was a motor force in many large hunts, and it does appear that those countries which convicted and executed witches in great numbers were known for their Christian militancy, their religious intolerance and their vigorous participation in either the Reformation or the Counter-Reformation. Differences between witch-hunting in New England and the other North American colonies, between England and Scotland, between Poland and Russia, and between Italy and Germany can all be attributed in some measure to these elusive differences in general religious 'enthusiasm'. These differences can in turn be linked to the religious stability of the countries in question, for it was areas that had experienced religious change or felt threatened by it that tended to pursue witches with the greatest determination. These areas were, moreover, much more likely than others to become preoccupied with diabolical witch-beliefs and to allow their magistrates to use torture in order to protect the Christian faith. In this way religious zeal tended to reinforce other reasons for intense witch-hunting, just as its absence allowed public officials to develop a more 'enlightened' and moderate attitude towards the whole process.

8 DECLINE AND SURVIVAL

During the late seventeenth and early eighteenth centuries European witchcraft prosecutions declined in number and eventually came to an end. The decline did not occur simultaneously in all European countries and regions. In the Netherlands, for example, the decline became evident early in the seventeenth century, whereas in Poland prosecutions did not begin to drop off until after 1725. Despite these differences in timing, the decline of witchcraft was a European-wide phenomenon, and its occurrence within a hundred-year period in every country that had experienced witch-hunting suggests that there are general reasons for the end of the great witch-hunt, just as there were general reasons for its beginning.

The decline of witchcraft prosecutions raises two major problems of interpretation. The first concerns the distinction between individual prosecutions and large hunts. There was a difference between the end of mass prosecutions that took scores, if not hundreds, of lives and the termination of all trials, no matter how small. The two developments are closely related, since many critics of witch-hunting opposed all trials, large and small, and because the negative reaction to some of the large panics contributed to the eventual termination of all witchcraft prosecutions. But the reasons for the decline of the two types of prosecution were not always the same. Large hunts came to an end as European communities, having experienced the social dysfunction that mass panics produce and having come to the conclusion that innocent people had suffered in the process, became determined to prevent the recurrence of such undertakings and establish legal procedures that would prevent the chain-reaction type of hunt from developing. These hunts also declined when the social, economic and religious conditions that helped to create a mood conducive to witch-hunting no longer prevailed. Individual witchcraft prosecutions, on the other hand, died out only after laws were passed prohibiting them or after the judicial authorities of a particular locality adopted a policy of refusing to try such cases. The decline of both types of witch-hunting required the emergence of a sceptical mentality, but the complete termination of witch-hunting was predicated upon a much more profound scepticism regarding the reality of witchcraft than that which caused the cessation of the large hunts.

The second problem of interpretation connected with the decline of witchcraft concerns the respective roles of the élite and the common people in the process. Traditionally historians have emphasized the part played by the ruling classes and the educated élite in bringing witch-hunting to an end. It was certainly within the upper levels of society that the new scepticism first took hold, and it was certainly these men who took the necessary political and legal steps to stop prosecutions completely. By way of contrast, popular witch-beliefs showed little sign of changing at this time, and on numerous occasions members of the lower classes pushed for the prosecution of alleged witches, only to be frustrated by the refusal of a sceptical magistrate to countenance the prosecution. Nevertheless, the lower classes may have had much more to do with the decline of witchcraft than has been previously acknowledged. One scholar has argued that the hysteria manifested during the witch-hunts was mainly that of the bureaucratic class and that enlightenment came from the more rational common people.[1] It is true of course that the most extreme witch-beliefs, those most capable of sustaining a witch-hunt, came mainly from the upper classes and were shaped and disseminated mainly by them. It is also true that throughout the period of witch-hunting there was a tradition of lower-class scepticism that emerged when officials tried to obtain confessions. At the very peak of a major Scottish witch-hunt, for example, a woman from Newbattle in Midlothian challenged the entire theory of the Devil's mark, claiming that everyone had such bodily imperfections.[2] Even more important, the common people could and did play an important role in stopping large witch-hunts. Since they helped to sustain the mood of large witch-hunts, and since they also performed the essential judicial functions of denouncing and testifying against their neighbours, the common people had the capacity to bring witch-hunts to an end whenever they realized that the trials were doing more harm than good.

One of the best examples of the way in which the people of a community could take steps to stop a witch-hunt comes from the small German town of Lindheim, where in 1661 the magistrate,

---

1 Baeyer-Katte, 'Historischen Hexenprozesse', pp. 220–31.
2 Scottish Record Office, CH2/276/4.

Georg Ludwig Geiss, executed a midwife and six other women for killing a child at birth and using the remains to concoct a magical ointment. He also arrested the mother and father of the child, who had testified that they did not suspect the midwife and had actually exhumed the baby's body to show that it was still intact. As the hunt developed (there were thirty executions in all) and when the father of the baby, a well-to-do miller, was tortured, sentiment in the town turned against the magistrate. The miller and a few other prisoners managed to escape and to present a counter-suit against Geiss at the imperial supreme court at Speyer, which ordered the witch-trials to cease. This action came too late to save the life of the miller's wife, but popular resistance to the trials became so strong that one man physically assaulted the judicial official who had come to arrest his wife, and Geiss himself was forced to flee.[3]

Although the lower classes did occasionally help to bring individual witch-hunts to an end, they cannot be credited with the primary responsibility for the long-term decline of witch-hunting. There is no evidence, for example, that European villagers of the late seventeenth and early eighteenth centuries gradually lost their magical beliefs and therefore became increasingly reluctant to accuse their neighbours of witchcraft. The number of formal accusations did in fact decline during these years, but this had nothing to do with popular scepticism or 'enlightenment'. Villagers made fewer witchcraft accusations against their neighbours either because they had little hope of prosecuting them successfully or because the conditions which encouraged them to do so no longer prevailed. In neither case could the villagers be considered to have actively caused the decline in accusations. Indeed, all the evidence regarding individual witchcraft prosecutions from the late seventeenth century until the end of the hunt suggests that they arose mainly in response to lower-class pressure and that any scepticism regarding the accusations came from the ruling classes and the educated élite.

It is tempting to claim that witchcraft prosecutions died of their own weight or that they contained the seeds of their own decline. To the extent that the conduct of the large hunts engendered criticism of the entire process of witch-hunting, this argument is certainly valid. But it would be misleading to assert that witch-hunts simply burned themselves out. The trials and even the large hunts went on long enough in the various regions of Europe to show that under certain circumstances the prosecution of witches could continue indefinitely.

3 Baschwitz, *Hexen und Hexenprozesse*, pp. 302–4.

What brought the trials to an end was not simply a recognition that witch-hunting could get out of control, but a series of significant changes in European judicial systems, in the mental outlook of the educated and ruling classes, in the religious climate that prevailed throughout Europe, and in the general conditions in which people lived.

JUDICIAL CHANGES

In dealing with the decline of witchcraft it is appropriate first to discuss the various changes that took place in the operation of European judicial systems, both in general and with specific reference to witchcraft. These judicial changes deserve primary consideration because in most cases it was objections to witchcraft prosecutions on legal and judicial grounds that first led to their reduction in numbers. Indeed, some of the early critics of witch-hunting based their case solely on legal grounds, insisting that their scepticism was in no way philosophical.[4] These men actually facilitated the decline of witchcraft without abandoning the notion that witchcraft was possible or that witches did in fact exist.

There were three main judicial and legal developments that contributed to the decline of witchcraft: (1) the demand for conclusive evidence regarding *maleficium* and the pact; (2) the adoption of stricter rules regarding the use of torture; and (3) the promulgation of decrees either restricting or eliminating prosecutions for witchcraft. The first of these, the demand for more solid evidence of witchcraft, expressed itself in many different ways. It could take the form of a judicial decision that there was insufficient evidence to justify the use of torture, an investigation to determine whether *maleficium* might have had natural causes, an insistence on infallible proof of the demonic pact, or a more general plea for special caution in witchcraft cases.[5] Sometimes the sceptical demand for evidence would be based on the difficulty of establishing the actual commission of *maleficium*. In the late seventeenth century, for example, a number of judges became increasingly reluctant to accept the occurrence of misfortune shortly after the expression of hostility as proof that sorcery had in

4 Thomas, *Religion and the Decline of Magic*, p. 576.

5 B. Shapiro, *Probability and Certainty in Seventeenth-Century England* (Princeton, 1983), pp. 194–226; Ginzburg, *Night Battles*, p. 126; Thomas, *Religion and the Decline of Magic*, pp. 574–5; P. Miller, *The New England Mind: From Colony to Province* (Cambridge, Mass., 1953), p. 205.

fact been practised. When we consider the fact that most charges of *maleficium* arose as attempts by neighbours to explain misfortunes that mysteriously beset them, the significance of this more demanding attitude becomes apparent. To prove the commission of *maleficium* one needed tangible evidence of magical intent, and without the actual instruments of magic (such as were often adduced in court against ritual magicians in the late Middle Ages) the case was difficult to prove. A similar scepticism arose regarding the demonic pact. Aside from confession itself, the main evidence regarding the pact was the Devil's mark. For more than a hundred years judges had accepted the mark as evidence of the pact, using it to allow torture and incorporating it into the libel or indictment. In the late seventeenth century, however, judges became increasingly reluctant to allow evidence of the Devil's mark to be admitted, thus making witchcraft prosecutions much more difficult to sustain.[6] A third type of evidence that was gradually excluded was spectral evidence, the testimony of an afflicted person that she could see the spectre or spirit of the offending party.

A second change in legal procedure that led to a significant reduction in witchcraft prosecutions and convictions was a growing reluctance to use torture as an instrument of judicial interrogation. The administration of torture had been criticized throughout the period of the great witch-hunt, both on humanitarian grounds and for the eminently practical reason that confessions adduced under torture were unreliable.[7] Nevertheless, the regular use of torture had persisted in most European jurisdictions, and it was because of torture, more than any other single factor, that large witch-hunts had been able to develop. During the seventeenth century, however, a number of European jurisdictions adopted much stricter rules than they had previously followed regarding both the application of torture and the admissibility of evidence obtained by it. Such rules were promulgated in Spain in 1614, in Italy in the 1620s and in Scotland in the 1660s.[8] Similar restrictions also emerged in various German principalities in the period after 1630, perhaps partially as a result of the publication

---

6 Mackenzie, *Laws and Customes* (1678), p. 91.

7 Even those who urged the prosecution of witches recognized the problems inherent in torture. See Peter Binsfeld, *De Confessionibus Maleficarum et Sagarum* (Treves, 1596), pp. 679–98.

8 Henningsen, *Witches' Advocate*, p. 373; Lea, *Materials*, II, pp. 960–1; *Register of the Privy Council of Scotland*, 3rd ser., pp. 187, 210.

of Friedrich Spee's *Cautio Criminalis,* a devastating critique of the procedures used in German witchcraft trials.[9]

Restrictions on the use of torture were followed ultimately by its complete abolition. This process, which was facilitated by the decline of non-capital punishments and a lower premium on confessions, occurred in Scotland in 1709, Prussia in 1740, Saxony in 1770, Austria in 1776, Belgium in 1787, Switzerland in 1803 and Bavaria in 1806. With the possible exception of Scotland, this final elimination of torture had little demonstrable effect on witch-hunting, if only because abolition came so late. Indeed, the desire to execute witches, which usually could not be accomplished unless confessions were forthcoming, was at least partially responsible for keeping the torture system functional. The abolition of torture became possible only when authorities no longer believed that witchcraft merited the death penalty.[10]

In addition to imposing restrictions on the use of torture, princes and legislative assemblies throughout Europe took deliberate steps in the late seventeenth and eighteenth centuries to reduce or eliminate witchcraft prosecutions. These proclamations often had a dramatic impact on the process of witch-hunting. An edict of Louis XIV of France in 1682, which prescribed mere corporal punishment for acts of divination and classified the practice of magic as mere 'superstition', was largely responsible for bringing a virtual end to witch-hunting in France. One of the reasons it had such an effect was that it applied to the entire country and thereby greatly reduced the amount of judicial discretion that both local courts and the regional *parlements* had traditionally exercised in the treatment of witchcraft.[11] The same was true for the Prussian decrees of 1714 and 1721, the efforts of Empress Maria Theresa to eliminate witch-hunting in Austria and Hungary between 1755 and 1768, and the Polish prohibition of 1776.[12] We must not, however, assign too

9 Bremen, where the first German translation of Spee's treatise took place, abandoned torture in witch trials in 1640. See Monter, *Ritual, Myth and Magic,* p. 30. For a translation of sections of the *Cautio* see Kors and Peters, *Witchcraft in Europe,* pp. 351–7.

10 See M. Damaska, 'The Death of Legal Torture', *Yale Law Journal,* 86 (1978): 873–8.

11 For the entire process of royal intervention in the provinces see Mandrou, *Magistrats et sorciers,* pp. 425–86.

12 See W.G. Soldan and H. Heppe, *Geschichte der Hexenprozesse,* ed. M. Bauer (Munich, 1912), II, p. 265; Lea, *Materials,* III, p. 1435; G. Klaniczay, 'Decline of Witches and Rise of Vampires in 18th-Century Habsburg Monarchy', *Ethnologia Europaea,* 17 (1987): 165–8; Damaska, 'Death of Legal Torture', p. 874 n. 28.

much significance to all such royal decrees and statutes, for some prohibitions of witchcraft trials were put into effect long after the trials had in fact ceased and therefore merely ratified an existing situation. The repeal of both the English and the Scottish witchcraft statutes by the British Parliament in 1736 had very little practical effect and went virtually unnoticed by contemporaries because prosecutions in both countries had by that time long since come to an end. Nevertheless, in dealing with the decline of witchcraft, we must be aware of the fact that princes, central councils and representative assemblies very often did use their power to keep the prosecution of witches under control and in some instances effectively ended witch-hunting in their countries.

THE NEW MENTAL OUTLOOK

At the same time that judges and princes were creating new rules of evidence, restricting the use of torture, and banning witchcraft trials, changes were taking place in the mental world of European élites which made them sceptical regarding the reality of witchcraft. These changes were in fact closely related to the judicial changes we have just described, since judicial caution in handling witchcraft cases, the reluctance to use torture and the prohibition of trials were often based on a scepticism regarding the reality of the alleged crime. Although some magistrates and judges insisted that their scepticism was strictly legal and that witches did in fact exist, many harboured deep doubts about the reality of such phenomena and therefore were more inclined to insist upon complete proof or voluntary confession before conviction. Perhaps the best example of the combination and interaction of judicial and philosophical scepticism regarding witchcraft is the work of Christian Thomasius, a professor at the University of Halle who in the early years of the eighteenth century criticized both the system of judicial torture and prevailing witch-beliefs.[13]

Although changes in mentality brought about a decline in witchcraft prosecutions only when they affected the magistrates and judges who were entrusted with criminal prosecutions, they were evident in a much broader cross-section of the European élite. Indeed, many of the early attacks on witch-beliefs were made by theologians, philosophers and scientists who had nothing to do with the prosecution of witches.

---

13 C. Thomasius, *Dissertatio De Crimine Magiae*, trans. R. Lieberwirth (Weimar, 1967); *Über die Folter*, trans. and ed. R. Lieberwirth (Weimar, 1960).

Their ideas, however, gradually spread among educated Europeans and eventually penetrated the ruling and magisterial classes.

It is important to note that scepticism regarding witchcraft was not new to the seventeenth century. Throughout the period of the great witch-hunt there had always been a few individuals who questioned the reality of alleged acts of harmful magic and diabolism. Indeed, many of the arguments against the reality of witchcraft that were advanced in the seventeenth and eighteenth centuries were the same as those used by Weyer, Scot and Montaigne in the sixteenth century. The difference between the two periods is that whereas in the sixteenth century the views of the sceptics were refuted by such advocates of witch-hunting as Bodin and Erastus, in the late seventeenth and eighteenth centuries their views were widely and often warmly embraced. The reason for the change is that during the intervening period the entire mental outlook of educated Europeans had changed in such a way that the traditional arguments against the sceptics no longer had persuasive force. Even more important, there was no need to refute the sceptics, for their views no longer posed a threat to religion, philosophy or the social order.

The changes that took place in the mental outlook of educated Europeans, when taken together, amounted to an intellectual revolution that destroyed scholasticism as the predominant philosophical system of Europe and, among other things, dissolved many of the beliefs that lay at the basis of witchcraft prosecutions. The first and most basic of these changes (and at the same time the most difficult to trace) was a growing tendency in all fields of thought to reject dogma and inherited authority – to question everything, even the basic principles upon which one's world-view is based. This tendency can be seen most clearly in the work of René Descartes, who in his search for certain knowledge abandoned reliance upon books, rejected the 'authority' of the ancients as well as of the scholastics, and built his philosophical system upon 'clear and distinct ideas'. Descartes denied that he was a sceptic, at least in the traditional Greek sense of doubting even that one could possess knowledge, since he arrived at a certain knowledge of his own existence and also that of God and the material world. But the process by which Descartes arrived at that certainty – the wholesale rejection of dogma and the systematic expression of doubt – became closely identified with him and with the Cartesianism that spread throughout Europe.[14]

---

14 See R.H. Popkin, *The History of Scepticism from Erasmus to Descartes* (Assen, 1960), pp. 174–216, especially. pp. 212–13.

Cartesianism as a philosophical system is important for our purposes, since it became the main rival of scholasticism in the seventeenth century, but the sceptical methodology that Descartes followed is even more important, for it reflects an attitude that was becoming increasingly prevalent in the seventeenth century. The seventeenth century, with all its religious intolerance and warfare, may strike us as a century of intense and uncompromising faith, and in a certain sense it was. But within the literate élite, among university-educated men, and especially among natural philosophers, it was a period of profound and pervasive doubt. When specific witch-beliefs and the religious and philosophical systems that sustained them became the target of such doubt, the prosecution of witches became increasingly difficult to justify.

A second change in the mental outlook of educated Europeans in the late seventeenth century was the growing conviction that the universe functioned in an orderly, regular fashion, according to fixed laws. This belief found support in the scientific discoveries of Copernicus, Galileo, Kepler and Newton, all of whom contributed to the dethronement of the old Aristotelian–scholastic cosmology in which a stationary earth remained at the centre of the universe, vulnerable to assault by all sorts of supernatural forces. The new mechanistic world-view made the earth part of a smoothly operating machine and it drastically reduced, if it did not completely eliminate, the role of spirits and demons in this universe. Descartes, who was one of the leading exponents of the mechanical philosophy, did not deny the possibility of their existence, but he did deny that they had anything to do with the operation of the universe or that they could take on bodies. Once demons were denied these powers, of course, the entire cumulative concept of witchcraft came under attack.[15]

The mechanical philosophy represented a serious threat to current religious belief, since it could easily lead its advocates from the denial of the existence of spirits to a rejection of miracles, the efficacy of prayer, the operation of Divine Providence and even the existence of God. As the English philosopher Henry More warned in an attack upon the extreme materialistic version of the mechanistic philosophy,

15 On the attractions of the new philosophy, which allowed men to appropriate nature rather than to be victimized by it, see Easlea, *Witch Hunting*, esp. pp. 196–252.

'No spirit, No God'.[16] The implicit danger of atheism might have prevented the widespread acceptance of the mechanical philosophy, had it not been for the determination of natural philosophers like Descartes to make it clear that there was a place for God in their universe and for the willingness of theologians and divines to accommodate the new philosophy. In England, for example, the Established Church and even the nonconformist sects proved to be surprisingly receptive to the new ideas. Latitudinarians rejected demonology, made every effort to reconcile faith with reason, and developed a sophisticated natural theology according to which God worked through the processes of nature.[17] Even biblical literalists endorsed the denial of the power of demons on Earth, since the Bible, while making few references to witchcraft as such, claimed that God – the sovereign God of reformed Protestantism – had chained up the Devil in hell and had thereby prevented him from interfering in human affairs. Religion, therefore, did not prove to be a serious obstacle to the reception of the mechanical philosophy, nor did it prevent educated Europeans from abandoning their belief in demonic power. The Dutch Protestant minister and Cartesian philosopher Balthasar Bekker was representing a growing body of religious opinion when in 1691 he wrote that both scripture and reason prove that 'the Empire of the Devil is but a chimera and that he has neither such a power nor such an Administration as is ordinarily ascribed to him'.[18]

Closely related to the belief in a regular, orderly universe was the growing conviction among educated Europeans that there were natural explanations for mysterious or apparently supernatural phenomena. In the fifteenth and sixteenth centuries the natural world was rather narrowly defined. Any phenomena which could not be readily explained in fairly simple 'naturalistic' terms were readily attributed to supernatural intervention of some sort – a mode of thought that scholasticism encouraged. The first challenge to this scholastic outlook came not so much from the mechanical

---

16 N. Brann, 'The Conflict between Reason and Magic in Seventeenth-Century England: A Case Study of the Vaughan–More Debate', *Huntington Library Quarterly*, 43 (1980): 114. For More, the existence of witchcraft and other forms of demonic activity provided proof of the existence of spirits and hence also of God. See A.R. Hall, *Henry More: Magic, Religion and Experiment* (Oxford, 1990), pp. 138–9.

17 See S.J. Fox, *Science and Justice: The Massachusetts Witchcraft Trials* (Baltimore, 1968), p. 32.

18 Quoted in Easlea, *Witch Hunting*, p. 218.

philosophy but from its rival, the magical cosmology of the neo-Platonists. It might seem surprising that neo-Platonism, a philosophy in which magic held such an important place, could be credited with uprooting a world-view that was in many ways more realistic. But by emphasizing the fact that substances had natural sympathies and antipathies which explain why they act in a certain way, neo-Platonists discouraged a reliance upon supernatural explanations of extraordinary events and encouraged an exploration of the natural world in a genuinely scientific manner.[19] Even when Renaissance magicians felt compelled to supplement natural with spiritual magic they helped to undermine the scholastic cosmology, since in the neo-Platonic world the learned magician could compel spirits to respond to his commands and not therefore remain a victim of capricious demonic forces. In the long run the magical world view of the neo-Platonists was successfully challenged by the other rival to scholasticism, the mechanical philosophy, according to which matter was completely inert and barren and incapable therefore of accommodating any type of magic, natural or spiritual. During its period of influence, however, neo-Platonism helped generations of intellectuals to gain the confidence that extraordinary phenomena had natural causes. It is interesting to note that Reginald Scot, the most radical critic of witch-beliefs and witchcraft prosecutions in the late sixteenth century, fully accepted the reality of natural magic. His credulity may not have helped him respond to his critics, but it does reveal how the theory of natural magic could lead to, or at the very least accommodate, a naturalistic challenge to witch-beliefs.[20]

At the same time that educated Europeans were adopting world-views that encouraged them to attribute extraordinary occurrences to natural causes, they were also beginning to discover that many of the unusual diseases and aberrant forms of behaviour that were customarily attributed to witchcraft could be explained without any reference to the supernatural. Beginning in the second half of the sixteenth century, a number of learned men, especially trained physicians, began to argue that many diseases which were allegedly caused by *maleficium* had natural causes; that individuals who made free confessions to witchcraft were either under the influence of drugs or suffering from some form of melancholy, depression or mental disorder; and that persons who were possessed by the Devil had

19 Trevor-Roper, 'European Witch-Craze', p. 181.

20 Easlea, *Witch Hunting*, p. 23. Weyer also praised natural magic, although he was hostile to diabolical magic. See L. Thorndike, *A History of Magic and Experimental Science* (New York, 1941), VI, 516.

in fact succumbed to some medical malady. The growth of such sentiment was by no means steady, and the medical community itself was divided on these questions.[21] Johann Weyer, whose views on the natural causes of alleged *maleficia* and the melancholy of confessing witches have won him enduring fame as an early sceptic, was effectively refuted by another physician, Thomas Erastus, while a doctor of medicine from Provence, Jacques Fontaine of Maximin, later proved to be even more credulous than Erastus.[22] It has even been suggested that doctors, finding themselves unable to explain a rash of epidemic diseases, actually *caused* the witch-craze.[23]

Nevertheless, doctors did eventually succeed in undermining witch-beliefs.[24] The English doctor Edward Jorden, in an attack upon popular witch-beliefs and the activities of the cunning men, showed that many of the maladies allegedly inflicted by witches were some form of what we would call hysteria, while John Cotta attributed some of the same symptoms to epilepsy.[25] It took some time before a large proportion of educated Europeans became convinced that all diseases had natural causes; even Cotta and Jorden were not willing to rule out certain supernatural maladies.[26] And since there remained a number of undiagnosed illnesses, the temptation to attribute them to preternatural forces was strong. Even when doctors were able to identify the natural causes of physical and mental disease, the belief that witchcraft was involved did not evaporate, for it was perfectly plausible to argue that the Devil worked *through* nature, just as the natural theologians made the same claim with respect to God. By and large, however, the educated élite became convinced that the diseases witches were said to cause, the behaviour that demoniacs manifested, and the wild confessions that some witches made all had natural causes and took place without any participation or cooperation of

21 On early medical opinion see Denis, *Toul*, pp. 13–15.

22 Thorndike, *History of Magic*, VI, pp. 553–4; Monter, *European Witchcraft*, pp. 61–3. On the credulousness of English physicians see G. Tourney, 'The Physician and Witchcraft in Restoration England', *Medical History*, 16 (1972), especially pp. 153–5.

23 See L.L. Estes, 'The Medical Origins of the European Witch-Craze: A Hypothesis', *Journal of Social History*, 17 (1984): 270–84.

24 For a list of physicians critical of witch-beliefs see J. Nemec, *Witchcraft and Medicine, 1484–1793* (Washington, 1974), pp. 4–5.

25 M. MacDonald, *Mystical Bedlam* (Cambridge, 1979), pp. 198–9. See also *Witchcraft and Hysteria in Elizabethan England*, ed. M. Macdonald (London, 1990).

26 For the attempt of Cardinal Barberini to ascertain whether a disease had natural or supernatural causes see Ginzburg, *Night Battles*, pp. 125–6.

spirits or demons. Even when the actual causes of the disease or exceptional behaviour were not yet known, men were optimistic and confident that those causes would eventually be discovered. By 1756 a Hungarian doctor was able to claim that 'these days physicians leave supernatural matters for the clergy'.[27]

The mental changes we have been describing – the growth of Cartesian doubt, the spread of the mechanical philosophy and the conviction that there were natural causes of supernatural phenomena – occurred primarily within the upper levels of European society. As far as we can tell, the witch-beliefs of the lower classes changed very little in the late seventeenth and eighteenth centuries. These were simply reclassified by the élite as 'superstition' and treated with contempt, a striking illustration of what Peter Burke has referred to as the withdrawal of the élite from popular culture.[28] Of course there was some inevitable percolation of upper-class ideas down to the lower levels of society, just as there had been in the fifteenth and sixteenth centuries when learned ideas of the demonic pact and the sabbath had been transmitted to the uneducated through the media of sermons, catechetical instruction, and even witchcraft trials themselves. It is possible that the two groups of educated or semi-educated persons with whom the members of the lower classes had contact – the clergy and physicians – were able to weaken some popular witch-beliefs. The clergy may have been able to convince their parishioners that God worked through the processes of nature and that demons were not constantly threatening men with physical harm, while the doctors may have achieved some success in helping their patients to realize that their diseases were not caused supernaturally, as the cunning men had always argued.[29] It would be rash, however, to assume that these two groups of educated professionals achieved a great deal of success in changing popular attitudes. Scepticism regarding the supernatural is much more difficult to instill in people than credulity, and most local clerics and physicians were probably not confident enough in their scientifically based sceptical views to mount any sort of effective assault on lower-class credulity and superstition.[30]

27 Quoted in Evans, *Habsburg Monarchy*, p. 405.

28 P. Burke, *Popular Culture in Early Modern Europe* (London, 1978), pp. 270–81.

29 Delumeau, *Catholicism*, p. 174, argues that the fear of the Devil diminished as the two Reformations filtered down to the parish level in the late seventeenth century.

30 For the success of one cleric, using the tactics of uninterest rather than persuasion, see J. Boswell, *Journal of a Tour to the Hebrides*, ed. R.W. Chapman (Oxford, 1970), p. 266.

The persistence of superstitious beliefs among the peasantry may have actually contributed, in a somewhat ironic way, to the triumph of scepticism among the élite. One of the tactics that sceptics such as Nicolas de Malebranche, Laurent Bordelon and Cyrano de Bergerac used to win support for their views was to ridicule the beliefs of the silly rustic shepherds and other peasants who continued to claim that witches were active in their communities.[31] The same tactics of ridicule and satire, it should be noted, were later used by William Hogarth and Francisco Goya in the paintings and engravings they made on the theme of witchcraft and superstition. The effect of this ridicule was to encourage members of the upper classes, even those who were not well-educated, to pay at least lip-service to the new scepticism so as to confirm their superiority over the lower classes. Scepticism, in other words, became fashionable. During the late seventeenth and early eighteenth centuries the barriers that separated the various social classes were raised and class divisions and conflicts became more acute throughout Europe. In order to put as much distance as possible between themselves and the common people, the members of the landed and middle classes, especially those who were upwardly mobile, did all they could to prove that they shared nothing with their inferiors. Knowledge of the latest scientific discoveries may have been one way to establish one's social and intellectual credentials, but scepticism regarding witchcraft, since it involved the expression of open contempt for the lower classes, was far more effective. The decline of witch-beliefs among the upper and middle classes may have had as much to do with social snobbery as with the development of new scientific and philosophical ideas.

THE NEW RELIGIOUS CLIMATE

We have already seen how the Reformation, while on the one hand serving to intensify the European witch-hunt, on the other hand planted the seeds of its decline. We have seen how the Protestant view of the sovereignty of God worked against the very possibility of *maleficium*, how the Christianization of the populace weakened the belief in magic; how biblical literalism led to a recognition of the Devil's impotence; and how conflicts between Catholic and Protestants over exorcism led many people to doubt the reality of possession, the Devil and witchcraft. While each of these religious

---

31 Monter, *European Witchcraft*, pp. 113–26; L. Bordelon, *L'Histoire des imaginations extravagantes de Monsieur Oufle* (Paris, 1710).

developments did make some contribution to the end of the great witch-hunt, the most important religious factor in the decline of witchcraft prosecutions was the change in the religious climate that occurred in the late seventeenth century. While it would be misleading to claim that Europe as a whole became more religiously tolerant at this time,[32] there is plenty of evidence to show that religious zeal and enthusiasm were waning in Europe after 1650. The clearest illustration of this was the decline of religious warfare after the Peace of Westphalia in 1648. After that time international conflict had much more to do with national self-interest and dynastic aggrandizement than with religious ideology. At the national level the same tendency can be observed in the sources of domestic unrest: after 1650 there were few religious wars in Europe. In theology the reaction to enthusiasm and zeal is evident in the emphasis on the reasonableness of religion,[33] while the most general indication of the new climate was the mistrust of men who claimed to be directly inspired or directed by the deity.[34] All of this suggests that the age of the Reformation, which had been marked by the intense expression of religious zeal, by religiously inspired warfare, by a preference for the emotional over the rational, and by the presence of ideologically inspired saints or fanatics, was gradually coming to an end and that a more secular, more rational age was dawning.

The decline of religious enthusiasm had a number of important effects on the process of witch-hunting. Among theologians, as we have seen, the desire to accommodate religion to philosophy and science led churchmen like the Latitudinarians in England to accept the mechanical philosophy and other cosmologies in which Satan had very little power. The growing distrust of individuals who claimed to have direct contact with the world of spirits made men sceptical of demoniacs, which in turn led people to question the reality of the witchcraft that was so often said to be its source. But the most important effect of the new religious outlook was a decline in the commitment of God-fearing Christians to purify the world by burning witches. It is true of course that not all witchcraft prosecutions required religious zeal or enthusiasm for their sustenance, especially those centring on the alleged practice of *maleficia*. But many witch-

32 See Drummond and Bulloch, *The Scottish Church 1688–1843*, (Edinburgh, 1973), Chapter 1.

33 G. Cragg, *From Puritanism to the Age of Reason* (Cambridge, 1960).

34 See M. Heyd, 'The Reaction to Enthusiasm in the Seventeenth Century: Towards an Integrative Approach', *Journal of Modern History*, 53 (1981): 258–80.

craft trials and hunts were inspired by the determination of magistrates, clergy and the entire community to purify the world by waging war on Satan's confederates. As this type of militancy and millenarianism declined, so too did the witchcraft prosecutions which they had encouraged.

SOCIAL AND ECONOMIC CHANGE

The effect of social and economic change on the decline of witchcraft prosecutions is extremely problematic. Part of the problem is that social and economic conditions had more of an impact on the original suspicions and accusations of witchcraft than on the actual prosecutions themselves, and it is difficult if not impossible to determine whether those accusations declined or whether officials simply refused to take action on the basis of them. The other part of the problem is that even if it could be shown that witchcraft accusations did decline in number in the late seventeenth and early eighteenth centuries, it would be difficult to identify those social and economic changes that made villagers and townsmen feel more secure and less vulnerable to the maleficent deeds of their neighbours. The effect of social and economic change on the decline of witchcraft is, in other words, very much a matter of speculation. Nevertheless, the fact that a number of social and economic conditions did play an important part in the growth of witchcraft prosecutions suggests that in corresponding fashion factors of this nature may have had something to do with their decline.

There are three different ways in which socio-economic change might have helped to bring the great witch-hunt to an end. The first is that a general improvement in living conditions in the late seventeenth and early eighteenth centuries may have reduced some of the local village tensions that lay at the basis of witchcraft prosecutions. During the final years of the great witch-hunt the economic circumstances of most Europeans were better than they had been during its peak. The price revolution levelled off, wages stopped declining and in some countries actually rose, the population declined slightly and then grew at a more steady pace, and climatic conditions improved. These changes may have made life a little more comfortable for the lower classes, but it is unlikely that they could have significantly reduced or eliminated the specific social tensions that led to witchcraft accusations. Throughout the eighteenth century there was more than enough economically based conflict in village communities, more than enough poverty and hunger, and certainly more than enough misfortune in daily life to sustain frequent and intense witch-hunting.

A second possibility is that villagers, while still having adequate cause to denounce neighbours as witches, no longer did so because the witches did not present the same type of threat as they had in the past. There may be some substance to this argument. Keith Thomas has shown, for example, that the full implementation of the Poor Law system in England by the end of the seventeenth century eliminated some of the guilt that villagers experienced when they refused to dispense charity. In such circumstances they had less reason to relieve that guilt by accusing the poor of witchcraft.[35] In a more general sense, there was less reason to accuse solitary and isolated women of witchcraft as they became more familiar features of early modern European villages and towns. Instead of viewing such persons with suspicion and fear, people chose rather to ignore them. And as early modern European towns and cities grew in size, they lost their character as intimate, face-to-face societies, the very types of communities in which most accusations of witchcraft originate.

A third possible effect of social and economic change on the decline of witchcraft is more indirect but perhaps of greater importance than the other two. As we have seen, the tremendous economic and social turmoil of the early modern period, when compounded with the political and religious instability of the age, produced a mood of pessimism and deep anxiety that affected all social classes. It made villagers and magistrates, acting both as individuals and as members of the community, identify, accuse and prosecute witches as a means of relieving that anxiety. Witches, therefore, served as scapegoats, not simply for the daily misfortunes of village life but for the more general ills of society at a time of rapid and fundamental change. By the end of the seventeenth century, many of the conditions that had given rise to all of this unease and anxiety no longer existed. Not only was there a reduction of inflation and an overall improvement in living conditions, but the great pandemic of plague that had had such devastating social effects on European life during the past 300 years finally began to work itself out and did not reappear again until the late nineteenth century. At the same time the religious turmoil of the Reformation period subsided, and the astonishing series of rebellions and revolutions that had occurred in the late sixteenth and early seventeenth century came to an end by 1660. Even international warfare, which had disrupted European

35 Thomas, *Religion and the Decline of Magic*, pp. 581–2.

society in countless ways during the period of witch-hunting, had somewhat less traumatic effects on European society after 1660.[36] European countries did not abandon warfare, but by 1700 they had virtually stopped the practice of sacking towns and villages.[37] The net effect of all this was that Europe after 1660 gradually entered a period of social, political, economic and religious stability, a period during which the absolutist states of Europe and the aristocracies that predominated within them discovered the means by which a more stable world could be maintained. In such an environment individuals and communities had less reason to lash out at their helpless neighbours to relieve their general fears, and even less reason to engage in a massive witch-hunt to eradicate an imaginary horde of Devil-worshippers who were threatening to turn the entire world and the social order upside down.

THE SURVIVAL AND REVIVAL OF WITCHCRAFT

The decline of witchcraft prosecutions was a gradual process. In most countries a period of intense prosecution gave way first to a period of occasional trials and sporadic small hunts and then to a cessation of both executions and trials. In France, for example, the decline of prosecutions began in the 1620s in the area subject to the jurisdiction of the *parlement* of Paris, but it was not as noticeable in other parts of the country until the edict of Louis XIV in 1682.[38] Even then, however, there were occasional trials, mainly for divination and ligature, until the last execution in 1745. In England, where the only large national hunt came to an end in 1646, occasional trials and executions continued until 1682. After that date there were only a few scattered trials, some resulting in convictions but not in executions, until the witchcraft statute of 1604 was finally repealed by Parliament in 1736. In Scotland, where witch-hunting had been more intense than in England, the decline began somewhat later, after the great hunt of 1661–62, and the last execution took place in 1722. It took even longer for witch-hunting to end in the German territories. Many German states, while never duplicating the mass

36 See J. Childs, *Armies and Warfare in Europe, 1648–1789* (New York, 1982), p. 2.

37 T. Rabb, *The Struggle for Stability in Early Modern Europe* (New York, 1975), p. 122.

38 Soman, 'Decriminalizing Witchcraft: Does the French Experience Furnish a European Model?', *Criminal Justice History*, 10 (1989): 7. The last legal execution in the jurisdiction of Paris took place in 1625.

slaughters of the 1620s and 1630s, executed considerable numbers of witches until well into the eighteenth century. King Frederick William I reduced the number of witchcraft trials in Prussia in 1714, but the last one did not occur there until 1728. In Würzburg the final execution took place in 1749, in Württemberg in 1751, and in all of Germany at Kempten in 1775. Somewhat surprisingly there were a few prosecutions for witchcraft in Spain and in both Spanish and Portuguese America in the late eighteenth century, although none of them resulted in executions.[39] There was an isolated prosecution in Sweden in 1763 and, even more belatedly, an execution – the last legal one in Europe – at Glarus in Switzerland in 1782. In 1793 two women were executed for witchcraft in the Polish city of Posen (recently acquired by Prussia), but the incident was not documented in the official record and appears to have been illegal.[40]

By the end of the eighteenth century the great European witch-hunt, which had reached its most intense point in the closing years of the sixteenth century and in the early years of the seventeenth, was a thing of the past. The hunt was, as we have seen in Chapter 1, a time-bound rather than a recurrent or eternal phenomenon. Nevertheless, certain components of the phenomenon have either persisted or recurred since the eighteenth century, giving subsequent generations a glimpse of the great hunt through contemporary glasses. One of the most enduring and widespread of these components has been the persistence of popular beliefs in witchcraft. These beliefs were never as extreme as those of the learned élite, but being based on the fear of *maleficia*, they proved to be much more durable. In the middle of the nineteenth century the Bishop of Orléans reported that in the countryside the belief in witchcraft and the reliance upon cunning men were as widespread as ever,[41] while even in the twentieth century popular witch-beliefs, many of them deeply rooted in antiquity, still flourished among the older inhabitants of Franconian Switzerland.[42]

On the basis of popular witch-beliefs local communities have occasionally taken illegal action against those people whom they suspected of witchcraft. In 1722, for example, some peasants in Grønning in Denmark burned a witch alive, long after legal executions

---

39 Monter, *Ritual, Myth and Magic*, pp. 101–4; A. Metcalf, 'Families of Planters, Peasants and Slaves: Strategies for Survival in Santana de Parnaiba, Brazil, 1720–1820' (University of Texas PhD thesis, 1983), pp. 90–1.

40 Sebald, *Witchcraft*, p. 49; Soldan and Heppe, *Geschichte*, II, 332.

41 Garrett, 'Witches and Cunning Folk', p. 57.

42 See Sebald, *Witchcraft*, passim.

had ceased.[43] A similar episode occurred in 1751 at Tring in Hertford-shire, England, when an innkeeper incited a mob to break into a workhouse and seize a poor old woman, Ruth Osborne, and her husband, both of whom were suspected of witchcraft. Like many English witches in the sixteenth and seventeenth centuries, Ruth Osborne had once asked the innkeeper for some milk but had been refused. Having stripped both Osbornes and tied their hands to their feet, the mob dragged them to a nearby stream and subjected them to the swimming test, an ordeal which resulted in Ruth Osborne's death. Three men were eventually tried for Osborne's murder and one of them, Thomas Colley, was convicted and executed.[44]

Incidents similar to that of the Osbornes, in which either individuals or groups of people assault men and women whom they suspect of practising harmful magic, have occurred from time to time ever since the eighteenth century, even in the recent past.[45] In Clonmel, Tipperary, in 1894 the husband, relatives and friends of a young woman, Bridget Cleary, beat and burned her to death on the suspicion that the real Bridget had been taken away by the fairies and that a witch had been put in her place.[46] Even more evocative of the witch-hunts of the sixteenth and seventeenth centuries was the assault on Elizabeth Hahn in a small German village in 1976. Hahn was a poor, elderly spinster who was widely suspected of being a witch and keeping familiars in the form of dogs. Her neighbours shunned her, threw rocks at her, threatened to beat her to death and eventually set fire to her house, badly burning her and killing all of her animals because they thought she was casting hexes on them.[47] One year later two brothers in a village near Alençon, France, were tried for murdering a village sorcerer who kept a cabin full of magical potions and who was known to throw salt on people's gardens.[48] In 1981 a Mexican mob stoned a woman to death after her husband accused her of using witchcraft to incite the attack that took place on the life of Pope John Paul II.[49]

43 G. Henningsen, 'Witchcraft in Denmark', *Folklore* 93 (1982) p. 133.

44 W.B. Carnochan, 'Witch-Hunting and Belief in 1751: The Case of Thomas Colley and Ruth Osborne', *Journal of Social History*, 4 (1970–71): 388–403.

45 See Sebald, *Witchcraft*, p. 52, n. 42, for an incident in 1818 in France.

46 P. Byrne, *Witchcraft in Ireland* (Cork, 1975), pp. 56–68.

47 Sebald, *Witchcraft*, p. 223.

48 Agence France-Presse, 13 May 1977. The case is discussed in Henningsen, *Witches' Advocate*, p. 18

49 *Newsweek*, 25 May 1981, p. 33.

All of these incidents recall in one way or another the belief in and fear of witchcraft that were such common features of early modern European life. The main difference between these episodes and the witchcraft prosecutions of the past is that the established judicial authorities in the communities where the incidents occurred have not participated in the assault upon the suspected witches but instead have prosecuted the assailants. Modern European witch-hunting has, in other words, become a form of popular, vigilante-style justice that magistrates have tried to control and prevent. If we wish to find parallels between the legal hunting of witches in the past and similar forms of prosecution today, we must look at the ways in which modern governments have subjected political dissidents and social nonconformists to a process of judicial terror. The victims of these campaigns are no longer witches; the growth of scepticism among the administrative classes of society has ensured that witch-hunting in the full sense of the word will not recur. But the judicial procedures that were once used against witches have been revived. In prosecuting these modern 'witches' authorities have violated many traditional safeguards of civil liberty and have used a variety of judicial tactics to harass, prosecute, convict and penalize a group of people who have become the object of widespread fear.

The judicial tactics most reminiscent of those used during the European witch-hunt are those employed by numerous governments around the world against political and military prisoners. In many countries these tactics include the use of torture – sometimes by means of the strappado and other time-tested methods – in order to obtain confessions and the names of accomplices.[50] Certainly one of the saddest and most frightening aspects of twentieth-century history has been the revival and increasing use of judicial torture. The episode in recent history which is most frequently compared to early modern European witch-hunts did not, however, involve the use of torture. The interrogation of hundreds of American citizens by congressional committees in the early 1950s in order to discover the presence of communists in the government, the armed forces and the entertainment industry has often been described as a witch-hunt. Indeed, one of the victims of that hunt, Arthur Miller, wrote a play, *The Crucible*, which was intended to illustrate the similarities between the hearings of these committees and the witch-hunt that had taken place at Salem in 1692.

50 *The Observer*, 15 June 1980.

Between these two episodes there were many grounds for comparison. In both cases politically prominent individuals distinguished themselves as witch-hunters and prosecutors; the threat was perceived to be both internal and external; and the stereotype of the witch/communist broke down as the hunt progressed, especially after military officers were implicated, thereby encouraging the growth of scepticism. But it was in the area of criminal procedure that the two hunts resembled each other most closely. Just as a special court had been established to hear witchcraft cases in Salem, so special congressional committees (the House Un-American Activities Committee and the Senate Permanent Investigations Committee), both of which had special powers of subpoena and interrogation that regular courts did not have, were established to deal with the communist menace. The legal proceedings of the 1950s, just like those of 1692, were based largely on the assumption of guilt, so much so that Senator Hubert Humphrey claimed that the committees were 'turning Anglo-Saxon jurisprudence upside down'. In both cases prosecutors used leading questions in the interrogation of witnesses, and most important, enormous pressure was brought to bear on witnesses to reveal the names of accomplices or like-minded associates. It was this pressure to name names (without torture but not without other forms of coercion) that most deeply disturbed Miller and many other victims of the communist-hunt, such as Lillian Hellman. It was also this feature of the hunt that most vividly evoked the horrific memory of the chain-reaction witch-hunt.[51]

The illegal treatment of accused witches by unauthorized mobs or vigilantes and the legal harassment and prosecution of witch-substitutes by authorized magistrates and politicians remind us that although the European witch-hunt was concluded more than 200 years ago, certain features of it reappear from time to time. We get another reminder, although one of a very different kind, when we observe the practice of magic and witchcraft in the contemporary world. Since the end of the Second World War, and even more so since the late 1960s, there has been a significant increase in the number of practising witches, especially in Britain and America. Although figures are difficult to obtain, it has been estimated that there are more than 200,000 American witches and half as many in Britain. It is not within the scope of this book to describe the various practices

51 L. Hellman, *Scoundrel Time* (Boston, 1976); A.R. Cardoza, 'A Modern American Witch-Craze', in *Witchcraft and Sorcery*, ed. M. Marwick (London, 1970), pp. 369–77.

of contemporary witches, to analyse the composition of the many different witchcraft movements, or to speculate on the reasons for the revival of interest in witchcraft and the occult at this time.[52] My only concern is to determine whether the modern practice of witchcraft is in any way a revival or continuation of past practice and whether the witches of today have anything in common with the people who were accused and prosecuted in the sixteenth and seventeenth centuries. If we use contemporary definitions of witchcraft as the basis of comparison, there does appear to be some common ground between them. Witches today can be broadly defined as persons who practise magic and who worship pagan gods or, in the case of the satanists, the Christian Devil. During the early modern period a similar definition of witchcraft could easily have been accepted by most contemporaries, although the magic that witches performed was considered to be mainly maleficent, and the object of their veneration was always considered to be the Devil. In both periods, however, witches could be defined as magicians who had rejected the Christian faith.

Although witches in the twentieth century can be defined in very similar terms as those of the sixteenth and seventeenth centuries, there are very few other similarities between the two groups. Some modern witches, especially the followers of Gerald Gardner, contend that early modern witches, just like themselves, were in fact practitioners of an ancient fertility religion, Wicca, rather than the Devil-worshippers the authorities claimed they were. This contention is based largely on the scholarly work of Margaret Murray, and it has therefore lost credibility as Murray's thesis has been destroyed by her critics. Not only is there no uncontaminated evidence that witches were in fact worshipping pagan gods, but there is not even any solid evidence that witches gathered collectively, like their modern descendants, for any purpose whatsoever. To the extent that modern witchcraft is organized into covens or even into local and regional organizations, it is qualitatively different from the witchcraft that was actually practised (as opposed to what was believed to be practised) in the past.

Aside from the lack of organization among early modern European witches, there are even more fundamental distinctions between them and their modern counterparts. Sixteenth- and seventeenth-century witches were always named by other people: one was *called* a witch, even if one did actually practise a certain amount of magic. In the

---

52 See M. Adler, *Drawing Down the Moon* (Boston, 1979), for a survey of modern witchcraft in America.

twentieth century, however, witches have defined themselves as such, perhaps reluctantly but nevertheless with a certain amount of pride. Once witchcraft became a self-defined rather than an other-defined activity, it also lost its malevolent character. Early modern European witches were regarded as essentially evil beings, whereas modern witches proclaim themselves to be essentially beneficent and have even established a witch anti-defamation league to counter the negative image that witches have inherited from the past. Modern witches insist that the magic they perform is invariably good, whereas the craft of the early modern witch, even if it was performed with good intentions or not performed at all, was represented to society as the quintessence of evil.

In this context it is worth noting that contemporary satanists, such as Anton LaVey, publicize themselves as being evil, but if LaVey's *Satanic Bible* is any guide, they consider themselves evil only by traditional Christian criteria. LaVey proposes a non-Christian, hedonistic but nevertheless non-aggressive ethic which neither he nor any objective observer could label as evil.[53] There are of course a few 'satanists' who have attracted attention by destroying animal and occasionally human life, but these persons do not typify the satanists, much less the broader witchcraft movement, and are probably best regarded as criminals or sadists rather than witches. Another group of reputedly evil satanists are those who allegedly engage in 'satanic-ritual abuse'. It remains unclear, however, whether such cults really do exist, or whether they, like the covens of the sixteenth and seventeenth centuries, are the figment of other people's, especially children's, imagination.[54]

Aside from the alleged evil of contemporary satanists, and the fantasies that others have developed regarding them, there are few similarities between the witches of the sixteenth and seventeenth centuries and their modern counterparts. Even the social status of the two groups is different. Early modern witches, as we have seen, came almost exclusively from the lower levels of society, whereas witches in America and Europe today come from all social classes and especially from among the university-educated. As one American observer has pointed out, 'It is well-educated, middle-class people who have nice homes and doctorates – people you wouldn't classify as

53 A.S. LaVey, *The Satanic Bible* (New York, 1969), pp. 46–54.
54 See J.S. Victor, *Satanic Panic: The Creation of a Contemporary Legend* (Peru, Ill., 1993); L. Wright, 'Remembering Satan', *New Yorker*, 17 May 1993: 60–81; 24 May 1993: 54–76.

cultural drop-outs – who are very much active in this area.'[55] And of course the most basic difference between the two groups of witches is that the modern ones do in fact engage in various magical and religious activities – organized or otherwise – whereas the early modern ones, while occasionally performing some acts of white or possibly even black magic, did not actually do most of the things they were accused of.

When we turn from technologically advanced European and American society to more underdeveloped or even primitive cultures in the world today, we encounter one more version of witchcraft that can be compared with witchcraft in the early modern period. Concerning African and native American witchcraft much anthropological work has been done, and this work has been used both imaginatively and productively by historians during the last two decades in exploring the social environment in which witchcraft accusations arose and in studying the sources of witch-beliefs. Since African witchcraft is basically an other-defined activity, based on only limited practice, it serves as a more valid standard of comparison for historical European witchcraft than the practices of self-defined ritual magicians and neo-pagans in western Europe and America. Historians who have studied witch-beliefs and witchcraft accusations among groups like the Azande have found striking similarities between the functions that such accusations served in those societies and those that they served in European villages. They also have discovered that many of the social structures which sustain the belief in witchcraft and which encourage certain patterns of accusation in African villages had parallels in early modern European communities. These similarities, which have greatly enriched our understanding of early modern European witchcraft accusations, nevertheless do have their limitations. To begin with, they deal much more with magic than with diabolism. Early modern European witchcraft acquired its distinctive character from the superimposition of a fairly sophisticated demonology on a body of peasant belief regarding magic and *maleficium*. This demonology had no equivalent in primitive cultures and for that reason extended comparisons between primitive and early modern European witchcraft break down. It is not surprising that the work of anthropologists on witchcraft has been applied most successfully

---

[55] *New York Times*, 15 November 1973. An anthropologist doing fieldwork among witches in London concluded that they were generally white, middle-class and intellectual. T.M. Luhrmann, *Persuasions of the Witch's Craft: Ritual Magic in Contemporary England* (Cambridge, Mass., 1989).

to the study of English witchcraft, where the crime was defined more in magical and less in diabolical terms than in any other place in Europe.[56]

A second difference between primitive and historical European witchcraft is that many of the fantastic beliefs and accusations associated with the European sabbath are absent from primitive cultures. Since most of these beliefs are rooted in Christian demonology, their absence in pagan cultures is not surprising. Now it is true that in some primitive cultures there are witch-beliefs which are strikingly similar to European witch-beliefs regarding the sabbath. Among a number of African tribes, most notably the Dinka of southern Sudan and the Lugbara of western Uganda, there exist not only beliefs regarding day-witches or simple sorcerers but another set of beliefs regarding night-witches. Night-witches, unlike their more pedestrian diurnal counterparts, are able to turn themselves into animals who can walk upside down, gather at night and feast on corpses, dance naked and go out at night in spirit and attack people, causing indiscriminate damage to crops and barrenness to women. The prevalence of such ideas in a non-Christian society only recently influenced by western theology suggests that all societies are capable of generating a fantasy of people reversing all social and moral norms and engaging in such activities as cannibalistic infanticide. To that extent the European image of the sabbath is just one version of a universal nightmare that haunts people whenever the social order appears to be in danger. It is important to note, however, that although the Dinka and the Ugbara can identify and take counter-action against day-witches, they cannot specifically identify and prosecute night-witches. When day-witches are named, moreover, there is never any attempt to attribute to them the activities of night-witches. Night-witches, in other words, exist only in these people's imagination.[57]

The inability of these African societies to identify and prosecute night-witches leads us to what is perhaps the single most important difference between early modern European witchcraft and witchcraft in contemporary primitive cultures. European society, unlike primitive African societies, developed systems of criminal procedure that were capable of discovering and prosecuting large numbers of individuals for thought crimes or for activities that never took place. African societies, to be sure, developed methods of combating witchcraft and

---

56 See A. Macfarlane, *Witchcraft in Tudor and Stuart England*.
57 See Mair, *Witchcraft*, pp. 36–42.

in the twentieth century have actually conducted large witch-hunts, interestingly enough without the official support of the government. But they have never succeeded in erecting legal machinery capable of sustaining the type of systematic, deadly and effective prosecution that took place in early modern Europe. This legal machinery was implemented in Europe only when the modern state had already reached a fairly advanced state of development and before the leaders of those states had become sceptical and secular. By the time modern states had been formed in Africa, the ruling class had become sufficiently sceptical of witchcraft – partially as the result of European intellectual influence – that they would not devote the judicial power of the state to the detection and prosecution of alleged witches. Just as in European society after the middle of the eighteenth century, retaliation against witches and the punishment of them remained a local, popular and technically (in so far as the state was concerned) illegal operation.

These differences between the legal environment of early modern Europe and that of primitive African communities, as well as the revival of witch-hunting against witch-substitutes in the twentieth century, underline the importance of legal procedures in the European witch-hunt. The reasons why that hunt took place are many and varied, as this book has argued. But the hunt was essentially a judicial operation and as such could not have taken place without the growth of the legal powers of Church and state, the introduction of inquisitorial procedure, and the development of torture and other forms of judicial coercion. It is also true that the hunt could not have occurred if the cumulative concept of witchcraft had not yet been formed. This book has shown that the fusion of various witch-beliefs by the end of the fifteenth century, coupled with the development of legal procedures at the same time, formed the two essential preconditions of the witch-hunt and explain more than any other factors why the hunt took place when it did. Of course these two preconditions were intimately connected, since it was only because of the development of new legal procedures that various witch-beliefs could be fused. Only when inquisitors were able to coerce individuals into confessing to their fantasies could the cumulative concept of witchcraft acquire the legitimacy that it needed to command credence.

If the adoption of legal procedures proved to be of crucial importance in the origin of the great witch-hunt, their elimination was of no less importance in its decline. As we have seen in this chapter, the real turning point in the great hunt occurred when magistrates and judges came to the conclusion that the judicial process had resulted in the execution of innocent human beings and therefore took steps to prevent such miscarriages of justice from ever happening again. At the same time a more fundamental philosophical and religious scepticism challenged the very system of belief upon which the great witch-hunt was based, but it is worth noting in conclusion that the decline of the European witch-hunt was much more the work of lawyers, judges and magistrates than of theologians or philosophers. And after the prosecution of witches had dwindled to an occasional prosecution for *maleficium*, it was a series of legislative acts and decrees that brought the European witch-hunt to an end, thus concluding one of the saddest chapters in the legal history of the West.

BIBLIOGRAPHICAL NOTE

The literature on European witchcraft is immense and continues to grow at a fast pace. This brief note is intended to draw attention to some of the works, especially those in English, which the reader might wish to consult for further study.

BIBLIOGRAPHIES

There is no comprehensive bibliography of the subject, but H.C. Erik Midelfort has listed 509 titles in 'Recent Witch-Hunting Research, or Where Do We Go from Here?', *Papers of the Bibliographical Society of America*, 62 (1968): 373–420, and has included additional items in 'Witchcraft, Magic and the Occult', in *Reformation Europe: A Guide to Research*, ed. S. Ozment (St Louis, 1982), pp. 183–209. There is a select bibliography of 1,140 titles in Rossell Hope Robbins, *The Encyclopedia of Witchcraft and Demonology* (New York, 1959), and Robert Mandrou lists 515 items in *Magistrats et sorciers en France au XVIIe siècle* (Paris, 1968), pp. 25–70. Robert Muchembled presents a much briefer but annotated bibliography of sixty-five titles in Marie-Sylvie Dupont-Bouchat et al., *Prophètes et sorciers dans les Pays-Bas XVIe–XVIIIe siècle* (Paris, 1978), pp. 33–9. Wolfgang Behringer has commented on much of the recent literature in 'Neue Historische Literatur: Erträge und Perspektiven der Hexenforschung', *Historische zeitschrift*, 249 (1989): 619–40.

GENERAL STUDIES

There are two anthologies in English that provide a good introduction to the subject of European witchcraft. *Witchcraft in Europe, 1100–1700: A Documentary History*, ed. Alan C. Kors and Edward Peters (Philadelphia, 1972), consists entirely of primary sources, including excerpts from witchcraft treatises, accounts of trials, and excerpts from philosophical works. *European Witchcraft*, ed. E. William Monter (New York, 1969), combines primary sources with excerpts from scholarly books and articles, some of which are not available elsewhere in translation. Henry Charles Lea, *Materials Toward a History of Witchcraft*, arranged and edited by Arthur C. Howland (3 vols, New York, 1957) consists of notes taken by Lea for the history of witchcraft he was planning to write when he died in 1909. The quotes and paraphrases from relatively rare witchcraft treatises and nineteenth-century secondary literature make these volumes an indispensable reference tool. Of all the encyclopedias of witchcraft and magic the most useful is by Rossell Hope Robbins, cited above. The best one-volume study of witchcraft in the West, which has a special emphasis on the Basque country, is Julio Caro Baroja, *The World of the Witches*, trans. O.N.V. Glendinning (Chicago, 1961). As for the witch-hunt or witch-craze itself, the brilliant but controversial essay by H.R. Trevor-Roper, 'The European Witch-Craze of the Sixteenth and Seventeenth Centuries' in *Religion, the Reformation and Social Change* (London, 1967), pp. 101–208, and in *The European Witch-craze of the Sixteenth and Seventeenth Centuries and Other Essays* (New York, 1969), pp. 90–192, emphasizes the formation and dissemination of learned belief. More recent syntheses, reflecting developments in social history and the history of popular culture, include Joseph Klaits: *Servants of Satan: The Age of the Witch Hunts* (Bloomington, 1985) and G.R. Quaife, *Godly Zeal and Furious Rage: The Witch in Early Modern Europe* (London, 1987). Other general interpretations appear in Jean Delumeau, *La Peur en occident XIVe–XVIIIe siècles* (Paris, 1978), pp. 346–88; Marijke Gijswijt-Hofstra, 'The European Witchcraft Debate and the Dutch Variant', *Social History*, 15 (1990): 181–94; Wolfgang Behringer, '"Erhob sich das ganze Land zu ihrer Ausrottung . . .": Hexenprozesse und Hexenverfolgungen in Europa', in *Hexenwelten: Magie und Imagination vom 16.–20. Jahrhundert*, ed. Richard van Dülmen (Frankfurt, 1987), pp. 131–69; and Robert Muchembled, 'Satan ou les hommes? La Chasse aux sorcières et ses causes' in *Prophètes et sorciers*, cited above, pp. 13–39. An earlier, but still valuable study is Kurt Baschwitz, *Hexen und Hexenprozesse* (Munich, 1963).

THE MEDIEVAL BACKGROUND

In recent years a number of books have been written in English on the period preceding the great witch-hunt. The most comprehensive of these, and one that defines witchcraft in very broad terms is Jeffrey Burton Russell, *Witchcraft in the Middle Ages* (Ithaca, 1972). Very different from Russell's book, both in its scepticism regarding the reality of organized witchcraft and in its emphasis on the role of ritual magic in the formation of the stereotype of the witch is Norman Cohn, *Europe's Inner Demons* (London, 1975). The figure of the magician and the way in which his crime was viewed by medieval writers receives detailed treatment in Edward Peters, *The Magician, the Witch and the Law* (Philadelphia, 1978). Richard Kieckhefer, *European Witch Trials: Their Foundations in Popular and Learned Culture, 1300–1500* (London, 1976), shows how popular beliefs can be distinguished from learned ones in the trial records and also includes a valuable calendar of witchcraft trials. The fullest discussion of the important fifteenth-century trials in parts of Switzerland is Andreas Blauert, *Frühe Hexenverfolgungen: Ketzer-, Zauberei- und Hexenprozesse des 15. Jahrhunderts* (Hamburg, 1989). The older works of Joseph Hansen, *Zauberwahn, Inquisition und Hexenprozess im Mittelalter* (Munich, 1900) and *Quellen und Untersuchungen zur Geschichte des Hexenwahns und der Hexenverfolgung im Mittelalter* (Bonn, 1901), are still of immense value. Carlo Ginzburg, *Ecstasies: Deciphering the Witches' Sabbath*, trans. Raymond Rosenthal (New York, 1991) argues that the idea of the witches' sabbath emerged as the result of an interraction between folkloric culture and the learned culture of the Church.

THE LITERATURE OF WITCHCRAFT

Owing largely to the efforts of the credulous witchcraft historian Montague Summers and the translator E.A. Ashwin, a number of the most famous witchcraft treatises have been translated into English. Among these are the *Malleus Maleficarum* of Heinrich Kramer and James Sprenger (London, 1928; repr. New York, 1971); Francesco Maria Guazzo's *Compendium Maleficarum* (London, 1929); Nicolas Rémy's *Demonolatry* (London, 1930); and Henry Boguet's *Examen of Witches* (London, 1929). Summers also edited Reginald Scot, *The Discoverie of Witchcraft* (London, 1930) and Matthew Hopkins, *The Discovery of Witches* (London, 1928). George Gifford's *A Dialogue Concerning Witches and Witchcraft* is included in *The Witchcraft Papers*, ed. Peter Haining (Secaucus, N.J., 1974), pp. 76–139. An abridged version of Pierre de Lancre's *Tableau de l'inconstance des mauvais anges et démons* has been edited by Nicole Jacques-Chaquin (Paris, 1982), but no English translation has been made either of that work or of Bodin's *Démonomanie*. The sceptical treatise by Johann Weyer, *De praestigiis daemonum*, has been translated as *Witches, Devils and Doctors in the Renaissance*, ed. George Mora

(Binghamton, N.Y., 1991). General studies of the literature of witchcraft appear in *George Lincoln Burr: Selections from his Writings*, ed. Lois Oliphant Gibbons (Ithaca, 1943), pp. 166–89, and in Lynn Thorndike, *A History of Magic and Experimental Science*, VI (New York, 1941), pp. 514–59. *The Damned Art: Essays in the Literature of Witchcraft*, ed. Sydney Anglo (London, 1977) is an excellent collection of essays. Siegfried Leutenbauer, *Hexerei- und Zaubereidelikt in der Literatur von 1450 bis 1550* (Berlin, 1972), deals extensively with the issues raised in the early witchcraft treatises, while different aspects of the *Malleus Maleficarum* are treated in *Der Hexenhammer: Enstehung und Umfeld des Malleus Maleficarum von 1487*, ed. Peter Segl (Cologne, 1988). Stuart Clark has illuminated various aspects of demonological thought, especially in 'Inversion, Misrule and the Meaning of Witchcraft', *Past and Present*, 87 (1980): 98–127 and 'Protestant Demonology: Sin, Superstition and Society (c. 1520 – c. 1630), in *Early Modern European Witchcraft: Centres and Peripheries*, ed. B. Ankarloo and G. Henningsen (Oxford, 1990), pp. 45–81.

REGIONAL AND LOCAL STUDIES

There is a great need for a bibliography of all the studies that have been done on witch-beliefs and witchcraft prosecutions in particular localities. For Germany there are hundreds of such studies, but very few in English. One exception is the excellent book by H.C. Erik Midelfort, *Witch Hunting in Southwestern Germany, 1562–1684: The Intellectual and Social Foundations* (Stanford, 1972). Also in English is a doctoral dissertation by Edward W.M. Bever, 'Witchcraft in Early Modern Württemberg (Princeton, 1983), and a study of witchcraft in Franconia both in the past and in more recent times by Hans Sebald, *Witchcraft: The Heritage of a Heresy* (New York, 1978). Lyndal Roper has emphasized gender in her study of witchcraft accusations in Augsburg, 'Witchcraft and Fantasy in Early Modern Germany', *History Workshop Journal,* 32 (1991): 19–43. Gerhard Schormann has written a survey of witch-hunting throughout Germany, *Hexenprozesse in Deutschland* (Göttingen, 1981) and also a regional study, *Hexenprozesse in Nordwestdeutschland* (Hildesheim, 1977). Wolfgang Behringer has written a comprehensive study of witch-hunting and witch-beliefs in southeastern Germany, *Hexenverfolgung in Bayern: Volksmagie, Glaubenseifer und Staatsräson in der Frühen Neuzeit* (Munich, 1987). Harmut H. Kunstmann has studied witchcraft in Nuremberg in *Zauberwahn und Hexenprozesz in der Reichs-*

stadt Nürnberg (Nuremberg, 1970). Friedrich Merzbacher, *Die Hexenprozesse in Franken* (Munich, 1957) is especially helpful in discussing legal procedure. For Austrian lands there is a study, arranged chronologically, by Fritz Byloff, *Hexenglaube und Hexenverfolgung in den österreichischen Alpenländern* (Berlin and Leipzig, 1934), and R.J.W. Evans has included a survey of witchcraft and magic in Austria, Bohemia and Hungary in *The Making of the Habsburg Monarchy, 1550–1700* (Oxford, 1979).

For France the major study, which emphasizes the role of the *parlement* of Paris in the decline of French witchcraft, is Mandrou's book, cited above. Alfred Soman, 'The Parlement of Paris and the Great Witch-Hunt (1565–1640)', *Sixteenth Century Journal*, 9 (1978): 31–44, serves as a valuable corrective to Mandrou. Soman has written extensively on French witchcraft, including 'Trente procès de sorcellerie dans le Perche (1566–1624)', *L'Orne littéraire*, 8 (1986): 42–57. Robin Briggs provides both a comprehensive study of French witchcraft and specific material on Lorraine in the first three chapters of *Communities of Belief: Social and Cultural Tension in Early Modern France* (Oxford, 1989). Clarke Garrett, 'Witches and Cunning Folk in the Old Regime' in *The Wolf and the Lamb: Popular Culture in France from the Old Regime to the Twentieth Century*, ed. J. Beauroy et al. (Stanford, 1976), pp. 53–64, deals with witchcraft at the popular level, especially in the later period.

On the French Low Countries Robert Muchembled has published a long and stimulating essay, 'The Witches of the Cambrésis: The Acculturation of the Rural World in the Sixteenth and Seventeenth Centuries', in *Religion and the People, 800–1700*, ed. James Obelkevich (Chapel Hill, 1979), while Marie-Sylvie Dupont-Bouchat has studied witchcraft prosecutions in Luxembourg in 'La Répression de la sorcellerie dans le duché de Luxembourg aux XVIᵉ et XVIIᵉ siècles' in *Prophètes et sorciers*, cited above. A collection of essays on witchcraft in the United Provinces of the Netherlands, edited by Marijke Gijswijt-Hofstra and Willem Frijhoff, has now been translated into English as *Witchcraft in the Netherlands from the Fourteenth to the Twentieth Century* (Rotterdam, 1991).

For the Jura region there is the superb study by E. William Monter, *Witchcraft in France and Switzerland: The Borderlands during the Reformation* (Ithaca, 1976). Guido Bader, *Die Hexenprozesse in der Schweiz* (Affoltern, 1945), presents an overview of Swiss prosecutions, but it has been superseded by later work. Andreas Blauert, *Frühe Hexenverfolgungen*, cited above, explores both the prosecutions and the development of learned witch-beliefs in western Switzerland in the fifteenth century.

For Italy the brilliant study by Carlo Ginzburg, *I Benandanti* (Turin, 1966) has been translated by John and Anne Tedeschi as *The Night Battles: Witchcraft and Agrarian Cults in the Sixteenth and Seventeenth Centuries* (Baltimore, 1983). Ruth Martin has explored witchcraft trials in Venice in *Witchcraft and the Inquisition in Venice, 1550–1650* (Oxford, 1989). A more general study for all of Italy is Giuseppi Bonomo, *Caccia alle Streghe* (Palermo, 1959). William Monter provides a brief survey in 'French and Italian Witchcraft', *History Today*, 30 (1980): 31–5.

For Spain there is a detailed investigation of the Basque witch-hunt by Gustav Henningsen, *The Witches' Advocate: Basque Witchcraft and the Spanish Inquisition (1609–1614)* (Reno, 1980). On Castile there is the older study of Castile by Sebastián Cirac Estopañán, *Los procesos de hechicerías en la Inquisitión de Castilla la Nueva* (Madrid, 1942), and for the lands outside Castile, William Monter, *Frontiers of Heresy: The Spanish Inqusiition from the Basque Lands to Sicily* (Cambridge, 1991), especially Chapter 12.

Concerning the British Isles the older studies by Wallace Notestein, *A History of Witchcraft in England* (Washington, 1911), and George L. Kittredge, *Witchcraft in Old and New England* (Cambridge, 1929), are still useful. Alan Macfarlane's book, *Witchcraft in Tudor and Stuart England* (London, 1970), a study of witchcraft in the county of Essex, demonstrates the application of anthropological theory to the study of European witchcraft. Keith Thomas's magisterial work, *Religion and the Decline of Magic* (London, 1971), which likewise employs anthropological theory, deals not only with witchcraft but all other forms of magic in England. Clive Holmes explores the relationship between learned and popular culture in 'Popular Culture? Witches, Magistrates and Divines in Early Modern Europe', in *Understanding Popular Culture*, ed. Steven Kaplan (Berlin, 1984), pp. 85–111. Christina Larner has written an excellent overview of witch-hunting in Scotland, *Enemies of God: The Witch-hunt in Scotland* (London, 1981), while I have studied the largest witch-hunt in Scottish history in Brian Levack, 'The Great Scottish Witch Hunt of 1661–1662', *Journal of British Studies*, 20 (1980): 90–108.

The literature on witchcraft in New England continues to grow steadily. In addition to Paul Boyer and Stephen Nissenbaum's study of village factionalism, *Salem Possessed: The Social Origins of Witchcraft* (Cambridge, 1974), John P. Demos has produced an innovative study, *Entertaining Satan: Witchcraft and the Culture of Early New*

England (New York, 1981). Richard Wiseman, *Witchcraft, Magic and Religion in 17th-Century Massachusetts* (Amherst, 1984), and Richard Godbeer, *The Devil's Dominion: Magic and Religion in Early New England* (Cambridge, 1992) both deal with magic as well as witchcraft, while Carol Karlsen has emphasized the importance of gender in *The Devil in the Shape of a Woman: Witchcraft in Colonial New England* (New York, 1987).

Returning to Europe, there are a number of essays on different aspects of Scandinavian witchcraft in *Early Modern European Witchcraft: Centres and Peripheries*, cited above. In this work there are English summaries of monographs by Bengt Ankarloo, *Trolldoms-processerna i Sverige* (Lund, 1971) on pp. 324–39, and Antero Heikkinen, *Paholaisen Liittolaiset* (Helsinki, 1969) on pp. 374–94. For Poland there is Bohdan Baranowski, *Procesy Czarownic w Polsce w XVII i XVIII Wieku* (Lodz, 1952), with a French summary on pp. 178–81. Gábor Klaniczay has written a number of articles on Hungarian witchcraft, most notably 'Hungary: The Accusations and the Universe of Popular Magic', in *Early Modern European Witchcraft*, cited above, pp. 219–56. For Russia there are a number of articles by Russell Zguta, including 'Witchcraft Trials in Seventeenth-Century Russia', *American Historical Review*, 82 (1977): 1187–1207.

PARTICULAR ASPECTS OF THE WITCH-HUNT

Regarding the religious aspects of the witch-hunt, Jean Delumeau's *Catholicism Between Luther and Voltaire: A New View of the Counter-Reformation* (London, 1977), especially Chapter 4, has had a lasting effect on witchcraft studies, especially in France. For England there is Keith Thomas's *Religion and the Decline of Magic*. For Germany, the older study by Nikolaus Paulus, *Hexenwahn und Hexenprozess, vornehmlich im 16. Jahrhundert* (Freiburg, 1910) has enduring value.

On the legal aspects of witch-hunting, Dagmar Unverhau has revealed the variety of legal procedures with which prosecutions could be conducted in 'Akkusationsprozess – Inquisitionsprozess: Indikatoren für die Intensität der Hexenverfolgung in Schleswig-Holstein', in *Hexenprozesse: deutsche und skandinavische Beitrage*, ed. C. Degn, H. Lehmann, and D. Unverhau (Neumünster, 1983). The best study of torture is Edward Peters, *Torture* (Oxford, 1985). John Tedeschi, 'Inquisitorial Law and the Witch', in *European Witch-craft*, cited above, pp. 83–118, deals with legal procedure in the Roman Inquisition.

On the question of women and witchcraft see E. William Monter, 'The Pedestal and the Stake: Courtly Love and Witchcraft', in *Becoming Visible: Women in European History*, ed. R. Bridenthal and C. Koonz (Boston, 1977), pp. 119–36; Clarke Garrett, 'Women and Witches: Patterns of Analysis', Signs, 3 (1977): 461–70; and Carol Karlsen, *The Devil in the Shape of a Woman*, (New York, 1987). Other works which emphasize the importance of gender as an analytical category in studying witchcraft are Marianne Hester, *Lewd Women and Wicked Witches: A Study in the Dynamics of Male Domination* (London, 1991); J.A. Sharpe, 'Witchcraft and Women in Seventeenth-Century England: some Northern evidence', *Continuity and Change*, 6 (1991): 179–99; Anne Barstow, *Witchcraze: A New History of the European Witch-Hunts* (New York, 1994); Susanna Burghartz, 'The Equation of Women and Witches: A Case Study of Witchcraft Trials in Lucerne and Lausanne in the Fifteenth and Sixteenth Centuries', in *The German Underworld*, ed. Richard J. Evans (London, 1988), pp. 57–74; and Carolyn Merchant, *The Death of Nature: Women, Ecology and the Scientific Revolution* (New York, 1980), Chapter 5.

On old age and witchcraft there are articles by Sona Rosa Burstein, 'Aspects of the Psychopathology of Old Age Revealed in Witchcraft Cases of the Sixteenth and Seventeenth Centuries', *British Medical Bulletin*, 6 (1949) and Edward Bever, 'Old Age and Witchcraft in Early Modern Europe', in *Old Age in Pre-Industrial Society* edited by Peter Stearns (New York, 1982), pp. 150–90. A more general study of the social identity of witches is Richard A. Horsley, 'Who Were the Witches?: The Social Roles of the Accused in the European Witch Trials', *Journal of Interdisciplinary History*, 9 (1974): 689–715.

A great deal has been written about the psychological and psychiatric aspects of witchcraft. Among these are George Rosen, 'Psychopathology in the Social Process: (I.) A Study of the Persecution of Witches in Europe as a Contribution to the Understanding of Mass Delusions and Psychic Epidemics', *Journal of Health and Human Behavior*, 1 (1960): 200–11; Robert D. Anderson, 'The History of Witchcraft: A Review with Some Psychiatric Comments', *American Journal of Psychiatry*, 126 (1970): 69–77; Thomas S. Szasz, *The Myth of Mental Illness* (New York, 1961), Chapter 12; and Evelyn Heinemann, *Hexen und Hexenglauben* (Frankfurt, 1986). The classic work on the psychology of the prisoners during the witch-hunt is Etienne Delcambre, 'La Psychologie des inculpes Lorrains de sorcellerie', *Revue historique de droit francais et étranger*, ser. 4,

34 (1954): 383–403, 508–26, parts of which have been translated in Monter, *European Witchcraft*, cited above.

On the decline of witchcraft three works are of particular value: Brian Easlea, *Witch-hunting, Magic and the New Philosophy: An Introduction to the Debates of the Scientific Revolution, 1450–1750* (Brighton, 1980); Barbara J. Shapiro, *Probability and Certainty in Seventeenth-Century England* (Princeton, 1983), Chapter VI; and Alfred Soman, 'Decriminalizing Witchcraft: Does the French Experience Furnish a European Model?', *Criminal Justice History*, 10 (1989): 1–22. On possession we have the classic study by Traugott K. Oesterreich, *Possession and Exorcism*, trans. D. Ibberson (New York, 1974), D.P. Walker's stimulating work, *Unclean Spirits: Possession and Exorcism in France and England in the Late Sixteenth and Early Seventeenth Centuries)* (Philadelphia, 1981), and Cécile Ernst, *Teufelaustreibungen: Die Praxis der katholischen Kirche im 16. und 17. Jahrhundert* (Bern, 1972).

The anthropological literature on witchcraft in pre-literate cultures would require a bibliography of its own, but a number of studies have attempted to relate material on African witchcraft to European witchcraft. There are two excellent collections of essays, *Witchcraft and Sorcery*, ed. Max Marwick (2nd edn, London, 1982), and *Witchcraft Confessions and Accusations*, ed. Mary Douglas (London, 1970). Geoffrey Parrinder, *Witchcraft: European and African* (London, 1958) and Lucy Mair, *Witchcraft* (New York, 1969) both deal with European material in depth.

BIBLIOGRAPHY

Adler, Margot *Drawing Down the Moon*. Boston, 1979.

Alver, Bente G. *Heksetro og Trolddom*. Oslo, 1971.

Anderson, Robert D. 'The History of Witchcraft: A Review with some Psychiatric Comments', *American Journal of Psychiatry*, 126 (1970).

Andreski, Stanislav 'The Syphilitic Shock', *Encounter*, 58 (1982).

Anglo, Sydney 'Evident Authority and Authoritative Evidence: the *Malleus Maleficarum*', in *The Damned Art: Essays in the Literature of Witchcraft* ed. S. Anglo. London, 1977.

Ankarloo, Bengt 'Sweden: The Mass Burnings (1668–1676)', in *Early Modern Witchcraft: Centres and Peripheries*, ed. Bengt Ankarloo and Gustav Henningsen. Oxford, 1990.

Ankarloo, Bengt *Trolldomsprocesserna i Sverige*. Stockholm, 1971.

Ankarloo, Bengt and Gustav Henningsen (eds) *Early Modern European Witchcraft: Centres and Peripheries*. Oxford, 1990.

Avis, P.D.L. 'Moses and the Magistrate: a Study in the Rise of Protestant Legalism', *Journal of Ecclesiastical History*, 26 (1975).

Bader, Guido *Die Hexenprozesse in der Schweiz*. Affoltern, 1945.

Baeyer-Katte, Wanda von 'Die Historischen Hexenprozesse: Der Verbüro-kratisierte Massenwahn' in *Massenwahn in Geschichte und Gegenwart*, ed. W. Bitter. Stuttgart, 1965.

Bainton, Roland *Women of the Reformation: From Spain to Scandinavia*. Minneapolis, 1977.

Baissac, Jules *Les Grands jours de la sorcellerie*. Paris, 1890.

Baranowski, Bohdan *Procesy Czarownic w Polsce w XVII i XVIII Wieku*. Lodz, 1952.

Barb, A.A. 'The Survival of the Magic Arts', in *The Conflict between Paganism and Christianity*, ed. A. Momigliano. Oxford, 1963.

Barstow, Anne L. *Witchcraze: A New History of the European Witch Hunts*. New York, 1994.

Bartlett, Robert *Trial by Fire and Water: The Medieval Judicial Ordeal*. Oxford, 1986.

Baschwitz, Kurt *Hexen und Hexenprozesse*. Munich, 1963.

Baxter, Christopher 'Jean Bodin's *De la Démonomanie des sorciers*: The logic of persecution', in *The Damned Art: Essays in the Literature of Witchcraft*, ed. S. Anglo. London, 1977.

Behringer, Wolfgang '"Erhob sich das ganze Land zu ihrer Ausrottung. . .":

Hexenprozesse und Hexenverfolgungen in Europa', in *Hexenwelten: Magie und Imagination vom 16.–20. Jahrhundert*, ed. Richard van Dülmen. Frankfurt, 1987.

Behringer, Wolfgang *Hexenverfolgung in Bayern*. Munich, 1988.

Behringer, Wolfgang (ed) *Hexen und Hexenprozesse in Deutschland*. Munich, 1988.

Behringer, Wolfgang 'Kinderhexenprozesse: zur Rolle von Kindern in der Geschichte der Hexenverfolgung', *Zeitschrift für Historische Forschung*, 16 (1988).

Behringer, Wolfgang 'Neue Historische Literatur: Erträge und Perspektiven der Hexenforschung', *Historische Zeitschrift*, 249 (1989).

Bettencourt, Francisco 'Portugal: A Scrupulous Inquisition', in *Early Modern Witchcraft: Centres and Peripheries*, ed. Bengt Ankarloo and Gustav Henningsen. Oxford, 1990.

Bever, Edward 'Old Age and Witchcraft in Early Modern Europe' in *Old Age in Pre-industrial Society*, ed. P. Stearns. New York, 1982.

Bever, Edward 'Witchcraft in Early Modern Württemberg', PhD dissertation. Princeton, 1983.

Binsfeld, Peter *De Confessionibus Maleficarum et Sagarum*. Treves, 1596.

Blackstone, William *Commentaries on the Laws of England*. Oxford, 1796.

Blauert, Andreas *Frühe Hexenverfolgungen*. Hamburg, 1989.

Blauert, Andreas (ed.), *Ketzer, Zauberer, Hexen: die Anfänge der Europäischen Hexenverfolgungen*. Frankfurt, 1990.

Bodin, Jean *De la Démonomanie des sorciers*. Anvers, 1586.

Boguet, Henry *An Examen of Witches*. trans. E.A. Ashwin, ed. M. Summers. London, 1929.

Bonomo, Giuseppi *Caccia alle Streghe*. Palermo, 1959.

Bordelon, Laurent *L'Histoire des imaginations extravagantes de Monsieur Oufle*. Paris, 1710.

Bossy, John 'Moral Arithmetic: Seven Sins into Ten Commandments', in *Conscience and Casuistry in Early Modern Europe*, ed. Edmund Leites. Cambridge, 1988.

Boswell, James *Journal of a Tour to the Hebrides*. ed. R.W. Chapman. Oxford, 1970.

Boyer, Paul and Stephen Nissenbaum *Salem Possessed: The Social Origins of Witchcraft*. Cambridge, Mass., 1974.

Brann, Noel 'The Conflict between Reason and Magic in Seventeenth-Century England: A Case Study of the Vaughan–More Debate', *Huntington Library Quarterly*, 43 (1980).

Braudel, Fernand *The Structures of Everyday Life*. New York, 1981.

Braudel, F. and P. Spooner 'Prices in Europe from 1450 to 1750', *Cambridge Economic History of Europe IV*. Cambridge, 1967.

Brauner, Sigrid 'Martin Luther on Witchcraft: a True Reformer?' in *The Politics of Gender in Early Modern Europe*, ed. J.R. Brink et al., *Sixteenth-Century Essays and Studies*, 12 (1989): 29–42.

Briffault, Robert *The Mothers*. New York, 1927.

Briggs, Robin 'Witchcraft and Popular Mentality in Lorraine, 1580–1630', in *Occult and Scientific Mentalities in the Renaissance*, ed. Brian Vickers. Cambridge, 1984.

Briggs, Robin *Communities of Belief: Cultural and Social Tension in Early Modern France*. Oxford, 1989.

Brucker, Gene A. 'Sorcery in Early Renaissance Florence', *Studies in the Renaissance*, 10 1963.

Burghartz, Susanna 'The Equation of Women and Witches: A case study of witchcraft trials in Lucerne and Lausanne in the fifteenth and sixteenth centuries,', in *The German Underworld*, ed. Richard J. Evans, London, 1988.

Burke, Peter *Popular Culture in Early Modern Europe*. London, 1978.

Burke, Peter 'Witchcraft and Magic in Renaissance Italy: Gianfrancesco Pico and his *Strix*' in *The Damned Art: Essays in the Literature of Witchcraft*, ed. S. Anglo, London, 1977.

Burr, George Lincoln 'The Fate of Dietrich Flade', in *George Lincoln Burr: Selections from His Writings*, ed. Lois Oliphant Gibbons, Ithaca. 1943.

Burstein, Sona R. 'Aspects of the Psychopathology of Old Age Revealed in the Witchcraft Cases of the Sixteenth and Seventeenth Centuries', *British Medical Bulletin*, 6 (1949).

Burton, Robert *Anatomy of Melancholy*. New York, 1932.

Byloff, Fritz *Hexenglaube und Hexenverfolgung in den österreichischen Alpenländern*. Berlin and Leipzig, 1934.

Byrne, Patrick *Witchcraft in Ireland*. Cork, 1975.

Cardano, Girolamo *De Rerum Varietate*. Basel, 1557.

Cardoza, A. Rebecca 'A Modern American Witch-Craze', in *Witchcraft and Sorcery*, ed. M. Marwick. London, 1970.

Carnochan, W.B. 'Witch-Hunting and belief in 1751: the Case of Thomas Colley and Ruth Osborne', *Journal of Social History*, 4 (1970–71).

Caro Baroja, Julio *The World of Witches*. trans. O.N.V. Glendinning. Chicago, 1965.

Carus, Paul *The History of the Devil and the Idea of Evil*. New York, 1969.

Cervantes, Fernando *The Idea of the Devil and the Problem of the Indian: The Case of Mexico in the Sixteenth Century*. London, 1991.

Childs, J. *Armies and Warfare in Europe, 1648–1789*. New York, 1982.

Cirac Estopañán, Sebastián. *Los procesos de hechicerías en la Inquisición de Castilla la Nueva*. Madrid, 1942.

Clark, Stuart 'King James's *Daemonologie*: Witchcraft and Kingship', in *The Damned Art: Essays in the Literature of Witchcraft*, ed. S. Anglo. London, 1977.

Clark, Stuart 'Inversion, Misrule and the Meaning of Witchcraft', *Past and Present*, 87 (1980).

Clark, Stuart 'Protestant Demonology: Sin, Superstition and Society (c. 1520 – c. 1630)', in *Early Modern European Witchcraft: Centres and Peripheries*, ed. B. Ankarloo and G. Henningsen. Oxford, 1990.

Cohn, Norman *Europe's Inner Demons*. London, 1975.

Coudert, Allison P. 'The Myth of the Improved Status of Protestant Women: The Case of the Witchcraze', in *The Politics of Gender in Early Modern Europe*, ed. J.R. Brink, et. al. (vol. 12 of *Sixteenth-Century Essays and Studies*), pp. 61–94.

Cowan, Edward 'The Darker Vision of the Scottish Renaissance' in *The Renaissance and Reformation in Scotland*, ed. I.B. Cowan and D. Shaw. Edinburgh, 1983.

Cragg, G.R. *From Puritanism to the Age of Reason*. Cambridge, 1960.

Currie, Elliott P. 'Crimes without Criminals: Witchcraft and its Control in Renaissance Europe', *Law and Society Review*, 3 (1968).

Daly, Mary *Gyn/Ecology: The Metaethics of Radical Feminism*. Boston, 1978.

Damaska, Mirjan 'The Death of Legal Torture', *Yale Law Journal*, 86 (1978).

Davis, Natalie Z. *The Return of Martin Guerre*. Cambridge, 1983.

Deacon, Richard *Matthew Hopkins: Witch-Finder General*. London, 1976.

Degn, Christian, Hartmut Lehmann, and Dagmar Unverhau (eds). *Hexenprozesse: Deutsche und scandinavische beiträge*. Neumünster, 1983.

Delcambre, Etienne 'La Psychologie des inculpes Lorrains de sorcellerie', *Revue historique de droit français et étranger*, ser. 4, 32 (1954).

Delumeau, Jean *Catholicism between Luther and Voltaire: A New View of the Counter-Reformation*. London, 1977.

Delumeau, Jean *La Peur en Occident XIVe–XVIIIe siècles*. Paris, 1978.

Demos, John P. 'Underlying Themes in the Witchcraft of Seventeenth-Century New England', *American Historical Review*, 75 (1970).

Demos, John P. *Entertaining Satan: Witchcraft and the Culture of Early New England*. New York, 1982.

Denis, A. *La Sorcellerie à Toul aux XVIe et XVIIe siècles*. Toul, 1888.

De Vries, Jan *European Urbanization*. Cambridge, Mass., 1984.

Dienst, Heide 'Magische Vorstellungen und Hexenverfolgungen in den österreichen Alpenländern (15.–18. Jahrhundert)', in *Wellen der Verfolgungen in der österreichischen Geschichte*, ed. E. Zöllner. Vienna, 1986.

Dömötör, Tekla 'The Cunning Folk in English and Hungarian Witch Trials', in *Folklore Studies in the Twentieth Century*, ed. V.J. Newall. Woodbridge, 1978.

Douglas, Mary *Witchcraft Confessions and Accusations*. London, 1970.

Drummond, A.L. and J. Bulloch. *The Scottish Church 1688–1843*. Edinburgh, 1973.

Duerr, Hans Peter *Dream Time: Concerning the Boundary between Wilderness and Civilization*, trans. F. Goodman. Oxford, 1985.

Dupont-Bouchat, Marie-Sylvie 'La Répression de la sorcellerie dans le duché de Luxembourg aux XVIe et XVIIe siècles', in M. Dupont-Bouchat et al., *Prophètes et sorciers dans les Pays-Bas XVIe-XVIIIe siècles*. Paris, 1978.

Dworkin, Andrea *Woman Hating*. New York, 1974.

Easlea, Brian *Witch Hunting, Magic and the New Philosophy: An Introduction to the Debates of the Scientific Revolution 1450–1750*. Brighton, 1980.

Eliade, Mircea *Occultism, Witchcraft and Cultural Fashions*. Chicago, 1976.

Erikson, Kai *Wayward Puritans*. New York, 1966.

Estes, Leland 'The Medical Origins of the European Witch Craze: A Hypothesis', *Journal of Social History*, 17 (1984).

Evans, A. *Witchcraft and the Gay Counterculture*. Boston, 1978.

Evans, R.J.W. *The Making of the Habsburg Monarchy, 1500–1700*. Oxford, 1979.

Filmer, Robert *A Difference betweene an English and Hebrew Witch*. London, 1653.

Flint, Valerie I.J. *The Rise of Magic in Early Medieval Europe*. Princeton, 1991.

Forbes, Thomas R. *The Midwife and the Witch*. New Haven, 1966.

Foucault, Maurice *Les Procès de sorcellerie dans l'ancienne France devant les jurisdictions séculières*. Paris, 1907.

Fox, Sanford J. *Science and Justice: The Massachusetts Witchcraft Trials*. Baltimore, 1968.

Gari Lacruz, Angel 'Variedad de competencias en el delito de brujería 1600–1650 en Aragón', in *La Inquisición Española: Nueva visión, nueva horizontes* ed. J. Perez Villanueva. Madrid, 1980.

Garrett, Clarke 'Witches and Cunning Folk in the Old Regime' in *The Wolf and the Lamb: Popular Culture in France from the Old Regime to the Twentieth Century*, ed. J. Beauroy et al. Stanford, 1976.

Garrett, Clarke 'Women and Witches: Patterns of Analysis', *Signs*, 3 (1977).

Gaudemet, J. 'Les Ordiales au moyen age: doctrine, législation et pratique canoniques' in *La Preuve* (Receuils de la Société Jean Bodin, Vol. 17) Brussels, 1965.

Gentz, Lauritz 'Vad förorsakade de stora häxprocesserna?', *Arv*, 10, 1954.

Gifford, George *A Discourse of the Subtle Practice of Devils by Witches*. London, 1587.

Gifford, George *A Dialogue Concerning Witches and Wtichcraft*. repr. in *The Witchcraft Papers*, ed. P. Haining. London, 1974.

Gijswijt-Hofstra, Marijke 'Witchcraft in the Northern Netherlands', in *Current Issues in Women's History*, ed. Arina Angerman et al. London, 1989, pp. 75–92.

Gijswijt-Hofstra, Marijke 'The European Witchcraft Debate and the Dutch Variant', *Social History*, 15 (1990): 181–94.

Gijswijt-Hofstra, Marijke and Willem Frijhoff (eds) *Witchcraft in the Netherlands: from the Fourteenth to the Twentieth Century*. Rotterdam, 1991.

Ginzburg, Carlo *The Night Battles: Witchcraft and Agrarian Cults in the Sixteenth and Seventeenth Centuries*, trans. John and Anne Tedeschi. Baltimore, 1983.

Ginzburg, Carlo *Ecstasies: Deciphering the Witches' Sabbath*. New York, 1991.

Glanvil, Joseph *Saducismus Triumphatus*. London, 1681.

Godbeer, Richard *The Devil's Dominion: Magic and Religion in Early New England*. Cambridge, 1992.

Goode, William *Religion among the Primitives*. Glencoe, Illinois, 1951.

Greenleaf, R.E. *Zumarraga and the Mexican Inquisition 1536–1543*. Washington, 1962.

Greenleaf, R.E. *The Mexican Inquisition of the Sixteenth Century*. Albuquerque, 1969.

Grien, Hans Baldung *Prints and Drawings*. ed. J.H. Marrow and A. Shestack. Chicago, 1981.

Guazzo, Francesco Maria *Compendium Maleficarum*, trans. E.A. Ashwin, ed. M. Summers. London, 1929.

Haining, Peter (ed.) *The Witchcraft Papers*. Secaucus, New Jersey, 1974.

Hall, David (ed.) *Witch-Hunting in Seventeenth-Century New England: A Documentary Collection, 1638–1692*. Boston, 1991.

Hansen, Chadwick *Witchcraft at Salem*. New York, 1970.

Hansen, Joseph *Zauberwahn, Inquisition und Hexenprozess im Mittelalter*. Munich, 1900.

Hansen, Joseph (ed.) *Quellen und Untersuchungen zur Geschichte des Hexenwahns und der Hexenverfolgung im Mittelalter*. Bonn, 1901.

Harley, David 'Historians as Demonologists: The Myth of the Midwife-Witch', *Social History of Medicine*, 3 (1990).

Harner, Michael J. 'The Role of Hallucinogenic Plants in European Witchcraft', in *Hallucinogens and Shamanism* ed. Michael J. Harner. London, 1973.

Harris, H.A. *Sport in Greece and Rome*. Ithaca, 1972.

Harris, Marvin *Cows, Pigs, Wars and Witches*. New York, 1974.

Heikkinen, Antero *Paholaisen Liittolaiset*. Helsinki, 1969.

Heikkinen, Antero and Timo Kervinen 'Finland: The Male Domination', in *Early Modern European Witchcraft: Centres and Peripheries*, ed. B. Ankarloo and G. Henningsen. Oxford, 1990.

Heinemann, Evelyn *Hexen und Hexenglauben*. Frankfurt, 1986.

Heinsohn, Gunnar and Otto Steiger 'The Elimination of Medieval Birth Control and the Witch Trials of Modern Times', *International Journal of Women's Studies*, 5 (1982).

Hellman, Lillian *Scoundrel Time*. Boston, 1976.

Henningsen, Gustav 'The Papers of Alonso de Salazar Frias', *Temenos* 5 (1969).

Henningsen, Gustav *The Witches' Advocate: Basque Witchcraft and the Spanish Inquisition, 1609–1614*. Reno, 1980.

Henningsen, Gustav 'Witchcraft in Denmark', *Folklore*, 93 (1982).

Herlihy, David and Christiane Klapisch-Zuber *Tuscans and their Families*. New Haven, 1985.

Hester, Marianne *Lewd Women and Wicked Witches: A Study of the Dynamics of Male Domination*. London, 1992.

Heyd, Michael 'The Reaction to Enthusiasm in the Seventeenth Century: towards an integrative approach', *Journal of Modern History*, 53 (1981).

Hitchcock, James 'George Gifford and Puritan Witch Beliefs', *Archiv für Reformationsgeschichte*, 58 (1967).

Hobsbawm, E.J. 'The Crisis of the Seventeenth Century', in *Crisis in Europe*, ed. Trevor Aston. New York, 1967.

Holmes, Clive 'Popular Culture?: Witches, Magistrates and Divines in Early Modern England', in *Understanding Popular Culture: Europe from the Middle Ages to the Nineteenth Century*, ed. S. Kaplan. Berlin, New York and Amsterdam, 1984.

Holmes, Clive 'Women: Witnesses and Witches', *Past and Present*, 140 (1993).

Holmes, George *Europe: Hierarchy and Revolt, 1320–1450*. New York, 1975.

Hopkins, Matthew *The Discovery of Witches*. London, 1928.

Horsley, Richard A. 'Who Were the Witches? The social roles of the accused in the European witch trials', *Journal of Interdisciplinary History*, 9 (1979).

Houlbrooke, Ralph R. 'The Decline of Ecclesiastical Jurisdiction under the Tudors', in *Continuity and Change*, ed. R. O'Day and F. Heal. Leicester, 1976.

Huxley, Aldous *The Devils of Loudon*. New York, 1952.

Jobe, T.H. 'The Devil in Restoration Science: The Glanvill-Webster Witchcraft Debate', *Isis*, 72 (1981).

Johansen, Jens Christian V. 'Denmark: The Sociology of Accusations', in *Early Modern Witchcraft: Centres and Peripheries*, ed. Bengt Ankarloo and Gustav Henningsen. Oxford, 1990.

Kamber, Peter 'La Chasse aux sorciers et aux sorcières dans le Pays de Vaud: aspects quantitatifs (1581–1620)', *Revue historique Vaudoise*, 90 (1982).

Kamen, Henry *The Spanish Inquisition*. New York, 1965.

Kamen, Henry *Inquisition and Society in Spain in the Sixteenth and Seventeenth Centuries*. Bloomington, 1985.

Kamensky, Jane. 'Words, Witches and Woman Trouble: witchcraft, disorderly speech and gender boundaries in Puritan New England', *Essex Institute Historical Collections*, 128 (1992).

Karlsen, Carol *The Devil in the Shape of a Woman: Witchcraft in Colonial New England*. New York, 1987.

Kearney, Hugh *Scholars and Gentlemen*. London, 1970.

Kenyon, J.P. *The Popish Plot*. London, 1972.

Kieckhefer, Richard *European Witch Trials: Their Foundations in Popular and Learned Culture, 1300–1500.* London, 1976.

Kieckhefer, Richard *The Repression of Heresy in Medieval Germany,* Philadelphia, 1980.

Kieckhefer, Richard *Magic in the Middle Ages.* Cambridge, 1989.

King James I *Daemonologie,* ed. G.B. Harrison. London, 1924.

Kirkton, J *The Secret and True History of the Church of Scotland.* ed. C.K. Sharpe. Edinburgh, 1917.

Kittredge, George L. *Witchcraft in Old and New England.* Cambridge, Mass., 1929.

Kivelson, Valerie A. 'Through the Prism of Witchcraft: Gender and Social Change in Seventeenth-Century Muscovy', in *Russia's Women: Accommodation, Resistance, Transformation,* ed. B.E. Evans, B.A. Engel and C.D. Worobec. Berkeley, 1991.

Klaits, Joseph *Servants of Satan: The Age of the Witch-Hunts.* Bloomington, 1985.

Klaniczay, Gábor 'Benandante-kresnik-zduhac-táltos', in *Ethnographia,* 94 (1983).

Klaniczay, Gábor 'Shamanistic Elements in Central European Witchcraft', in *Shamanism in Eurasia,* ed. Mihaly Hoppal. Göttingen, 1984.

Klaniczay, Gábor 'Decline of Witches and Rise of Vampires in 18th-century Habsburg Monarchy', *Ethnologia Europaea,* 17 (1987).

Klaniczay, Gábor 'Hungary: The Accusations and the Universe of Popular Magic', in *Early Modern European Witchcraft,* ed. B. Ankarloo and G. Henningsen. Oxford, 1990.

Konig, David *Law and Society in Colonial Massachusetts,* Chapel Hill, N.C., 1980.

Kors, Alan C. and Edward Peters (eds) *Witchcraft in Europe, 1100–1700.* Philadelphia, 1972.

Kramer, Heinrich and James Sprenger *The Malleus Maleficarum,* trans. and ed. M. Summers. London, 1928; repr. New York, 1948, 1971.

Kunstmann, Harmut H. *Zauberwahn und Hexenprozess in der Reichsstadt Nürnberg.* Nuremberg, 1970.

Kunze, Michael *Der Process Pappenheimer.* Ebelsbach, 1981.

Kunze, Michael *Highroad to the Stake: A Tale of Witchcraft,* trans. William E. Yuill. Chicago, 1987.

Lamont, William *Godly Rule.* London, 1969.

Lancre, Pierre de *Tableau de l'inconstance des mauvais anges et démons,* ed. Nicole Jacques-Chaquin. Paris, 1982.

Langbein, John *Prosecuting Crime in the Renaissance.* Cambridge, Mass, 1974.

Langbein, John *Torture and the Law of Proof.* Chicago, 1977.

Langbein, John 'The Criminal Trial Before the Lawyers', *University of Chicago Law Review,* 45, (1978).

Lange, Ursula *Untersuchungen zu Bodins Démonomanie.* Frankfurt, 1970.

Larner, Christina 'James VI and I and Witchcraft', in *The Reign of James VI and I*, ed. A.G.R. Smith. London, 1973.

Larner, Christina '*Crimen exceptum?* The crime of witchcraft in Europe', in *Crime and the Law*, ed. V. Gattrell et al. London, 1980.

Larner, Christina *Enemies of God: The Witch-hunt in Scotland*. Baltimore, London, 1981.

Larner, Christina *Witchcraft and Religion: The Politics of Popular Belief*. Oxford, 1984.

Larner, C., C.H. Lee and H.V. McLachlan. *Source-Book of Scottish Witchcraft*. Glasgow, 1977.

Laslett, Peter *The World We Have Lost*. 3rd edn. New York, 1984.

Lassen, A. 'The Population of Denmark in 1660', *Scandinavian Economic History Review*, 13 (1965).

LaVey, Anton S. *The Satanic Bible*. New York, 1969.

Le Roy Ladurie Emmanuel. *Les Paysans de Languedoc*. Paris, 1966.

Lea, Henry C. *A History of the Inquisition in Spain*, 4 vols. New York, 1906–7.

Lea, Henry C. *A History of the Inquisition in the Middle Ages*, 3 vols. New York, 1955.

Lea, Henry C. *Materials toward a History of Witchcraft*, arr. and ed. Arthur C. Howland, 3 vols. New York, 1957.

Lea, Henry C. *The Ordeal*, ed. Edward Peters. Philadelphia, 1973.

Lea, Henry C. *Torture*, ed. Edward Peters. Philadelphia, 1973.

Lenman, Bruce and Geoffrey Parker. 'The State, the Community and the Criminal Law in Early Modern Europe', in V. Gattrell et al., *Crime and the Law*. London, 1980.

Leutenbauer, Siegfried *Hexerei- und Zaubereidelikt in der Literatur von 1450 bis 1550*. Berlin, 1972.

Levack, Brian P. 'The Great Scottish Witch-Hunt of 1661–1662', *Journal of British Studies*, 20 (1980).

Levy, Leonard W. 'Accusatorial and Inquisitorial Systems of Criminal Procedure: The Beginnings' in *Freedom and Reform*, ed. H. Hyman and L. Levy. New York, 1967.

Lorenz, Sönke, *Aktenversendung und Hexenprozess: Dargestellt am Beispiel der Juristenfakultäten Rostock und Greifswald (1570/82–1630)*, 2 vols. Frankfurt, 1982–83.

Luhrmann, T.M. *Persuasions of the Witch's Craft: Ritual Magic in Contemporary England*. Cambridge, Mass, 1989.

McCaghy, C. *Deviant Behavior*. New York, 1976.

MacDonald, Michael *Mystical Bedlam*. Cambridge, 1979.

MacDonald, Michael (ed.) *Witchcraft and Hysteria in Elizabethan England*. London, 1990.

Macfarlane, Alan *Witchcraft in Tudor and Stuart England*. New York, London, 1970.

Mackenzie, Sir George *The Laws and Customes of Scotland in Matters Criminal*. Edinburgh, 1678.

Mair, Lucy *Witchcraft*. New York, 1969.

Mandrou, Robert *Magistrats et Sorciers en France au XVII siècle*, Paris, 1968.

Martin, Ruth *Witchcraft and the Inquisition in Venice, 1550–1650*. Oxford, 1989.

Marx, J. Jean *L'Inquisition en Dauphiné*. Paris, 1914.

Marwick, Max (ed.) *Witchcraft and Sorcery*. London, 1970.

Masters, R. *Eros and Evil*. New York, 1966.

Merchant, Carolyn *The Death of Nature: Women, Ecology and the Scientific Revolution*. New York, 1980.

Merzbacher, Friedrich *Die Hexenprozesse in Franken*. Munich, 1957.

Metcalf, Alida 'Families of Planters, Peasants and Slaves: Strategies for Survival in Santana de Parnaiba, Brazil, 1720–1820', PhD dissertation, University of Texas at Austin, 1983.

Michelet, Jules *Satanism and Witchcraft*. trans. A.R. Allison, New York, 1939.

Midelfort, H.C. Erik 'Recent Witch Hunting Research, or Where Do We Go from Here?', *Papers of the Bibliographical Society of America*, 62 (1968).

Midelfort, H.C. Erik *Witch Hunting in Southwestern Germany, 1562–1684: The Social and Intellectual Foundations*. Stanford, 1972.

Midelfort, H.C. Erik. 'Witch Hunting and the Domino Theory' in *Religion and the People, 800–1700*, ed. James Obelkevich. Chapel Hill, N.C., 1979.

Midelfort, H.C. Erik 'Heartland of the Witchcraze: Central and Northern Europe', *History Today*, 31 (1981).

Midelfort, H.C. Erik 'Witchcraft, Magic and the Occult', in *Reformation Europe: A Guide to Research*, ed. S. Ozment. St Louis, 1982.

Midelfort, H.C. Erik. 'Johann Weyer and the Transformation of the Insanity Defense', in *The German People and the Reformation*, ed. R. Po-Chia Hsia. Ithaca, 1988.

Miller, Perry *The New England Mind: From Colony to Province*. Cambridge, Mass., 1953.

Monter, E. William (ed.) *European Witchcraft*. New York, 1969.

Monter, E. William 'La Sodomie à l'époque moderne en Suisse romande', *Annales*, 29 (1974).

Monter, E. William *Witchcraft in France and Switzerland: The Borderlands during the Reformation*. Ithaca, 1976.

Monter, E. William 'The Pedestal and the Stake: Courtly Love and Witchcraft', in *Becoming Visible: Women in European History*, ed. R. Bridenthal and C. Koonz. Boston, 1977.

Monter, E. William 'Witchcraft in France and Italy', *History Today*, 30 (November 1980).

Monter, E. William *Ritual, Myth and Magic in Early Modern Europe*. Athens, Ohio 1983.

Monter, E. William *Frontiers of Heresy: The Spanish Inquisition from the Basque Lands to Sicily.* Cambridge, 1990.

Muchembled, Robert 'Satan ou les hommes?' La Chasse aux sorcières et ses causes', in M. Dupont-Bouchat et al., *Prophètes et sorciers dans les Pays-Bas XVIe–XVIIIe siècle.* Paris, 1978.

Muchembled, Robert 'The Witches of the Cambrésis: the Acculturation of the Rural World in the Sixteenth and Seventeenth Centuries', in *Religion and the People, 800–1700*, ed. James Obelkevich. Chapel Hill, N.C., 1979.

Muchembled, Robert *Les Derniers bûchers: un village de Flandre et ses sorcières sous Louis XIV.* Paris, 1981.

Muchembled, Robert *Popular Culture and Elite Culture in France, 1400–1750*, trans. L. Cochrane. Baton Rouge, 1985.

Muchembled, Robert 'Satanic Myths and Cultural Reality', in *Early Modern European Witchcraft: Centres and Peripheries*, ed. B. Ankarloo and G. Henningsen. Oxford, 1990.

Murray, Alexander 'Medieval Origins of the Witch-Hunt', *The Cambridge Quarterly*, 7 (1976).

Murray, Margaret A. *The Witch-Cult in Western Europe.* Oxford, 1921.

Murray, Margaret A. *The God of the Witches.* London, 1933.

Murray, Margaret A. *The Divine King of England.* London, 1954.

Naess, Hans E. 'Norway: the Criminological Context', in *Early Modern European Witchcraft: Centres and Peripheries*, ed. B. Ankarloo and G. Henningsen. Oxford, 1990.

Nauert, C.G. *Agrippa and the Crisis of Renaissance Thought.* Urbana, Illinois, 1965.

Nemec, J. *Witchcraft and Medicine, 1484–1793.* Washington, 1974.

Newes from Scotland. London, 1591.

Notestein, Wallace *A History of Witchcraft in England.* Washington, 1911.

Nottingham, Elizabeth K. *Religion: A Sociological View.* New York, 1971.

Oates, Caroline 'The Trial of a Teenage Werewolf, Bordeaux, 1613', *Criminal Justice History*, 9 (1988).

Oberman, Heiko A. *Masters of the Reformation.* Cambridge, 1981.

Oberman, Heiko A. *Luther: Man between God and the Devil*, trans. E. Walliser-Schwarzbart. New Haven, 1989.

Oesterreich, Traugott K. *Possession and Exorcism*, trans. D. Ibberson. New York, 1974.

O'Keefe, Daniel L. *Stolen Lightning: The Social Theory of Magic.* New York, 1982.

O'Neil, Mary 'Magical healing, Love Magic and the Inquisition in Late Sixteenth-Century Modena', in *Inquisition and Society in Early Modern Europe*, ed. Stephen Haliczer. Totowa, N.J., 1987.

Ozment, Steven *When Fathers Ruled.* Cambridge, 1983.

Parke, F.N. 'Witchcraft in Maryland', *Maryland Historical Magazine*, 31 (1936).

Parker, Geoffrey 'Some Recent Work on the Inquisition in Spain and Italy', *Journal of Modern History*, 54 (1982).

Parrinder, Geoffrey *Witchcraft: European and African*. London, 1958.

Paulus, Nikolaus *Hexenwahn und Hexenprozesse, vornehmlich im 16. Jahrhundert*. Freiburg, 1910.

Pearl, Jonathan L. 'Witchcraft in New France in the Seventeenth Century: The Social Aspect', *Historical Reflections*, 4 (1977).

Pearl, Jonathan L. 'Humanism and Satanism: Jean Bodin's Contribution to the Witchcraft Crisis', *Canadian Review of Sociology and Anthropology*, 19 (1984).

Pearl, Jonathan L. 'Bodin's Advice to Judges in Witchcraft Cases', *Proceedings of the Annual Meeting of the Western Society for French History*, 16 (1989).

Perkins, William. *A Discourse of the Damned Art of Witchcraft*, in *Works*, III. Cambridge, 1613.

Peters, Edward *The Magician, The Witch and the Law*. Philadelphia, 1978.

Peters, Edward *Torture*. Oxford, 1985.

Peters, Edward *Inquisition*. Berkeley, 1989.

Pfister, C. 'Nicolas Remy et la sorcellerie en Lorraine la fin du XVI siècle', *Revue historique*, 93, 94 (1907).

Pitt-Rivers, Julian 'Honour and Social Status', in *Honour and Shame: The Values of Mediterranean Society*, ed. J.G. Peristiany. Chicago, 1966.

Pitts, John L. *Witchcraft and Devil Lore in the Channel Islands*. Guernsey, 1886.

Pohl, Herbert *Hexenglaube und Hexenverfolgung im Kurfürstentum Mainz*. Geschichtliche Landeskunde, 32 (Stuttgart, 1988).

Pollock, Adrian 'Social and Economic Characteristics of Witchcraft Accusations in Sixteenth- and Seventeenth-Century Kent', *Archaeologia Cantiana*, 95 (1979).

Popkin, Richard H. *The History of Scepticism from Erasmus to Descartes*. Assen, 1960.

Rabb, Theodore *The Struggle for Stability in Early Modern Europe*. New York, 1975.

Radford, G.H. 'Thomas Larkham', *Reports and Transactions of the Devonshire Association*, 24 (1892).

Remy, Nicolas *Demonolatry*. trans. E.A. Ashwin, ed. M. Summers. London, 1930.

Riezler, S. *Geschichte der Hexenprozesse in Bayern*. 1896. Stuttgart; repr. Aalen, 1968.

Robbins, Rossell Hope *The Encyclopedia of Witchcraft and Demonology*. New York, 1959.

Roper, Lyndal 'Witchcraft and Fantasy in Early Modern Germany', *History Workshop Journal*, 32 (1991).

Rose, Elliot *A Razor for a Goat*. Toronto, 1962.

Rosen, George 'Psychopathology of the Social Process: (I) A study of the persecution of witches in Europe as a contribution to the understanding of mass delusion and psychic epidemics', *Journal of Health and Human Behavior*, 1 (1960).

Rothkrug, Lionel 'Religious Practices and Collective Perceptions: Hidden Homologies in the Renaissance and Reformation', *Historical Reflections*, 7 (1980).

Rothkrug, Lionel 'Icon and Ideology in Religion and Rebellion, 1300–1600: *Bauerfreiheit* and *religion royale*', in *Religion and Rural Revolt*, ed. J.M. Bak and G. Benecke. Manchester, 1984.

Russell, Jeffrey B. *Witchcraft in the Middle Ages*. Ithaca, 1972.

Ruthven, Margaret *Torture: The Grand Conspirarcy*. London, 1980.

Sabean, David W. *Power in the Blood: Popular Culture and Village Discourse in Early Modern Germany*. Cambridge, 1984.

Sawyer, Ronald C. '"Strangely handled in all her lyms": Witchcraft and Healing in Jacobean England,' *Journal of Social History*, 22 (1989).

Schormann, Gerhard *Hexenprozesse in Nordwestdeutschland*. Hildesheim, 1977.

Schormann, Gerhard *Hexenprozesse in Deutschland*. Göttingen, 1981.

Scot, Reginald *The Discoverie of Witchcraft*. ed. M. Summers. London, 1930; repr. New York, 1972.

Scribner, Bob 'Witchcraft and Judgement in Reformation Germany', *History Today*, 40 (1990).

Sebald, Hans *Witchcraft: The Heritage of a Heresy*. New York, 1978.

Segl, Peter *Der Hexenhammer: Enstehung und Umfeld des Malleus Maleficarum von 1487*. Cologne, 1988.

Seth, Ronald *Children against Witches*. New York, 1969.

Seymour, St John *Irish Witchcraft and Demonology*. Dublin, 1913.

Shapiro, Barbara *Probability and Certainty in Seventeenth-Century England*. Princeton, 1983.

Sharpe, J.A. 'Witchcraft and Women in Seventeenth–Century England: Some Northern Evidence', *Continuity and Change*, 6 (1991).

Sharpe, J.A. *Witchcraft in Seventeenth-Century Yorkshire: Accusations and Counter-Measures*. Borthwick Paper No. 81. York, 1992.

Shumaker, Wayne *The Occult Sciences in the Renaissance*. Berkeley, 1972.

Silverblatt, Irene *Moon, Sun and Witches: Gender Ideologies and Class in Inca and Colonial Peru*. Princeton, 1987.

Soldan, Wilhelm G., and Heinrich Heppe. *Geschichte der Hexenprozesse*. ed. M. Bauer. Munich, 1912.

Soman, A.F. 'The Parlement of Paris and the Great Witch Hunt (1565–1640)', *Sixteenth Century Journal*, 9 (1978).

Soman, A.F. 'Trente procès de sorcellerie dans le Perche (1566–1624)', *L'Orne littéraire*, 8 (1986).

Soman, A.F. 'Witch Lynching at Juniville', *Natural History*, 95 (1986).

Soman, A.F. 'Le Rôle des Ardennes dans la décriminalisation de la sorcellerie en France', *Revue historique ardennaise*, 23 (1988).

Soman, A.F. 'Decriminalizing Witchcraft: Does the French Experience Furnish a European Model?', *Criminal Justice History*, 10 (1989).

Souza, Laura de Mello, E. *O diabo e a terra de Santa Cruz.* São Paulo, 1987.

Stafford, Helen 'Notes on Scottish Witchcraft Cases 1590–91' in *Essays in Honour of Conyers Read*, ed. N. Downs. Chicago, 1953.

Stearne, John *A Confirmation and Discovery of Witchcraft.* London, 1648.

Summers, Montague *The History of Witchcraft.* New York, 1956.

Szasz, Thomas *The Myth of Mental Illness.* New York, 1961.

Tazbir, Janusz *A State without Stakes.* trans. A.T. Jordan. Wydawniczy, 1973.

Teall, John L. 'Witchcraft and Calvinism in Elizabethan England: Divine Power and Human Agency', *Journal of the History of Ideas*, 23 (1962).

Tedeschi, John 'Preliminary Observations on Writing a History of the Roman Inquisition', in *Continuity and Discontinuity in Church History*, ed. F.F. Church and T. George. Leiden, 1979.

Tedeschi, John 'Inquisitorial Law and the Witch' in *Early Modern European Witchcraft: Centres and Peripheries*, ed. B. Ankarloo and G. Henningsen. Oxford, 1990.

Thomas, Keith *Religion and the Decline of Magic.* London, 1971.

Thomasius, C. *Über die Folter*, trans. and ed. R. Lieberwirth. Weimar, 1960.

Thomasius, C. *Dissertatio de Crimine Magiae.* trans. R. Lieberwirth. Weimar, 1967.

Thompson, Roger *Unfit for Modest Ears.* London, 1979.

Thorndike, Lynn *A History of Magic and Experimental Science*, 8 vols New York, 1923–58.

Tourney, Garfield 'The physician and Witchcraft in Restoration England', *Medical History*, 16 (1972).

Trevor-Roper, H.R. 'The European Witch-Craze of the Sixteenth and Seventeenth Centuries', in Trevor-Roper, *The European Witch-Craze of the Sixteenth and Seventeenth Centuries and Other Essays.* New York, 1969; and in *Religion, the Reformation and Social Change.* London, 1967.

Unverhau, Dagmar 'Kieler Hexen und Zauberer zur Zeit der großen Verfolgung (1530–1676)', *Mitteilungen der Gesellschaft für Kieler Stadtgeschichte*, 68 (1981).

Unverhau, Dagmar 'Akkusationsprozess–Inquisitionsprozess: Indikatoren für die Intensität der Hexenverfolgung in Schleswig-Holstein', in *Hexenprozesse: deutsche und skandinavische Beitrage*, ed. C. Degn, H. Lehmann, and D. Unverhau. Neumünster, 1983.

Valentinitsch, Helfried (ed.) *Hexen und zauberer: Die große Verfolgung – ein europäisches Phänomen in der Steiermark.* Graz, 1987.

Veith, Ilza *Hysteria: The History of a Disease.* Chicago, 1965.

Volk, Franz *Hexen in der Langvogtei Ortenau und der Reichsstadt Offenburg.* Lahr, 1882.

Wakefield, W.L. and A.P. Evans (eds) *Heresies of the High Middle Ages*. New York, 1969.

Walker, D.P. *Spiritual and Demonic Magic: From Ficino to Campanella*. London, 1958.

Walker, D.P. *Unclean Spirits: Possession and Exorcism in France and England in the Late Sixteenth and Early Seventeenth Centuries*. London, Philadelphia, 1981.

Walzer, Michael *The Revolution of the Saints*. Cambridge, Mass., 1965.

Watkins, S.C. 'Spinsters', *Journal of Family History*, 9 (1984).

Wesley, John *The Journal of the Rev. John Wesley, A.M.* New York, 1906.

West, Robert H. *Reginald Scot and Renaissance Writings on Witchcraft*. Boston, 1984.

Weyer, Johann *Witches, Devils and Doctors in the Renaissance*: Johann Weyer's *De Praestigiis Daemonum*, ed. George Mora. Binghamton, 1991.

White, Lynn, Jr 'Death and the Devil', in *The Darker Vision of the Renaissance*, ed. R.S. Kinsman, Berkeley, 1974.

Whitelocke, B. *Memorials of the English Affairs*. London, 1682.

Wiers-Jenssen, Hans *Anne Pedersdotter: A Drama in Four Acts*. trans. John Masefield. Boston, 1917.

Williamson, Arthur *Scottish National Consciousness in the Age of James VI*. Edinburgh, 1979.

Willock, I.D. *The Origins and Development of the Jury in Scotland*. Edinburgh, 1966.

Wiseman, Richard *Witchcraft, Magic and Religion in Seventeeth-Century Massachusetts*. Amherst, 1984.

Wright, A.D. *The Counter-Reformation*. New York, 1982.

Wüst, Wolfgang 'Inquisitionsprozess und Hexenverfolgung im Hochstift Augsburg im 17. und 18. Jahrhundert', *Zeitschrift für bayerische Landesgeschichte*, 50 (1987).

Yates, F. *The Occult Philosophy in the Elizabethan Age*. London, 1979.

Zagorin, Perez *Rebels and Rulers, 1500–1660*, 2 vols. Cambridge, 1981.

Zguta, Russell 'Was there a Witch-Craze in Muscovite Russia?', *Southern Folklore Quarterly*, 40 (1977): 119–27.

Zguta, Russell 'Witchcraft Trials in Seventeenth-Century Russia', *American Historical Review*, 82 (1977).

Zika, Charles 'Fears of Flying: Representations of Witchcraft and Sexuality in early Sixteenth-Century Germany', *Australian Journal of Art*, 8 (1989–90).

Zilboorg, G. *The Medical Man and the Witch during the Renaissance*. New York, 1941.

MAP

Europe in the early seventeenth century.

INDEX